JO-ANN®

Your Guide to Creativity™

"Celebrate the special occasions

in your life, and

bring beauty to the world."

–Debra E. Garner

Crafting · Decorating · Quilting · Sewing

Your Guide to Creativity

Better Homes and Gardens®
CREATIVE COLLECTION

Editor-in-Chief   Beverly Rivers
Editorial Manager   *Art Director*
Debra E. Garner   Patricia Church Podlasek

Assistant Art Director   Jan Michalson
Editorial Project Coordinator   Barb Hickey
Administrative Assistant   Lori Eggers
Contributing Writers   Judy Friedman, Susan Adams Bentley
Contributing Graphic Designers   Studio P2, Susie Rider, Emily Sheeder
Copy Editors   Diane Doro, Maria Duryee, Dave Kirchner, Susan J. Kling, Nancy McClimen, Margaret Smith
Illustrators   Glenda Aldrich, Marcia Cameron, Chris Neubauer
Indexer   Barbara L. Klein
Photographers   Craig Anderson, Marcia Cameron, Kathie Lentz Photography, Hastings–Willinger & Associates
Silver Lining Studio, Perry Struse, Steve Struse, The Reuben Group
Project Editors   Laura Holthorf Collins, Julie Keith, Jil Seversen
Proofreaders   Maria Duryee, Angela Ingle, Rachel Lopez, Ann Smith, Marcia Teeter

Publisher   Maureen Ruth
Senior Marketing Manager   Suzy Johnson

JO·ANN stores inc®

Chairman, President and CEO   Alan Rosskamm
Executive Vice President of Merchandising and Marketing   Dave Bolen
Vice President, Marketing   Barbara B. Semen

Director of Sales and Promotion   Tom Kuypers
Content and Education Specialist, Contributing Editor   Debra Green

Meredith CORPORATION

Vice President, Publishing Director   William R. Reed

Chairman and CEO   William T. Kerr

Chairman of the Executive Committee   E.T. Meredith III

Publishing Group President   Stephen M. Lacy
Magazine Group President   Jerry Kaplan

Production   Marjorie J. Schenkelberg
Book Retail Marketing Administration and Sales   George Susral
Circulation Newsstand   Gary Koerner

WELCOME

Finally—a reference for everything creative about crafts, decorating, and sewing! Compiled by the industry's leading sewing, crafts, and decorating retailer, this book is a veritable encyclopedia of ideas and techniques that teach, demonstrate, and inspire. Driven by Jo-Ann's decades of experience, it's the product of many talented hands. Let it be your helping hand to a lifetime of creative self-expression.

Whether you're arranging blooms for a wedding shower, designing draperies for a gracious guest room, or braving the basics to create an heirloom quilt, you'll find everything you need in *Your Guide to Creativity*™.

Detailed instructions and photos explain valuable techniques and tricks that will guide you to success—one step at a time. You'll also learn about recommended tools and materials that will enhance your skills and save you time.

Jo-Ann's veteran employees even share their personal tips and secrets gleaned from years of perfecting their own projects and helping people just like you.

With this resource in hand, you'll further nurture your creative passions and discover new talents just waiting to be tapped. We'll show you "how" so you can create the "what"—from candles and clothing to pillows and paintings that will enrich your surroundings and your life.

Nowhere else will you find a book with this breadth and depth of techniques for so many crafts, decorating, and sewing

pursuits. Written for beginners and experts alike, it's much more than a random collection of projects. It's a series of carefully presented how-to techniques that you can apply to your own creations, no matter how simple or complex.

Refer to the detailed subject index for your specific areas of interest, or browse through the sections for techniques and ideas you'd like to try right away:

- Crafts
- Decorating
- Home Decor Sewing
- Quilting
- Fashion Sewing

As you turn to this book again and again, we hope you'll come to see that it's more than a comprehensive reference. It's your roadmap to creative self-expression. You'll find every project enjoyable and rewarding, thanks to the details, insider shortcuts, and expert tips.

We hope you'll rely on *Your Guide to Creativity*™ not only for its comprehensive, thorough approach to crafts, decorating, and sewing, but also for the way it reveals the secrets behind beautiful things. Keep it for yourself or give it to a family member or friend, and celebrate the joy of imagination!

Although the tools and materials called for in this book usually are available at Jo-Ann stores, they're listed for illustration purposes only. If you can't find a specific item at your local store, we encourage you to substitute a similar fabric, notion, or product.

19

Table of CONTENTS

150

CRAFTS

Crafting is one of life's greatest pleasures.

With numerous techniques to choose from,

you can spend many happy hours

exploring the ideas and creative processes.

From metal to mosaics,

from crochet to candy,

there's an inspiring technique

for you to learn

and enjoy.

CAKE and CANDY
Making

Learn the fundamentals
of creating fabulous cakes

and elegant candies. Once you know the basics,
put what you've learned into practice
by making beautifully decorated cakes
and mouth-watering candies in your own kitchen.

Cake *Decorating*

Cake decorating has grown in popularity in the past decade. As a result, supplies and ingredients are readily available to consumers. By mastering a few techniques, anyone can achieve professional results.

Tools and Materials

Bag and Couplers – A
The featherweight bag is made of a flexible material that can be washed by hand or in the dishwasher. A grooved ring with an inner coupler base attaches to a decorating bag and holds the metal tip on the bag.

Cake Leveler and Spatulas – B
A cake leveler is used to cut off the crown of a cake, and for torting or cutting a single layer in half. Spatulas are used to stir icing, apply icing on cakes, blend colors, and fill decorating bags.

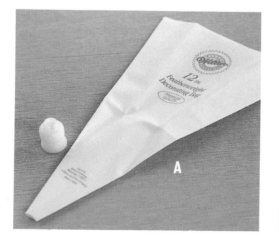

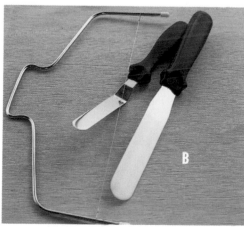

9

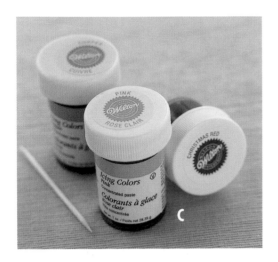

Colorants – C
Colorants can be blended to achieve almost any shade of icing.

Combs – D
Combs create decorative effects on cake edges and sides by pulling them through the frosting.

Flower Nail – E
A flower nail is a metal tool with a flat top used to create icing flowers by rolling between the fingers.

Metal Tips – F
Metal tips are small metal cones shaped to produce various designs when icing is pressed through them. They are available in a variety of sizes and shapes.

Meringue Powder and Piping Gel – G
Used in royal icing, meringue powder makes a frosting that holds a shape well and dries very hard. It is often used to make flowers. Piping gel is transparent and can be tinted any color, making it ideal for writing on or decorating cakes.

Smoothing Tools – H
Smoothing tools are wooden rollers and wide spatulas that even the frosting for a perfect surface every time. Wide smoothing tools give more control when working with large cakes. The roller is also used to roll out dough-like fondant icing and gum paste. Use confectionary or small cutter tools to cut confectionary flowers and shapes out of rolled fondant and gum paste.

Turntable – I
Turntables are designed to make frosting a breeze. With the turn of your hand, you achieve professional results.

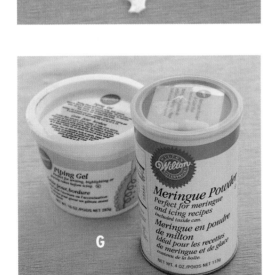

Cake Decorating Basics

Icing Consistency
There are three icing consistencies: Thin is used to ice cakes, write on cakes, and make floral stems; medium consistency is used to make borders and flowers directly on a cake; and stiff consistency is used to make dimensional flowers and petals.

Preparing the Bag
To prepare the bag for a coupler, unscrew the ring from the coupler, open the top of the bag, and push the coupler down inside the bag as far as it will go with the

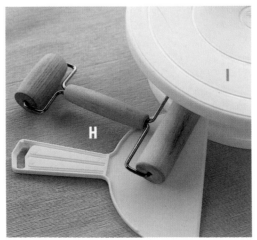

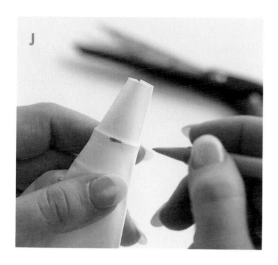

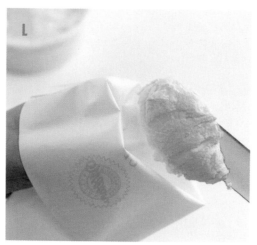

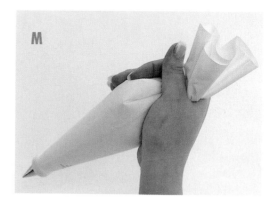

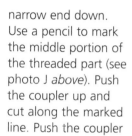

narrow end down. Use a pencil to mark the middle portion of the threaded part (see photo J *above*). Push the coupler up and cut along the marked line. Push the coupler back down into the bottom opening of the bag, place a tip on the base, and screw on the coupler ring (see photo K). Changing tips is as simple as unscrewing the ring, replacing the tip, and securing the ring in place again.

Types of Icing
Buttercream: This popular type of icing has a shortening base and is flavored with powdered sugar and extracts.

Royal icing: Royal icing is made with powdered sugar and water. It is used to make flowers that will dry hard and that can be stored to place on a cake later.

Fondant icing: Fondant has a soft, clay-like consistency, is rolled into a sheet, and then is used to cover cakes to give them a smooth, flawless finish. Fondant also can be molded and draped to achieve a spectacular look.

Buttercream Icing Recipe
1 teaspoon vanilla extract
2 tablespoons water
1 cup shortening
1 tablespoon meringue powder
1 pound sifted confectioner's sugar (4 cups)
1 teaspoon butter extract (optional)
This recipe makes a stiff consistency icing and yields 3 cups.

To make a medium-consistency icing, add one additional tablespoon of water to make a full recipe.

Colored Icing
Dip the tip of a toothpick into the coloring container. Run the toothpick through the icing; discard the toothpick and stir the icing. Repeat with a fresh toothpick to darken the frosting.
***Note:** Icing color will continue to darken for up to 2 hours after it is mixed.*

Filling and Holding the Bag
Holding the bag with one hand, fold down the top of the bag with the other hand to form a cuff over the top of your hand. Add icing to the bag with a spatula, inserting the icing below where you are holding the bag (see photo L). Pinch the bag closed from the

outside while pulling out the spatula between your index finger and thumb. Avoid filling the bag more than half full to prevent the icing from squeezing out the top. To properly close the bag, twist the top of the bag tightly and hold (see finger position, photo M). Your fingers will be on top of the bag, pushing against the icing. Continue twisting as you use the frosting, pushing the icing down to the tip of the bag.

Bag Positions
The correct position for holding the bag will be either a 45-degree angle (see photo M) or a 90-degree angle (see p hoto N).

Use the hands of a clock as a guide to hold the bag in the correct position. Imagine your work surface as the face of a clock. When the instructions indicate to place the bag in the 3 o'clock position, the back of the bag would point to 3. Decorate by working from right to left, unless you are writing.

Types of Cake Decorating Tips

Tips are grouped into family types and are assigned numbers. Tips within the same family have the same type of opening, with varying sizes (see example F, page 10).

Some popular families of tips include round, rose, leaf, basket weave, star, ruffle, and drop flower. The higher the tip number, the larger the tip opening. Using this information, you can vary the design by increasing or decreasing tip size within the same family.

Decorating tips are used for a variety of creative decorating designs. Use them in the following ways or make unique designs of your own.

Round tips can be used for writing, outlining, piping and filling, balls, dots, beads, strings, vines, flower centers, and other floral work.

Rose tips are narrow at one end and have a wide opening at the other. Use this tip to make petals for flowers such as a rose, pansy, carnation, and more.

Leaf tips are made with a v-shaped opening designed to make plain, ruffled, and stand-up leaves.

Ruffle tips are shaped like a teardrop and are used to create ribbons, bows, scallops, ruffles, and other special effects.

Star tips have deep grooves that work well for making stars, rosettes, fleur-de-lis, shells, and some kinds of flowers.

Drop flower tips make quick, one-squeeze flowers. The number of cuts in the tip indicate the number of petals the flower will have. This tip will make a simple flower, or turn the bag while squeezing to make a swirl flower.

Look for other specialty tips for making interesting designs. You'll be surprised how many unique decorations you can create.

Leveling and Torting the Cake

To prepare the cake for frosting, allow the cake to cool and remove it from the pan. Using a cake leveler, adjust the wire to the appropriate notch so that it is at the point where it will remove any bulge from the top of the cake (see Photo A). The legs should remain on the surface of the table while you move the leveler in a back and forth sawing motion across the cake.

To torte the cake (split a single-layer cake into more than one layer), adjust the wire to the halfway point of the layer and repeat the sawing motion (see photos B and C).

Filling the Layers

Icing can be spread between the cake layers or you can use a filling. To fill the cake, create a well of icing around the rim of the cake to prevent the filling from seeping out

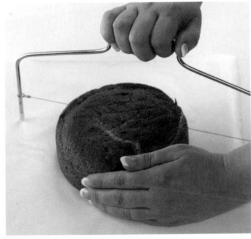

Photo A

Photo B

Photo C

Photo D

Photo E

Photo F

Photo G

the sides (see Photo D *opposite*). Use a bag fitted with a coupler, minus the tip, and pipe out a line of icing around the edge. Using a spatula, spread a filling such as mousse, pudding, or fruit puree into the center of the cake (see Photo E).

Icing the Cake

Start with a large amount of icing in a thin consistency. Use the spatula to evenly spread the icing across the top to the edges and down the sides (see Photo F). Strive to keep the spatula in contact with the icing, not the cake. Let the cake set for about 10 minutes. The cake will "crust" during this time, meaning when it is touched the icing should not stick to your finger. This is referred to as the crumb coat. Frost the cake a second time with the same icing and technique.

Smoothing the Icing

Smooth the icing by lightly scraping across the surface with the edge of a spatula while the icing is wet (see Photo F). An optional method is to wait for the top coat to crust, then use a roller lightly dipped in cornstarch to roll over the icing until the surface is smooth (see Photo G).

Comb the Icing

To create a decorative effect, comb the icing while the icing is still wet.

Getting Started

Writing – Photo H

Note: *Clock positions in parentheses indicate positions for left-handed users.*
You will need:

    Tip #3
    Icing Consistency – Thin
    Bag Position – 9 o'clock (3 o'clock)
    Bag Angle – 45 degrees

Hold the bag using a steady, even pressure as you squeeze a straight line of icing. Begin by touching the tip down slightly on the cake surface. Keep your wrist and fingers stationary and move your entire arm to create the letters. To stop, touch down on the surface of the cake. To prevent tails, stop squeezing before the tip touches the surface, then lift. Try freehand writing or use a toothpick to create a pattern on the cake to follow.

Swirl Flower – Photo I

You will need:

    Tip #2D (Drop this large tip directly in the
        bag without a coupler.)
    Tip #3
    Icing Consistency – Medium
    Bag Position – 9 o'clock (3 o'clock)
    Bag Angle – 90 degrees

Drop the #2D tip in the bag. Hold the bag in an upright position with the flat of your knuckles at 9 o'clock (3 o'clock). Squeeze the bag and turn one-quarter turn at the same

Photo H

Photo I

time the frosting is pushed through the tip. Stop squeezing and pull away to make each petal, until you have completed one entire flower. The turning motion creates the swirled petals. To create the flower center, remove the #2D tip and replace it with the #3 tip. Hold the tip slightly above the center of the flower and squeeze until a round ball forms (the icing will come up and around the tip). When the flower center is the correct size, stop squeezing and lift the tip.

Shell – Photo J

You will need:

Tip #21
Icing Consistency – Medium
Bag Position – 6 o'clock (same)
Bag Angle – 45 degrees

Hold the bag at 6 o'clock or upright so that you can pull it toward you. With the tip on the cake surface, squeeze out icing with heavy pressure, then arc the tip slightly as you move to the top of the shell. As the icing fans out, ease off on the pressure and pull the tip toward you. Stop squeezing the bag before you pull away to create a teardrop shape.

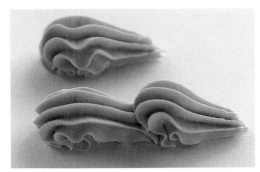

Photo J

Rose – Photo K

You will need:

Tip #12
Tip #104
Icing Consistency – Stiff
Bag Angles – Center base, 90 degrees
Bag Position for petals – 3 o'clock
(9 o'clock)

Cut several 1½-inch squares from waxed paper. Secure one square atop the flower nail with a dab of icing.

Base of rose: Start by making the rose base on the flower nail with tip #12. Holding the bag at a 90-degree angle, squeeze out icing to the size of a dime. Slowly raise the tip, squeezing with decreasing pressure to create a cone a little over ½ inch high. The cone should resemble a chocolate candy kiss.

Center wrap (forming the center of the flower): Switch to the #104 tip. Hold the bag with the tip in a vertical position (the #104 on the tip will be on top). With the bag in one hand and the nail in the opposite hand, position the wide angle of the tip at the same angle as the cone: 45 degrees. Spin the flower nail to the end of your fingers as you squeeze out a ribbon of icing all around the top portion of the cone. When you return to the starting point, move the tip down the icing mound and stop squeezing, then pull away.

Photo K

Petals, 1st layer: Make three petals to wrap around the center. As you hold the bag, the larger side of the tip should be on the bottom, and the small side should be straight up. While squeezing the bag, turn the nail to the end of your fingers, moving the nail up and down in an arcing motion, and going one third of the way around (the arc creates the petal). Slightly overlap the start of the next petal, and repeat for the next two.

Photo L

Photo M

Petals, 2nd layer: For the second layer, hold the bag with the large end down and touch the base just below completed petals. Tilt the little end up and slightly out and away from you. Again, turn the flower nail to the end of your fingers as you arc the nail slightly up and down, going one fifth of the way around. Overlap petals and repeat four times, for a total of five petals. Make more intricate roses by adding a third layer with seven petals. Remove the waxed paper and let the flower dry.

Picot – Photo L

You will need:

Tip #1
Icing Consistency – Thin
Bag Angle – 90 degrees

Hold the tip slightly above the cake surface. Squeeze the bag until a ball forms and envelops the tip. Stop squeezing and pull away. Continue with the same technique to form a triangle with the dots: 3 then 2 then 1.

Leaf – Photo M

You will need:

Tip #67
Icing Consistency – Thin
Bag Angle – 45 degrees
Bag Position – 6 o'clock (same)

Hold the tip on the surface and squeeze the bag to build up a base. Relax pressure and pull the tip toward you until the leaf narrows at one end. Stop squeezing and pull away.

Bow – Photo N

You will need:

Tip #104
Icing Consistency – Medium
Bag Angle – 45 degrees
Bag Position – 6 o'clock (same)

With the wide end of the tip touching the cake surface and the small end on top, squeeze the bag and move it in a figure eight to create the bow loops. Make straight or wavy streamers.

Photo N

Candy *Making*

Design creamy chocolate, marzipan, and other sweet confections with just a little practice. Learn to make mouth-watering treats that will elicit cheers of joy from your family and keep them asking for more.

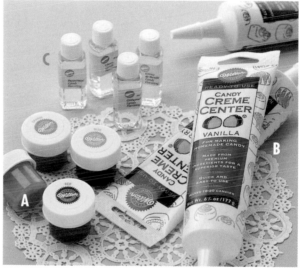

Tools and Materials

Candy Coloring – A
Use oil-base, not water-base, coloring when making candy for special colors or color combinations.

Candy Creme Center Filling – B
Use these premade cremes, available in many flavors, to fill candy centers.

Candy Flavorings – C
Add flavorings specifically designed for candy to enhance the taste.

Candy Disks – D
Melt and use colored candy disks to create fancy candy designs. Paint the colors on the inside walls of the candy cup molds or on top of the candy.

Candy Melting Plate – E
This is a bubble palette used to melt different colors of candy in the microwave oven.

Disposable Pastry Bags – F
Disposable pastry bags are used to pipe melted candy and to fill candy cups.

Electric Skillet – G
This household appliance is convenient for melting candy. A double boiler or microwave oven can also be used.

Latex Gloves – not shown
Wear these when handling candy to prevent fingerprints on the confections.

Lollipop Sticks – H
Lollipop sticks are used to create a handle for candies, particularly lollipops. The sticks are often used with lollipop molds.

Molds – I
Molds are available in a wide variety of styles and sizes for making special shapes.

Paintbrushes – not shown
These brushes are FDA approved for use with food. A small brush is used to apply candy to various sections of each candy cup in a mold.

Toothpicks – not shown
Use toothpicks to dip into food coloring, then mix with white candy to create a variety of additional colors.

Squeeze Bottle – J
Use a squeeze bottle to fill candy cups and pipe melted candy into decorative molds.

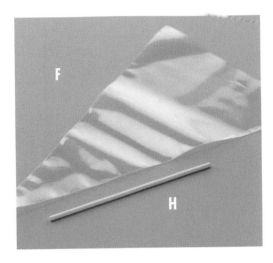

Candy Making Basics

Make sure all of the tools are dry, because water will harden the candy.

In addition, keep the candy from getting too hot; it will thicken and clump. To return it to its proper consistency, add 2 teaspoons of hydrogenated solid shortening to every 14 ounces of candy. Never thin candy with water or other liquids.

Use only flavorings and colorings specifically made for candy that are oil-base rather than water-base. Once the candy is made, handle it with latex gloves to keep it shiny and free of fingerprints.

Getting Started

Melting
Use one of these three methods to melt candy:

1. Microwave oven: This is the quickest way to melt candy; use caution to avoid over-heating. Place candy in a microwave-safe container and heat for one minute at the defrost setting. Stir and continue to heat and stir at the defrost setting for 30-second intervals until the candy is pourable.

2. Double boiler: Simmer water in the lower pan; remove from heat. Place the candy in the top pan and stir until melted.

3. Electric Skillet: Use this method for extended candy making that uses colors. Turn the skillet on low and place the glass containers of colored candy inside. Fill the skillet with water to halfway up the sides of the containers. Heat on low, stirring the candy until it is melted.

Coloring
Using colors designed for candy making, dip a toothpick in the color and run it through

Photo A

Photo B

colors to prevent colors from smudging. When all the cavities are painted and set, fill with candy. Let the candy set, then unmold.

Lollipops

Fill lollipop molds as desired. Place lollipop sticks in the mold indentations (see Photo D). Rotate the sticks to cover them with candy. Refrigerate or freeze to set. Gently unmold the lollipops. For a unique presentation, make a bouquet of delicious edible flower confections (see Photo E).

the melted candy. Discard the toothpick and stir the candy. Repeat to darken the color.

Molding and Unmolding

Fill the mold cavity with melted candy using a spoon, squeeze bottle, or pastry bag. Tap the mold on the counter several times or use a toothpick to remove invisible air bubbles. Make sure the candy is level and the edge of the cavity is clean. Place the mold in the refrigerator or freezer to set. Remove candy from the mold when the candy appears frosty (see Photo A). Turn the mold over, holding it about one inch above the counter, and gently tap or flex the mold to release the candy. Empty larger, more fragile pieces onto a towel.

Filled Centers

Make a candy shell by painting candy on the bottom and up the sides of the mold (see Photo B). Place the mold in the freezer to set. After it is set, fill the mold with the candy center almost to the top; then pour melted candy over the top, tapping to make it settle. Freeze the candy until set. Unmold.

Painting

Use a paintbrush, disposable bag, or squeeze bottle to paint or pipe color in the mold areas (see Photo C). Refrigerate or freeze the mold to harden and set each color before adding

Photo C

Photo D

Photo E

Crafts – Candy Making

CANDLE
Making

Light up your indoor
and outdoor spaces

with the relaxing, flickering glow
of beautiful candles you create yourself.
Follow these techniques to find out how easy it is
to make the shapes and scents to suit your
own personal tastes.

Candle *Making*

Tools and Materials

Beeswax and Paraffin – A & C
Wax is available in numerous forms, from large blocks of paraffin (C) and small bags of colored beads to flat sheets of beeswax (A).

Candle Melting Pot – B
A pot for melting wax is one of the most important parts of candle making. There are specific containers for melting wax on a stovetop.

Candle Thermometer – D
The candle thermometer is used to monitor the temperature of the wax. Without a thermometer you run the risk of heating the wax to the flash point, which is dangerous.

Candle Fragrance – E
Scent blocks add fragrance to the candles. Shave small slivers of the block into the melted wax.

Candle Color Block – F
Add color to the candle by shaving small bits from the blocks and putting them into the melted wax.

Learn the basics of block and container candle making, and discover how easy and fun it is to create your own custom candles.

Candle Wax Release – G
Wax release powder makes it easy to remove the candle from the mold. The powder is usually mixed in with the melted wax.

Molds and Mold Cleaner – H
Metal and acrylic candle molds are available in various sizes and shapes, and usually come with a screw for attaching the wick through the bottom hole. Use candle wax remover to clean molds, tools, and other accessories during candle making. Keep molds clean and dust free so future candles will remain as pure as possible.

Mold Sealer –
refer to page 20, Photo B
Sealer is a thick, gum-like substance used to seal the bottom of the mold where the wick is attached. It prevents the mold from leaking.

Wick Dowels – I
Wick dowels are small sticks that are laid across the top of a mold with a wick suspended from the stick.

Wicks – J
Wicks come in numerous sizes, including wicks with metal on the end and rolls of wick material that can be cut to the desired length.

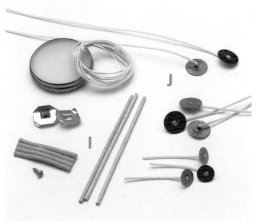

Getting Started

1. Cut a length of wick 2 inches longer than the height of your mold. Tie one end of the wick onto a dowel or insert it in a wick holder, and thread it through the mold and out the hole at the bottom. Insert a screw in the hole, and wrap the wick counter clockwise around the screw (see Photo A). Tighten the screw and trim the wick end to 1 inch long.

2. Place a small amount of mold sealer over the screw and spread it out with your fingers (see Photo B). Be sure to cover the entire screw and wick, making a tight seal.

3. In the melting pot, heat the wax to the pouring temperature specified on the wax package. Add any desired additives at the temperature specified in the manufacturer's directions. After the wax has melted, if desired, add shavings of color and scent, and pour the wax into the mold (see Photo C).

4. After pouring the wax into the mold, you can let the mold sit to harden the candle, or you can speed the process by using a cool-water bath. Fill a pot with cool water to a height a few inches shorter than your mold. Carefully lower the mold in the cool-water bath.

5. As the wax hardens, you will notice that the center of the mold will begin to sink,

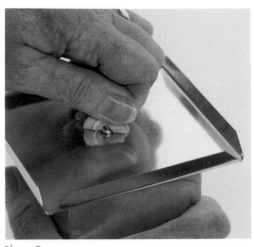
Photo A

Photo B

Photo C

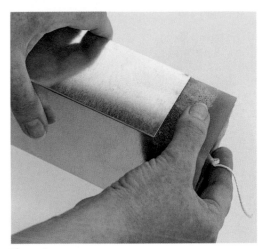
Photo D

forming a well. This is normal; you can fill the well with leftover wax. Reheat the reserved wax and pour just enough of it into the center of the mold to fill only the well (be careful not to overfill). Allow the wax to harden and refill any other wells that appear.

6. After the candle has completely hardened, remove it from the mold as follows (see Photo D): Remove the mold

sealer and screw from the bottom of the mold, and release the wick from the dowel or wick holder. Place the mold with the top down on a block of scrap wood. Lifting the mold and the block together, release the candle from the mold by firmly tapping the pieces onto a hard countertop or table. The block of wood will prevent the mold from denting and will protect your work surface. To finish, lightly scrape off any imperfections using a paring knife.

Polymer CLAY

Once you become skilled
in the basics of cane-work,

pinrolls, and resizing clay,
you'll be ready to experience the versatility
of this medium as you make
your own jewelry, home accessories,
and so much more.

Polymer *Clay*

Knead, shape, and cut tactile polymer clay, using a minimum of materials to create one-of-a-kind items. This captivating technique borrows supplies and techniques used in other craft media. Let your imagination guide your hands in making your own unique designs.

Tools and Materials

Note: Do not allow small children to use sharp cutting tools.

Adhesives – not shown
Use cyanoacrylate-type (strong holding) glue to affix metal findings to cured clay pieces.

Use a glue that that bonds to porous surfaces to attach raw clay to such surfaces as wood or terra cotta. It is not necessary to apply adhesives to join raw clay to raw clay; the clay bonds to itself.

Carving and Cutting Tools
Ball Stylus – A
  Use this multipurpose tool to shape clay.
Dockyard V-gauge – B
  Use this fine, sharp tool to texture raw clay or to carve cured clay.
Needle Tool – C
  To make holes in beads, you'll need at least one needle tool. You can use the blunt end of a carpet needle, a bamboo skewer, or round toothpicks to bore various-size holes through raw clay.
Clay Shaper – D
  Use this rubber-tipped tool to sculpt clay.
Ripple Blade – E
  Use this novelty blade to cut squiggles and impress patterns into clay.
Nublade – F
  Use this sharp tool to cut millefiori canes.

Brayers and Clay Rollers – G & H
These tools form uniformly thick sheets of clay and smooth surfaces. Clay resists building up on acrylic rods. Although wooden rolling pins and brayers can be used, they require frequent cleaning.

Clay – I
Polymer clay is a responsive plastic material used for a variety of craft projects. Because the baking temperature is so low, you can cover almost any material to create a new look. Polymer clays are often identified with their manufacturers because each brand exhibits its own properties.

Clay Gun – J
The clay gun is used to create logs, hair, flowers and other designs by using 19 interchangeable discs to make the shapes.

Electric Buffer – not shown
The buffer is used to polish finished pieces to a satin or gloss sheen.

Glaze – K
Use a liquid glaze specifically developed to make clay projects shine and to protect the finished project. Glazes are available in matte, satin, and gloss finishes.

Marxit – L
This tool has grooves marked along the sides to help measure off clay segments to make uniform size clay sheets, strips, widths, canes, and beads.

Pasta Machine – M
A pasta machine conditions and makes uniformly thin sheets of clay. Although more of an investment than other supplies (the machine cannot be used for food preparation after using it for clay), a pasta machine is a valuable and useful clay tool.

Pattern Cutter Set – N
Roll the clay and press the cutters to create shapes.

Sandpaper – not shown
Use wet/dry 400- and 600-grit automotive sandpapers to sand and polish cured clay.

Work Surfaces – not shown
Use nonstick surfaces that are light and portable, and resist clay build-up with clays that tend to get warm and sticky. Acrylic

boards, plastic laminate, marble, and smooth ceramic tile work well.

Other Tools

Look for other tools in your kitchen or crafts supplies that will work to roll, cut, and shape clay.

Polymer Clay Basics

Safety

Polymer clays that bear the AP nontoxic and ASTM-D labeling have been tested and found to be safe when used properly. Invest in an oven thermometer to calibrate your oven and a timer to bake clay at the recommended time to prevent burning. If the clay burns, open the windows, take the burnt items outside, and vacate the area until the air clears.

Curing

Curing temperatures vary by brands. To reach maximum fusion and strength, follow the clay manufacturer's instructions. Because clay items are most fragile while they are warm, avoid handling them until they have completely cooled.

Cure the clay in an oven dedicated for this purpose, if possible. Otherwise, you might want to protect your cooking oven by using disposable aluminum baking trays or oven baking bags to reduce the odor.

Note: It is not mandatory to use baking bags and does not affect the outcome of the project. Always bake clay in a well-ventilated area, as some fumes may be emitted.

To prevent flat, shiny spots on the clay, place baking parchment, an index card, a file folder, or polyester batting on the bottom of a baking tray before placing the clay on the tray. Set the tray in a baking bag and tightly seal the bag (to reduce the odor of the baking clay). Place the tray in the oven. Keep the area properly ventilated while baking the clay.

Conditioning

To achieve maximum cured strength, condition polymer clays prior to use. Condition the clay by kneading and warming it in your hands until it is soft and pliable, or repeatedly fold and roll the clay through the pasta machine until it is soft and pliable.

Ease of conditioning and clay strength vary by brands. Clay brands also differ in texture and stickiness. Experiment with brands to determine which ones you prefer. After the clay is conditioned, it is ready to be shaped and cut.

Sanding and Polishing

Use wet/dry 400- and 600-grit automotive sandpapers to sand and polish cured clay items. Place a sponge in water and lay 400-grit paper on the sponge to sand the item against the paper. Repeat with 600-grit paper. Rinse and dry the item thoroughly.

For high-gloss finishes, sand and polish the cured clay or apply a water-based surface gloss glaze. Sand beads prior to glazing them to avoid amplifying surface imperfections.

Photo A

Photo B

Photo C

Photo D

Photo E

Getting Started

Checkerboard Cane

Perfect this fun technique with only a little practice.

1. Referring to Photo A, above, and using two colors, roll each color into a sheet. The thickness of the sheets depends on the desired size of the completed checkerboard. It is important that both colored sheets be the same thickness. Trim the sheets and alternately stack them in four layers.

2. Gently press the stacked layers and turn the stack (see Photo B). Cut approximately ⅛-inch thick slices (see Photo C). Turn over every other slice and restack the clay into a square (see Photo D). Slice the checkerboard

into the desired thickness (see Photo E). Roll with a brayer to reduce the thickness, if desired.

Bull's-Eye Cane

One of the easiest canes to make, the Bull's-Eye Cane also allows for a great deal of creativity.

1. Roll the clay into a ball. Elongate the ball to form a log (see Photo F).

2. Roll a second color of clay into a sheet ¹⁄₁₆-inch thick and wrap it around the log (see Photo G). Roll the cane on a work surface to seal the wrap. (Use additional colors around the second color, if desired.) Slice the log into the desired widths (see Photo H).

Skinner Blend Bull's-Eye

Make canes of color gradation using the Skinner Blend technique, named for designer Judith Skinner.

1. Roll two separate sheets of each color through the pasta machine at the thickest setting to condition it. Cut each color into a triangle (see Photo I).

2. Join the two triangles to form a rectangle. Press together the edges and trim off the protruding tabs (see Photo J). Roll the rectangle through the pasta machine at the thickest setting, making sure that both colors touch the rollers.

3. Fold the rectangle from top to bottom (see Photo K). Place the folded side of the rectangle on the pasta machine rollers and roll the clay through again (see Photo L).

4. After rolling the clay ten times, striping is apparent (see Photo M); after rolling twenty times, stripes blend with graduated color (see Photo N). The clay strip should be thin and delicate.

5. Determine which color you want on the outside of the cane and begin rolling from the opposite end to form the Skinner Blend into a pinwheel. To make a bull's-eye like the one shown in Photo O, *opposite,* cut the sheet at the point where the red begins to change to eliminate some of the red clay. Begin rolling at the red end to tightly roll

Photo F

Photo G

Photo H

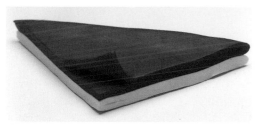

Photo I

Photo J

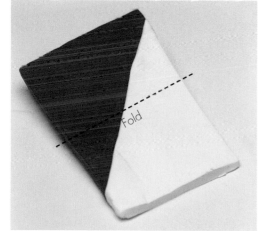

Photo K

Photo L

Photo M

Photo N

Photo O

the sheet, ending with white to the outside.

Gently roll and smooth the cane until swirls are blended and the roll is the desired size.

6. Cut cane slices to the desired thickness.

Making a Bead

Clay beads have endless design variations and uses. This technique uses leftover clay, adds a colorful cover, and results in a beautiful bead.

1. Make a cane (see Photo P), which provides the color and bead design. Roll scrap clay into a ball to form a base (see Photo Q, green clay).

2. Cut uniformly thin slices from the canes and place them on the base (see Photo P and Photo Q). To reposition slices, gently lift them from the base. After the slices are arranged, gently roll and smooth the surface with the acrylic rod to join the slices.

3. Lightly mark a hole placement with a needle tool or a bamboo skewer (see Photo R). Place a finger on the bead opposite from the mark. Use a drilling motion with the tool to make a hole in the bead. When the tip of the needle protrudes, withdraw the tool, turn the bead around, and drill the hole from the opposite side.

4. Place the bead on polyester batting on a baking sheet (to prevent flat, shiny spots on the bead). Follow the manufacturer's instructions to bake the clay.

5. Let the bead cool completely before handling to it avoid breaking it or distorting the shape.

Photo P

Photo Q

Photo R

Millefiori Flower Beads

1. Flower center: Roll a sheet of white and a sheet of orange clay through the thickest setting of the pasta machine. Trim the edges, stack the white on top of the orange (see Photo A), then roll the sheet again through the pasta machine on the thickest setting. Reset the machine to a thinner setting and roll the clay again. At one end, roll the strip into a jelly roll (see Photo B), then pleat the sheet back and forth while forcing it into a cane (see Photo C). Wrap in white and set the cane aside.

2. Flower petals: Use one half package of white and one half package of red clay. Following the instructions to make a Skinner Blend Bull's-Eye, page 24, roll a very thin sheet colored from red to white through the thin setting of a pasta machine. Cut the sheet at the point where the red begins to change to eliminate some of the red clay. Begin rolling at the red end to tightly roll the sheet, ending with white to the outside (see Photo O, page 25).

3. Reduction: A millefiori cane is a rod or loaf that contains an image, and canes may be reduced in diameter to miniaturize the image. To reduce the shaded bull's-eye flower center and flower petal canes, flatten the ends of the canes by pinching to help reduce the waste (see diagram, *right*).

Photo A

Photo B

Photo C

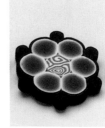

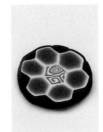

Photo D

Photo E

Photo F

Photo G

Photo H

Photo I

Photo J

Gently roll the center of the canes on the work surface to approximately 12 inches long, and until the middle section is the same diameter as the ends. Reduce canes only as you need them; canes cannot be enlarged.

4. Cut the canes: Cut off the ends of the reduced canes. Cut the flower petal canes into six equal lengths; cut the flower center to the same length (see Photo D).

5. Flower assembly: Press six petal canes around the flower center cane (see Photo E). Wrap a thin sheet of black clay around the petal cluster (see Photo F), pressing the black clay between the petals with a needle tool similar to Photo I, *opposite*.

Roll black clay into a long thin cylinder. Cut it into six equal lengths to fill in between the petals (see Photo G). Roll the cane to smooth the black clay (see Photo H). Indent the tip of the flower petals with a needle tool (see Photo I). Roll the cane to smooth the edges (see Photo J).

6. Leaf assembly: Make a Skinner Blend Bull's-Eye (see page 24) using two shades of green, lighter green to the outside (see Photo K). Wrap a thin sheet of white around the green (see Photo L). Slice the cane to make two half circles (see Photo M). Place a white sheet between the halves (see Photo N) and pinch the halves together to create a leaf (see Photo O). To form the leaves, pinch one side of the half circle to form a leaf tip while gently pinching the opposite end to reduce the shape. Press the leaf against the work surface to reduce the leaves and to maintain uniform thickness around each leaf. The finished sizes of the millefiori components is optional. The finished sizes for the project shown are approximately ½ inch for the flowers and ⅜ inch for the leaves. The size can be changed by reducing the green cane, then wrapping the cane with white clay as shown in Photo D, *opposite*. Cut the leaf cane into three equal segments. Press the segments to the flower cane (see Photo P). Slice the cane into the number of flower segments desired and make holes in each segment. Bake and cool according to the manufacturer's directions.

Photo K

Photo L

Photo M

Photo N

Photo O

Photo P

Drawer Pulls

Use the millefiori canes without reducing them to decorate objects such as the drawer pulls, *below*.

1. Apply glue to the surface. Roll a thin black clay base and carefully lay it on the glue-covered surface. Shape to fit. Cut very thin slices of the millefiori flower cane and place on top of the black clay base. Cut thin short pieces of the leaves and add to the outer edge of the flower. Add a colorful twisted coil around the edges.

2. Bake the project according to the clay manufacturer's instructions. Let the clay cool before handling it.

Creative Tip

Be sure to wash your hands and the work surface before and after working with each color of polymer clay. Otherwise, one color could be transferred to the next color of clay used. Baby wipes work really well.

– Team Member, Mentor, Ohio

Crafts – Polymer Clay

Mokume Gane Technique

The Mokume Gane technique (pronounced *Mo-kú-meh Gá-neh*) has gained great popularity among polymer clay enthusiasts. Many variations and materials—such as heat-set paints, powders, and metal leaf—can be incorporated into this design.

1. Roll each clay color through the thickest setting of a pasta machine or hand roll the clay to approximately 1/8-inch thickness. Stack the colors and trim them into a rectangle (see Photo A). Thin the stack to about half its thickness using an acrylic rod, then roll it through the pasta machine (see Photo B). Cut the stack in half. Stack one half on the other half and repeat the rolling process two times (see photos C and D for side views of stacked layers).

2. Use a rubber stamp (see Photo E) or other impressing tool (see Photo F) to deeply impress a design into the clay slab. Sprinkle baby powder or cornstarch on the rubber stamp to prevent the clay from sticking to it. Roll the top of the clay smooth with an acrylic rod or brayer (see Photo G). *Note: Although a stamp with words will create an interesting design in the clay, the words will not be legible.*

3. Cut and remove a couple of paper-thin slices from the top of the slab using the Nublade to reveal the marbleized pattern

and discard. Then cut slices from the center section of the stack to use in the project (see Photo H).

4. Roll a medium thin sheet of clay (white is used) with an acrylic rod. Place the smaller thin marbled slices on the solid color clay and roll the layers smooth (see Photo I). Cut out a shape.

5. For a backing, roll a sheet of clay through the thickest setting of the pasta machine (or hand roll the clay to approximately 1/8-inch thick). Place the cutout shape on the clay sheet (black is used). Inspect to make sure there are no air pockets between the shape and the sheet. Roll the layers smooth with the acrylic rod. Cut out the sheet around the shape (see Photo J).

6. To edge a shape with a solid color, knead a small ball of clay and roll the clay into a coil with the palm of your hand. Lightly and quickly roll the coil back and forth to the desired thickness. Wrap the coil around the shape. Trim the ends neatly. Roll another coil and taper the ends into curlicues. Press the curlicues along the sides and across the shape (see Photo K).

7. Place the clay on a flat baking surface and bake following the clay manufacturer's instructions. Let the clay cool completely before handling it.

8. To finish as a necklace (shown), cut black cording to length. Slip the cording through the side loops and knot the cording ends to wear the Mokume Gane as a necklace.

Photo A

Photo B

Photo C

Photo D

Photo E

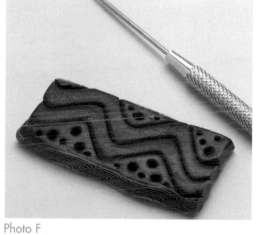

Photo F

Photo G

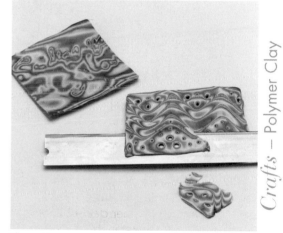

Photo H

Photo I

Photo J

Photo K

DECOUPAGE

This well-known French
art of bonding paper cutouts

to a surface can be accomplished by anyone.
Practice your skills on a small plate or box,
then graduate to furniture and walls for home
decor projects with panache.

Decoupage

Tools and Materials

Antiquing Medium (optional)
This aging medium comes in liquid, gel, stain, and paste formulas. Wipe it onto a surface that has been painted, following the manufacturer's instructions.

Cutting and Application Tools
Cutting Tools – A
Choose either small, fine manicure scissors or embroidery scissors. Both allow you to make tiny, tight cuts. You'll also find a crafts knife or razor blade useful for making inside cuts.

Smoothing Tools – B
Use a smooth-edge tool such as a burnisher (blue triangular tool, *right*) or an old credit card to work out any bubbles from under the applied papers.

Paintbrushes – C
Use foam brushes to apply decoupage medium to cut papers. Small, flat, synthetic brushes work well to apply glue to small pieces of paper.

Decoupage Glue or Medium – D
Most decoupage mediums are a three-in-one solution that includes a water-base sealer, glue, and final finish. Available in satin or gloss, some manufacturers label them mediums, although other containers are labeled decoupage glue. Read the manufacturer's label to determine whether to follow up with a good varnish.

Measuring Tool – E
Use rulers for accurate measurements, and as cutting guides for straight edges on decoupage papers.

Papers – F
Suitable papers include specialty decoupage papers, gift wrap, printed die cuts, and color copies of copyright-free images. Thick paper will not work well for decoupage. Make sure that the ink on all papers will not smear when moistened.

Paint (optional)
Before adding decoupage images, you can choose to paint the project surface. Turn to pages 183–229 for painting ideas.

Water-Base Varnish – not shown
After the decoupage medium dries completely, you can add several coats of varnish for a protective finish.

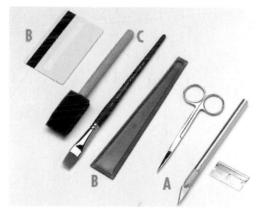

Originating in the late fifteenth century, the technique of decoupage is derived from the French word *découper*, which means "to cut out." By cutting and adhering paper images to a base, then applying a coat of finish over the top, you can transform a plain surface into a work of art.

Decoupage Basics

Decoupage yields beautiful results with minimal artistic talent. You can apply cut papers to any finished surface or you can start with your own creative paint treatment to serve as a decoupage background. (See page 193 for Paint Basics.)

Note: *Do not try to decoupage over wet or fresh paint. The moisture in the decoupage medium might cause the paint to peel. Allow 24–48 hours for the paint to cure.*

Getting Started

1. Cut out the desired elements from sturdy decoupage paper, gift wrap, prints, or whatever printed paper you are using. Select images that have print on one side only—otherwise, the image beneath might show through when you apply the medium. Most decoupers find it easier, when cutting small pieces, to move the paper instead of moving the scissors. It is helpful to cut tiny inside cuts before cutting out the basic shapes—the paper is less likely to tear.

Plan the overall design before adhering the elements. Apply decoupage medium to the back of the cutout with a sponge brush (see Photo A).

2. Press the cutouts in place, smoothing out as many of the air bubbles by hand as possible. Then use a burnisher or the edge of a smoothing tool (such as an old credit card) to flatten the images and pull out as much of the medium as possible. Work from the cutout center to the edges (see Photo B).

Be careful not to rub the image hard enough to scratch or tear it. Gently wipe away excess glue with a damp paper towel or sponge.

Photo A

Photo B

Photo C

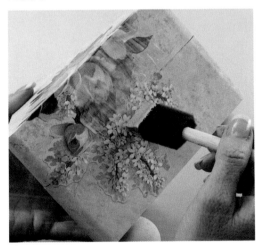

Photo D

If a paper crosses over an opening onto two sections of your project, slice through the paper along the opening and separate the two sections, allowing the medium to dry (see Photo C).

3. After pasting all papers, gently wipe away the excess medium and allow the surface to dry completely.
Note: *When working on glass, it is especially important that you remove excess medium from the glass before it dries to avoid an unwanted milky finish.*

4. Coat the surface with multiple coats of decoupage medium applied over the entire project surface (see Photo D). The first coat should be thin. Subsequent coats can be heavier. Open the lid slightly to dry thoroughly between coats. Keep the lid open with tooth picks or use a piece of wax paper. The objective is to make the overall surface as smooth as possible.

5. Apply antiquing, if desired. See Antiquing and Distressing beginning on page 214 for more information about antiquing.

6. Follow with a coat of varnish. Some manufacturers suggest that you let the decoupage medium cure for several weeks before applying varnish.

Faux GLASS

Once reserved
for specially trained artisans,

glass crafts can now be created by anyone
with spectacular results. The products, such as
pre-cut glass shapes, liquid leading, and etching creams,
are readily available.
All you need is a little inspiration!

Faux *Glass*

If cutting pieces of expensive, colored glass to make windows seems intimidating, here's a beautiful alternative that looks just as professional. It is applied like paint, but dries to a translucent finish. Use any stained-glass window pattern, or create a design of your own that mimics elements of your furnishings and your home's interior.

Tools and Materials

Crafts Knife or Razor Blade – A
Use a crafts knife or a single-edge razor blade to cut the leading-strip material.

Glass or Plexiglas®– not shown
Both glass and Plexiglas are ideal surfaces for liquid leading and window paint.

Instant Leading – B
Use precut, self-clinging strips of instant leading to form the design on the glass.

Liquid Leading – C
Use liquid leading to squeeze lead lines directly from a bottle to join or "solder" glass pieces for an authentic look.

Window Paint – D
Formulated specifically for stained-glass projects, this paint looks milky from the container, but dries translucent as glass.

Masking Tape – not shown
When you are not working on an installed window, tape holds the pattern and the glass or Plexiglas firmly to the work surface.

Toothpicks and Paper Towels – not shown
Use toothpicks to redirect the window paint if it "bleeds" beyond your pattern lines, or to push color into tight corners. A damp paper towel is necessary for quick clean ups.

Faux Glass Basics

Work on an existing window or take an easier route and work on glass or Plexiglas that will be installed with glazing points or thin molding into an existing window space. If you work on a separate piece of material, precut the material about ⅛ inch smaller than the existing window frame to ensure a good fit. It's difficult to trim later.

Clean the surfaces. Use only a damp cloth on Plexiglas. Do not use household cleaners, which may dull the surface. To clean glass, use glass cleaner. Mistakes may be easier to remove from glass than from Plexiglas after the paint dries.

To remove a section of color, use a razor blade to score around the dried color close to the lead lines to break the seal. Then "peel" it off the window. Be careful not to scratch the glass or Plexiglas surface, because scratches will show through the completed window design.

To create a pattern, select a design from a copyright-free pattern book, or draw your own motifs. Copy the pattern on white paper, then place the pattern securely under or on the reverse side of the glass. Use it as a guide and apply the leading, following the lines of the pattern.

Instant leading clings to the glass when pressed in place. Leading lines are further secured with the liquid-lead joints and paint. Begin and end lead lines at appropriate and obvious junctures, and avoid breaks midpoint in design lines.

To use liquid leading, place a piece of ruled paper on cardboard, or purchase a grid designed to create lines. Cover the ruled paper with non-clinging plastic (a dry-cleaning bag works). Tape securely. Following the paper lines, squeeze liquid leading directly from the bottle. Let the leading dry.

Getting Started

1. Size a printed pattern or create a pattern to fit the window. Copy the pattern onto white paper. Cut the glass or Plexiglas to the size and shape needed to accommodate the window.

Position the pattern under the glass and tape the edges of both the pattern and the glass to the work surface. Cover all pattern lines with the leading strips (see Photo A), using a crafts knife or razor blade to cut the joints. Consider how real stained glass windows are leaded, and try not to break lines that should be continuous. Do not stretch the leading strips.

2. Carefully fill in gaps between the leading strips with the liquid leading. Hold the leading bottle in your hand as you would a pencil, just above the glass surface. Gently squeeze the bottle with even pressure to "solder" the joints (see Photo B). Let the leaded joints dry thoroughly before adding window color.

3. When the liquid leading is dry, fill in the leaded areas with window paint colors. Do not shake or stir the paint. Using the paint bottle as an applicator, fill in the entire leaded area with paint so the paint touches the leading (see Photo C). Complete each section before moving to the next.

Remove bubbles by carefully combing through them with a toothpick. (If you get paint on your clothes, wash it out immediately.) Let the paint dry for a minimum of 24 hours or until the milky look disappears. Newly applied puddles of paint will dry lighter.

Note: You may mix colors for a variegated look, or combine any color with white for an opalescent appearance. Test the color mix on scrap glass so you know how it will look when it dries.

Let the window cure for one week before cleaning it with a soft, damp cloth. Install the design with glazing points or molding strips that have been painted or stained to match the window.

Photo A

Photo B

Photo C

Glass *Etching*

Transform ordinary stemware, vases, windows, or mirrors into elegant frosted home decor accessories.

Tools and Materials

Etching Mediums

Frost Spray – A

Create a semi-transparent frosted look with this one-step spray paint.

Etching Cream – B

Etching cream creates a reaction with the glass that forms a permanent design on the surface of the glassware. Allow the cream to remain on the glassware for the time stated. Take care when using etching cream. Wear gloves and goggles to avoid contact with eyes and skin and use it in a well-ventilated area.

Frosted Liquid Paint – C

This is an easy, non-toxic way to create the etched-glass look. Apply a coat of conditioner to the surface. Avoid touching the prepared surface of the glassware. Use tape or shelf paper to mask the areas of the glassware, and use a wedge-shape foam sponge to apply the water-base paint to the surface. If you desire a more frosted look, apply a second coat of paint, or apply the frosted paint to a flexible rubber stamp.

Note: Glass-etch rub-ons are available at your fabric store to help you create the look without actually etching the glass.

Tape or Self-Adhesive Vinyl Shelf Paper – not shown

Use frosted tape or adhesive-back vinyl shelf paper as a mask to contain frost paint or etching cream in certain areas of the glass.

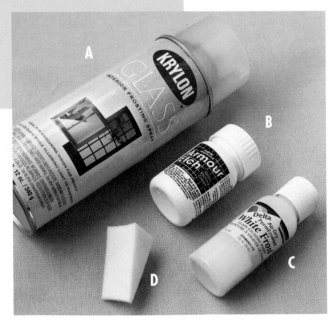

Wedge-Shape Foam Sponge – D

Use wedge-shape sponges to apply the liquid frost paint on glass.

Glass Etching Basics

Create beautiful designs on glass by designing a pattern freehand, masking off areas with tape, or using self-adhesive vinyl shelf paper. To make designs with curved lines, cut a piece of shelf paper large enough to cover the entire glass surface. Trace the design onto the shelf paper, planning the position of the design on the glass surface. Use a crafts knife or sharp scissors to cut out the design to make a stencil. Remove the backing paper and press the stencil onto the glass surface.

Getting Started

1. Wash the glass and dry thoroughly with lint-free paper towels or cloth. Tape works best to create the straight lines shown on the glass surface (see Photo A).

2. Use a wedge-shape foam sponge to apply the liquid frost paint or etching cream to the unmasked areas (see Photo B) or spray the areas with frost spray. Allow the glass to dry for the amount of time specified by the manufacturer before removing the tape or stencil.

Photo A

Photo B

Simple Elegance

Creating your own beautiful
frosted designs on glass
are so simple with new
easy-to-use etching products.

Glass *Inlay*

Glass inlay is a quick and easy way to create a mosaic look with less effort. The readily available, precut pieces allow you to adhere colored glass shapes to clear surfaces, letting light shine through. Glass pieces also can be applied to trays, tabletops, and other home-decorating accessories.

Tools and Materials

Buffer – A
The buffer pad wipes away any remaining solder after it has dried without harming the surface of the glass pieces. It is also used to polish the finished project.

Cutters – B
Use glass cutters to cut the glass chips into small pieces as needed for the project. The cutters will cut straight lines without shattering the glass.

Precut Glass Chips – C
Precut glass chips come in a variety of shapes and colors that can be used as is or cut to different sizes as needed for your project. Kits are available that contain precut chips, a pattern, and instructions.

Inlay Glue – see photos A and B
Adhere the glass pieces to the surface with inlay glue, which dries clear.

Paintbrush – D
A paintbrush is used to apply glue to the glass pieces, and to apply sealer to the finished inlay project.

Safety Glasses – E
Use safety glasses to protect your eyes when cutting glass pieces or tiles.

Solder Grout – see Photo C
Mix powdered solder with water. Use the compound to fill spaces between glass pieces to achieve the traditional soldered appearance of stained glass.

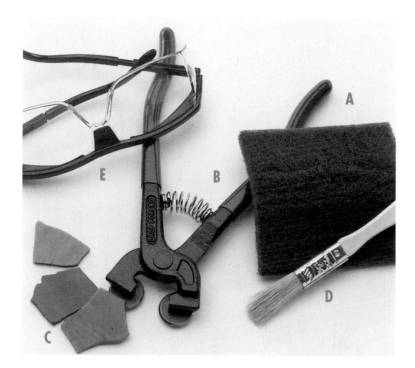

Photo A

Base Surfaces

Glass or Plexiglass is used to create faux glass projects. Look for these surfaces at your home center or frame shop.

Glass Inlay Basics

Purchased glass inlay pieces have no sharp edges, so they are safe and easy to use. Because they are precut to a variety of appealing shapes, there is minimal waste. You'll find a wide range of colors available.

Choose a pattern from a magazine or book, or create your own, using motifs from your home-decorating fabrics or wallpapers. Size the pattern to fit your project surface.

For a project base, cut a piece of thin glass or Plexiglas to the size and shape needed to accommodate the pattern, or work directly on terra-cotta, wood, or other base surfaces. Position and tape the pattern to the back of the glass. If you are not working on glass, use the pattern as a guide, or copy the lines onto the project surface with transfer paper.

Getting Started

1. Glue precut glass pieces on the front of the glass or Plexiglas, using inlay glue and the pattern as a guide (see Photo A).

2. Select background pieces. Wearing safety glasses, use the glass cutters to cut smaller pieces to fill in the background. Glue the glass chips to the glass, leaving small spaces between the pieces (see Photo B). Let the inlay glue dry completely.

3. Mix the solder (grout) with water according to the manufacturer's instructions. Use a spatula or brush to spread the solder over the glass (see Photo C), completely filling in all the spaces between the glass pieces and around the outside edges.

Let the solder dry following manufacturer's directions. Use a damp sponge to wipe away the excess from the surface. Use the buffer pad to remove any remaining solder and to polish the glass. Apply a coat of sealer with the paintbrush for protection against stains or the weather.

Photo B

Photo C

Crafts – Glass Inlay

GILDING

Looking for a way
to add elegance to an object?

Apply a layer of gold or silver using specialty paints,
foils, or gilding pastes to add shine
to a simple urn, dish, or picture frame.

Gilding *Finishes*

The richness of gold is at home in almost any decor. Liquid, leaf, and rub-on gilding products have made the application of metallic finishes easy and enjoyable. If you prefer other metallic colors, you'll find the same products in silver, bronze, and other finishes.

Tools and Materials

Adhesive – not shown
Gold-foil adhesive resembles crafts glue and it is the medium to which the gold leaf sticks.

Antiquing Medium – A
Antiquing medium is used to antique the gold finish if you prefer a dark, aged look. See page 214 for more about antiquing.

Foil Gold Leaf – B
Gold leaf or foil comes in sheet form. Cut it into manageable-size pieces. When pressed facedown on top of dry adhesive, the foil transfers to the project surface.

Liquid Leaf – C
This gilding product is easy to apply with a paintbrush and provides solid coverage, if desired, or can be dry-brushed for highlights.

Gilding Paste – D
Easy to apply with your finger or with a cloth, gilding paste adheres to most surfaces. Let it dry, then buff to a shine.

Paint – E
Change the project base-coat color by applying acrylic paint prior to gilding.

Paintbrushes – F
Use disposable sponge brushes when possible. Designate brushes for gilding and do not use them with other paint products.

Sealer – not shown
Use sealer to prevent decorative finishes from seeping into porous surfaces, such as wood, plaster, or papier-mâché. Apply sealer before base-coating with acrylic paint or applying a gilding product.

Gilding Basics

If your decorating feels a bit dull, polish it with a glint of gold. Whether it's a subtle rubbed-wax finish or glitzy gold foil, gilding can warm up your accessories for any room.

There are numerous products available; always read the manufacturer's label before beginning your project. Start by accenting a picture frame or floral container, then consider gilding furniture, walls, and even decorative moldings.

Getting Started

Gold Foil

1. Apply a coat of sealer to any porous surface such as wood, plaster, or papier-mâché. When the sealer is dry, paint the surface with the base-coat color of your choice (see Photo A). Let the base coat dry.

2. Apply a coat of adhesive to the surface (see Photo B). Let the adhesive dry until it is no longer a milky color, and then apply a second coat of adhesive. Let the second coat dry for one hour.

3. With the shiny side up, place the foil on the adhesive-covered surface (see Photo C). Press and rub the foil onto the surface with your fingers. Use the back of a spoon to burnish flat areas and a toothpick or other small object to press foil into recesses.

4. Peel off the foil, leaving the metallic finish on the surface (see Photo D). Use a cloth or a large brush to dust off any loose foil pieces. Apply a light coat of sealer to the foiled surfaces. If desired, apply antiquing medium to the sealed surface, wipe off the excess, and finish with another coat of sealer.

Liquid Leaf

Achieve an elegant result by applying liquid gold paint to a surface with a foam brush (see Photo E).

Gilding Paste

Gilding paste is an almost effortless way to add a metallic accent. Simply use your finger or a clean cloth to rub the paste onto the surface where desired (see Photo F). After it dries, buff the finish with a soft, clean cloth.

Photo A

Photo B

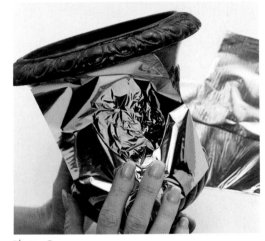

Photo C

Photo D

Photo E

Photo F

JEWELRY, METAL and WIRE

Have you been admiring
the imaginative jewelry

and metal objects you see in boutiques and art galleries?
Make them yourself!
Follow the techniques in this chapter to turn fun and
funky designs into works of art.

Jewelry *Making*

Express your personal style with jewelry you make yourself. Experiment with the variety of beads and charms available to make funky, formal, or casual accessories.

Tools and Materials

Choosing materials for a jewelry project is a bit like being a kid in a candy store. The vast array of beads, charms, and findings make the design choices nearly unlimited.

Bead Board – A
A bead design board allows you to first lay your materials in the center compartments to see how the components relate to one another, and then arrange the design along the outer grooves before stringing. If you plan to string several projects, this is an essential tool. To complete a single project without investing in a bead board, place the beads in small containers and line them up on a towel or piece of felt.

Bead Identification – *opposite*
By rows from left to right:
B   10/0 Rocaille, transparent rainbow seed, teardrop, and wooden.
C   Silver-lined bugle, inside rainbow seed, European glass, and bone.
D   Bugle, cut silver-lined, 3mm gold vacuum plated, and letter.
E   Silver-lined Rocaille, E beads, antique silver, and semi-precious (amethyst).

Earring Findings – *below*
F   Flat-pad posts with scroll backs (also called clutch)
G   Kidney wires (also called French wires)
H   Ball posts with scroll backs (also called clutch)
I   Clip backs
J   Fish hook ear wires (also called ball hooks)

A

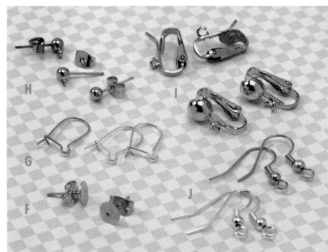

B

C

D

E

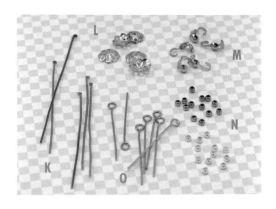

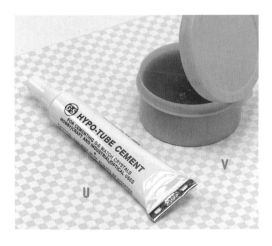

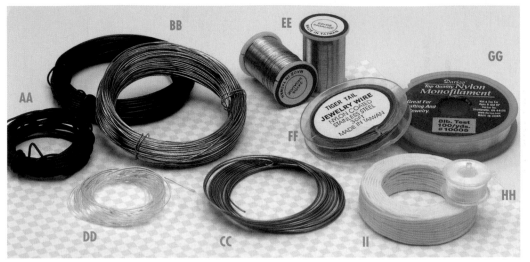

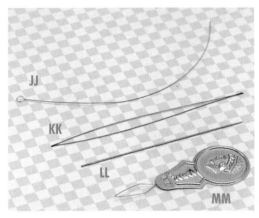

crimping tool or pliers to hold the cord in place.

O Eye pins have a loop on the end so that additional items can dangle from the bead strand. They also are used to make dangles.

Findings, Miscellaneous – *left middle*

P A jump ring is a single ring with a split in the center for linking components that will have minimal weight or stress.

Q Split rings are double-loop rings that look like miniature key chains. They are much stronger than jump rings and work well to link items that add weight or stress, or to attach dangling charms.

R Pin backs are used to sew or glue beads onto the base for a pin or brooch.

S Spacers hide the knots between the beads and the clasp.

T Crimp-coil necklace ends attach and conceal the necklace thread.

Glue and Wax – *left middle*

U Jeweler's glue is used to secure flat-backed gems or stones to mounts. The end of threading material also can be dipped in the glue. After it dries, the end will be stiff enough to run through the beads and the string will not fray.

V Beeswax keeps fine threads from tangling. Rub the thread over the wax before and during beading.

Fasteners – *top left*

K Head pins in gold and silver (similar to dressmaker's pins) have a flat end and are used to keep the last bead in a row intact. They generally are used to make dangles on earrings and necklaces.

L Bell caps in gold and silver are placed over the ends of beads for decoration or emphasis. They can be glued in place or strung on both sides of the bead.

M Double-cup connectors in gold and silver (also called clamshells) conceal the knot and attach the beaded strand to the clasp.

N Crimp beads in gold and silver secure the cording to the clasp. The cord runs through the crimp bead, around the hook of the clasp, and back through the crimp bead, forming a loop. The soft metal crimp bead is compressed with a

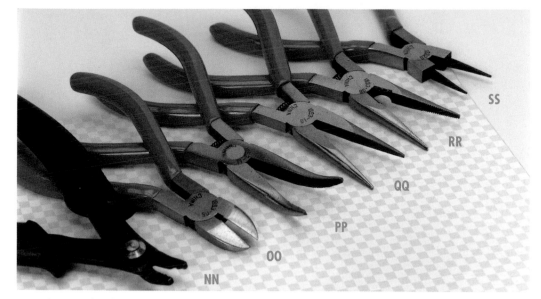

Pliers and Tools – *left*

The right tools make the job easier, but you don't necessarily need a chest of tools to complete a project. Start with commonly used pliers and tools, and add to your collection as your skills grow.

NN A crimper tool secures crimp beads to cording, and holds fasteners in place.

OO Wire cutters cut wire and tiger tail.

PP Curve-nose pliers work in awkward spots.

QQ Flat-nose pliers hold wire without creasing or making marks.

RR Needle-nose or snipe-nose pliers are for general use.

SS Round-nose pliers make smooth loops.

Threading Materials – *below*

The threading or stringing material used for beading depends on the final look you want, whether the stringing material will be visible, the weight of the beads, and the size of bead openings.

TT Metallic cord is used for necklaces that focus on a single bead or item.

UU Shiny nylon cord is soft to the touch and ideal for colorful clusters of beads.

VV Hemp cord is a natural fiber often used with stones and hand-crafted beads.

WW Craft lacing, shown in green and pink, is a plastic cord ideal for children's beading.

XX Metallic thread is used when stringing material will be visible through clear or luminous beads, or with metallic beads.

Hooks and Clasps –
lower left, opposite

W Spring rings (also called bolt rings) are for necklaces and bracelets.

X Barrel or screw clasps are for necklaces.

Y Lobster clasps are for necklaces or bracelets.

Z Filigree clasps (also called triple box clasps) are for necklaces.

Jewelry Wire – *opposite top*

Different wires are used to string beads, make findings, or as decorative elements.

AA Use soft imitation leather black cording to display beads or special elements. Gentle against the skin, it is ideal when stringing material is visible.

BB Craft wire (shown in blue and silver) is multipurpose and used for stringing material and for wrapping beads to combs, barrettes, etc.

CC Memory wire keeps its shape (coil) for bracelets; it can be cut into single or multiple coils and strung with beads.

DD Jelly cord is a strong, stretchy cord used when no stringing material is visible.

EE Narrow-gauge wire, gold and silver, is best for stringing small (20 to 40 gauge) items with no visible stringing material.

FF Tiger tail is a nylon-coated wire used to string heavy or sharp beads. Because it is stiff, it is also used to maintain a basic shape for bracelets or watchbands. It

does not work well for necklaces that have a fluid look.

GG Nylon monofilament beading thread is used for twisted necklaces, and to achieve a fluid look.

HH Beading thread is ideal for clear beads and semi-precious stones.

II Waxed linen thread helps make stringing beads fast and easy.

Needles and Threaders –
opposite middle

Beading needles are very fine so they will slide easily through small openings.

JJ Wire bead threaders are ultra-fine and flexible, making them ideal to string semiprecious stones, pearls, and beads with small openings.

KK Big-eye needles are split in the center to make them easy to thread.

LL Beading needles often look like sewing needles, but are longer and finer.

MM Needle threaders come in handy because beading needles can be difficult to thread.

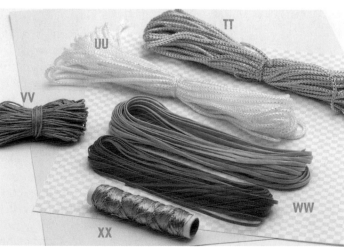

Jewelry Making Basics

Decorative Materials

When choosing beads for a necklace, it is helpful to select one bead as the focal point for the center. Or, design a necklace in which the shape is the focal point and the beads are all similar. Remember that the pattern of all of the beads is important because it draws the eye upward toward the face and gives the necklace a unified look.

For bracelets, no focal point is needed. Keep all the beads a similar and practical size and weight for comfort.

Weight and length are key factors when making earrings. Earrings that are too long or too heavy are uncomfortable to wear. Use post or clip backs with heavy beads.

Findings

The clasps, hooks, earring bases, and other structural workings of jewelry are referred to as findings. Match the style and weight of the findings to the beads and finished design. For example, a heavy necklace will require a sturdy clasp for security; a fine necklace will require a small clasp to blend with the design.

Putting it Together

Stringing materials also should be matched to the beads and the design. Wire and tiger tail work well for heavy or rough beads, although both have stiffer shapes and do not drape well. Cotton or linen string, thread, and cording drape well but are less strong.

Soft metal tubes called crimping beads are the main tool to attach the clasp to strung necklaces and bracelets. Knots also can be used and often are covered by special beads at the end of a strand.

Jump and Split Rings

To open jump rings (shown on page 46, photo P), pull one side toward you and the other side away. Close the ring by pinching it shut with pliers. Do not open the ring by spreading it wider.

Slide an item onto a split ring by slipping it into the opening in the same manner as placing a key on a key ring, then slide it around until it reaches the center of the ring. If your project calls for several split rings, purchase split ring pliers at fishing supply stores for just a few dollars. They spread apart the rings to make working with the rings easier.

Knots

Overhand knot: This is the weakest of the three knots shown. Make a loop in the cord. Bring one end through the loop and tighten it. Overhand knots often are used to end a section, strand, or to separate beads.

Square knot: This is the next strongest knot of the three shown. Bring the left cord over

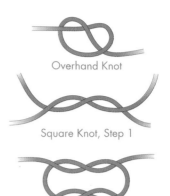

Overhand Knot

Square Knot, Step 1

Square Knot, Step 2

Surgeon's Knot

and under the right cord; bring the right cord (the same one used) over and under the left cord. Pull to tighten it. Square knots are used to join two strands.

Surgeon's knot: This is a stronger version of the square knot. Begin in the same manner as a square knot, left over right and under and then right over left and under. Go through the loop one more time with the right cord. Pull to tighten.

Crimp Beads

1. Thread a crimp bead onto the strand after the last bead. Run the cord through the ring of the clasp and back through the crimp bead, forming a loop. Slip the cord end through the next several beads and pull it to tighten the loop.

2. Place the crimp bead in the wide hole of crimping pliers and squeeze to compress the bead.

3. Turn the crimp bead 90 degrees and place it in the small hole of crimping pliers. Compress it again to create a tight ending and round shape. If you do not have crimping pliers, use needle-nose pliers, making the crimp as tight and round as possible.

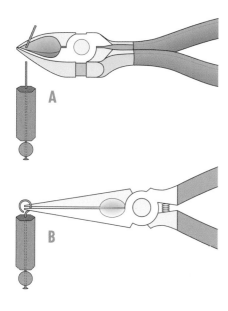

Making Loops

1. To make a loop in the end of an eye pin, head pin, or wire, cut the wire ¼ inch above the last bead (see diagram A).

2. Grip the tip of the pin or wire with round-nose pliers and rotate the pin around the pliers to form a loop (see diagram B). Make the loop as small and complete as possible.

Getting Started

Twisted Necklace

Color and motion are the attractions of this necklace made of assorted small beads.

1. Join three 22-inch strands of beading thread in an overhand knot (see Photo C). Secure the knot with a dot of glue and trim the ends. Feed the threads through the bottom opening of a double-cup connector and close the connector to encase the knot.

2. String the threads with assorted small beads (see Photo D).

3. Lightly braid the strands (see Photo E). Pull all three threads through the bottom opening of a second double-cup connector. Tie the threads in several surgeon's knots and add a dot of glue to secure the knots. Trim the ends and close the connector to encase the knots. Attach a lobster clasp to one connector and a jump ring to the other connector.

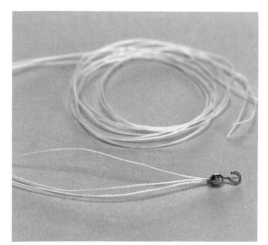

Photo C

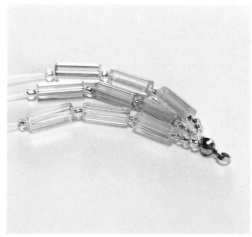

Photo D

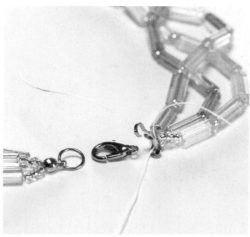

Photo E

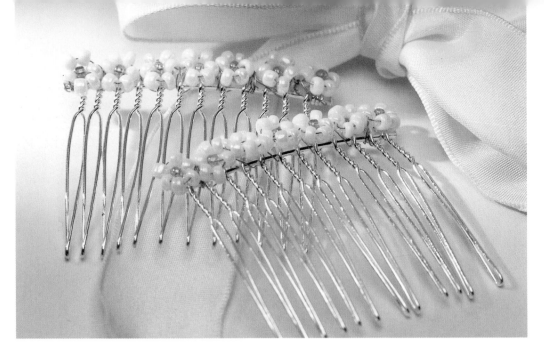

Daisy Chain Comb

A row of beaded daisies is wired to a comb for a dainty springtime hair ornament.

1. Slide 3 white and 1 green seed bead onto a 17-inch strand of 32-gauge silver beading wire, leaving a 3-inch tail. Go back through the first white bead (see Photo A).

2. Add 3 white seed beads and go through the last seed bead to create a daisy. Continue this pattern, placing the daisies close together. Make a strand long enough to fit across the top of the hair comb (see Photo B).

3. Wrap the 3-inch tail around one end of the comb to anchor the daisy chain. Use the other end to wire the remainder of the chain across the top of the comb, slipping the wire between each flower (see Photo C). Finish by wrapping the remaining 3-inch tail around the end of the comb.

Multi-strand Necklace

1. Join three 22-inch strands of beading thread in an overhand knot. Secure the knot with a dot of glue and trim the ends. Feed the threads through the bottom opening of a double-cup connector and close the connector to encase the knot (see Photo D).

2. String 1–1½ inches of one thread with assorted small beads (see Photo E). Repeat the pattern on the other two strands. Join the three strands with several larger beads. Repeat this pattern to near the center of the necklace. At the center, thread all three strands through a series of larger beads to create a focal point. String beads on the remaining thread following the previous pattern.

3. Pull all three threads through the bottom opening of a second double-cup connector. Tie the threads in several surgeon's knots and add a dot of glue to secure the knot. Trim the ends and close the connector to encase the knot. Attach one end of a barrel clasp to each connector (see Photo F).

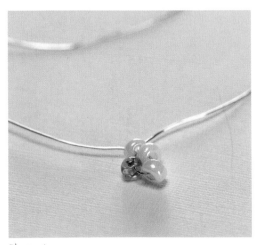

Photo A

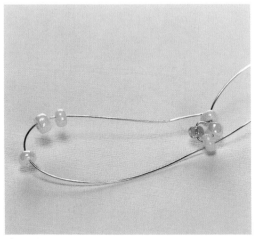

Photo B

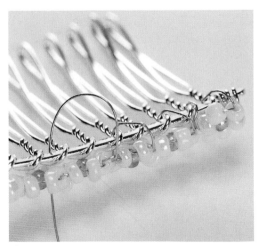

Photo C

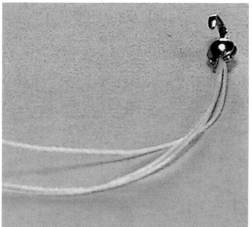

Photo D

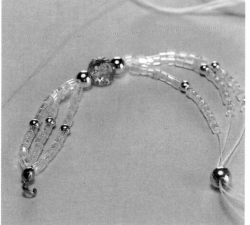

Photo E

Photo F

Metal *and Wire*

Once relegated to a few shelves at the hardware store, wire has emerged as a versatile and fun crafts product. Use it for jewelry, home decor projects, and gifts.

Tools and Materials

Eyelet Punch – not shown
Use this tool to grip fabric and to punch uniform eyelets.

Files – A
Use files to smooth the tips of sharp wire or to shape wire into a point.

Hammer – B
Use a nylon hammer to flatten large areas of a design. The nylon coating prevents scratches and damage to the wire.

Hand Tools
Nylon Jaw Pliers – C
Use these nylon-coated pliers to smooth out or flatten wire without damaging it. If the wire gets little bends or kinks in it, place the wire between the jaws of the pliers and press down.

Round Nose Pliers – D
The basic wire craft tool, round nose pliers are used to make loops in the wire.

Bent Chain Nose Pliers – E
The bent shape of these pliers allows you to grasp and manipulate wire easily, especially in small, intricate areas. They also are ideal for opening and closing small loops.

Wire Cutters – F
It is important to have sharp, pointed, flush wire cutters. Use specially made cutters that are small enough to fit into hard-to-reach places. When cutting small pieces of wire, hold the wire in an enclosed area, such as a trash bin. Wear safety goggles while using and cutting wire.
Note: Always point the wire away from your face and other people while cutting.

Flat Nose Pliers – G
With the tips, these pliers create sharp angles in wire as well as grip and bend wire.

Jig – H
The jig is a platform used to design and shape wire. Pegs fit into the holes of the jig and are arranged depending on the shape to be created. Pegs, available in four sizes, determine the size of the loop in the design.

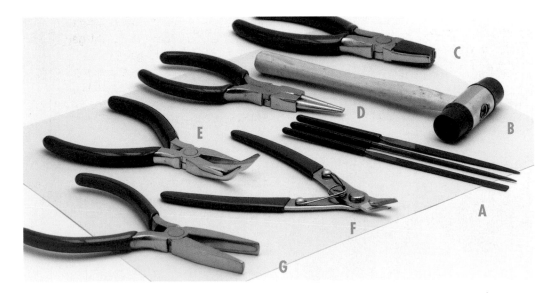

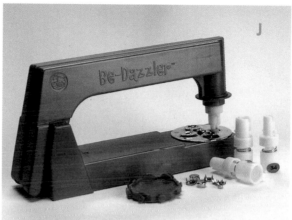

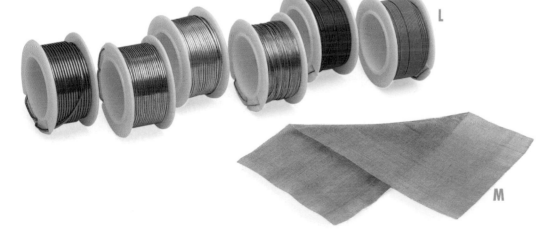

Stud-Setting Tool – I

Use this tool to push studs through fabric and to close the prongs on the back of the studs.

Stud and Rhinestone Setting Machine – J

Quickly attach a variety of studs to fabric using four sizes of plungers. With a quick press, this handy tool also will attach rhinestones to fabric.

Twist- and Curl-Making Tool – K

The twist-making tool coils wire and wire beads. The tool comes with an assortment of bars, each creating a different size and shape of coil.

Wire – L

Copper wire is available in many colors and weights. The higher the gauge number, the thinner the wire. For example, 24-gauge wire is thinner than 18-gauge wire. Generally, heavy gauges work well on a jig, and fine gauges work well to make wire beads. Practice with gauges to determine which works best for your project.

Woven Metal Fabric – M

This sturdy yet pliable fabric is woven from varying weights of wire. Use sharp cutting tools to cut the fabric, and bend and shape it for a multitude of crafting uses.

Metal and Wire Basics

Creating a Basic Anchor Loop

This loop begins wire designs and is used as an anchor loop on the jig. To create a basic anchor loop (see Photo A-1), grip an end of wire between the handles of the round nose pliers, about ¼ inch down from the tip of the nose. Carefully wind the wire around the nose of the pliers to create a loop. This can be done by either turning the pliers or by pulling the wire around. Pull the loop off the nose of the pliers, then squeeze the loop between the tips of the pliers to flatten the end.

Eye Loops

The eye loop (see Photo A-2) is often used at the end of the beaded link. To create this loop, bend the end of the wire ⅜ inch from the end at a right angle. Use the round nose pliers to make a loop that is centered over the straight end of the wire.

Wire Rings and Jump Rings

To make a small wire ring or jump ring (see Photo A-3), create a basic loop. Use wire cutters to trim off the straight end of the wire under the loop. Always open a wire ring sideways—never pull it open wide by pulling apart the ends. Use pliers to squeeze the opening closed.

To make several jump rings, use the large metal rod of the Twist- and Curl-making tool (see Photo C). Create a coil that is tightly wound so that the rounds of wire are as close as possible (see Photo A-3). Remove the coil from the tool. Use wire cutters to

cut one complete round from the coil for each jump ring needed.

Bead Links

A bead link is any number of beads on a wire with a loop at each end (see Photo A-4). Bead links can be attached to each other to form a chain or they can be attached to other wire shapes.

Creating a Spiral

To create a spiral, make a basic loop at the end of the wire (see Photo A-5). Grip the loop between the jaws of the nylon jaw pliers. Shift the position of the loop as you circle the wire around. Repeat until the spiral is the desired width. Make tightly or loosely wound spirals.

Getting Started

Wire & Bead Stretch Bracelets

1. To make the bracelet in Photo D, *opposite*, follow the manufacturer's instructions with the Twist- and Curl-making tool (see Photo C). Use the smallest metal bar and make a long coil with blue or copper wire (see Photo B). Cut the coil into ½-inch lengths to create the coil beads.

Photo B

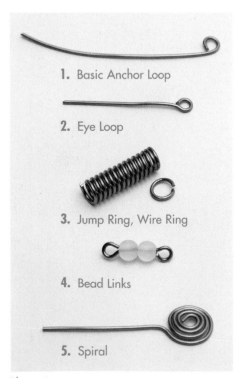

1. Basic Anchor Loop

2. Eye Loop

3. Jump Ring, Wire Ring

4. Bead Links

5. Spiral

Photo A

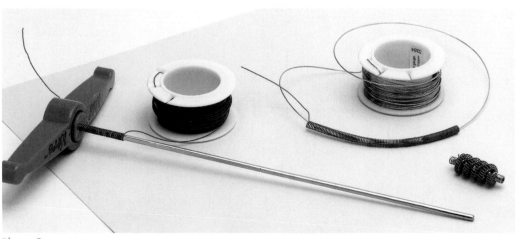

Photo C

2. Thread beads onto elastic, alternating wire beads and glass beads, to make the bracelet long enough to fit around a wrist (see Photo D).

3. Knot the ends of the elastic securely and trim the excess elastic.

Double Coil Bead Bracelets

1. To make the bracelet in Photo E, follow the manufacturer's instructions for the twist- and curl-making tool (see Photo C, *opposite*). Refer to Photo B, *opposite*, for a close-up view of coils. Use the smallest metal bar to make double beads. Use 26-gauge bare copper wire for the first coil (see Photo E), and use 24-gauge tinned copper wire for the second coil. Use five or six double coil wire beads, depending on the finished size of the bracelet.

2. Thread wire beads onto 20-gauge wire, alternating wire beads with glass beads.

3. To form the hook, bend back one end of the 20-gauge wire approximately 1¾ inch from the end. Form a tight hairpin turn and gently press the double wires together. Hold the nylon-jaw pliers across both wires, about ¾ inch from the end of the shorter wire. Tightly wrap the shorter wire around the long wire two or three times; cut off the excess wire. Use the round nose pliers to bend the loop in half to create a hook. Turn up the end of the hook.

4. To form the eye clasp at the opposite end of the bracelet, make a loop with the round nose pliers. Wrap the excess wire two or three times around the base of the loop and cut off the excess wire.

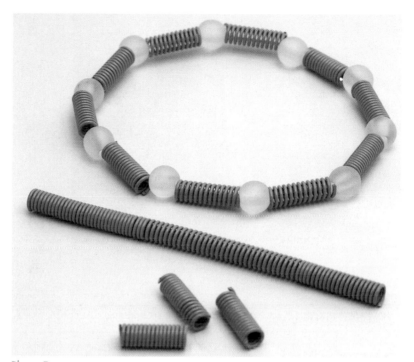

Photo D

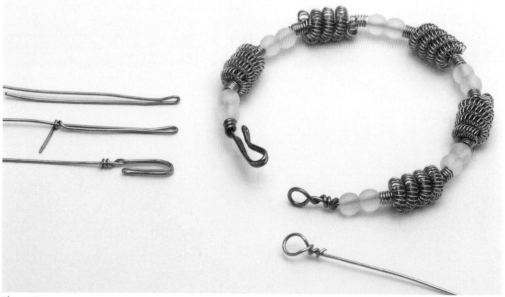

Photo E

Wire & Bead Candlesticks

Insert rolled woven metal fabric into the candlesticks. Starting at the candlestick base and leaving 4-inch wire tails at the top and bottom, coil wire around the candlesticks. Add beads and crimp the wire to secure the beads as you wrap the wire. Spiral the wire tails, and insert studs at the bases of the candles.

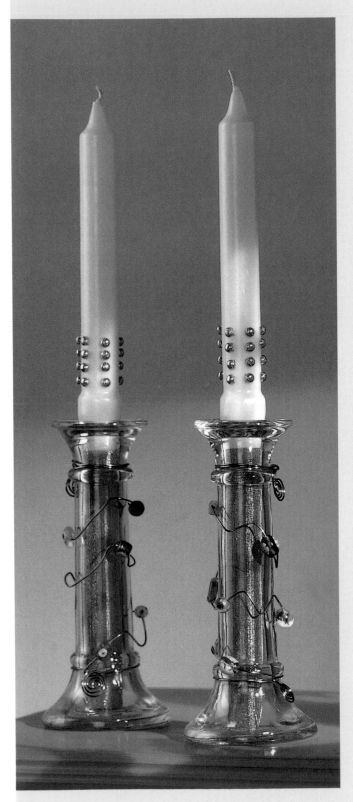

Frame & Candleholder

Layer woven metal fabric around photo frames and candles to form attractive casings. Secure the metal fabric layers with eyelets, and trim the eyelets with wire and bead coils.

Table Cover or Shawl

Trim a large fabric square with wide tape and cording. Use the stud-setting hand tool to attach nail heads and square studs along the borders and corners. Trim purchased tassels with coiled wire and beads to add decorative appeal and weight to the fabric corners.

Stud-Embellished Pillow

Trim a fabric square with nail heads and square studs, using the stud-setting hand tool. Sew on a fringe, join the square to backing fabric, and insert a pillow form.

Lampshade

Cover a lampshade with fabric, then glue trim to the top and bottom edges of the shade. Space studs evenly around the lower edge. Wire beads to spirals and use jump rings to attach the dangling spirals to the shade.

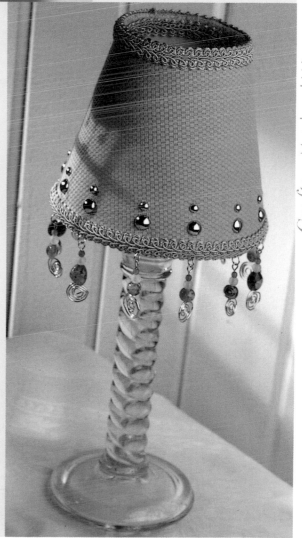

CROSS-STITCH
and
NEEDLEPOINT

Easy and enjoyable,
the age-old stitching techniques

of cross-stitch and needlepoint never go out of style.
Study the basic stitches in this chapter to start
making your own heirloom pieces that will last
for generations.

Elegant *Cross-Stitch*

Tools and Materials

Fabrics – A

Fabrics from left to right: 28-count Monaco, 22-count Hardanger, 18-count Aida, 14-count Aida, 14-count Damask Aida, 8-count Aida, and 6-count Aida.

Background fabrics for cross-stitching come in a variety of thread counts (threads per inch), colors, and fiber contents. Fabrics such as Aida cloth, Hardanger, linen, and assorted even-weave fabrics are traditional choices.

When determining the amount of fabric to purchase, keep in mind the method you plan to use for finishing the piece, and add at least 3 inches to each side.

Aida cloth

Aida cloth is a woven fabric designed in a pattern of overall squares. Each cross-stitch is worked over one fabric square by inserting a threaded needle into distinct corner holes. Aida cloth, available in 6, 8, 11, 14, 16, and 18 squares per inch, is recommended for beginners.

Closely-woven fabrics

Counted cross-stitch also can be done on closely-woven fabrics, such as fleece, wool, cotton, and satin, using waste canvas as a temporary grid.

Even-weave fabrics

Even weaves are woven from single-ply threads of the same size, characteristics that make the fabric easier to stitch than linen or Hardanger. Even-weave fabric such as Brittany, Jobelan, and Monaco are good choices for beginners.

Hardanger

Hardanger is another traditional choice for counted cross-stitch. It is woven from a fine two-ply thread and has a thread count that is always 22 threads per inch.

Linen

With fine thread counts ranging from 26 to 40 threads per inch, linen appeals to advanced stitchers. Although the fabric can be difficult to stitch because of its uneven weave, the finished work has an elegant look.

Waste canvas

Waste canvas is a stiff temporary canvas grid with 6 to 16 squares per inch. Cover waste canvas edges with masking tape before placing it on the fabric to prevent threads from catching on the raw edges as you stitch. Align the grid with the fabric grain and baste the canvas to the fabric.

Note: *Before cross-stitching on fabrics with give (such as knits), stabilize the fabric with iron-on backing.*

Everyone who loves needlework appreciates a beautifully stitched piece. These pages are filled with tips, techniques, and information on tools and materials to help you cross-stitch with ease and perfection.

A

Use a sharp chenille needle to pierce closely-woven fabric under the waste canvas. After stitching is completed, moisten the canvas and pull out the horizontal threads, one at a time and in sequence. Repeat to remove the vertical threads.

Hoops and Frames – B
Hoops
Embroidery hoops are available in plastic, wood, metal, and spring-tension styles. They vary in size, ranging from ornament size (3 inches in diameter) to large lap models (23 inches in diameter).

Although hoops are portable and easy to use, they tend to leave marks on the fabric. To discourage this, cover the piece when stitching is interrupted briefly, and remove the fabric from the hoop when

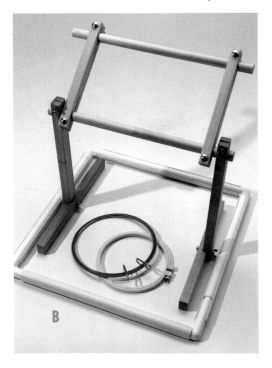

you stop stitching for longer periods. Another way to keep stitchery clean is to stretch the fabric over the hoop, then turn the hoop over. Work the design from the back side of the fabric.

In addition to hand-held hoops, there are freestanding floor hoops and tabletop hoops. Both allow you to work with both hands, but they lack the portability of hand-held hoops.

Mounting frames
Mounting frames are available in many sizes and varieties. The fabric is secured at the top and bottom, and the piece is rolled as the stitching progresses.

Q-Snaps
Q-Snaps are plastic L-shape bars that slip together at the corners. Four long curved pieces of plastic snap over each bar, holding the fabric in place. They are available in assorted lengths.

Stretcher Bars
Wooden stretcher bars are sold in pairs so you can purchase the length and width to accommodate the piece. The bars interlock at the corners snugly and the fabric is mounted with brass tacks. Stretcher bars keep stitchery clean and crease-free.

Needles – C
Chenille Needles (Not shown)
When cross-stitching closely woven fabrics with waste canvas, use chenille needles. Chenille needles are similar to tapestry needles, except they have sharp tips that pierce fabric.

Embroidery Needles (C-3,C-4)
Embroidery needles have the long eye of chenille needles, but are slimmer and

have a sharp point. They can be used for cross-stitching, but the sharp tip may snag fabric and result in uneven stitches. Embroidery needles range from sizes 1 through 10.

Tapestry needles (C-1,C-2)
Tapestry needles work best for cross-stitching even-weave fabrics. They have a long eye and blunt tip that doesn't snag or catch fabric threads. They are available in sizes 13 to 26, with the larger numbers indicating the finer needles.

Scissors – D

Use sewing scissors to trim fabric and small, sharp-pointed embroidery scissors to cut and clip threads.

Threads – E, F, G, and H
Embroidery Floss – E
Cross-stitch is most often worked with six-strand cotton embroidery floss. Available in a variety of colors, including variegated shades, threads usually are separated into strands for stitching.

Metallic Thread – G
Used alone or in combination with other threads, metallics add sparkle to the stitches.

Pearl Cotton – F and H
Pearl cotton is a highly mercerized, twisted, non-divisible 100-percent cotton thread. Pearl cotton is available in four sizes: #3 and #5, which are sold in skeins, and #5, #8, and #12, which are sold in balls. Size 12 is the thinnest.

Note: *Rayon floss (not shown) is highly lustrous thread that is 100-percent rayon and comes in six-strand skeins. When working with rayon, use short lengths and lightly dampen the threads. Rayon embroidery floss is slippery, and recommended for experienced stitchers.*

Other types of less commonly used threads are three-ply Persian wool, silk, narrow satin ribbon, and silk ribbon.

Purchase all the thread for a project at one time to ensure that threads come from the same dye lot. Keep a record of color numbers in case you need to purchase additional amounts or for reference.

Colorfast Testing of Thread

Although most threads are colorfast, occasionally some dark shades bleed. Check the threads before beginning to stitch, especially if the design will be laundered. Stitch on a scrap piece of fabric and dip the fabric into tepid water. If the color bleeds, determine whether to use the thread, choose a different shade of thread, or avoid laundering the finished work.

Cross-Stitch Basics

Preparing the Fabrics

Press out fabric wrinkles and creases, and trim the edges. With a threaded needle, overstitch the edges to prevent the fabric from raveling. Or bind the fabric edges with masking tape, being aware that tape may leave a permanent residue when left on fabric for long periods.

Preparing the Threads

Cut threads into manageable lengths. For embroidery floss, pearl cotton, and wool,

18 inches is adequate. For metallics, rayons, silks, ribbons, and threads that might wear or tangle with repeated stitching, use shorter lengths. Experiment on a scrap of fabric to determine the best length.

When you work with embroidery floss, separate all six plies. Combine the suggested number of lengths to work the cross-stitches and to keep stitches smooth and untwisted.

Threading a Needle

Thread a needle with an even number of floss lengths: Cut a 30– to 36-inch length of floss and separate only half as many strands. Fold the strand in half, and thread the cut ends through the needle.

Loop Knot (see diagram, below)

Holding the folded end (the loop), work the first half of a cross-stitch. As you return the needle to the back of the fabric, slip the point through the loop and pull the thread to secure the loop knot.

Thread a needle with an uneven number of floss lengths: Hold the needle in your left hand (if you are right handed), and loop the floss over the end of the needle. Pinch the looped floss with your thumb and

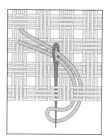

Loop Knot

forefinger, then slide it off the needle. Insert the pinched loop through the eye.

Starting and Ending a Stitch

Working with an uneven number of floss lengths: When you stitch with an uneven number of floss lengths, begin stitching with a waste knot—a temporary knot that is clipped when you complete the first length of floss (see the diagram, below).

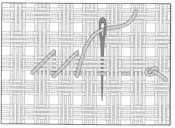

Waste Knot

Knot the end of the threaded floss. Push the needle into the right side of the fabric, then bring the needle up through the fabric several inches to the left of the knot. Work the first series of stitches (from left to right), catching the thread on the wrong side of the fabric. Clip the waste knot.

When you complete the floss length or a color, secure by weaving the thread under the stitches on the wrong side of the piece (see the diagram, *below*). Clip the thread close to the fabric rather than leaving thread tails that may tangle in the stitching or be pulled to the right side of the fabric.

To begin the next thread length, weave the thread under previous stitches on the wrong side of the piece, similar to ending the previous thread.

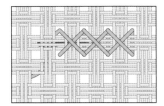

Shown from fabric front

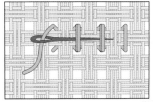

Shown from fabric back
Securing Thread

Choosing a Starting Point

If the piece has a border, work the basic lines first to make sure the stitches connect, then stitch border details. Stitch the inner design, counting stitches from the border.

If the design has no border, begin stitching at the design center or begin in a corner and work horizontally across the piece.

Stitching Method

The punch-and-poke method is most often used to do cross-stitch. To do this, keep the right hand (if you are right handed) on top of the fabric and the left hand below. Insert the threaded needle into the wrong side of the fabric with the left hand. Pull the needle through to the right side with the right hand. Push the needle to the wrong side using your right hand, and pull it through with the left. With a little practice, the punch-and-poke method becomes second nature, and the stitches will be uniform. Using this method, the stitches are more likely to be worked in the holes, rather than caught in the fabric threads.

Laundering the Finished Piece

If the finished piece is soiled or has hoop marks, wash it in lukewarm water using a mild detergent. Thoroughly rinse the detergent from the fabric. *Note: See page 61 for colorfast testing of threads.*

You can still wash the finished piece even if you have not checked the threads for colorfastness. If a color begins to bleed, hold the stitchery under cool running water. Flush water through the piece until the color stops running.

Lay the piece flat. When it is almost dry, press it with a hot iron and a press cloth.

If the finished piece does not require laundering, press it with a damp press cloth and a hot iron.

Framing Stitchery

Determine whether to frame the finished piece using glass or with the design exposed. Glass protects the finished work from dirt and dust; however, it also captures moisture that damages threads over time. Use acid-free matting or spacers to prevent the glass from touching the fabric. Although moisture still can get inside the frame, the mat and spacers lessen the problem.

For a cross-stitch piece that will be displayed in a home without air-conditioning or in an area with high humidity, omit the glass. Pad the finished cross-stitch with batting to raise and soften the appearance while concealing the mounting board beneath.

Getting Started

Refer to the diagrams, *below* and *opposite*, and the stitched examples on page 64 to practice.

Most cross-stitch charts feature symbols that represent one cross-stitch for each symbol shown. Color-coded symbol keys designate the color of floss to be used.

Basic Cross-Stitch: Bring the needle up at 1, down at 2 to create the first diagonal, then up at 3 and down at 4 to create the first cross-stitch. On linens, Hardanger, and even-weave fabrics, count over two threads and up two threads of the fabric as shown in the diagram, *below*.

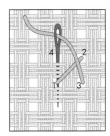

Basic Cross-Stitch

For Aida cloth, work one stitch over each square of fabric. (The first leg of a cross-stitch is a half cross-stitch.) You can work the cross-stitch in the reverse manner, so the top leg runs from the lower left corner to the upper right corner. Work the stitches consistently, with the top leg of every stitch worked in the same direction.

Cross-Stitch in Rows: Work a line of diagonal stitches in one direction as shown in Step 1. Then cover with top diagonals in the opposite direction on your second journey (see Step 2).

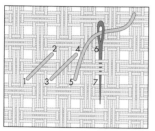

Step 1

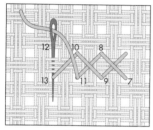

Step 2
Cross-Stitch in Rows

Backstitch: Backstitches are usually worked with a single strand of dark color floss to outline, define, and sharpen cross-stitch motifs and designs. Follow the diagram, *below*, to work the stitches.

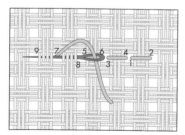

Backstitch

Half Cross-Stitch: A half cross-stitch is a single diagonal stitch or half a cross-stitch. Half cross-stitches are indicated by a diagonal line on charts. Follow the diagram, *below*, to work the stitches.

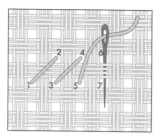

Half Cross-Stitch

One-Quarter Cross-Stitch: On linen, Hardanger, and even-weave fabrics, a quarter cross-stitch extends from the corner to the center intersection of the threads. To make quarter cross-stitches on Aida cloth, estimate the center of the square (see the diagram, *below*), and end the stitch there.

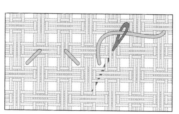

One-Quarter Cross-Stitch

Three-Quarter Cross-Stitch: Three-quarter cross-stitches combine one quarter cross-stitch with one half cross-stitch. The quarter stitch can be worked on either side of the half cross-stitch. A cross-stitch piece designed with three-quarter cross-stitches is more realistic-looking than one designed in basic cross-stitch. See the diagram, *below*.

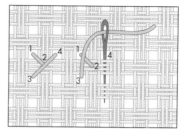

Three-Quarter Cross-Stitch

ᴥreative Tip

Fill in the completed sections of your cross-stitch graph with a highlighter to mark your progress.

– Team Member, Springfield, Pennsylvania

Stitched Examples

Photo A: Basic Cross-Stitches on 28-count even-weave fabric stitched over two threads.

Photo B: Cross-Stitches and Backstitches on 11-count Aida cloth stitched over one square. (Leaves outlined in black and tulip in dark pink.)

Photo C: Half Cross-Stitches on 14-count Aida cloth stitched over one square.

Photo D: Quarter and Three-Quarter Stitches on 22-count Hardanger fabric stitched over two threads.

Tools and Materials

Canvas – A

Needlepoint canvas is a stiff, loosely woven grid made from cotton, silk gauze, synthetics, or plastic. There are two basic types: mono (single-thread) canvas and Penelope (double-thread) canvas.

Mono canvas

Ranging in size from 10 to 40 stitches per inch, mono canvas comes in two styles: regular and interlock. Regular mono canvas

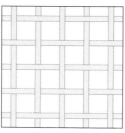

Mono canvas

consists of single threads woven together. (One thread is referred to as one mesh.) This canvas style is prone to shifting and may not be suited for some needlepoint stitches. Interlock mono canvas is similar to regular mono, except it is secured at the mesh intersections and is therefore more stable.

Penelope canvas

Consisting of double threads woven together, Penelope canvas is available in sizes 3½ through 12, with 8, 10, and 12 the most common.

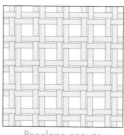

Penelope canvas

It is especially strong and can be worked the same as mono canvasses; however, its

Needlepoint

The steady rhythm of working a needlepoint project can be relaxing and satisfying. Learn these simple needlepoint stitches and complete your first project in no time.

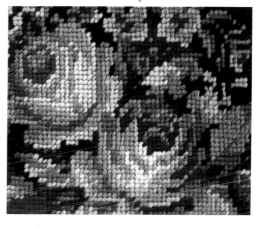

paired threads also make it possible to stitch two sizes of needlepoint in a single piece. For example, Penelope 10 (also referred to as Penelope 10/20) allows for 10 stitches per inch as well as 20 stitches per inch.

On Penelope canvas, the paired threads running in one direction are slightly closer together than the perpendicular threads. Work Penelope canvas with the closely woven threads held vertically.

Needlepoint is categorized by canvas size. Ranging from finest to coarsest, they are: petit point, worked on mono canvas ranging from 16 to 40 stitches per inch and on Penelope 10/20; gros point, worked on mono canvas ranging from 8 to 14 stitches per inch; and quickpoint, worked on rug canvas ranging from 3½ to 7 stitches per inch.

Masking Tape – not shown

Cover canvas edges with masking tape to prevent threads from catching on the edges.

Mounting Frames or Stretcher Bars – D

There are many styles from which to choose—hand-held to freestanding. Scroll frames are freestanding and generally made from wood. The canvas is secured at the top and bottom, and rolled as work progresses.

Needles – B

Use tapestry needles for needlepoint. They have a long eye, a blunt tip, and they come in assorted sizes.

Needlepoint Yarn and Threads – C

The threads most frequently used in needlepoint are yarns, including four-ply tapestry, three-ply Persian, two-ply crewel, and three-ply rug yarn. Less common choices range from pearl cotton and cotton floss to novelty yarns and metallics.

Scissors – E

Use an old pair of scissors for trimming the canvas and small, sharp-pointed embroidery scissors to cut and clip yarns.

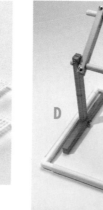

Needlepoint Basics

Preparing the Canvas

Add a 3-inch margin (for framing) all around the stitching area and cut the canvas to size, cutting between the meshes in a straight line. Cover the edges of the canvas with masking tape.

Preparing the Yarn

Cut yarn into 18-inch lengths. For specialty yarns and threads that might wear or tangle with repeated stitching, use shorter lengths. Experiment on scrap canvas before cutting all of the yarn.

Mounting the Canvas

Mount the needlepoint canvas on stretcher bars or on a scroll frame. If portability is important, you may choose to work the canvas in your hands.

Starting and Ending a Stitch

Use a waste knot to begin the first thread of the needlepoint piece (refer to the diagram in the Cross-Stitch section on page 61). Knot the end of the threaded yarn. Push the needle through the fabric from the right side, placing the knot several inches to the left of the first row of stitches. Bring the needle up through the fabric (to the right of the knot). Work the first row of stitches from right to left, catching the thread tail on the wrong side. When you complete the yarn length or a color area, finish it by pulling the yarn under previously worked stitches on the wrong side. Clip the waste knot and trim any excess yarn.

Beginning a Design

A needlepoint design can be worked in a variety of ways. One method is to stitch the primary design in continental stitches, then fill in the background with continental or basketweave stitches. Another method is to work the primary design and the background in basketweave all at one time. Start stitching in the upper right corner and work to the lower left corner (or work in the reverse).

Stitching Methods

Work the stitches with a single in-and-out motion of the needle or in the punch-and-poke method. The latter method is done with two hands and is described in the cross-stitch section on page 62.

Getting Started

Although hundreds of decorative stitches exist in an adventuresome needlepointer's repertoire, the two most commonly used stitches are continental and basketweave. Both stitches look the same on the right side and are worked by taking a diagonal stitch over each mesh intersection.

Basketweave Stitch is worked diagonally in rows, starting in the upper right corner (see Photo A and refer to the Basketweave Stitch diagram, *below*). It looks like the continental stitch on the right side, but the back appears woven. It may distort the canvas somewhat, but the distortion isn't as severe as that from the continental stitch.

Photo A: Basketweave Stitch

When you work from top to bottom, the needle should be held in a vertical position. Make a diagonal stitch over one intersection of canvas, then bring the needle out two holes downward to begin the next diagonal stitch. As the next row from bottom to top is worked, the needle is held horizontally. Make a diagonal stitch over one intersection, then bring the needle out two holes to the left and begin the next stitch.

Continental Stitch (or tent stitch) is worked horizontally in rows from right to left, completely covering the back of the

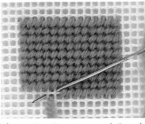

Photo B: Continental Stitch

canvas. Bring the needle to the right side and make a diagonal stitch, going in one hole up and to the right (see Photo B and refer to the Continental Stitch diagram, *below*). Come out again on the bottom row hole further to the left. Continue to the end of the row. Turn the canvas upside down and work the next row.

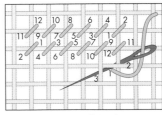

Continental Stitch

Blocking Needlepoint

Whether the piece is slightly or severely distorted, it will require blocking to square it. Do this yourself or take the finished work to a professional needlework or frame shop.

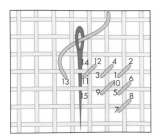
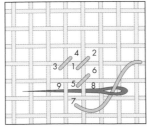
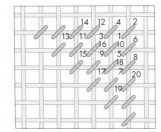

Basketweave Stitch

KNITTING
and CROCHET

Make your own
knitted and crocheted sweaters,

scarves, hats, and afghans to keep you warm
when winter's chill is in the air. No longer an old-fashioned
craft, even the younger generation is begging to
learn these techniques.

Knitting

No longer a needle craft for just your grandmother, knitting is enjoying a resurgence in popularity. Learn to create the latest fashion wear seen in department stores at a fraction of the cost. All you need is needles and yarn; the rest is up to you.

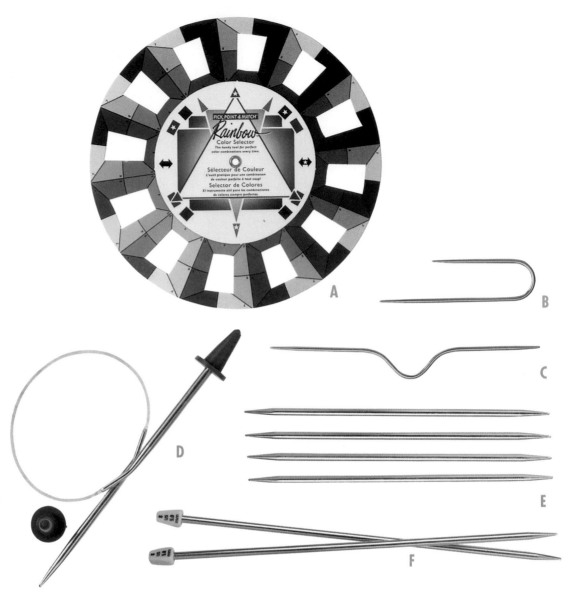

A

B

C

D

E

F

Tools and Materials

Color Wheel – A
The color wheel is designed for use with fiber and fabric.

Cable Hook – B
This tool is used for transferring or manipulating stitches in cable and Aran patterns.

Cable Needle – C
Used for the same purpose as a cable hook (see *above*).

Needles – D, E and F
Knitting needles are identified by two numbers. The first, the circumference size in millimeters, is universal. The United States uses a second series of identifying numbers usually ranging from 0–19 with a smaller number indicating a smaller diameter.
Circular Needle – D
Circular needles are used for circular or tubular knitting, and for row knitting on wide pieces such as afghans.

G

H

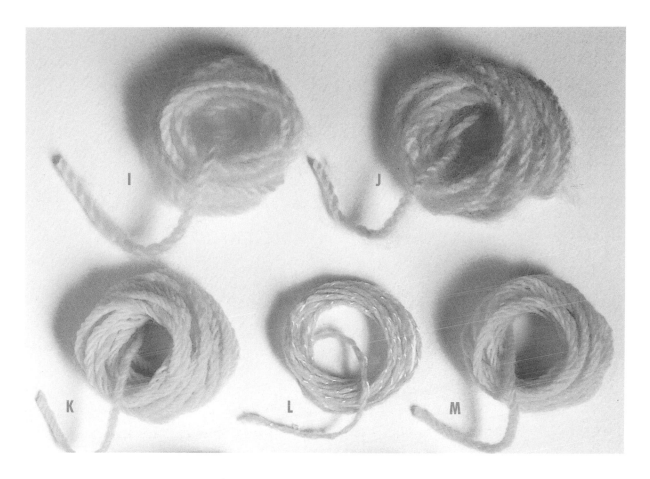

Note: A point protector is shown on the needle and next to the needle and is used to prevent stitches from slipping off the needle; use both point protectors to store projects in process.

Double-Point Needles – E

Double-point needles are used to knit small tubular projects, such as socks.

Straight Needles – F

Straight needles are used for knitting in rows.

Tapestry Needle – G

Tapestry needles are used to seam pieces together, and for working in ends of yarn.

Ring Markers – H

Ring markers are slipped on the needles to mark changes in pattern repeats, increases or decreases, or the beginning of rounds in circular knitting

Yarn – I to Q

Before beginning your project, choose from a wide variety of yarns available. Whenever possible, use the type of yarn recommended by your pattern maker. Follow the manufacturer's directions for yarn care.

Acrylic – I & J

This soft, 100 percent acrylic yarn is available in solid and variegated colors. The mohair-like appearance makes this a good choice for baby garments and afghans.

Blended Four-Ply Worsted – K

This yarn, a 4-ply worsted weight blend of soft, warm lamb's wool and durable acrylic, is a good choice for children's clothing, and comfortable accessories such as socks, mittens, and hats.

Cotton – not shown

Cotton yarns make garments that wear well, are non-allergenic, absorbent, and have excellent washing qualities. One type of yarn is mercerized cotton that is made to be extra strong and has a soft sheen. However, there is very little stretch to the yarn, which should be taken into consideration when knitting or crocheting a garment. Look for other cotton yarns such as 4-ply worsted, medium-weight,and cotton chenille. Use cotton yarns for children's garments, summer sweaters or vests, and other lightweight garments.

Sport-Weight Yarn – L

Sport-weight yarn is suitable for baby and children's garments and afghans. It is shrink-proof and non-pilling.

Worsted Weight Acrylic – M

This 4-ply, 100 percent acrylic yarn is soft to the touch and a good choice for children's and baby garments, home decor pieces, and accessories.

Wool and Acrylic Blend – N

This chunky blend is perfect for quick-to-make projects, jackets, vests, and home decorating items.

Worsted Wool – O

The clear stitch definition achieved with this 100 percent wool, 4-ply worsted weight yarn makes it a good choice for traditional sweaters, accessories, and home decor. Hand wash 100 percent wool.

Chenille – P

This soft, plush, super-chunky chenille has the look and feel of velvet, making it ideal for vests and wraps. Worked on large-sized needles, chenille is great for quick projects. Hand wash chenille.

Acrylic/Rayon Blend – Q

This richly textured, soft, chunky yarn is available in solid or blended shades, and is designed for afghans, throws, and home decor items.

Getting Started

Making a Slip Knot – A

1. Leaving a 6-inch length of yarn, make a loop and allow the working end of the yarn to hang down behind. Reach through the loop with your knitting needle and catch the yarn, pulling it forward through the loop (see Photo A-1).

2. Pull downward on the working yarn, tightening the knot (see Photo A-2).

Photo A-1

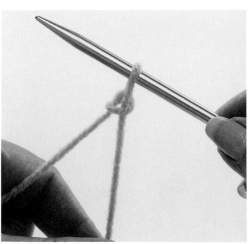

Photo A-2

Long Tail Knitting Cast On (co) – B

1. Draw out a tail of yarn, allowing one inch for every stitch to be cast on. Make a slip knot and follow these instructions: Hold needle with slip knot in your right hand, and hold the tail and working yarn in your left hand as shown (see Photo B-1).

2. Insert the tip of the needle upwards along the thumb, and through the loop on the thumb as shown (see Photo B-2).

3. Swing the needle up and over the inside strand around your index finger (see Photo B-3).

4. Bring this loop forward through the circle formed by the yarn around your thumb (see Photo B-4).

5. Spread the tail and working yarn with your thumb and index finger, tightening the stitch (see Photo B-5). Repeat for the number of stitches needed.

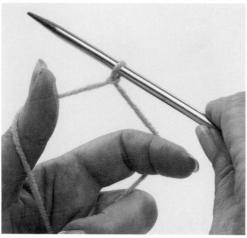

Photo B-1

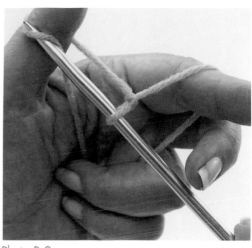

Photo B-2

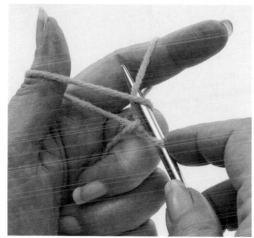

Photo B-3

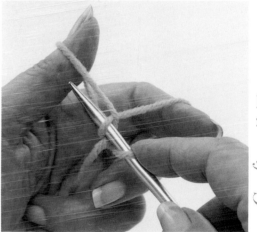

Photo B-4

❧Creative Tip

Slip your knitting onto stitch holders to prevent the yarn from

"memorizing" the needle shape.

– Team Member, Springfield, Pennsylvania

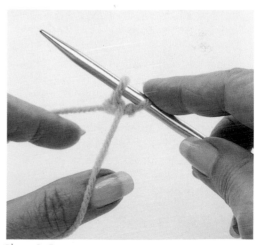

Photo B-5

How to: Hold the Yarn – C

1. Generally both right- and left-handers hold the needle with the cast on or completed stitches in their left hand. Photo C-1 shows the working yarn being held in the right hand, commonly called the American method. Start by looping the working yarn over your little finger.

2. Rotate your hand so the yarn lays under your two middle fingers and over your index finger, then pick up the remaining needle (see Photo C-2). Let the working yarn feed through your fingers to maintain a consistent tension, which keeps your knitting smooth.

How to: Make a Knit Stitch (k) – D

1. Holding the needle with the cast on or completed stitches in your left hand, and keeping the working yarn in back of the work, insert the point of the right-hand needle into the first stitch from front to back (see Photo D-1).

2. Wind a loop of yarn under, then over the point of the right-hand needle in a clockwise motion (see Photo D-2).

3. Draw this loop toward you through the stitch on the left-hand needle (see Photo D-3).

4. The newly completed stitch remains on the right-hand needle. As you slide the stitch worked from the left-hand needle, it now appears on the right-hand needle in the row below the newly completed row of stitches.

Continue working into the row of stitches on the left-hand needle until all stitches have been worked and transferred to the right-hand needle (see Photo D-4).

Photo C-1

Photo C-2

Photo D-1

Photo D-2

Photo D-3

Photo D-4

The piece of knitting you see in Photos D-1 to D-4 is called stockinette. It is created by making knit stitches on one side of the work (the side seen facing you in the pictures), and making purl stitches on the other side.

How to: Make a Purl Stitch (p) – E

1. Holding the needle with the cast on or completed stitches in your left hand and keeping the working yarn in front of the work, insert the point of the right-hand needle into the first stitch from back to front (see Photo E-1).

2. Wind a loop of yarn over and around the point of the right-hand needle in a counterclockwise motion (see Photo E-2).

3. Push this loop away from you through the stitch on the left-hand needle (see Photo E-3).

4. The newly completed stitch remains on the right-hand needle. As you slide the stitch worked from the left-hand needle, it now appears on the right-hand needle in the row below the newly completed row of stitches (see Photo E-4).

Continue working into the row of stitches on the left-hand needle until all stitches have been worked and transferred to the right-hand needle.

The piece of knitting you see in photos E-1 to E-4 is called reverse stockinette. It is created by making purl stitches on one side of the work (the side seen facing you in the pictures), and making knit stitches on the other side.

Photo E-1

Photo E-2

Photo E-3

Photo E-4

✂Creative Tip

Always work a gauge swatch before you begin knitting or crocheting your project starting with the recommended needle or hook size. If the swatch is too large, use a smaller needle or hook; if it is too small, use a larger needle or hook. Otherwise, the pattern will not be true to its intended size.

– Team Member, Garden Grove, California

Photo F-1

Increasing and Decreasing

To make a knitted garment fit, it will be necessary to increase or decrease stitches in areas such as the neck, armholes or other rounded areas. The pattern will tell you when and where this is necessary.

Increase: Yarn Over (yo) From the Knit Side – F

Bring the yarn forward between the two needles to the front of the work (see Photo F-1). Keep it in that position while you knit the next stitch in the usual way.

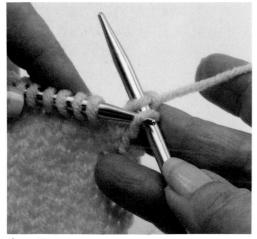

Photo G-1

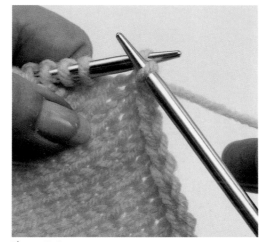

Photo G-2

Photo H-1

Photo I-1

How to: Bind Off (BO) – G

1. Holding the yarn and needles in the usual working position, work two new stitches onto the right-hand needle. Using the point of the left-hand needle, lift the first stitch worked up and over the second stitch, and off the needle (see Photo G-1). One stitch remains on the right-hand needle.

2. Work the next stitch on the left-hand needle and repeat the process of lifting one stitch over the other until you have one stitch remaining on the right-hand needle (see Photo G-2). Cut the working yarn at about 4 inches, pull through the loop, and tighten. Weave in the end with a tapestry or yarn needle.

Working in Ends – H

Thread the end to be hidden through a tapestry or yarn needle. Skim the needle under the surface of 2 to 3 inches of stitches (see Photo H-1) and draw the end through the stitches. Stretch the work slightly before trimming.

Seaming: Mattress Stitch – I

One way of seaming the row edges of pieces together is called Mattress Stitch. Thread a yarn or tapestry needle with matching color. (Contrast yarn has been used in the Photo I-1 for clarification). With the right side of both pieces facing you, secure the yarn at the lower edge of one piece. Run the needle under the first two cross bars between the edge stitch and second stitch, and draw up. Repeat on the other side (see Photo I-1). Continue this process, alternating between sides until the entire seam has been joined. Fasten off and weave in the end.

Note: When worked as a stitch in the next row, a yarn over will result in an additional stitch. It is often used as an increase in lace work because it creates a small hole. If, on the next row, it is worked together with the stitch on either side, it can be used as an eyelet or small buttonhole without altering the number of stitches.

Photo J-1

Photo K-1

Photo K-2

Photo K-3

Photo L-1

Photo L-2

Increase: Yarn Over (yo) From the Purl Side – J

Lay the yarn over the top of the right-hand needle and around between the needles to the front of the work again (see Photo J-1). Purl the next stitch in the usual way.

Increase: Knit Into Front and Back of the Same Stitch (kfb) – K

1. This technique will produce a one-stitch increase without creating a hole. Knit a stitch into the next stitch on the left-hand needle, but do not slide it off (see Photo K-1).

2. Insert the point of the right-hand needle into the back of the same stitch. Knit it from this position, then slide it to the left-hand needle (see Photo K-2).

3. Additional stitch made (see Photo K-3).

Decrease: One-Step Slip, Slip, Knit (ssk) – L

1. Insert right-hand needle into the front of the first stitch on the left-hand needle (see Photo L-1). Leave stitch on left-hand needle.

2. Now insert the point of the right-hand needle into the back of the second stitch on the left-hand needle (see Photo L-2). Draw the yarn forward through the loops of both stitches, then off the left-hand needle. One stitch decreased.

Note: Often decreases are used in pairs at necklines and armholes. The stitch the needle goes through first determines the direction of the slant. Thus a "knit two together" will slant right and an SSK will slant left.

Crafts – Knitting

Photo M-1

Decrease: Knit Two Together (K2tog) – M

You can decrease one stitch by knitting two stitches together. Insert the point of the right-hand needle through the fronts of the first two stitches on the left-hand needle and complete the knit stitch as usual (see Photo M-1). The same procedure can be worked from the purl side and is called P2tog.

Picking Up a Dropped Stitch –N

1. A dropped stitch in stockinette stitch will become a "run" if not caught and brought back up to the current row (see Photo N-1).

2. Working with the knit side facing you, insert a crochet hook from front to back into the dropped stitch. Push the hook under the horizontal thread above the dropped stitch and use the hook to draw this thread through the dropped stitch (see Photo N-2).

3. Continue until each ladder has been made into a loop and the stitch is even with the last row worked (see Photo N-3). Transfer the last loop to the left-hand needle to be worked as usual.

Photo N-1

Photo N-2

Photo N-3

Creative Tip

When repeats are part of a knitting pattern, write the number of repeats completed on a sticky note, and attach it to the instructions when you lay the project down. You will never have to recount your stitches.

– Team Leader, Harbor City, California

Classic Turtleneck

A simple classic turtleneck sweater using a knit stitch and soft variegated yarn in watery aqua and pale lavender colors, is the perfect project for a beginner.

Crochet

Learn to crochet and you'll never have idle hands. From the beginning basics of single stitches to triple crochet and beyond, you'll be surprised how simple it is to get started, and in no time, you'll find that you can't put your new hobby away. Check out your local craft store to see all the new colors and textured fashion yarns.

Tools and Materials

Crochet Hooks – A

Crochet hooks come in a variety of sizes. Small hooks used for lace are usually made of steel. Very large hooks for novelty crochet are often made of plastic. Hooks are identified by the millimeter size of the shank, a number size, and a letter size, in ascending order from small to large. For instance, a hook with a 3.5mm shank is also known as an "F" hook.

Shown in Photo A is a set of aluminum hooks in a range of frequently used sizes from *top to bottom*, an "F" hook (3.75mm) to a "K" hook (6.5mm).

Color Wheel – see page 68, Knitting Section

Yarns – see pages 69-70, Knitting Section

Holding the Hook –B

There are two basic ways to hold the hook: in the pencil position (see Photo B-1).With the end of the hook in the space between your thumb and index finger; or in the knife position (see Photo B-2), with the hook held as if grasping a knife.

Whichever option you choose, your thumb and either your index finger or third finger grasp the hook in the flattened finger rest. Either position will provide good support and allow you to develop a comfortable rhythm. Try both positions to determine which one you like best. Your free hand will control the yarn supply.

Size F (3.75mm)

Size G (4.00mm)

Size H (5.00mm)

Size I (5.50mm)

Size J (6.00mm)

Size K (6.50mm)

Photo A

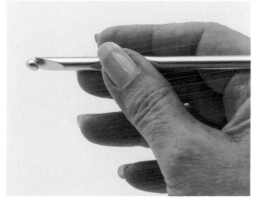

Photo B-1

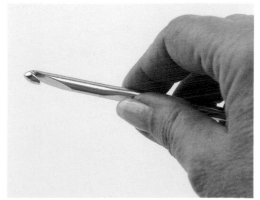

Photo B-2

Photo C-1

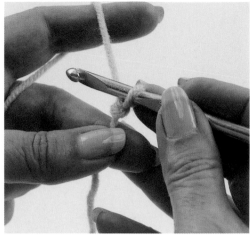

Photo D-1

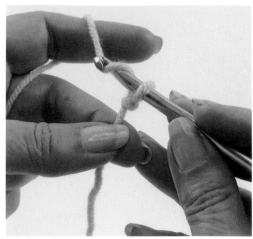

Photo E-1

Making a Slip Knot – C

Leaving a 6-inch length of yarn, make a loop and allow the working end of the yarn to hang down behind. Reach through the loop with your crochet hook and catch the yarn (see Photo C-1), pulling it forward through the loop and tightening the knot.

How to Hold the Yarn – D

Photo D-1 shows the slip knot completed. The photo shows the yarn threaded through the fingers and is ready to begin making a chain.

Shown is only one of many ways to hold the yarn that will give good tension and control. Loop the working yarn over the index finger of your free hand and hold it loosely with your last two fingers, or loosely wrap it around your little finger. Grasp the slip knot with your thumb and middle finger. As you crochet, the yarn will feed through your fingers to form new stitches. To maintain tension, continue to hold your thumb and middle finger just below the stitch you are working into.

If you find holding the yarn in a different way is easier, do it as long as you are able to maintain a consistent tension.

Yarn Over (yo) and Starting the Chain (ch) – E

Catching the yarn with the hook and drawing it through to form a stitch is part of every crochet stitch. It is important to always catch the yarn in the same way so your stitches look consistent. Bring the yarn over the top of the hook from back to front, catching the yarn inside the hook. Turn the hook slightly toward you to help prevent the yarn from slipping off the hook (see Photo E-1).

Pull the yarn through the loop and onto the shank. One chain is made, and one loop

Photo F-1

remains on the hook. It is important that the hook be extended through the loop to the shank, as this is what determines the size of the chain. If it only goes through to the throat, the loops will be too tight.

Making and Counting the Chain – F

Continue in this same manner to create a foundation chain. To maintain tension and produce even chains, continue to move your thumb and middle finger so that they are holding the completed chains right under the chain being worked into.

The chains formed should be loose enough for the hook to go back through easily, and should be even in appearance.

When counting the number of chains, do not count the loop that is on the hook. Count the loop that is just below the hook as one, then count each loop down to the one just above the slip knot. There are three chains shown in Photo F-1.

Turning Chain (tch) – not shown

Crochet stitches are formed by making various loops that give each stitch a different height. At the start of each row or round, chains are worked to raise the hook to the height of the first stitch of the next

Photo G-1

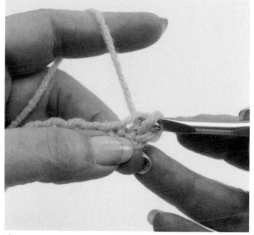

Photo H-1

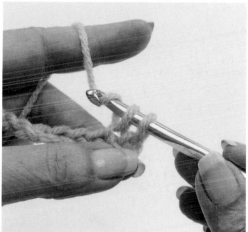

Photo I-1

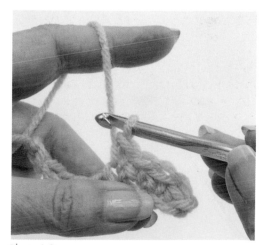

Photo I-2

row or round. Each basic stitch has a recommended number of chains to equal the height of the stitches to be worked in the coming row or round.

Depending upon the height of the stitch and the pattern, the turning chain is sometimes counted as a stitch. Your pattern will tell you how many chains to work for the turning chain and whether to count it as a stitch. If the turning chain is counted as a stitch, you will begin crocheting in the second stitch.

Counting Stitches – G
To determine the correct number of stitches at the end, it is important to understand how to count stitches.

The first stitch is the one at the base of the turning chain. Three chains have been made for the turning chain and there are five stitches clearly visible in the picture (see Photo G-1).

How to: Make a Slip Stitch (sl st) – H
The slip stitch is the shortest of all the crochet stitches and is not commonly used to produce fabric. It is used for joining, shaping, and carrying the yarn from one place to another.

To form a slip stitch, insert the hook into the first stitch as shown in Photo H-1, or into the second chain from the hook, if working from a beginning chain.

Yarn over the hook and draw through both the work, or chain, and the loop on the hook. One loop remains on the hook and one slip stitch is complete.

How to: Make a Single Crochet (sc) – I
To form a row of single crochet stitches onto a chain, insert the head of the hook from front to back into the second chain from the hook. Bring the yarn over the hook from back to front (see Photo I-1) and pull the yarn through the chain, but not through the loops on the hook. Two loops remain on the hook.

Bring the yarn over the hook again from back to front and draw it through both loops (see Photo I-2). One single crochet is complete. Repeat in each chain. When working across a row of stitches, insert the hook from front to back under both loops of the stitch unless directions state otherwise.

For the turning chain, chain one at the beginning of a row starting with a single crochet.

How to: Make a Half Double Crochet (hdc) – J

To form a row of half double crochet stitches onto a chain, yarn over, then insert the head of the hook from front to back into the third chain from the hook (see Photo J-1).

Yarn over and draw through all three loops on the hook at once. One loop remains on the hook and one half double crochet is complete. Repeat in each chain or stitch across row. For the turning chain, chain two at the beginning of a row starting with a half double crochet.

How to: Make a Double Crochet (dc) – K

1. To form a row of double crochet stitches onto a chain, yarn over, then insert the head of the hook from front to back into the fourth chain from the hook. Bring the yarn over the hook from back to front and pull the yarn through the chain, but not through the loops on the hook. Three loops remain on the hook.
Note: Since the beginning of a double crochet is the same as a half double crochet, your stitch at this step will look like Photo J-1 except that the hook will have

been inserted into the fourth chain from the hook instead of the third.

2. Yarn over and draw through two loops on the hook at once (see Photo K-1). Two loops remain on the hook.

3. Yarn over and draw through two loops on the hook again. One loop remains on the hook and one double crochet is complete. Repeat in each chain or stitch across row (see Photo K-2).

For the turning chain, chain three at the beginning of a row starting with a double crochet.

How to: Make a Triple (tr) – L
(Also Known as a Treble)

1. To form a row of triple stitches onto a chain, yarn over twice, then insert the head of the hook from front to back into the fifth chain from the hook (see Photo L-1). Yarn over and pull the loop through the chain, but not through the loops on the hook. Four loops remain on the hook.

2. Yarn over and draw through two loops on the hook at once Three loops remain on the hook (see Photo L-2).

3. Yarn over and draw through next two loops on the hook at once Two loops remain on the hook (see Photo L-3).

4. Yarn over and draw through last two loops on the hook at once. One loop remains on the hook and one triple crochet is complete. Repeat in each chain or stitch across row (see Photo L-4).

For the turning chain, chain four at the beginning of a row starting with a triple crochet.

Changing Yarn or Colors –M

When joining a new yarn or color, work the previous stitch until there are two loops left on the hook. Complete the stitch by drawing the new yarn through the last two loops (see Photo M-1).

Working In Ends – N

Thread the loose end through a tapestry or yarn needle. Skim the needle under the surface of 2 to 3 inches of stitches (see Photo N-1) and draw the end through the stitches. Stretch the work slightly before trimming.

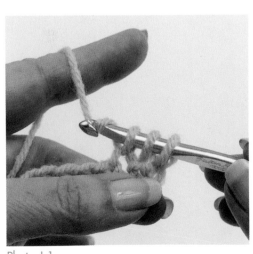

Photo J-1

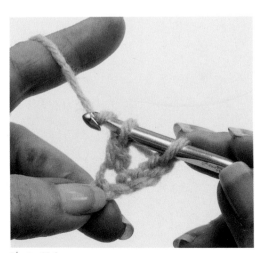

Photo K-1

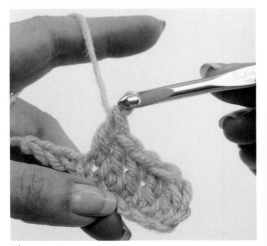

Photo K-2

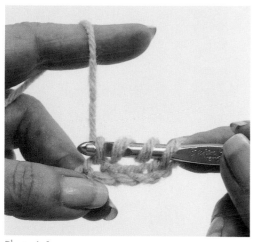

Photo L-1

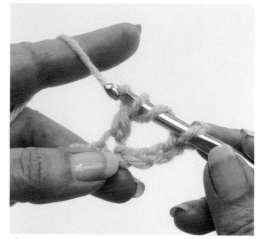

Photo L-2

Photo L-3

Photo L-4

Photo M-1

Photo N-1

Elegant Granny-Square Afghan

Made with double and triple crochet stitches and
a large needle, this soft and elegant granny-square
afghan uses variegated yarn squares outlined with
velvety chenille.

Ribbon and Traditional
EMBROIDERY

Whether you thread your needle
with cotton floss or silk ribbon,

when you learn a few simple stitches,
you'll be able to use the techniques to add
decorative embellishments to linens,
home accessories, and clothing.

Ribbon *Embroidery*

Often you'll find the most elegant (and expensive) wearables and home furnishings embellished with beautiful ribbon embroidery. With an understanding of the materials used and a few basic embroidery stitches, you'll be able to duplicate this intricate-looking technique.

Tools and Materials

Beads and Pins (optional) – A
A variety of sizes and shapes of beads are available to embellish your embroidery designs. To accent padded surfaces, such as the embroidered velvet box shown on page 84, push the beads into place with straight pins.

Fabrics
Any knit or woven fabric is suitable for ribbon embroidery, although some tightly woven fabrics, such as silk pongee and taffeta, are more difficult to work with than less tightly woven fabrics. Solid colors and tone-on-tone textured and printed fabrics are preferable to print fabrics with dominant designs, such as florals.

Frames and Hoops – B
Hoops are a matter of personal preference. If the design is small and the fabric is lightweight, a hoop may be necessary. On most fabrics, however, a hoop will leave a mark. It may be helpful to fuse a very lightweight interfacing to the back of the fabric before embroidering. If you are embroidering on a ready-to-wear garment, don't use a hoop.
Note: When using velvet, allow for extra fabric around the perimeter of the design area, as the hoop will crush the velvet.

Needles – C
The eye of the needle must be large enough for the ribbon to lie flat when threaded through. The barrel of the needle must create a hole in the fabric large enough for the ribbon to pass through when stitching. A needle that is too small is difficult to pull through the fabric and ultimately shreds the ribbon. In needle sizing, the higher the number, the smaller the needle. Use either a chenille or tapestry needle when you are working ribbon embroidery.

Ribbons and Floss – D
The standard ribbon sizes used for embroidery are 4mm (similar to ⅛-inch wide) and 7mm (similar to ⅜-inch wide). Size 13mm is used for large-scale ribbon embroidery. Most embroidery ribbons are 100-percent silk. There are high-quality substitutions available. Narrow widths of sheer, bias cut, and textured ribbons also may be used for embroidery.

Cotton embroidery floss is sold in six-ply skeins and is available in a wide range of colors. It separates into single or multiple plies for stitching. Floss is used in combination with ribbon to make a variety of stitches such as stems, outlining, French knots, and for fine detail.

Scissors — E

Use small, sharp embroidery scissors to cut ribbon and embroidery threads and to manipulate ribbon as you work.

Ribbon Embroidery Basics

Ribbon embroidery is a forgiving needle art and invites creativity. Exact stitch placement is usually not crucial.

For most stitches, the ribbon must be kept flat and smooth. Broaden the ribbon with each stitch by sliding the needle underneath it several times. Untwist and smooth the ribbon between stitches.

When stitching, gently pull the ribbon through the fabric so that the completed stitch lies softly on the surface. To keep from pulling a stitch too tightly, place your thumb over the ribbon on the front of the fabric where it is being pulled to the back. If the stitch "sinks" or is too tight, make another stitch over the first.

Work with 18-inch ribbon lengths to prevent fraying. When stitching, do not carry ribbon over more than 1 inch of fabric.

Stitch Layering

The key to beautiful ribbon embroidery is the layering of stitches. Stitched elements should look as though they belong together. To layer stitches, tuck entry points underneath or directly next to previous stitches to integrate leaves and petals.

Threading and Securing the Needle

Locking the Ribbon

Trim one ribbon end at a diagonal. Thread the trimmed end through the eye of the

Locking the Ribbon

needle and pull it through the eye to beyond the needle tip. Pierce the trimmed ribbon end with the needle about 1 inch from the ribbon end, *above*. Pull the untrimmed end, causing the ribbon to lock itself around the eye of the needle. Do not lock heavy or textured ribbon onto the needle because you'll have trouble pulling it through the fabric. Instead, hold it securely.

Soft Knot

Working with the free ribbon end, fold the ribbon back onto itself about 1 inch (see Soft Knot, Step 1, *opposite*). Pierce the needle through both layers of the folded ribbon. Gently pull the ribbon through the folds, leaving a soft loop knot at the ribbon end (see Soft Knot, Step 2, *opposite*).

Ending the Ribbon

Bring the ribbon to the back of the fabric. Lay the ribbon across the back of the nearest stitch (see Ending the Ribbon, Step 1, *opposite*). Stitch through the ribbon and through the back of the nearest stitch simultaneously (see Ending the Ribbon, Step 2, *opposite*). Repeat; trim the ribbon ¼ inch from the ending stitch.

Transferring a Design

Transfer only the integral design parts to the fabric. Sometimes it is difficult to fully cover transferred marks because the ribbon often has a mind of its own. Stems, flower centers, a small spray of French knots, and the starting point for large leaves are main design elements.

To transfer, place the original or the photocopy of a design onto a light source, such as a light table or at a window during the day. Position the fabric, right side up, over the design diagram. Trace the main elements onto the fabric with a pencil,

Soft Knot Step 1

Soft Knot Step 2

Ending the Ribbon Step 1
(Wrong Side of Fabric.)

Ending the Ribbon Step 2
(Wrong Side of Fabric.)

Ribbon Embroidery Box Color Key

 Rosette

 Spiderweb Rose

Pointed-Loop Petal Stitch

Bullion-Tipped Lazy Daisy

 Gathered Rose

French Knot

Twisted Straight Stitch

Seed Beads

Bugle Bead

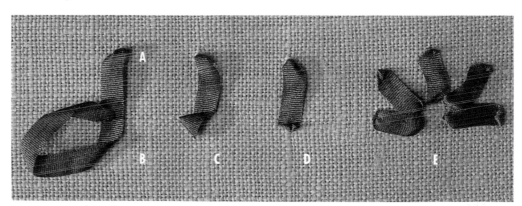

Japanese-Leaf Stitch

a gel pen (heat set after tracing), or a disappearing ink pen.

Cleaning
Hand wash or dry clean embroidered garments, depending on the garment fabrics and the fiber content of the ribbon.

Japanese-Leaf Stitch – *above*
1. Bring the needle to the front at the inner point of the design line (A). Extend the ribbon to lie flat on the fabric, giving the ribbon a little slack. With the needle, pierce

the center of the ribbon at the desired stitch length end (B).

2. Gently pull the ribbon through to the back of the fabric (C).

3. Stop pulling the ribbon through when the end of the stitch has a slight curl (D). Don't pull the stitch tight, or the ribbon curl will disappear.

4. To make flower petals, complete multiple stitches (E).

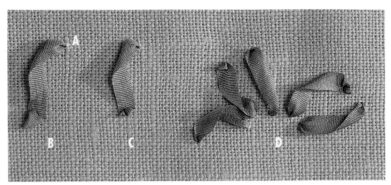

Twisted Straight Stitch

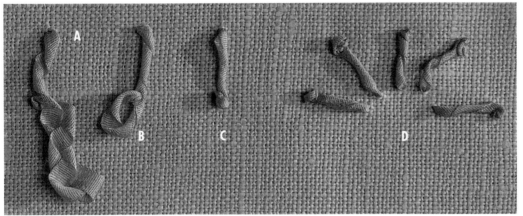

Twisted-Ribbon Variation Stitch

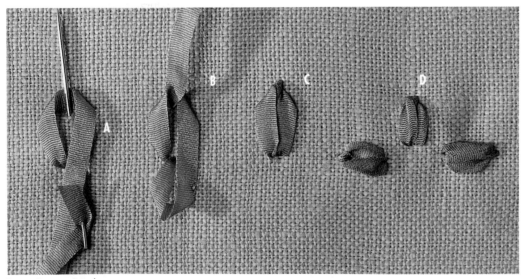

Lazy Daisy Stitch

Twisted Straight Stitch – *top left*

1. Bring the needle to the front at the inner point of the design line (A). Extend the ribbon to lie flat on the fabric surface. Twist the ribbon once, changing the shape from straight to bent (B).

2. Give the ribbon a little slack, and pierce the center of the ribbon at the desired stitch length end. Gently pull the ribbon through to the back of the fabric (C).

3. Stop pulling the ribbon when the end of the stitch has a slight curl (D). Don't pull the stitch tight, or the curl will disappear.

4. Make several stitches to complete the pattern. See the finished box lid on page 84 for an example.

Twisted-Ribbon Variation – *middle left*

1. Pull the needle through to the front at the inner point of the design line. Twist and coil the ribbon length (A). Extend the twisted ribbon flat on the fabric surface and pierce the center of the ribbon on one end at the desired stitch length (B).

2. Give the ribbon a little slack. Gently pull the coiled ribbon through to the back of the fabric.

3. Stop pulling the ribbon through when the end of the stitch looks like a knot (C). Uncoil the remaining ribbon before proceeding with the next stitch. Make several stitches together to form spiked petals (D). Layer a variety of colored petals for such flowers as chrysanthemums and asters.

Lazy Daisy Stitch – *bottom left*

1. Bring the needle to the front at the inner point of the design line. Re-insert the needle into the fabric next to the entry point. In one motion, back it out through the fabric at the desired stitch length end. Before pulling the ribbon through, lay the ribbon flat underneath the needle and loop it back around toward the entry point. Keep the ribbon flat as shown (A).

2. Hold the ribbon flat with your thumb and pull the needle through (B).

3. Take a small stitch over the top to anchor the loop (C).

4. Make several stitches for petals or make individual stitches for leaves (D).

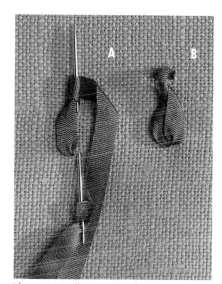

Photo 1: Bullion-Tipped Lazy Daisy

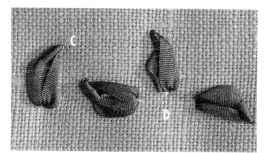

Photo 2: Bullion-Tipped Lazy Daisy

Bullion-Tipped Lazy Daisy – *above*

1. Begin as with a traditional lazy daisy stitch (A). Before pulling the ribbon through, loosely wrap the ribbon twice around the pointed end of the needle as if to make a French knot (B).

2. Hold the ribbon flat with your thumb and pull the needle through (B). The tip of the stitch forms a bullion that can be curved by drawing it to the left or to the right of center.

3. Stitch through to the back at the uppermost tip of the bullion to secure (C). See the box lid on page 84 for examples.

4. Make several bullion-tipped lazy daisies to form a flower (D). See the flower on the sweater detail, page 89.

French Knot – *right*

1. Bring the needle to the front on the mark (A). Loosely wrap the ribbon one to two times around the needle, depending on the desired size of the knot (B). Keep the ribbon looser than you would to wrap floss for traditional embroidery French knots.

2. Hold the ribbon off to one side and push the needle through to the back directly next to the entry point (C).

3. Gently pull the needle through the wraps (D) to form a completed knot (E).

Spiderweb Rose – *below*

1. Use one ply of matching floss to make an extended fly stitch. Add two additional legs to make a five-spoke base (A).

Photo E
Completed French Knot

French Knot

2. With ribbon, bring the needle to the front at the center of the spokes. Weave ribbon over and under the spokes, making certain to skip every other spoke when weaving. Loosen the ribbon as you work outward. If the ribbon twists while weaving, it adds to the texture of the rose (B).

3. When the spokes are covered (C), stitch through to the back, hiding the exit point under a petal. Secure stitches on the back. See the roses on the box lid on page 84.

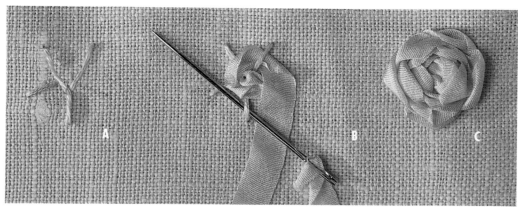

Spiderweb Rose

Crafts – Ribbon Embroidery

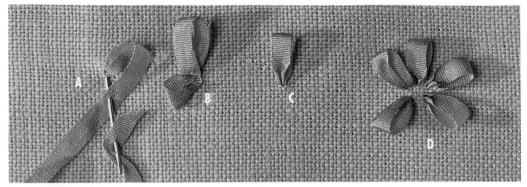

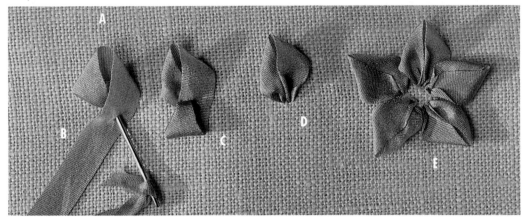

Loop-Petal Stitch

Pointed-Loop Petal Stitch

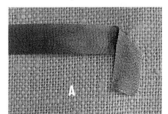

Rosette

Loop-Petal Stitch – *top left*

1. Bring the ribbon to the front at the inner point of the design line. Fold the ribbon forward to form a small loop. Pierce the center of the ribbon directly in front of the entry point (A).

2. Gently pull the ribbon through to the back (B).

3. Stop pulling the ribbon through when the end of the stitch has a slight curl (C). Don't pull the stitch tight, or the ribbon loop will disappear.

4. Make a series of stitches for flowers or use one single stitch for a leaf (D).

Pointed-Loop Petal Stitch – *middle left*

1. Bring the ribbon to the front at the inner point of the design line. Extend the ribbon and fold it under at a 90-degree angle (A). Hold the angled fold with your thumb while folding the ribbon forward at a 90-degree angle, to make a pointed loop. Pierce the center of the ribbon at the end of the loop, directly next to the entry point (B).

2. Gently pull the ribbon through to the back of the fabric (C).

3. Stop pulling the ribbon through when the end of the stitch has a slight curl (D). Don't pull the stitch too tight, or the loop will disappear.

4. Cluster stitches to form a flower (E). See the box lid on page 84 for pointed-loop leaves.

Rosette – *bottom left*

Note: Make the rosette, then handstitch it to the fabric base.

1. Fold one end of a 9-inch length of 7mm ribbon forward at a 45-degree angle, leaving a short tail for working (A). Fold the ribbon over (B). Roll the ribbon to form the flower center (C) and stitch through the base of the roll to hold it together.

2. Fold the ribbon back diagonally and wrap the fold around the roll (D).
Note: The first steps are similar to the Ribbonwork Basics technique on page 97. Continue to wrap and roll for half of the ribbon length, securing each wrap with matching thread (E).

3. Working from the back of the wrapped rose center, gather the remaining ribbon along the same edge as the secured ribbon, tapering the thread to the ribbon end (F). Tighten the gathers and wrap them around the rose center (G).
Note: It is easier to position the gathers when working with the rose upside down. Secure the gathers to the back of the finished rose (H).

Cascading Ribbon – *above right*

1. Working with the desired ribbon length, tie a small bow near the ribbon center and hand tack the bow knot in place on the fabric (A).
Note: The bow is optional.

2. Thread a needle with one ribbon end and secure it as described on page 84. A short distance from the bow center, take a very small stitch through the fabric. Pull the ribbon through, allowing some slack as the ribbon naturally twists (B).

3. Continue to randomly cascade ribbon, backstitching each time (C), until you are pleased with the effect (D). Repeat with the other ribbon end.

Gathered Rose

1. Use a running stitch and sew a line along one edge of the ribbon. Pull the thread until the ribbon is half the original length, even out the gathers, and secure the thread with a knot.

2. Place the gathered ribbon on the fabric and loosely coil into a rose shape. Create the center of the rose by anchoring the ribbon with a couple of small stitches.

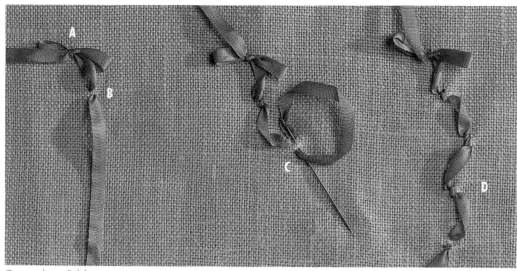

Cascading Ribbon

Gathered Rose

Spiral the ribbon around the center and secure the ribbon to the fabric with several small stitches. Secure the thread in back with a knot.

Ribbon-Embroidered Sweater

This sweater features bullion-tipped lazy daisies, twisted ribbons, cascading ribbons, and decorative beads.

Traditional *Embroidery*

For generations, stitchers have been embellishing clothing and home furnishings with simple embroidery. From elaborate designs on christening gowns to simple outline-stitched quilts, this handwork is passed from generation to generation with great pride.

Tools and Materials

Embroidery Needles – A

Embroidery needles have a long eye, a sharp point, and are slender so they pass through closely-woven fabrics with ease. They come in sizes 1 through 10, the higher number indicating the smaller needle.

Fabrics

Most closely-woven fabrics, such as cotton, wool, satin, or linen, are suitable for embroidery work. However, it is always best to work a few stitches on a swatch before you begin any project. If you choose a fabric with "give," you'll need to prepare it with an iron-on tear-away stabilizer sheet first (see instructions under Preparing the Fabric, *opposite*). Fabrics with a tighter weave work best.

Hoops and Frames – B

Hand-held Embroidery Hoops: Embroidery hoops are available in a wide variety of sizes, ranging from 3 to 23 inches in diameter. They're available in wood, metal, and plastic styles. Because hoops are so portable, they're a popular choice.

Designs worked in hoops have a tendency to acquire hoop marks from the moisture of hands and general house dust. It is wise to cover embroidery whenever it's set aside, and to remove the hoop for overnight storage.

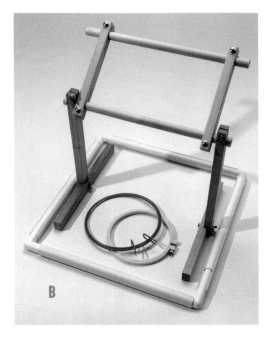

Freestanding Hoops: If you enjoy stitching with both hands, free-standing floor and tabletop hoops are options. Neither style has the portability of hand-held hoops, since you must sit up to them to stitch.

Q-Snaps: Q-Snaps are plastic, L-shaped bars that slip into one another at the corners. Long, curved pieces of plastic snap over each bar, holding the fabric in place. They come in assorted lengths. Because the design is stitched within the bars, the piece is not as easily soiled as designs worked in embroidery hoops.

Stretcher Bars: Wooden stretcher bars are sold in pairs so you can purchase the length and width best suited to your design. The bars interlock tightly at the corners. Brass tacks or staples hold the fabric to the bars. Stretcher bars are less likely to soil a design since the design is worked entirely within the frame. Leave additional fabric all around for mounting.

Scissors – C

You'll need two pairs of scissors: sewing shears for cutting fabric and a small, sharp-pointed pair of embroidery scissors for cutting threads.

Threads – D, E, F and G

Embroidery Floss – D: The most widely used floss for embroidery is six-stranded cotton, a divisible thread made of double mercerized, long staple cotton. It's available in a wide variety of colors.

Metallic Thread – F: Metallic thread is available on spools (see Photo F) and in six-ply skeins (not shown). A blend of shiny polyester metallic and viscose, it comes in a limited color palette.

Pearl Cotton – E and G: Pearl cotton is a highly mercerized, twisted, non-divisible 100-percent cotton thread. It is available in skeins in sizes #3 and #5, and in balls in sizes #5, #8, and #12. Size 12 is the thinnest.

Note: Rayon floss (not shown), a highly lustrous thread, is 100-percent rayon and comes in six-strand skeins. When working with rayon, use short lengths and lightly dampen the threads. Rayon embroidery floss is slippery, and recommended for experienced stitchers.

Embroidery Patterns – not shown

Iron-on embroidery designs as well as pre-printed items like pillowcases and dresser scarves are available for purchase. Transfer the design to your fabric with an iron and you are ready to begin.

Embroidery Basics

Preparing the Fabric

If your fabric is prone to raveling, overcast the edges or tape them with masking tape.

For fabrics with a lot of "give," use a baste-on or iron-on temporary tear-away stabilizer. First, trace the design onto the stabilizer with a fine-tip permanent black marking pen. Fuse or baste the sheet to the front side of the fabric, following the manufacturer's instructions. Then proceed with the embroidery. When all of the stitching is complete, gently pull away the stabilizer material.

Preparing the Threads

When working with six-strand floss, it is best to separate the strands prior to stitching. First, cut an 18-inch length of floss, then separate it into individual strands. Regroup the desired number of strands and thread the needle. Separating the strands helps keep stitches smooth and free of twists.

Threading the Needle

Loop the thread over the eye of the needle. Pinch the looped floss with your thumb and forefinger, then slip it from the needle. Thread the pinched loop through the eye of the needle.

Starting and Ending a Thread

To begin a thread, weave it in an area that will be covered by stitches or behind already worked areas. End the thread in the same manner. Trim any loose ends close to the piece.

Transferring a Design

Trace the design onto tracing paper using a permanent black marking pen. Tape the pattern to a light box or a window. Tape fabric over the top of the design. Retrace the design using a water-soluble marker.

Getting Started

Your chosen pattern will usually indicate which stitches to use for different areas. If not, we have included a few suggestions with each stitch. However, much of the enjoyment of traditional embroidery lies in the fact that you can choose any stitch or stitches that fit into the design.

✂ Creative Tip

Listen to a book-on-tape while you're stitching. It's like reading and stitching at the same time.

– Team Member, Woodbridge, Virginia

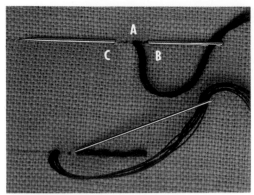
Backstitch

Backstitch

1. Bring the needle up through the fabric at A. Take the needle down at B. All stitches should measure the length of stitch AB.

2. Bring the needle up at C. The distance between C and A should be equal to the length of AB. Continue working stitches in this manner.

Common uses: Use the backstitch for doing lines and outlines.

Blanket Stitch

1. Bring the needle up through the fabric at A. Insert at B and come up at C in a single motion, keeping the thread under the tip of the needle.

2. Pull the needle through the fabric. Continue making vertical stitches in this manner.

3. To finish a row of stitches, take a tiny stitch over the last stitch.
Note: When stitches are placed next to one another, the stitch is called a buttonhole stitch.

Common uses: The blanket stitch is used for edging hems and buttonholes. It also can be used as a decorative stitch for scalloped designs.

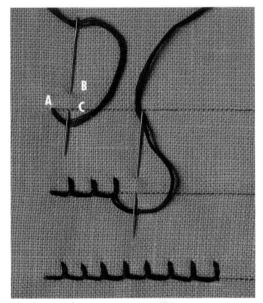
Blanket Stitch

Bullion Knot (Caterpillar, Worm, Coil, Post, or Roll Stitch)

1. Bring the needle up through the fabric at A (top of knot).

2. Insert the needle into the fabric at B (bottom of knot) and bring it up at A. Do not pull the needle through the fabric.

3. Wrap the thread around the end of the needle multiple times. (The wrapped area must equal the length from A to B.)

4. Lightly hold the wrapped area to the fabric with your left thumb. Pull the needle tip through the wrapped thread, keeping the wrapped area flat and as close to point A as possible.

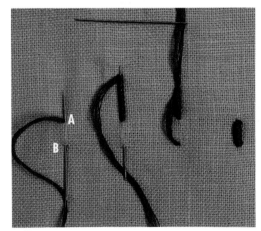
Bullion Knot

5. Lift the needle thread up, bringing the wrapped thread back to B. Insert the needle into B. Pull the needle through fabric.

Common uses: The large, long bullion knot can be used in the same way as a French knot to create greater emphasis and dimension.

Lazy Daisy (Detached Chain Stitch)

1. Bring the needle up through the fabric at A. Re-insert the needle at A and bring it up at B, keeping the thread under the tip of the needle.

2. Pull the thread to form a loop.

3. To secure the loop, take a tiny stitch over the top.

Common uses: This stitch is most often used to make flower and leaf shapes. The stitches may be scattered to use as filler.

Bullion-Tipped Lazy Daisy

1. Work Step 1 for the lazy daisy stitch.

2. Before pulling the needle through, wrap the thread around the tip two or more times.

3. To secure the loop, take a tiny stitch (with the wrapped thread) over the top of the loop.

Common uses: This stitch can be used in the same places as the lazy daisy, with the additional bullion stitch creating more texture and dimension.

Cross-Stitch (Sample Stitch)

1. Bring the needle up through the fabric at A and down at B. Continue to the end of the row.

2. Come up through the fabric at C and go down at D. Continue across to the end of the row.

Note: You can work the cross-stitch in the reverse manner, so the top leg runs from the lower right corner to the upper left corner. Work the stitches consistently, with

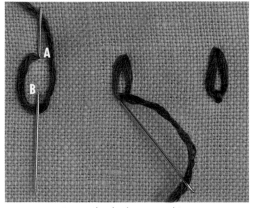

Lazy Daisy (Detached Chain Stitch)

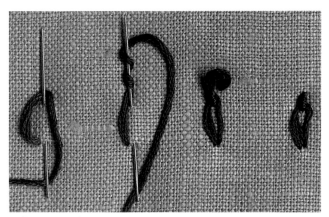

Bullion-Tipped Lazy Daisy

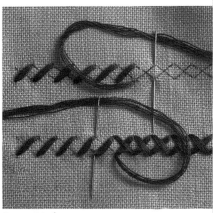

Cross-Stitch

the top leg of every stitch worked in the same direction.

Common uses: This is one of the most well-known stitches and can be used for filling, outlines, borders and motifs.

Feather Stitch (Single Coral Stitch)

1. Bring the needle up through the fabric at A. Insert the needle at B, but do not pull the thread taut. Bring the needle up at C (in the middle of stitch AB, and slightly below) to create a curved stitch.

2. Make stitch DE to create a second curve to the right of the first curve. Continue in this manner until the shape is filled.

Common uses: This light, delicate stitch is used as a filling stitch where a feather-like appearance is desired. Also use this stitch for backgrounds and outlines.

French Knot (Knotted Stitch)

1. Bring the needle up through the fabric at A.

2. Hold the tip end of the needle about 1 inch above A. Wrap the thread over the tip end one to three times, depending on the size of the desired knot.

3. Insert the needle close to A. Keep the excess floss taut as you work and keep the knot close to the fabric.

4. Pull the needle through the fabric, keeping the excess floss taut as you pull.

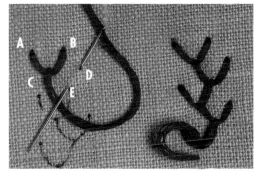

Feather Stitch

Don't pull too tight, or the knot will disappear into the fabric.

Common uses: This stitch is most often used for scattering or sprinkling effects, to indicate dots, or to add texture and dimension.

Satin Stitch

1. Bring the needle up through the fabric at A. Insert the needle at B, then come up at C, placing the needle as close to A as possible. Continue in this manner to fill the shape.

Common uses: This stitch is most often used for filling in designs, shading, and outlining.

Padded Satin Stitch

1. Work steps 1 and 2 of the Satin Stitch.

2. Using the same color (two colors are shown to help define the steps), work a second layer in the opposite direction.

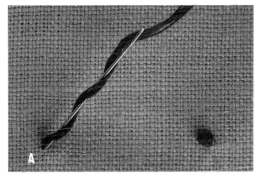

French Knot

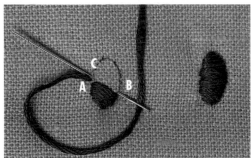

Satin Stitch

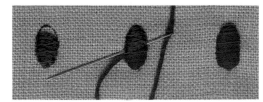

Padded Satin Stitch

Common uses: This stitch is used in the same manner as the satin stitch, but creates more dimension.

Crafts – Traditional Embroidery

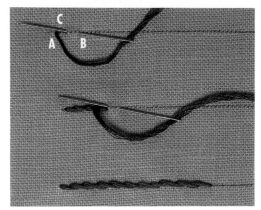

Stem or Outline Stitch

Stem Stitch (Outline or Crewel Stitch)

1. Bring the needle up through the fabric at A. Insert at B, then come up at C halfway between A and B.

2. Work consecutive stitches in the same manner, making each stitch the same length. Always enter and exit the needle on the line, and keep the running thread to one side of the needle—above or below. *Note: Be consistent when you are working this stitch.*

Common uses: This stitch is commonly used for making stems, outlining, lines, filling, and shading.

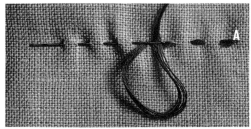

Running Stitch

Running Stitch

1. Bring the needle up through the fabric at A. Load the needle with as many stitches at a time as possible, then pull the needle through the fabric. Make the stitches as evenly spaced as possible. They should look the same on both sides of the fabric.

Common uses: This basic stitch is most often used for lines, outlines, basting and quilting.

A Baby Coverlet

This enchanting duck was stitched with six strands of floss. Outline stitches define the body and features, satin stitches give texture to the feet and bill, and padded satin stitches make the bow center and bonnet stem. Also used are French knots for the bow dots, lazy daisy stitches for flower petals, blanket stitches for the bonnet, and feather stitches for the centers of the leaves.

Serenity Pillow

On natural linen, this pillow was stitched with six strands of floss to backstitch the lettering, three strands for outline stitches that define the stems, two strands for the bullion-tipped lazy daisy and bullion knots in the lavender, and a single strand of floss for the satin stitches that define the small leaves.

RIBBON FLOWERS

Elegant, realistic, and everlasting

satin-ribbon flowers are perfect for
floral arrangements and corsages.
Add them to gift packages, or use them
as fashion accessories.

Ribbon *Flowers*

Most of us have used ribbons in myriad ways—bows for dresses and hair, edging for pretty linens, and decorations for gift packages. History tells us that our ancestors also used elaborate ribbon embellishments for clothing and home decoration. Expand your knowledge of ribbons and create beautiful flowers that will enhance your surroundings.

Tools and Materials

Crinoline – not shown
Crinoline is a stiff open-weave fabric used for backings, interlinings or as a base for ribbon flowers.

Needles – A
Milliner's sharp size 10 needles work best for ribbonwork.

Ribbons – B
Experiment with a variety, including wired, non-wired, silk, ombré (two-tone), velvets, solids, and cross weaves. Keep assorted widths and colors on hand. Buy a minimum of two yards of each ribbon.

Ruler or Tape Measure – C
Measure the amount of ribbon needed for each leaf or blossom.

Scissors – D
You'll need sharp sewing scissors and pointed embroidery scissors for embroidery.

Stamens – E
Purchase floral stamens for the blossom centers, or make stamens with beads and wire.

Thread – not shown
Use white quilting thread or beading thread because it is stronger than sewing thread.

Thread-Covered Wire – F
Choose thread-covered wire in 22- or 32-gauge weight for making stamen stems.

Wire Cutters – G
Use household wire cutters to cut wire stems, not scissors.

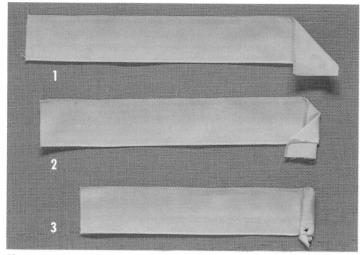

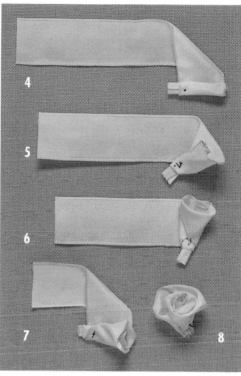

Photo A

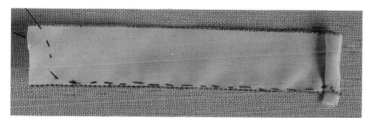

Photo C

Photo B

ꙅCreative Tip

When threading a small-eyed needle, cut the thread at an angle, making a point on the end. You may not see the point, but the needle will!

– Team Member, Phoenix, Arizona

Photo D

Photo E

All the petals and leaves are individually stitched. The assembly of the petals into flowers is also done with stitching; in some cases you can use hotmelt adhesive for this process.

Ribbonwork Basics

During the 1920s, ribbons were often used to make flowers for ball gowns, boxes, hats, and many other beautiful items. The ribbon can be gathered, ruched, pleated, or embroidered for flower trimmings.

To make petals and leaves for ribbonwork, you need to know only two stitches—the backstitch on page 92 and the running stitch on page 94. The beginning and ending stitches are always backstitched, and gathering is done with running stitches.

Getting Started

Folded Rose – Photos A and B

Photo A-1: For the rose center, fold down the right end of the ribbon.

Photo A-2: Fold this end across itself.

Photo A-3: Roll the ribbon into a cylinder (forming the flower center) and secure with stitches.

Photo B-4: Fold the ribbon down on the right end so that the cylinder is horizontal and a 45-degree angle is created at the fold.

Photo B-5: Fold the flower center down as shown.

Photo B-6: Roll the cylinder until the ribbon on the left becomes straight again. Secure with stitches.

Photo B-7: Repeat the folding and rolling steps until the rose is the desired size.

Photo B-8: Stitch the raw edge into the base of the rose.

Note: For a bud, roll only once or twice.

Coiled Ribbon Rose – Photos C, D, and E

Photo C: If the ribbon is wired, remove the wire at the bottom edge by gently pulling it out. Add a running stitch from the upper edge down and across the bottom. Make a ribbon center by referring to the steps for folding a ribbon to make a rose.

Photo D: Gather the remaining length of ribbon and secure the gathering with stitches.

Photo E: Coil the ribbon on itself until all the ribbon is coiled. Stitch the end of the ribbon into the base of the rose.

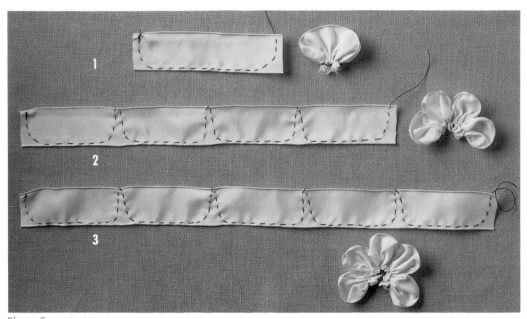

Photo F

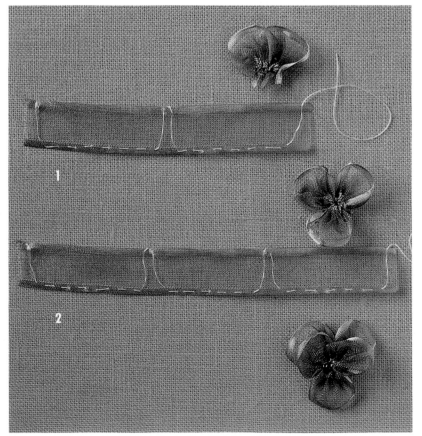

Photo G

U-Gathers for Petals – Photo F

Photo F-1: A single U-gather makes a petal for a poppy or a tea rose. If the ribbon has wire in the edges, remove the bottom edge wire. Stitch the pattern as shown, using a simple running stitch. Gather the ribbon tightly to form a petal shape. Secure the gathering with stitches.

Photo F-2 and F-3: For multiple petals, divide the ribbon equally and create the appropriate number of U-gathers as shown. Use 4- and 5-petal U-gathers for roses. Roll a coiled flower center (see Photo E on page 97) or use stamens, *opposite*. Stitch the gathered petals around the rose center.

U-Petal Pansies – Photo G

Photo G-1: Make one two-petal U-gather for the back two petals of a pansy. If the ribbon has wire in the edges, remove the bottom edge wire. Divide the ribbon into two equal sections with a crease. Stitch the two-petal pattern as shown. Gather tightly; secure the gathering with stitches and sew the petals to a small piece of crinoline fabric.

Photo G-2: Make a three-petal U-gather for the front three petals of a violet. Remove the wire from the bottom edge; divide the ribbon into three sections with creases. Stitch the three-petal pattern and gather tightly. Secure the gathering with stitches. Join the first and last petal together at the gathering line. Stitch the three-petal clusters to the two petals attached to the fabric. Add a bead for the flower center.

Dipped Corner Petal – Photo H

Photo H-1: Fold the ribbon in half and take a few stitches at the edges as shown.

Photo H-2: Turn the ribbon inside out and keep the corners tucked in.

Photo H-3: Pleat the bottom of the petal and secure it with stitches.

Note: This ribbon example is used for the tea roses (see page 100).

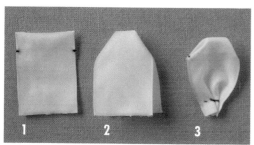

Photo H

Stamens – Photo I

Photo I-1: Wrap purchased stamens with thread or wire. Fold them in half and secure with thread-covered wire.

Photo I-2: Attach to the flower petal with stitches or glue.

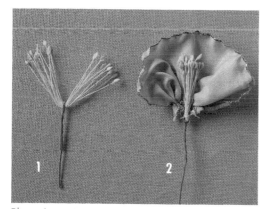

Photo I

Tent Leaves – Photo J

Tent leaves are basic ribbon leaves. Use them for any type of flower.

Photo J-1: Use 3 inches of 1½-inch-wide wired ribbon to make one leaf. If the ribbon is wired, remove the wire on the bottom edge.

Photo J-2: Fold down the ribbon on one side. Fold down the opposite side of the ribbon. Sew across the base of the triangle, catching all the layers of ribbon in the stitching.

Photo J-3: Pull the gathering stitches tight; then wrap the thread around the base of the leaf and secure with stitches.

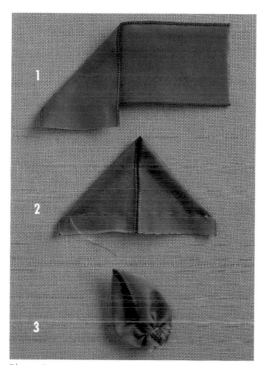

Photo J

Note: *If stemming the leaf, glue a 3-inch piece of wire to the inside of the base before wrapping the thread around the leaf base. Wrap the wire with floral tape.*

Boat Leaves – Photo K

Boat leaves are so named for the shape of the stitch pattern. Use these leaves with any flower.

Photo K-1: Use 5 inches of 1-inch-wide wired ribbon to make one leaf. Remember to remove the wire on the bottom edge. Fold the ribbon in half.

Photo K-2: Fold up the bottom corners of the ribbon to form a boat shape. Stitch the ribbon as shown.

Photo K-3: Gently pull the gathering thread until the boat shape disappears. Open the leaf and adjust the gathering to the desired shape. Secure the leaf with stitches. Trim the ribbon tabs at the back of the leaf and crimp the edges, if desired.

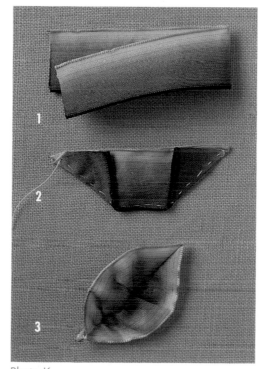

Photo K

Creative Tip

When you're hand sewing, finger pricks are inevitable, and you'll most likely bleed on your work. To remove the bloodstain, put a bit of your own saliva on it. Enzymes in your saliva will break down your blood and the stain will wash away.

– Store Team Member, Fairmont, West Virginia

Elegant Poppies

Soft pastel poppies are made from three colors of ribbon to make them look realistic, yet they are so simple, a beginner can make them. The flowers were first made, then stitched to crinoline to form a pleasing floral composition. The crinoline can be stitched to a cushion or base of your choice. Create the poppies by following the instructions for U-gathered petals shown in Photo F-1 on page 98. Using 1½-wide ribbon, make two petals using 6-inch lengths of ribbon and two petals using 7-inch lengths of ribbon. Make a stamen center, following the instructions for Photo I on page 99. Glue or stitch the petals around the stamen. Complete the composition with boat leaves, following the instructions for Photo K on page 99.

Kissing Ball

Make a kissing ball by covering a foam ball with moss. Make coiled roses using 10-inch lengths of 1-inch-wide wired ribbon, following the instructions for photos C, D, and E on page 97. The folded roses are made with 10 inches of 1-inch wide-wired or unwired ribbon. Follow the instructions for photos A and B on page 97. If desired, add pansies following the instructions for Photo G on page 98. Hang and embellish with ribbons and pearl head pins.

White Tea Roses

Tea roses are exquisite when they are made from two ribbon colors in two widths, and utilizing three ribbon techniques. Create these delicate tea roses by following the instructions for U-gathered petals shown in Photo F on page 98 and dipped corner petals shown in Photo H on page 99. Make the center stamens for the roses and the tent leaves with instructions given for Photo I and Photo J on page 99. Finish the base of the rose and the stem with floral tape.

Handmade
PAPER

With just a few tools

and materials, you can make

your own one-of-a-kind note cards, gift wrap, paper castings,
and other crafts projects. Family and friends will enjoy
receiving your special greetings and sentiments when they are
written on your very own paper creations.

Handmade *Paper*

In the past, papermaking was little more than a way of creating a surface for printing, lettering, or painting. Today, you can manipulate paper pulp and add texture and color to create dynamic and innovative handmade papers to use for special invitations, announcements, and mementos.

Tools and Materials

Blotting and Drying Materials – A
From top to bottom:
Press Bar
  A press bar made of wood, metal or plastic is used to press the remaining water from the newly formed sheet.
Sponge
  Use a sponge to help remove the water from the sheet.
Cover Screen
  The cover screen (gray) is a piece of non-metallic screen larger than the sheets of paper you're making. Lay the screen over the new sheet of paper while removing most of the water.
Blotting Paper (Couching Sheet)
  Choose absorbent materials such as thick paper towels or blotter sheets for removing the moisture from the paper.

Casting Lint and Embellishments – B
Often referred to as cotton linter, this convenient pulp is available in packages as linter squares or bulk linters, and can be easily processed in your blender. Embellishments such as the mica flakes shown can also be added to the pulp.

Deckle and Molds – C
From top to bottom:
Pour Mold (with wide deckle)
  A pour mold is placed in a empty pan and water with pulp is poured into the mold. This type of mold requires a wide deckle (the removable top part of a hand mold, shown at top of photo C, *right*) to hold the water as it is poured into the mold. A deckle determines the size and shape of the paper.

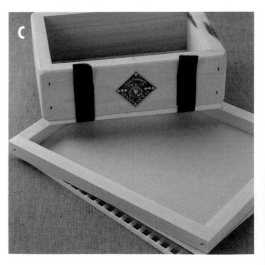

Dip Hand Mold
Use a dip hand mold to make a paper sheet by lowering the dip hand mold into a vat full of water and pulp.

Note: A mold commonly consists of a deckle, a papermaking screen, a cover screen, and a plastic support grid.

Dried Flowers, Leaves, and Glitter – D
Pretty elements can be blended into the paper for visual appeal and texture.

General Household Items – E
Blender
Use a blender to prepare the pulp.
Iron
A household iron is used to help dry paper or to smooth it for writing.
Shallow Tub or Dishpan
Referred to as the "vat," the hand mold is dipped into this container.
Shallow Tray
Use a tray, baking sheet, or something similar as your drain tray.

Templates (optional) – F
Purchase templates for making note cards, envelopes, and special shapes.

Handmade Paper Basics

Deckle and Mold
The mold is the outer wooden framework that holds the screen and deckle in place. The size and shape of the mold determines the dimensions of your paper. The deckle sits in the mold on top of the drain screen, and is the papermaking screen where the paper pulp comes to rest.

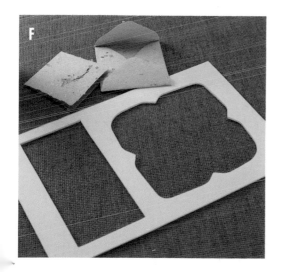

Pulp
Pulp for handmade paper is readily available to purchase in packages, or you can look for it in your waste paper or trash. Have fun adding colored bits and pieces of scavenged papers gathered from parties where napkins, tissue, and wrapping paper are available for the taking. Other papers that work great for papermaking include computer paper, art and copier paper, crepe paper, egg cartons, colored envelopes, and paper bags. Papers that you might want to avoid are heavily printed papers, glossy magazine pages, brochures, cardboard, and newsprint (unless you want to cut off the printed areas and use the plain paper).

Color Additives
Once you start making paper, you will also want to think about all of the wonderful things that can be added to enhance the color, texture, and fragrance. Papers such as napkins, crepe paper, and tissue paper come in an abundance of colors and work well to colorize the pulp medium. Water-soluble textile dyes are also available, along with inks, water-soluble paint powders, and even food coloring.

Natural dyes work well; however, they might fade over a period of time. Tea and coffee are the most common, but consider onion skins for a warm, golden tone.

Embellishments
Create beautiful papers by adding decorative textural elements gathered from nature. Fresh or dried flowers, leaves and ferns, small stems, herbs, seeds, and grasses make interesting sheets of paper. Some items will release their own color into the paper. If this is not acceptable, try boiling them for a few minutes; then lay them out to dry on paper towels. If they still bleed, repeat the procedure. Rose petals and other delicate flowers should not be boiled, but placed in the microwave oven on paper towels and cooked on high for three to four minutes before adding them to the pulp. Small additions of potpourri work well, but be cautious of the oils that are often added

to these mixtures because they might stain the paper.

Jazz up your paper with additions of glitter, pieces of ribbon, metallic threads, raffia, or anything you choose. For delightful fragrances, consider adding dried herbs, orange peel, or lemon peel.

Getting Started

1. Place the mold (we used a pour mold in the photographs *opposite*) upside down on a flat surface and assemble according to the manufacturer's instructions. Fill a shallow tub full of water and lower the mold into the water. The water should come within ¼ inch of the top of the mold.

Choose a piece (or pieces) of paper to recycle that is slightly larger than the paper sheet you intend to make, or use bags of purchased paper pulp. Tear the paper into small pieces and place it in the blender with 2 cups of water. Blend the paper on high speed for approximately 20 to 30 seconds; then pour the paper water into the mold (see Photo A).

2. Spread the pulp evenly in the mold by wiggling your fingers in the mold, or gently stir with a spoon. Lift the mold out of the pan (see Photo B) as a sheet of paper forms on the papermaking screen (the fine-woven white screen).

3. Quickly move the mold to a tray, open the mold, and remove the white screen and deckle (see Photo C).

4. Set aside the mold and place the screen and deckle on the tray. Gently lay a cover screen (gray color) over the newly formed paper to protect it. Place a damp household sponge on top of the screen, and press over the entire surface to

remove excess moisture from the paper (see Photo D). Continue pressing and wringing the sponge until all the excess water has been removed from the paper.

5. Carefully lift the corner of the papermaking screen and peel it off the paper sheet (see Photo E).
Note: If the sheet of paper comes up with the screen, try to get it to release at one of the other corners.

Turn the papermaking screen (with the new paper on it) facedown on a dry couching sheet. The new sheet will be between the screen and the couching sheet. Using the sponge, firmly press down to remove as much water as possible (see Photo F).

6. Gently remove the couching sheet, then the papermaking screen (the new paper will be laying on the bottom couching sheet). Lay a dry couching sheet directly on top of the new paper (see Photo G) and, using a press bar, apply firm pressure over the entire surface of the new sheet (see Photo H).

7. Remove the top couching sheet from the new paper and carefully peel the new paper off the bottom couching sheet. If the new paper seems too fragile, repeat the step seen in Photo G.

8. With an iron set at high temperature, lay the new paper on an ironing board or flat surface, and slowly iron until the new paper is dry (see Photo I).
Note: You might want to place a pressing cloth between the ironing board and the paper to prevent stains on your ironing board cover.

New paper might look nicer when placed between couching sheets and slowly dried under the pressure of a stack of books. Protect the books from moisture and change the couching sheets when they become damp.

Photo A

Photo B

Photo C

Photo D

Photo E

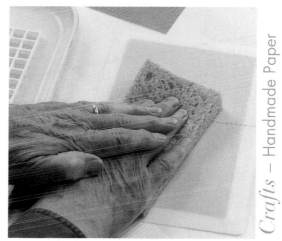

Photo F

Photo G

Photo H

Photo I

Crafts – Handmade Paper

Paper Casting Basics

A paper casting is created when wet pulp is pushed into a form and left to dry, so that it retains the shape and detail of the mold. Because of the texture of the paper fiber, it is easily manipulated into the crevices of a mold and is capable of reproducing fine details.

For paper casting, it is recommended that white rather than colored fibers be used because the white will show more detail. Cotton linters work best, although white recycled paper, such as white paper bags combined with cotton linters, works well.

You can make a paper casting with a few simple tools. Use a small strainer to drain the lint, a terry cloth towel and sponge to remove moisture, and a paper casting mold to form the shape (see Photo A).

Many molds are ordinary kitchen items, such as cookie cutters and candy molds. Other items include seashells and antique molds of various kinds.

Photo A

Getting Started

1. To make one casting, blend six linter squares (¼ cup of bulk linters) with 1½ cups of water. Pour the mixture into a large cup or glass. Slowly pour from the cup into a sieve that has been positioned over an empty container (see Photo B). Let the water drain.

2. Place a casting mold, image side down, on top of the sieve. Flip the sieve over so that the casting mold is on the bottom and the sieve is on top (see Photo C). Tap the sieve so the linter mass falls onto the mold, and remove the sieve.

3. Gently press the wet linter mass against the face of the mold using a damp sponge (see Photo D). Continue pressing to remove the water so that the linter mass begins to conform to the image on the mold. Remove the sponge and press the casting with a terry cloth towel to further remove the moisture. Allow the casting to air dry or, to speed the process, microwave for 2 minutes at medium power. Remove the casting from the mold when it is dry.
Note: If you have difficulty releasing the casting, try using a nonstick cooking spray, a silicone spray, or petroleum jelly on the inside of the mold. Be sure to wipe off any excess before beginning the casting process.

Photo B

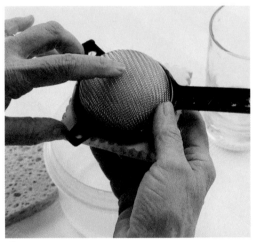

Photo C

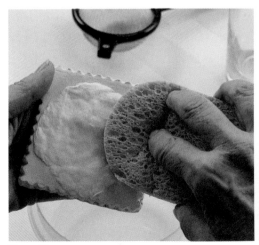

Photo D

SCRAPBOOKING

If friends
were flowers,
I'd pick you!

Capture
all of the important moments

of your life in colorful, dimensional scrapbooks.
They're fun to make, offer endless design possibilities,
and best of all,
they provide a record of your personal history
for future generations to explore.

Scrapbooking

Capture fond memories of family, friends, and special events in scrapbooks that are fun to assemble.

Tools and Materials

Adhesives – A

Scrapbooking glues and tapes should be labeled "photo-safe" and be free of acid, lignin, and PVC. Glue sticks, pens, and wands make applying adhesive neat and easy. Some set up instantly; others are repositionable so that items can be safely lifted off and rearranged. Double-sided tape comes in a roll-on dispenser that lays down a strip of tape when pressed to a photograph or paper. Look for photo stickers with a peel-away backing in the scrapbooking department. This is one of the quickest ways to permanently apply photos to a page.

In some cases, you might want to remove an antique, heirloom, or other special photograph from the scrapbook at a later date. Use photo corners or photo sleeves for these special items.

Die Cuts – B

Precut paper shapes called die cuts come as frames, borders, and solid shapes. Use them on a page to set the theme, highlight a photograph, or draw attention to journaling. Die cuts are available in almost any shape imaginable—numbers, letters, geometrics, borders and bands, animals, special interests, and holiday shapes—and a wide range of colors and patterns.

To add dimension to a page, place one or more raised self-adhesive dots under a die cut.

Paper Punches and Scissors – C, D, E, F, and G

Paper punches are available in all different shapes, edge cutters shape corners of photographs and papers, and decorative-edge scissors add unlimited interest to a scrapbook page. Punches can be used

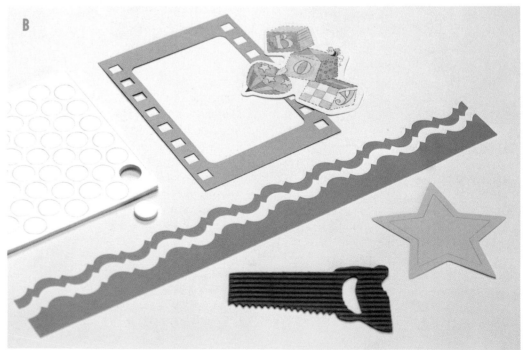

to produce a negative (punched out) or positive (glued to the page as an accent) effect.

Pens, Pencils, and Markers – H to M

Writing supplies designed especially for scrapbooking and paper crafts will resist bleeding and fading. Roller gel pens are easy to use and come in a wide variety of colors (see H and I). Pens with felt tips on both ends (J) are used to apply color directly to a stamp or color in a stamped image after it's been placed on the paper. Pigment pens are the most basic writing tool and come in a variety of colors, sizes, and tips (K). Metallic pens are available in colors such as gold, copper, and silver (L). Red eye-reducing pens help neutralize the eye glow that sometimes results from flash photography (M). Some companies make different pens for human eyes than for animal eyes.

Use only graphite or artist-quality pencils for decorating a page. Dye-base markers are appropriate for embellishing or stamping but should not be used for journaling. They might fade if exposed to light for long periods of time.

Cutters – N, O, and P

Rotary cutters and mats identical to the ones used by quilters can be used on larger pieces. Decorative blades work in the same manner as a plain straight blade. Use a different blade for cutting paper than for cutting fabric—paper dulls the blade and makes it difficult to use on material. Small, circular paper cutters and mats (N) come in handy when cropping photographs or trimming background papers. A circle-cutting wheel is designed to

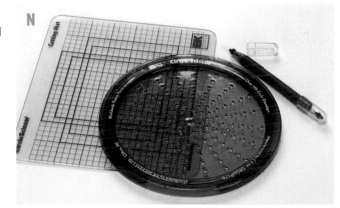

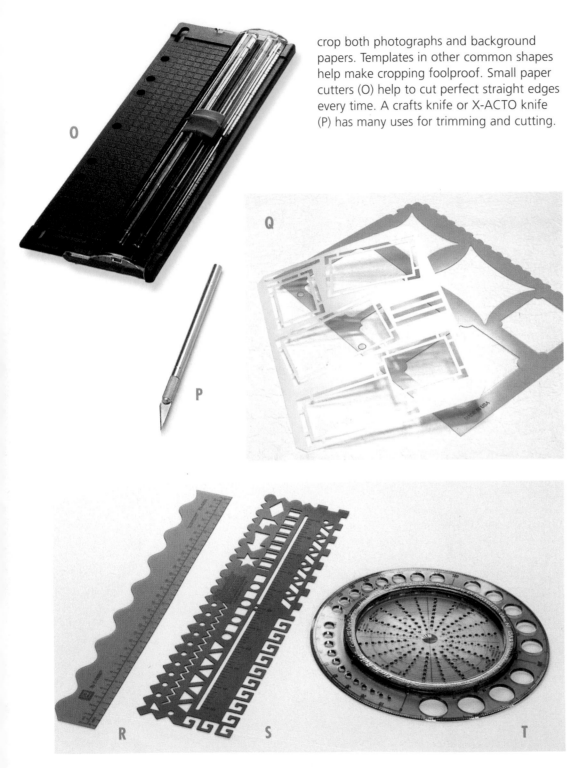

crop both photographs and background papers. Templates in other common shapes help make cropping foolproof. Small paper cutters (O) help to cut perfect straight edges every time. A crafts knife or X-ACTO knife (P) has many uses for trimming and cutting.

Rulers and Templates — Q, R, S, and T

Many templates are cut from plastic sheets and are similar to stencils. Center the template over the photograph or background paper; then trace the shape and cut it out. There are also templates for shaping long items like the edge of a page or pocket (Q). Rulers with shaped edges and stencil-like templates (R and S) make it easy to add borders to a page. A circular rule allows you to trace small circles or draw larger ones for cropping (T).

Scrapbooking Basics

Acid-free and archival-quality products are designed to last for generations and not damage other materials in the scrapbook. A few key terms to look for when purchasing papers, glues, inks, and decorative items are:

Acid-free: Look for products with a pH between 7 and 8.5. More acidic papers (above 8.5) will become brittle over time and might cause photographs to discolor.

Lignin-free: Lignin is naturally present in most papers. It is believed that paper that has not had the lignin removed will yellow when exposed to ultraviolet light.

Buffered: Acid-free paper might become acidic over time as it is exposed to acids from memorabilia included in the scrapbook. Buffered paper reduces the break down over time and prevents the paper from becoming acidic.

Albums
Albums come in an almost endless selection of sizes, shapes, and cover

designs, the most common sizes being 8½×11 inches or 12×12 inches. Make sure whatever album you choose is photo friendly and acid-free.

Binders: These are built like your old school notebook where the rings snap apart to insert pages. They are often larger than other albums and can have a wider variety of papers used for pages, including pages you make and punch yourself.

Spiral-bound: Because these books have a set number of pages, they are ideal for one-topic scrapbooks such as wedding, anniversary, or vacation albums. Extra pages can be torn out.

Post-bound: Screw-style posts bind the pages together and allow you to add or rearrange the pages. More pages can be added up to a certain thickness, but the size of the page is limited.

Strap-style: Plastic straps woven through staples and attached to the pages construct these albums. The pages lay flat and close together when open, making these albums ideal for larger layouts.

Almost all albums except spiral-bound can have page-protecting sleeves slipped over the pages. If your album will be handled or transported often, be sure to use pages that are compatible with page protectors.

Embellishments
Decorative punches and scissors, pretty papers, stickers, die-cut shapes, rubber stamps, and colored pens and pencils are just a few of the items that can enhance your pages. New items hit the market almost weekly, so check with your Jo-Ann Store often.

Getting Started

Adding handmade touches to a page not only makes it more fun and attractive, it often makes it more useful. Once you understand the basic steps, you will find unlimited ways to modify and personalize them.

Photography
Do your initial cropping with your camera if possible. By focusing on what you really want to remember—a building, an expression, or a landmark, for example—and eliminating the background clutter from the photograph, you'll have a larger, clearer image. In other cases, background is as important as the subject of the photograph because it sets the tone or location. A flurry of color and activity behind a child eating cotton candy at a carnival, the trees behind the picnic table at a campsite dinner, or the Statue of Liberty in the background of a portrait are vital elements to the overall photograph.

To add variety and interest, use different camera angles (see Photo A). Consider placing the subject matter slightly off center. Everyone photographs the Eiffel Tower dead center with the people directly in front. Take a different approach and have the person stand slightly to the side of the landmark subject of your photograph. When photographing children, pets, or flowers, get down on their level and shoot straight on instead of downward.

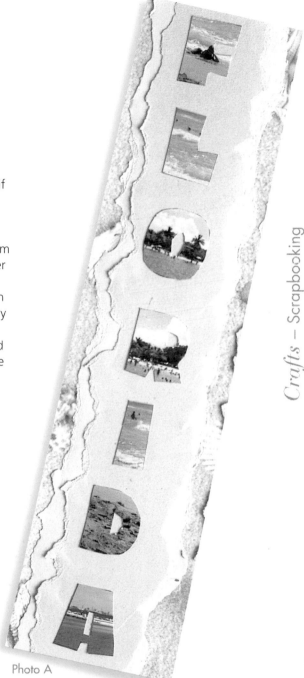

Photo A

Color Copying

When working with one-of-a-kind photographs, fragile items, heirloom documents like birth (see Photo C) and wedding announcements, or newspaper clippings, it is best to use a color photocopy instead of the original. Take advantage of this tool and use it to enlarge, reduce, or otherwise alter your image. Always copy onto good-quality, pure white, acid-free paper.

Photo B

Journaling

Journaling, or telling a story, is what separates a scrapbook from a fancy photo album (see photos B and C). Use your own handwriting (it will mean more to future generations to see the story in your own hand) and a pigment pen. Journaling can range from clever photo captions, to a short memory of an event, to a detailed account of someone's life. Intersperse photographs and memorabilia that apply to the event. Journaling can be set off by a box drawn with a template, by a die cut, or even a separate piece of paper glued to the page.

Cropping

Trimming a photograph to enhance an image is called *cropping* (see Photo D). If the background clutter detracts from the central image, simply cut it away. Cropping can also be used to fit more images and journaling on

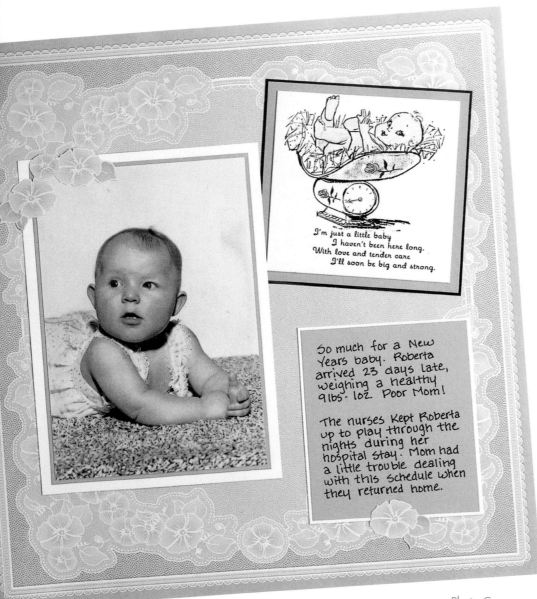

I'm just a little baby
I haven't been here long.
With love and tender care
I'll soon be big and strong.

So much for a New Years baby. Roberta arrived 23 days late, weighing a healthy 9 lbs.- 1 oz. Poor Mom!

The nurses kept Roberta up to play through the nights during her hospital stay. Mom had a little trouble dealing with this schedule when they returned home.

Photo C

a page. Never crop the only copy of a photograph; have a reprint or color photocopy made. Do not crop Polaroid photographs because of the chemicals they contain. Start by cropping a small amount, then trim away more if needed.

Templates can be used as a cropping guide. Center the template over the photograph, then trace the shape onto the photograph and cut along the lines. Freehand cutting can be done with a straightedge or a crafts knife, plain or decorative-edge scissors, a rotary cutter and mat, or a paper cutter. Silhouette-style cropping (see the photos, *upper left and right*) cuts away all the background, leaving only the primary image.

Original Photo

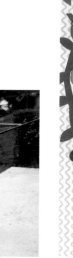

Photo D

Photo Coloring

Tint black-and-white or sepia photographs for an old-fashioned hand-colored look using photo-coloring brush markers (see Photo E). Using matte-finish paper, make a color copy of the photograph. Lightly brush the photograph, highlighting the focal points and a few background or other elements. For the best results, work quickly and in small areas. Remember to keep most of the photograph its original color or you will lose the effect of hand tinting. In the photograph (see Photo E) the skin, shoes, hair, and toy were colored and the cheeks were slightly blushed, but all else was left natural. If your colors streak, even them out with a cotton swab. Let the color dry for 24 hours before handling.

Original Photo

Photo E

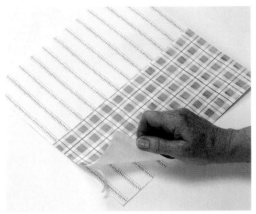

Photo F

Pockets

Make your pages more efficient by adding pockets to hold invitations, announcements, programs, or other mementos (see Photo F and finished page, *right*). Cut the pocket paper in half or slightly larger than what it needs to hold. Attach the pocket with acid-free, double-sided tape, or glue it to the base paper along the short sides and bottom and decorate it as desired.

Windows and Doors – Photos G, H, and I

Windows and mats accent a scrapbook photo or journal phrase just as a picture frame draws the eye to a piece of art. To create a window, crop the photograph, leaving a small margin on each side. Cut a window piece to fit your page. Place the window piece on a cutting mat and cut out an opening slightly smaller than the photograph. Glue or tape the photograph under the opening in the window and adhere the window to the page.

Photo G

Photo H

Photo I

For fun, add a door or flap over the window. Use a template, sticker, or other guide to draw an image larger than the window opening. If needed, add a flap to one side for a single-opening door (see photos G and H, made with a sticker) or two sides for a double-opening door (see Photo I). For a double-opening door, cut the door along the center line. Make a crease along the flap line and glue the flap to the window.

Make a moving part for the window by attaching the door with a brad fastener (see photos J and K).

Photo J

Photo K

Keepsake Pockets and Packets

Manufacturers have made it easy to display three-dimensional items that should be sealed because they are fragile or not free of acid. Clear envelope-style keepsake pockets (see Photo L) often have adhesive backs and are great for storing flatter items like a single coin, stamps, a lock of hair, or ticket stubs. Simply place the item in the envelope, seal it shut, remove the backing material, and press it in place.

Photo L

For bulkier items, choose three-dimensional holders (see Photo M). Many come with template patterns, or you can cut your own templates. Cut a window to fit the holder following the Windows and Doors instructions, *opposite*. If desired, cut a backing piece that is slightly smaller than the window from cardboard. Cut a liner piece to fit inside the holder using paper that will highlight your item.

Place the item inside the holder and snap the top to the bottom. Slip the window over the holder and glue it in place. If desired, glue the holder to the cardboard. Glue the holder to the page.

Photo M

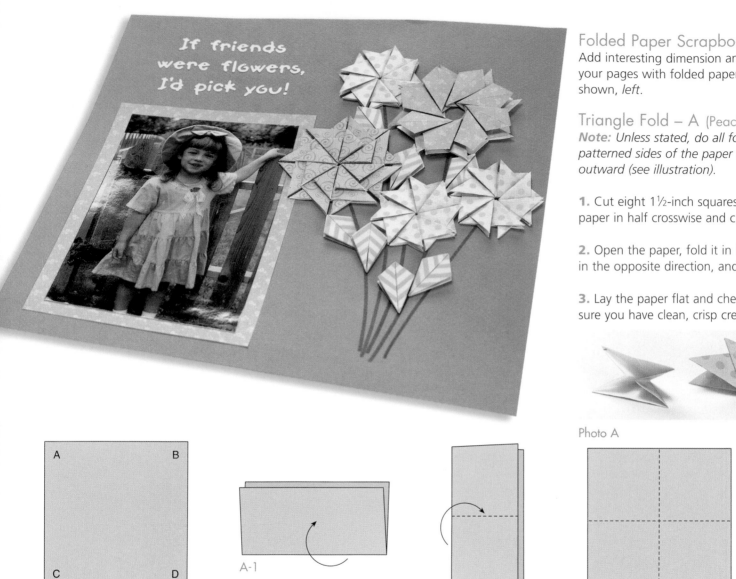

Folded Paper Scrapbook Page

Add interesting dimension and texture to your pages with folded paper designs as shown, *left*.

Triangle Fold – A (Peach Flowers)

Note: Unless stated, do all folds with the patterned sides of the paper facing outward (see illustration).

1. Cut eight 1½-inch squares. Fold the paper in half crosswise and crease.

2. Open the paper, fold it in half lengthwise in the opposite direction, and crease.

3. Lay the paper flat and check to make sure you have clean, crisp creases that show.

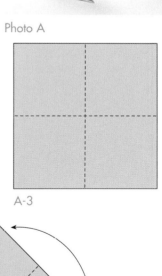

Photo A

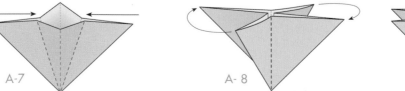

4. With the pattern side out, fold the upper left corner to the lower right corner, forming a triangle, and crease.

5. Open the paper square and repeat, folding the lower left corner to the upper right corner, forming another triangle, and crease.

6. Hold the triangle in both hands with the folded side parallel to the table.

7. Push the folded edges up and toward the center, collapsing the triangle.

8. Turn the flaps following the direction of the arrows in the diagram. The front flap is folded to the left and the back flap is folded to the right, forming a smaller layered triangle.

9. One triangle fold has been completed.

To assemble a peach flower, hold two triangles with the closed points facing downward. Slide the top flap of the right triangle between the two flaps of the other triangle (see Photo A). Arrange the triangles

until the flower is complete, then carefully glue the petals in place with the points flush.

Single Stair Fold – B (Pink Flower)

1 through **9**: Cut eight 2⅛-inch squares. To make this Single Stair Fold, first follow the nine steps for making the Triangle Fold petals, *opposite*.

10. Hold the triangle fold with the point facing down.

11. Grasp the upper right corner (top flap only) and fold it down toward the point as shown.

12. Turn the small flap to the left side as shown. Assemble the flower petals in the same manner as the peach flowers (see Photo B).

Kite Fold – C (Blue Flower)

1 through **9**: Cut eight 2-inch squares. To make this Kite Fold, first follow the nine steps for making the Triangle Fold petals, *opposite*.

10. Hold the triangle fold with the point facing down.

11. With the folded point facing down, grasp the upper right corner (top layer only) and bring the flap forward as shown.

12. Open and separate the edges of the raised flap with a pencil lead pushed all the way down to the point. Begin pressing down on this section with your hand as you remove the pencil and flatten the paper, creating a kite shape.

13. Turn the triangle over and repeat for the other side.

To complete the blue flower, hold two triangles with the points facing downward. Slide the left edge of the right triangle under the kite shape of the left triangle. Offset the points by about ¼ inch. Glue the triangles in place (see Photo C). Repeat until the blue flower is complete. There should be a small center opening.

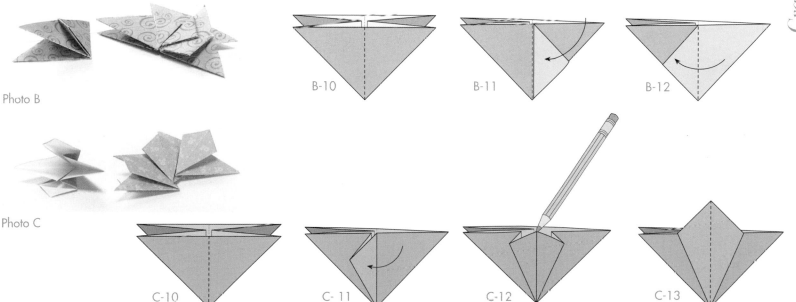

Photo B

Photo C

B-10

B-11

B-12

C-10

C-11

C-12

C-13

Leaf Fold – D (Green Leaves)

1 through **9**: Cut one 2-inch square for each leaf. To make the Leaf Fold, first follow the nine steps for making the Triangle Fold petals, on page 116, then follow the instructions for making the Kite Fold on page 117.

10. Hold the Kite Fold with the point facing down.

11. Fold the right and left flaps in between the front and back kite shapes.

12. With the right and left flaps tucked in, crease the paper.

13. Bring the right fold forward so that the edge aligns with the center crease.

14. Bring the left fold forward so that the edge aligns with the center crease.

15. and **16.** Turn the triangle over and repeat on the other side.

17. With the triangle shape facing as shown in D-16, fold the right flap to the left side. Repeat for the back side.

18. Completed leaf fold.

To finish the photo album cover shown on page 116, draw stems with a green marker and glue the leaves to the stems where desired.

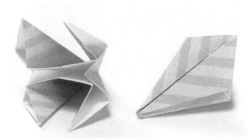

Photo D

ॐCreative Tip

Save all acid-free paper scraps to make

punched shapes for decoration.

– Team Member, Martinsville, Virginia

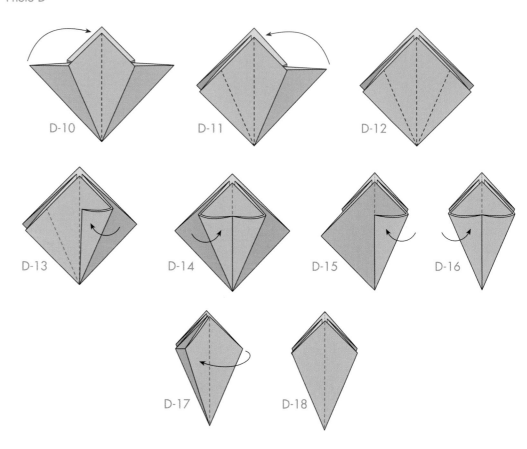

D-10

D-11

D-12

D-13

D-14

D-15

D-16

D-17

D-18

Folded Paper Frame

Decorate your favorite photo by creating a unique frame that will add color and dimension to your scrapbook page. Follow the instructions for the Triangle Folded paper (peach flowers) on page 116.

The points of each triangle should be offset farther than the flower project to create a large opening for the photo. Work on a flat surface. Do not glue the triangles together until you have reached the desired size for the center opening.

Paper Punch Wedding Page

An assortment of punches and a doily mat complement this wedding photo without overpowering it. Five colors of paper (violet, lavender, gold, sage, and dark green) are punched with swirl and floral punches and assembled to create borders and corner motifs. The white paper doily is double-matted with the sage and violet papers to anchor the page, and the names of the bride and groom and their wedding date finish it nicely.

Handmade
SOAP

Give an assortment
of colorful and fragrant handmade soaps

to a friend, or use them to decorate
your bathroom and kitchen.
You'll love experimenting with the different shapes,
essential oils, and gift-making ideas these
soap techniques offer.

Tools and Materials

Soapmaking is faster and easier when convenient materials are used, allowing you to direct your energies toward creativity instead of searching for obscure products.

Base Soap – A
Blocks and bars of soap for soapmaking are designed to melt easily and evenly. Precolored, white, and clear glycerin bases are available in a variety of block sizes.

Color – B
Liquid color allows you to develop a custom color and can be added to either the white or colored bases. Coloring agents are highly concentrated, so only a few drops are needed to make most colors.

Embellishments – C
Finely ground glitters are added to give sparkle to handmade soaps.

Fragrance – D
Highly concentrated oils allow you to add your favorite fragrance to the soap. Only a few drops are needed for each project, and

Handmade *Soaps*

Easy and elegant handmade soaps dress up any bath, whether you design them for your own home or make them in batches as gifts. Molds, premixed fragrances, and microwavable base products are designed to make this craft a snap.

scents can be mixed to create your own special blend.

Kitchen Tools – E
A sharp knife, a cutting board, a large glass measuring cup or spouted bowl, a large spoon, a microwave oven, and a newspaper or an old plastic tablecloth for easy cleanup are the basic equipment needed for soapmaking. None will be damaged by the process, and a thorough cleaning makes them ready for regular kitchen use after the soap is made.

Molds – F
Firm, level molds are used to shape the soap. A wide range of bar shapes is available, as well as long loaf forms that can be sliced after the soap has cured. A variation on the bar mold has designs indented into the form, creating a raised pattern on the bar (see the examples, *above left*). Other fun shapes are two-part, three-dimensional molds and small detailed embedments that can be used to make fancy guest soaps or floating designs in clear glycerin bars.

Handmade Soap Basics

Soapmaking has come a long way since Grandmother's day of cooking lye and fat in an outdoor kettle. Today the focus is on making a decorative product that also is functional. Precolored bricks of soap provide a base that can be melted in the microwave oven and poured into an assortment of decorative molds. Coloring agents and fragrances are readily available, too, making it possible to personalize soaps.

Adding Color
Although it might be tempting to add food coloring to the soap base, resist the urge. Food coloring fades when exposed to sunlight. Instead, use dyes specially made for soapmaking which are also skin-friendly. Look for colors that are labeled as cosmetic grade.

Creating Shapes
Loaf molds are sliced into individual bars after the soap cools, allowing you to make soaps as thin or as thick as you want. Allow the loaf to cool a few hours, but cut the soap while it is still soft and pliable. Be sure to use

a knife blade with the same thickness at the top as the sharp edge so the slices will be straight and even.

Soap also can be shaped by hand for a rustic look. Allow the melted soap to cool so it is comfortable to handle, then shape it into balls with your hands, compressing it as if you were working with modeling clay. Reshape the soap every few hours as it settles and the shape changes. To make a bar, allow the soap balls to cool 10 to 15 minutes, then flatten them with your palm. Smooth any cracks by dampening your fingers with water or oil and rubbing over the cracks, or leave the cracks for a natural look and texture.

Adding Fragrance

Creating your own fragrance combinations makes soapmaking fun, but adding too much fragrance is a common mistake. Use only 10 to 15 drops (about ¼ teaspoon) per pound of soap. To experiment with a combination of scents, place a few drops of each fragrance in a zipper-style plastic bag and write down the formula. Let the fragrance set for a few days; then smell. If you find the scent pleasing, use your formula to make enough for a complete batch of soap.

Adding Embellishments

Two or more colors can be mixed and swirled once they are poured into the mold, or smaller soaps can be embedded into larger clear glycerin bars. Glittery or pearlescent powder also can be added for a festive appearance.

Getting Started

One basic melting and shaping technique allows you to make soaps of all different shapes and complexities. Start with the basic soapmaking technique, then spread your wings and try more complicated designs.

Photo A

Photo B

Photo C

Photo D

1. Spray the mold with a release agent, such as nonstick cooking spray (see Photo A). Wipe away any excess oil that accumulates in crevices with a paper towel. A very thin coat of petroleum jelly also can be used. Use the release agent sparingly. If the soap does not release easily from the mold, place the mold in the refrigerator (not the freezer) for one hour, then pop out the soap.

2. Cut the soap base into cubes of similar size (see Photo B). Slice the block into several smaller pieces, then cut each slice into smaller cubes.

3. Place the cubes in a microwave-safe measuring cup (see Photo C); one with a handle and spout works best. Microwave the soap for 15 seconds. Stir and continue microwaving and stirring at 5-second intervals. If you are melting a large batch, increase the initial time to 30 seconds and the interval times to 10 seconds. Avoid allowing the soap to boil; if some of the soap boils before the rest is melted, select a lower temperature on the microwave oven.

4. To add color, stir a single drop of soap colorant into the melted soap. The soap will

Photo E

Photo F

Creative Tip

For a neat gift, take three or four of your homemade soaps and gather a new washcloth around them. Tie the top with a pretty ribbon and decorate with a floral pick.

– Store Associate, Martinsville, Virginia

Photo G

Photo H

Photo I

darken slightly as it cools. If needed, add additional color one drop at a time. To add fragrance, allow the soap to cool and to form a thin skin. Add a few drops of fragrance and stir it into the soap, mixing it thoroughly.

5. Pour the melted soap into the mold (see Photo D, *opposite*). If the mold has a raised design, the soap can be poured in all one color, or a contrasting color can be poured into the design area and cooled before the main color is poured into the mold. Allow the soap to cool for one

hour, then pop it from the mold (see photos E and F).

Loofah Slices

1. A loofah sponge saturated with soap is ideal for gardeners, crafters, and people who need to scrub at the end of a task. Dampen a long loofah sponge and reshape it into an even circular shape before making the soap.

2. Wrap the sides and bottom of the loofah in plastic wrap and secure it with rubber bands. Place it in a jar or other cylindrical

container (see Photo G). Melt the soap base and add color or scent, if desired. Let the soap cool and form a top skin. Pour soap over the loofah, completely covering it. Allow the soap to cool.

Remove the plastic wrap. Slice the loofah into ½- to 1-inch slices (see photos H and I).

Crafts – Handmade Soaps

Photo J

Photo L

Photo M

Photo K

Photo N

Embedments

Float one soap within another for a magical touch. Both clear and opaque soaps can be used, or the two may be combined.

1. Pour melted soap base into embedment molds (see photos J and L). Let the soaps cool, then pop them out of the molds.

2. To place an embedment on top of the soap, lay an opaque shape in the bottom of the mold (see Photo M). Lightly spray the

shape with rubbing alcohol. Fill the mold with clear soap base. Let the bar cool for one hour, then pop it from the mold.

3. To place the embedments in the center of the bar (see Photo N), pour clear soap base into the mold, filling it halfway. Place the embedment shapes in the bar. Transfer a small amount of rubbing alcohol to a spray container. Lightly mist the soap in the mold with the rubbing alcohol, and continue filling the rest of the mold.

Loaf Soap

Add swirls of color, embedments, or other embellishments to loaves of soap and each slice will be different.

Place the melted soap base in the loaf mold. To add embedments, pour in a small amount of soap, then add some shapes. Lightly spray the surface with rubbing alcohol and add a little more melted soap base. Add more embedments. Continue in this manner until the loaf mold is filled. Add layers of color, swirls, or glitter in the same manner.

Let the soap cool for 1 to 3 hours. Remove it from the mold. While the soap is still pliable, slice it into bars with a thin-blade knife (see Photo N).

Gift Giving

When you devote time to making soaps, consider packaging them creatively for gifts. Choose a basket and include a pretty sponge, rubber-stamp a clever bag and tuck the soaps inside, or purchase clear plastic gift boxes and wrap them with gold elastic cord.

STAMPING and EMBOSSING

Stamps have become much more
than simple motifs added to note cards.

Emboss them, add paint or
colored-pencil accents,
use metallic treatments, and
even apply them to wall or fabric surfaces—you're only
limited by your imagination.

Stamping *and Embossing*

Create fabulous greeting cards and notes that will be cherished by your friends and family. Or use a little paint and a stamp or two to make a quick crafts project on wood or fabric. When you use acid-free inks and papers, you can combine stamping with your scrapbook projects.

Tools and Materials

Acrylic Paint – A
Expand your options with water-soluble acrylic paints. Available in many colors, these paints are ready to use and dry quickly to a permanent, water-resistant surface. Use with foam stamps.

Adhesives – B
Glue sticks work well when adhering light-to medium-weight papers together. Use glue pens to layer thin papers and to add glitter. An alternative is double-sided tape (not shown). Use masking or artist's tape to mask off areas that you want to protect.

Box Templates – C
Boxes are great surfaces for stamping. Use templates to make several sizes and shapes of boxes. Cut out the shape, score, and fold along the indicated lines.

Brayer – D
Use a brayer to roll color onto paper.

Brush Art Markers and Colored Pencils – E
Use water-base markers, available in a rainbow of colors and many tip sizes, to color stamped images or to apply color directly to the rubber stamp. For a soft look, color the stamped images with colored pencils, achieving light to dark colors by varying the pressure. Colored pencils work well on all papers except coated ones.

Creasing Tool – F
The creasing tool is made of bone or plastic. Use the point to score paper and the long flat edge to make a sharp crease in the paper.

Cutting Tools and Punches – G
The paper cutter is an indispensable tool for making straight cuts. Because you measure and cut at the same time, it makes quick work of cutting rectangles and squares. Scissors are available in an enormous selection of straight and decorative blades. Use these to cut interesting shapes and to finish project edges. To cut a continuous pattern, realign the blade carefully after each cut. Hole punches also come in a variety of sizes and may be used to punch holes for threading ribbon and cording.

Embossing Heat Tool – H
This convenient tool quickly and safely melts embossing powders. It emits intense heat without blowing air and can be directed at the surface of the stamped image.

Embossing Powders – I
Choose from a multitude of colors, including clear and metallics. The powders are sprinkled over an image stamped with a slow-drying pigment or embossing ink. After the powder is applied, it is heated to the melting point, which creates a raised, shiny finish. The embossed image becomes the color of the powder or, if you're using clear powder, the color of the ink.

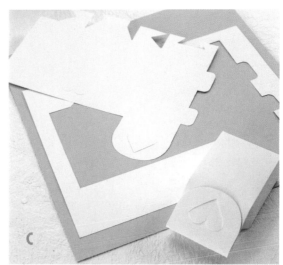

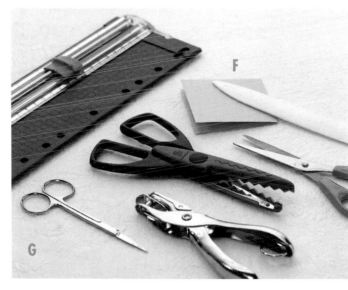

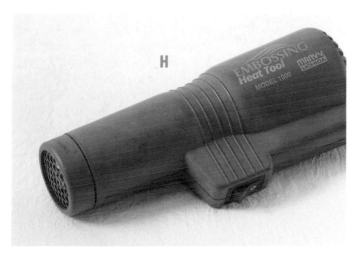

127

both to stamp and for layering. Choices include card stock, glossy, uncoated, sticker, vellum, handmade, tissue, and mulberry.

Rubber/Foam Stamps – K

There are thousands of stamps available for every occasion and mood. The most popular are wood-handled stamps with a rubber die adhered to a foam cushion and mounted on a wood block. Foam-handled stamps are mounted on a dense piece of foam. They are very pliable and work well on curved surfaces. There are picture or word stamps, with either line drawings or solid images.

Sponges – L

Wedge-shaped foam sponges are used to apply ink to the stamp. They also are used directly on stamping surfaces to create backgrounds. These backgrounds can range from soft watercolor effects to solid blocks of color. Find the sponges at art and crafts stores or in cosmetic departments. Natural sea sponges provide a wide range of textures, and they are most often used to add color to background areas and large shapes.

Pop Dots – see page 133, Photo J

Use pop dots to create dimension with your stamping designs. The pop dots are made of thin pieces of foam with glue on both sides to make application easier.

Papers – J

Paper is by far the most popular surface to stamp. Stampers may select from a huge variety of solid-color and patterned papers,

M

N

✂Creative Tip

Store stamp ink pads upside down so the ink will stay on top of the pad surface. Stamp the color of the ink pad onto a label and stick it to the bottom of the pad so you know what color it is without having to turn it right side up.

– Team Member,
Torrance, California

Stamp Pads – M

Stamp or ink pads come in many sizes and shapes and in a rainbow of colors, including metallics. Usually the surface of the pad is higher than the edge of the container so you can ink any size stamp. There are many different types of inks. The type you select is determined by the stamping surface.

Rainbow ink pads (see Photo M, *top*) contain individual blocks of colored inks arranged side-by-side to make one ink pad. Multi-colored ink pads are available with pigment and dye inks.

Pigment inks are thick and slow-drying (see Photo M, *lower left*). They work well on all types of papers and with clear embossing powder. Pigment inks are available in clear and vivid colors.

Dye-based inks are water-based and fast drying (see Photo M, *lower right*). They can be used on all papers, but may bleed on absorbent papers such as tissue paper or construction paper.

Stamp Cleaner – N

Stamp cleaners are specially formulated to safely remove ink from rubber stamp surfaces. Clean the stamp when you change ink types or colors. Use an old toothbrush to remove dried ink from stamp crevices.

Stamping Rulers, Stylus, Crafts Knife – O

Rulers are handy to measure paper and for using as a straightedge with a knife or a creasing tool. The stamp positioner is a clear acrylic tool that looks like a T-ruler; it helps to position a stamp image exactly where you want it on the stamping surface. The stylus has two metal ends that are used when making cards from card stock. Use it to score the paper before folding. A crafts knife is useful to make exact cuts and for interior slits in a project.

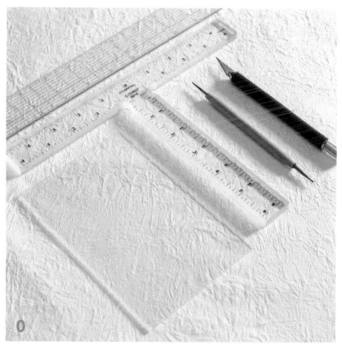

O

Stamping and Embossing Basics

Painting Technique

When stamping with acrylic paint, it is best to use foam stamps. Shake the paint well and squeeze a puddle of paint onto a disposable foam plate. Mix textile medium with the paint to stamp on fabrics, following the manufacturer's instructions. Use a wedge-shape foam sponge to dab the paint onto the stamp, being careful not to get paint in the crevices. Stamp the image on the stamping surface (see Photo A), applying an even, firm pressure. Reapply paint after each impression.

Multi-Color Stamping Technique

Randomly stamp the image multiple times on the stamping surface using a variety of colors (see Photo B). Clean the stamp carefully when you change ink colors.

Masking Technique

1. Stamp the image on the stamping surface. Then stamp the same image on a separate piece of notepaper. Cut the second image (this is the mask) out with scissors and place over the first image (see Photo C).

2. With the mask covering the original image, stamp an image with part of the stamp on the mask (see photo D). Photo E shows placement of the image (in black ink) prior to removing the mask. Remove the notepaper image; the second image will appear to be behind the original image as shown with the finished box in Photo F.

Photo A

Photo B

Photo C

Photo D

Photo E

Photo

Photo G

Photo H

Creative Tip

Looking for a card stock to match a specific color ink pad? Swipe the ink pad across the lighter colored card stock until you get the color you want. This way, you can layer the front and add embellishments, and everything matches.

– Team Member, Richland, Virginia

Coloring Stamped Images

1. Ink the stamp by pressing it onto the surface of the pad several times for complete ink coverage. Stamp the image onto the card stock, applying even, firm pressure (see Photo G). Do not rock or wiggle the stamp. Carefully lift the stamp straight up.

2. When the stamped image is dry, use markers or colored pencils to color the image (see Photo H).

3. Cut complementary papers in graduated sizes for layering, creating a 1/8- to 1/2-inch border around the stamped piece and the layered papers (see Photo I). Use decorative-edge scissors to finish the edges of the papers.

4. Using a glue stick, mount the stamped piece on the complementary papers, then on a folded piece of card stock for a card, or fold the stamped card stock into a note card.

Photo I

Photo A

Photo B

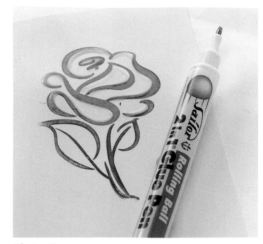

Photo C

Photo D

Photo E

Marker and Glitter Technique

1. Use brush markers to apply ink directly on the rubber die. Start with the lightest color and work toward the darkest (see Photo A).

2. Before stamping the image, lightly breathe on the stamp to remoisten the ink. Stamp the image onto the stamping surface, applying even, firm pressure (see Photo B). Do not rock or wiggle the stamp (it may smear). Carefully lift the stamp straight up.

3. Use a glue pen to apply glue to the areas to receive glitter (see Photo C). Immediately sprinkle glitter on the wet glue. Tap off the excess glitter and let the glue dry (see Photo D).

4. Mount the stamped design on layers of complementary papers. Use decorative-edge scissors, if desired, to finish the edges of the papers (see Photo E).

Creating Dimension Technique

1. Roll a brayer across the rainbow ink pad several times, moving it slightly to the left and right so the colors overlap on the roller (see Photo F). You also may color or draw on the brayer with brush markers.

2. Roll the brayer back and forth across the card stock several times, starting and stopping off the edge of the paper to avoid lines (see Photo G). Repeat this process until the stamping surface reaches the desired intensity, re-inking the brayer as necessary. Ink one piece of card stock for the background and one for stamping.

3. Ink the stamp with black ink or any color that will be visible on the rainbow-colored card stock (see Photo H). Stamp the image multiple times on one of the pieces of card stock, re-inking after each impression.

4. When the ink is dry, cut out the stamped images (see Photo I).

5. Cut a piece of complementary paper about 1 inch smaller on all sides than the background card stock. This will later be attached to the card stock. Apply pop dots to the back of some of the stamped images to create dimension (see Photo J).

6. Mount the complementary paper on the background card stock with a glue stick. Arrange and mount the stamped images on the complementary paper (see Photo K). *Note: Glue a couple of the images to the complementary paper without the pop dots.*

Photo F

Photo G

Photo H

Photo I

Photo J

Photo K

Crafts – Stamping and Embossing

Photo A

Photo B

Art Deco Place Mat

Create a set of stamped place mats,

napkins, and matching napkin rings

in an afternoon, and use them for

entertaining that evening.

Photo C

Heat Embossing Technique

1. Ink the stamp with pigment ink or embossing ink, and stamp the image onto the stamping surface (see Photo A).
Note: Clear embossing powder will pick up the color of pigment inks.

2. Immediately pour a generous amount of embossing powder over the stamped image to cover the wet ink (see Photo B). Tilt the paper on edge and tap off the excess powder onto a piece of clean scrap paper. Pour the excess powder back into the jar to use again. Use a small paintbrush to dust off any stray specks of powder.

3. Heat the powder with an embossing heat tool until the powder melts, creating a raised, shiny, or metallic finish (see Photo C). Hold the tool about 1 to 2 inches from the image and constantly move in a sweeping motion over the image. Be careful not to overheat the powder.

4. Leave the embossed image as it is, or color the design with art brush pens or colored pencils (see Photo D).

Photo D

Butterfly Gift Box

Make someone feel special

with personalized gift wrap

made just for her.

Personalized Notecards

Send creatively designed cards with personal

messages to friends and family members.

Gift Bag

With paper sacks and a few

supplies, you'll have the

ingredients to make fabulous

looking gift bags in a matter

of minutes.

DECORATING

Decorate with style and grace,

and you will not only improve

the visual quality of your living space,

you'll also give it personality.

It's easy to add a fresh new look

to your favorite rooms with florals,

paint, and frames.

Find out what you can do

to transform your space into

a stylish self-expression.

FLORAL

Learn the basics
of floral elements and design,

and make your arrangements look like they were
created by a professional designer.

Dry Foam – A

Dry foam is used specifically for dried and silk flower arranging. The dry foam will hold flower or greenery stems at any angle without the use of glue or floral picks. It is easily cut into any shape and placed into any size container.

Floral Spray Paints – B

Floral spray paints designed for dried, silk, and fresh flowers come in a rainbow of colors, including metallics and glitter. These sprays are used for changing the color of flowers or adding special color effects and glitter highlights.

Floral Spray Sealer – C

A crystal clear spray used in floral arranging to help seal surfaces and create a shine on matt finishes.

"Frog" or Kenzan – D

The "frog" or kenzan is a metal device with lots of sharp pins pointing upward. It is used when dry foam will not work, such as in a clear glass bowl or on a plate. The frog is held into place with sticky clay, then the flower stems are placed into the frog between the steel pins.

Floral arranging is easy when you have all the materials you need. The more familiar you are with the necessary tools and supplies, the more at ease you'll be when you are creating your own designs.

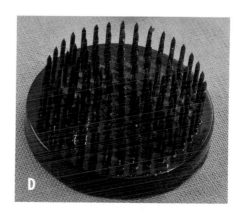

Glass Marbles and River Rock – E

These polished glass and stone accents can be embedded into the Liquid Illusion resin for color and also can be used in and around arrangements for texture. They also add interest in the bottom of clear glass vases and containers and hide stem ends.

Glue Gun and White Crafts Glue – F

A glue gun and hotmelt adhesive are indispensable tools that work well for silk and dried flower arrangements. The hotmelt adhesive dries quickly and is almost invisible. No crafter's toolbox should be without one. White glue can also be used for the same purpose as a hot-glue gun, but it dries more slowly.

Greening Pins (Ferning Pins) – G

Greening pins (also called ferning pins) are used for stabilizing moss and securing other materials to straw or dry foam. The pins may have a "U" shape at the top (see Photo G) or an "S" shape (not shown).

Liquid Illusion – H

Liquid Illusion is used to create the illusion of water in clear glass containers while firmly holding the stems of silk flowers in place. Be sure to follow the manufacturer's instructions for mixing. Glass floral marbles are often embedded in the hard resin for color.

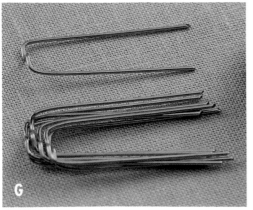

Moss

Spanish – I

Spanish moss has a warm brown color, and can be used to cover the foam and mechanics of design in a permanent botanical arrangement. As a general rule, Spanish moss is used either for its specific texture or color, working best with cool colors like blues, purples, and grays.

Sheet – J

Sheet moss is a green moss with applications that are similar to those of Spanish moss, but it works best with warmer colors like reds, golds, and oranges.

Reindeer – K

Reindeer moss is a gray-green, sponge-like moss that grows on the ground about 1 to 4 inches in height. Reindeer moss is used to support a focal point in arrangements or mixed with other mosses as filler.

Natural Excelsior – L

Used for the same purpose as moss, excelsior is made from wood shavings. It is used to cover dry foam for silk and dried floral arrangements or in baskets as filler.

Pearl-head Corsage Pins – M

Pearl-head corsage pins are used in making corsages and boutonnieres.

Pick Tool and Metal Picks – N

This handy tool will crimp a sharp metal pick onto the stem of floral materials and makes arranging flowers a breeze.

Pew Clips – O

Small plastic hangers designed to hold small floral arrangements and clip onto the ends of pews. Shown colored and clear.

Pillar and Taper Holders – P

These handy candle cup holders have a pointed tip underneath the cup that sticks into the dry foam and securely holds pillar or taper candles (3-inch pillar shown).

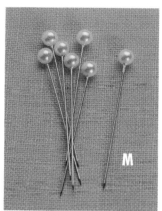

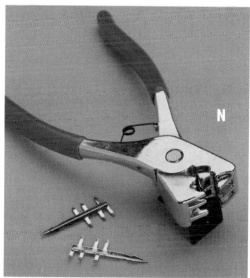

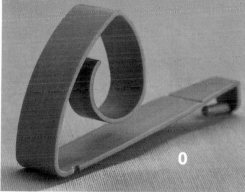

Tapes and Clay

Floral Tape or Stem Tape – Q

Floral tape is a stretchable tape that is used for covering wire and flower stems primarily in corsage and wedding work. The tape sticks to itself for a smooth finished look on wire. Available in several colors.

Waterproof Tape – R

Available in ¼-inch width, this tape is used to secure foam into a container by securing the tape to one side of the container, over the foam, then securing it to the other side. Most often, it is criss-crossed for added stability. It also can be used to anchor pillar and taper holders securely in place.

Sticky Clay – S

Sticky clay is just that: sticky. It is used to anchor frogs, prongs, and floral foam to dry containers.

Wire Cutters – T

Use wire cutters when shortening wire and trimming several thicknesses of wire. Scissors are not recommended for these tasks.

Wire and Picks

Wood Picks – U

Wood picks are slender stakes 3 inches or longer. They will add strength to weak and/or fragile stems. Secure stems to picks with attached wire.

Floral Wire – V, W, and Y

Floral wire is available in several different gauges and lengths. It is commonly used for holding up the heads of flowers and lengthening the stems for corsage and bouquet work. Some floral wire is fabric covered (V). Floral wire is usually found rolled on spools (W). Heavier wire often comes in cut lengths (Y). The advantage of spool wire is that it can be used for a garland in one continuous length.

Chenille Stems – X

Chenille stems (or pipe cleaners) are used to secure the ribbon for making bows.

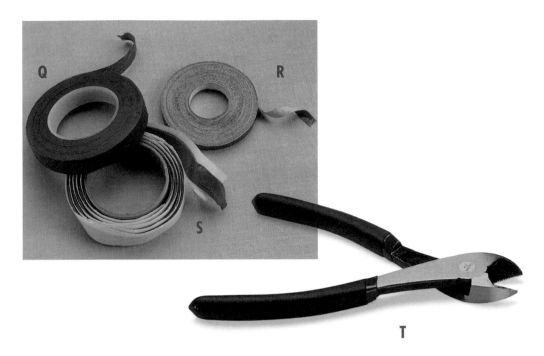

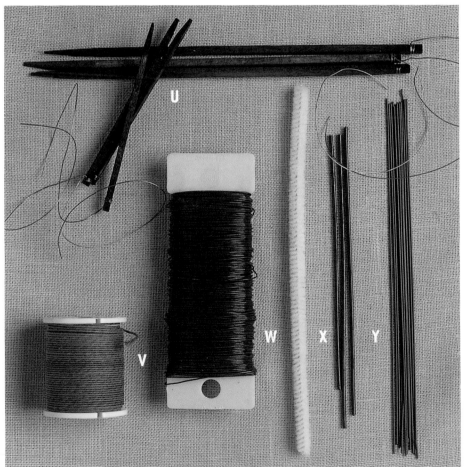

Floral Design *Elements*

Photo A - Harmony

Photo B - Symmetry

C - Asymmetry

Floral arranging requires an understanding of basic elements such as line, form, and texture. Keeping these elements in mind as you design your floral arrangements will give you beautiful results each time.

Line

Line refers to the curves or directional movement of the arrangement. Consider the decor and architectural elements of the room where the flowers are to be placed. This will help determine the design lines and overall look of straight or curved lines. For example, rooms with tall windows, columns, or other vertical decor call for florals with tall thin lines that imitate the dominant features in the room.

Form

Form applies to the fundamental shape of an arrangement such as a ball, triangle, "L", or "S" shape. Free-form designs have materials that fall outside of basic shapes.

Harmony

Floral designs that tie the colors, elements, or textures of a room together create a harmonious theme in the surrounding decor. For example, use the room's wall color within the arrangement to achieve decorator results (see Photo A).

Balance

Balance refers to the correct proportion of flowers to the vase as it relates to the height and width of the floral composition. Balanced floral designs fall into two categories: symmetrical or asymmetrical. As a rule of thumb, the arrangement should be about one and a half times the height of the container.

Symmetrical: These designs are created so that both sides of the design are equal. If a line were drawn down the center of the arrangement, both sides would have a similar look (see Photo B).

Asymmetrical: Arrangements containing different design elements on each side are considered to be asymmetrical. This type of arrangement must still have the correct weight on both sides to be visually pleasing (see Photo C).

Texture

Texture helps set the tone of the arrangement. Surfaces, containers, and floral elements that are smooth, shiny, reflective, and glittery are best used in formal or elegant settings. Natural or dried materials, raffia, straw, burlap, wire, or rough textures such as wood are informal, and lend themselves to a more relaxed decor. Be sure that the type of flowers or other materials used in the arrangement are compatible with the container and the room decor.

Size of Elements:
The size of the flowers determines their significance within the arrangement. Larger flowers carry greater visual weight, while it takes

Photo D

several small flowers to equal a single large flower. It is important to realize that both sizes are needed to achieve the correct balance (see Photo D).

Similarity of Elements: Similar elements are close in size, texture, and color. Having different flowers that meet this criteria gives you the freedom to substitute one for the other or use a mix of both (see Photo E).

Photo E

Color of Elements: Determining the use of light and dark flowers in an arrangement is critical to the balance. Dark-colored flowers carry greater weight than light-colored flowers. Therefore, it may take at least two or more light-colored flowers to equal one dark flower (see Photo F).

Photo F

Contrast
Arrangements with flowers of contrasting color create dramatic statements and draw attention to the design (see Photo G).

Proportion & Scale
The height and size of the floral arrangement should relate to the size and style of the container. The flowers and the

accessories must be in correct size relationship to other elements of the design. Also, consider the placement of the arrangement in the room, and the purpose for which it is intended (see Photos G and H).

Keep a design low for a dining room table where guests will be eating and talking. Tall arrangements are more appropriate for areas such as corner and entry tables, or fireplace mantels.

Weight
Visual weight is determined by the relationship of the larger flowers to the smaller filler flowers within the arrangement. Each flower has a certain degree of importance which is determined by the size, similarity of elements, and color.

Dried Flowers in Silk Arrangements
Permanent Botanicals is a widely used term for working with silk and dried flora in the same arrangement. When creating a silk or artificial design, the inclusion of dried flowers gives added reality to the design. By using moss, pods, or other dried materials, the artificial flowers are given credibility by the real floral materials.

Photo G

Photo H

Color In Florals

Color is an integral part of flower arranging basics. The best floral designs follow the correct elements of design, and also pay careful attention to color.

Special occasions such as weddings will probably use more white or neutral tones with the addition of soft pastel colors, while other celebrations tend to call for brighter colors. For help with color, refer to the Color Theory chapter on page 190.

Basic Flower Types

There are four basic types of flowers:

Line Flowers
Named for their tall, thin, long, line-like look, line flowers include gladiola, delphinium, and larkspur.

Mass Flowers
Mass flowers are named for mass/bulk and majority of use; most are round flowers such as peonies, open roses, carnations, daisies, and asters.

Form Flowers
Form flowers are named for their unique shape and form; they include iris, lilies, anthurium, and bird of paradise.

Filler Flowers
Filler flowers fill in the areas between the more major floral placements; examples include statice and baby's breath.

Some flowers can actually fall into two categories. Roses, when in bud form, are form flowers; when they are open, they are mass flowers. Limonium or spray asters are known as filler, but depending on their use in the design, also can be considered line material.

Arrangement Recipe

Line Materials

Line materials are the first elements placed in the design. They help establish the height and width of the arrangement. If no line materials are used in the design, the other flowers are used in the same manner as the line materials.

Floral Arranging *Basics*

Knowing the basics of flower arranging makes it easier to create beautiful, well-designed arrangements. Carefully study all components, including the container, to make sure that elements complement each other.

Dominant Materials

Inserted after the line materials, these are usually form flowers like lilies or iris and mass (round) flowers like peonies. Be sure to insert the dominant items within the form established by the line materials.

Secondary Materials

Secondary materials usually consist of smaller mass flowers spaced evenly between the dominant materials in the design.

Filler Materials

Filler materials occupy open spaces around the other flowers in the composition; however, filler flowers are by no means mandatory in your design.

Accent Materials

Accent material is the one thing that stands out in the design. It could be simply the use of color or the focal point of the composition. When a statue or figurine, such as a bird, is added to a design, it automatically becomes the accent to the design.

Special Materials

Add items such as vine, grapes, and visible moss to create added texture and visual interest.

Note: *When working with only mass or form flowers, use the flowers as you would when working with line materials. Establish the top and outer boundaries. Place special importance on the visual balance of the design by spacing identically on all sides.*

145

Containers *and Forms*

With the wonderful choices of containers available, it may be challenging to determine the best one for your project. When you are looking for a container, be sure to consider the line, shape, and size of the arrangement. The container should complement the design, not detract from it. If you like the shape and size, but not the color, consider changing it with a distressed or painted finish. (See pages 210–223.)

Baskets – A
Baskets are available in a never-ending supply of shapes, sizes, and colors. From baskets made of natural materials to beautiful, elegant wire and brass creations, all are readily available at reasonable prices. Wire baskets allow you to insert floral materials into the container at a myriad of levels, creating endless design possibilities.

Bowls – B
Bowls are great containers to use for dried or silk arrangements. The dry foam is placed into the bowl and secured with a hot-glue gun or sticky tape. Bowls work best for placement on round tables or small coffee tables.

Foam Shapes – C
A wide variety of foam shapes is available for floral arranging. For swags, wreaths, topiaries, and other floral pieces, foam makes designing quick and easy. Simply use picks to attach moss, leaves, and flowers.

Glass and Ceramic Vases – D
Always popular and the most common containers for flower arrangements, these vases are available in every shape and color imaginable.

Grapevine Forms – E
This is one of the most popular forms used in floral arranging. Inexpensive and easy to work with, grapevines are readily available in a wide variety of sizes and shapes.

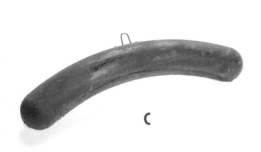

C

D

E

Metal Containers – F
Most metal containers are either brass, pewter, or a combination of inexpensive metals. Decorative containers of this type are often bright and shiny, with designs molded into the sides for added interest. Other metal containers are made very smooth and simple for more formal types of occasions.

Novelty Containers – G
Novelty containers are available in numerous shapes and sizes, and add interest and charm to floral arrangements. Most often made from plaster molds, they tend to be heavier than many containers; thus helping to prevent an arrangement from tipping over. Filling these types of containers with dry foam may require some ingenuity and careful thought if they are an odd shape, but the results are worth additional steps.

Terra-Cotta Pots – H
At one time, terra-cotta was only considered for live plants and mostly used out-of-doors. In recent years, terra-cotta pots have begun to show up in stores where they are purchased for both silk-flower and dried-flower arrangements. While terra-cotta looks great naturally, many people like to paint and embellish it with bold and bright designs.

Trays or Boxes – I
A tray or box is a great container when the height of the arrangement needs to be kept to a low profile.

Urns – J
Urns are perfect containers for giving height to an arrangement, or making an impressive statement regardless of where they are placed.

Wire Forms – K
In recent years, wire forms have gained in popularity and are used in the same ways as foam shapes. Rather than using picks, you wire the flowers and greenery to the forms.

Small painted pieces of chicken wire are available for purchase in floral departments. This wire can be cut and shaped to meet your particular designing needs.

I

J

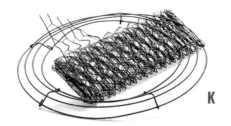

K

Bow-Making *Basics*

Knowing how to make beautiful bows is an important part of floral arranging and crafting. Bow making has become much easier with the wire edge that helps give body and shape to the ribbon. With a little patience and practice, you can learn to make perfect bows every time.

Perfect Bow

1. Loop a length of ribbon and hold the loop between your thumb and index finger, with the ribbon tail at the back several inches longer than the front tail.

With your opposite hand, pick up the long tail and wrap it around the loop to begin the knot (see Photo A).

2. Use the index finger of the same hand to push a loop through the knot (see Photo B) in front of the thumb holding the first loop.

3. Extending your thumbs through both of the loops, gently pull the back of the loops with your thumbs and index fingers to tighten the knot (see Photo C). Trim the ribbon ends.

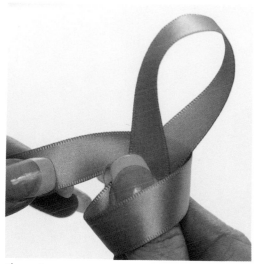

Photo A

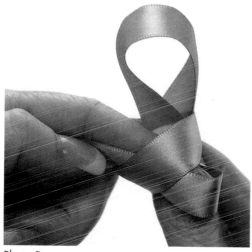

Photo B

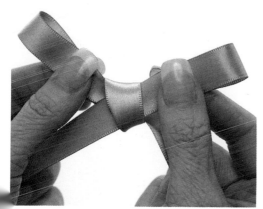

Photo C

Pleated Bow

Make this easy bow when you are working with ribbon that is difficult to knot.

1. Starting on the smallest top loop, fold the tail under so that it is a little more than half the length of the first loop (see Photo D).

2. Continue folding the ribbon back and forth, making each successive loop slightly larger. End the bow with the tail of the ribbon tucked under on the bottom side.

3. Place a staple in the center of the ribbon. Using a contrasting ribbon (see the photo *above*), wrap it around the center of the bow, and secure it with double-sided tape or a dab of hot glue.

Photo D

Creative Tip

If I'm having trouble deciding on the colors or flowers for a live or silk arrangement, I select a pretty ribbon, then match flowers to it.

– Accounts Payable Team Member, Hudson, Ohio

Floral – Bow-Making Basics

149 ❦

Photo A

Photo B

Basic Looped Bow

Determine the length of the ribbon you will need for your project. For a 6-loop bow, 1-inch wide plus tails (*above*), you will need approximately 1½ yards of ribbon. If you have chosen a two-sided ribbon, you will need to make a twist in the ribbon each time it passes between your thumb and index finger. This will keep the ribbon right-side-out.

1. Create a small loop between your thumb and index finger. This will become the center or "knot" of the bow (see Photo A).

2. Make the first loop of the bow, twist the ribbon and hold the twist between your fingers, make a loop on the other side,

twist the ribbon and hold the twist between your fingers (see Photo B). Continue twisting and making loops until there are three on each side, plus the center loop. The loops should be made smaller in the center, then each slightly larger than the previous one. An odd number of loops will make a better-looking bow.

3. Slip a piece of wire or chenille stem through the small loop or "knot" in the center of the bow and twist the wire to secure the bow (see Photo C). Fluff the bow and use the wire or chenille stem to secure the bow to your project.

Optional: Cover the chenille stem with a floral embellishment. (See the photo *above*.)

Photo C

Beyond the Bow

For an elegant ribbon-wrapped bouquet for a flower girl or bridesmaid, first secure the stems with wire to keep them in place. Trim the stems to the same length. Fold ½ inch of ribbon over the end of the stem, wrap the ribbon over the folded piece, and begin wrapping the ribbon at an angle up the stem. Keep the overlapped ribbon tight. At the top, cut and secure the end with a dab of hot glue. Add the Perfect Bow (see pages 148–149).

Elegant *Urns*

While we most often think of roses and urns for formal arrangements in traditional decorating schemes or for use on elegant occasions, often it is the combination of the flowers and the container that dictates the style. Fill an urn with daisies, and the same arrangement fits into a Country French or casual decor.

To create a painted finish on your urn, see Faux Finishes, beginning on page 210.

Traditional Urn

1. Fill an urn with dry foam. Cover the foam with Spanish moss and secure the moss with greening pins (see Tools & Materials, pages 139–142). Begin placing flowers in the urn by first positioning the line flowers (see Floral Arranging Basics, page 145) in a symmetrical design. Your line flowers, or first-inserted flowers, establish the basic shape of the arrangement (see Photo A). Be careful not to cut them all the same length. The height of the line flowers will determine the height of the finished arrangement.

Photo A

2. Add the dominant flowers (see Floral Arranging Basics, page 145) between and around the line flowers (see Photo B). Create the depth and shape of the arrangement by cutting the flower stems at different lengths as you design.

3. Cut pieces of greenery to fill in around the base of the urn. Allow longer pieces to "spill" over the edge of the container. It is very important to also place some greenery to the inside of the arrangement so it doesn't look hollow.

Continue filling out the design with smaller mass flowers, placing them deep inside the arrangement as well as around the outside. Finally, add the filler flowers (see page 145). Vary the height and length of the flowers to create visual interest.

Photo B

Basket *Arrangements*

Wire and woven baskets add an element of interest and texture to floral designs. Arrangements created in baskets made of natural woven materials such as reeds, vines, and bamboo tend to be more informal, while those made of gold, silver, or painted wire add elegance to formal flower displays. With wire, you can secure the foam in the bottom, then insert floral stems into the shape at any and all levels of the container.

Photo A

Photo B

Wire Basket

1. Fill a wire basket with dry foam. If the basket is round it may require two bricks of dry foam to fill it. Lay the dry foam side by side and set the bottom of the container on top of it. Gently press the bottom of the container into the dry foam until it makes a depression in the foam. With a serrated knife, cut around the shape and inset the foam into the container. Secure with sticky tape if necessary. Cover the dry foam with Spanish moss and secure with greening pins.
Note: *You may need to tuck extra Spanish moss into the sides of the basket to cover the dry foam.*

2. Establish the height and width of the arrangement by first inserting the line materials (see page 145). Begin by inserting pieces of greenery into the dry foam at opposite sides of the wire basket (see Photo A). Define the shape of the arrangement by gradually clipping shorter pieces of greenery to insert around the outside of the wire basket. Establish the maximum height of the arrangement by placing the "line" flower (burgundy larkspur) in the center of the design (see Photo B).

3. Add the dominant flowers down inside the basket. Remember to keep the arrangement light and airy by cutting the stems in a variety of lengths. Add secondary flowers to help further define the shape of the centerpiece, allowing them to spill over the edge of the basket. Tuck small filler flowers into the greenery (see Photo C).

4. Continue adding other colors of dominant and secondary flowers with different shapes and textures. Don't be afraid to let some of the flowers come through the sides of the basket, but allow the top edge of your basket to show.

5. When you are satisfied with the arrangement, add fruit and berries for additional interest. Allow the fruits to spill over the top and through the sides of the basket. If necessary, wire the fruits and berries to wooden wired picks.

Photo C

⊱Creative Tip

When using ribbon in a basket-container centerpiece, hold the ribbon in place on the handles or on any spot on the basket using "Cling," a green floral tacky putty.

– Accounts Payable Team Member, Hudson, Ohio

Creative *Container*

Add extra color and interest to a floral arrangement by embellishing the container. This plain and simple vase takes on a whole different look when striped ribbons are artfully woven up the sides, creating a light and airy feeling that becomes an active part of the arrangement.

Woven-Ribbon Vase

1. Measure your container and add 1½ inches to the measurement. Cut 12 lengths of ⅝-inch-wide ribbon. Using a hot-glue gun, attach three vertical ribbons to one side of the bottom and top of the container (see Photo A). Continue on the remaining three sides. Allow the glue to cool. Weave coordinating ribbon horizontally through and around the container. Cut and glue the woven ribbon, overlapping the ends to secure.
Note: *Do not pre-cut the horizontal ribbons. The lengths will vary.*

2. Make a 6-loop bow from a coordinating 1½-inch-wide ribbon, referring to Bow-Making Basics on pages 148–151. Leave ample length for the tails. Hot glue the bow to one corner of the container and wrap the tails loosely to the opposite bottom corner of the container (see Photo B). Make a smaller 3-loop bow and glue it to the container.

3. Fill the container with dry foam. Cover the dry foam with Spanish moss and secure with greening pins. Cut the stems of three dominant flowers to 4 inches and push them into the dry foam to establish the shape of the arrangement.

4. Cut the stems of the secondary flowers. Insert the smaller flowers, allowing them to fall over the edge of the container in free form. Continue to place the secondary flowers between the dominant flowers.

5. Add small 3-inch pieces of greenery to the top of the arrangement. Cut filler flowers, attach them to 3-inch wooden wired picks, and insert into the arrangement, letting them remain longer to create a loose, airy feeling.

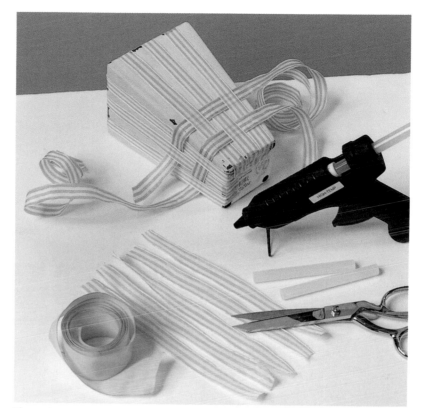

Photo A

Photo B

Unusual *Shapes*

Uniquely shaped containers add interest and drama to the most simple arrangement. Containers with uncommon shapes may also present design challenges. Choose flowers that do not overpower the container in either color or size; test the flowers in the arrangement before securing them into the foam.

To add a distressed or faux-painted finish to a container, see pages 210–223.

Note: *Containers shown are examples only, and not available in all stores.*

Creative Containers

1. Fill the container opening with dry foam. Cover the foam with Spanish moss and secure with greening pins. Allow some of the Spanish moss to spill over the side of the opening (see Photo A). Clip the stems of the dominant flowers to the desired length and insert in the dry foam. The length of the stems should be in proportion to the size of your container.

2. Cut the stems of the secondary flowers, and tuck in between the dominant flowers. Let some flowers spill over the sides (see Photo B).

3. Cluster and wire green leaves, referring to the Elegant Centerpieces Rose Topiary directions on pages 174–175. Add them to the arrangement (see the photo of the finished arrangement, *opposite*). Clip grape clusters from a stem of grapes, and using a 3-inch wooden wired pick, add them to the container, allowing the grapes to spill over the side (see the photo, *opposite*). Fill in with green leaves as desired.

4. Make a loop bow with two different colors of ¼-inch velvet ribbon. Secure with 22-gauge wire and push it into the arrangement where desired (see the photo, *opposite*).

Photo A

Photo B

Topiary *Shape*

The topiary is a tree or shrub that is clipped or trimmed into ornamental shapes. Often displayed in pairs, topiary trees can be made on a small scale for a buffet or side table as well as on a large scale for the patio or front porch.

Cascading Topiary

It is very important that the topiary base be firmly secured to the container to prevent it from tipping over. If the container is heavy, floral foam and tape should be adequate. For a lightweight container, secure the foam with plaster of Paris.

If you are using dry foam, be sure it fills the entire cavity of the urn. Pieces of the dry foam can be placed in the bottom of the urn and a larger block placed at the top.

1. To make a topiary tree, use a precast foam topiary form and secure it in the container with tape. Cover the base, trunk, and ball with Spanish moss using greening pins (see Photo A). To cover the wooden stake, snip a long piece of greenery and attach a pick to both ends. Pick one end of the greenery into the base, wrap the greenery around the trunk, and finish by picking the other end into the underside of the ball (see Photo B).

2. Cut the greenery apart and, using picks, cover the ball with single leaves of different sizes. Continue picking the greenery into the ball until you are pleased with the look. Pick long and short trailing pieces into the base. Bend the longer pieces down to spill over the sides of the container. Remember: Greenery doesn't grow in perfect symmetry.

3. Add artificial fruit to the base. Finish the topiary tree with a bird's nest and bird. Pick a nest into the ball with a wired wood pick. Hot glue will work as well.

Photo A

Photo B

Optional: If you want to use ribbons, place a bow (see Bow-Making Basics on pages 148–151) on the underside of the ball and allow the tails to trail down through the greenery.

Easy *Wreaths*

Using a foam base,
create a wreath to
complement your front
door or interior decor.
With a variety of
materials such as moss,
ribbon, or dried leaves,
cover the base, add
embellishments, and it's
ready to hang.

Moss-Covered Wreath

1. For a hanger, cut a length of heavy floral wire 6 inches long, make a "U" shape, then bend the wire prongs at a 90 degree angle (see Photo A). Push the hanger into the foam ½ inch from the edge of the wreath and secure with hotmelt adhesive. Glue green reindeer moss onto the wreath using a glue gun and hotmelt adhesive (see Photo B).

2. Cut the stems of several berry sprays various lengths, and attach them into the foam base using greening pins.
Note: *Save some berry sprays for later use. Be sure to bend each spray so that it follows the curve of the wreath (see Photo B). All floral elements should radiate out from the point where the bow attaches, with the larger flowers near the bow. (See Creative Tip below right.)*

Trim the stems of three dominant blooms to measure 3 inches. Insert the stems directly into the foam at the top of the wreath, covering the ends of the berry sprays (see Photo B). Make a 7-loop satin bow, referring to Bow-Making Basics on pages 148–151. Secure the bow with 22-gauge wire, and insert the bow into the top of the wreath between two of the dominant blooms. Leave the tails of the bow long, and cut them off once you've completed the wreath.

3. Clip large color-coordinated leaves from a silk greenery bush. Wrap the leaves around a single bloom filler flower and hold together with hot glue (see Photo C). Wrap the stem with floral tape and cut the stem to the desired length. Using a hand-held pick tool, attach a steel pick to the stem and insert it into the wreath as desired.
Note: *If you do not have a hand-held pick tool, use wooden wired picks.*

4. Add small amounts of the remaining berry spray by clipping the berries and attaching steel picks (see Photo D). Fill in all spaces with berries. Cut the ribbon to the desired length,

Photo A

Photo C

Photo B

and attach the tails of the bow to the bottom of the wreath with small dabs of hot glue. **Note:** *Use minimal amounts of hot glue, as it will cause spots on the ribbon.*

Photo D

Floral – Easy Wreaths

Creative Tip

One of the main differences between European Design and American Geometric Design is that, in European Design, more than one axis or growth point is evident. In American Geometric form, only one axis is used. In one axis, radiation is the term for movement of all materials in and out of the axis or growth point. Think of a bulb that is planted in the soil, watered, and given sunshine. When the bulb blossoms, the part that comes up out of the ground is the axis or growth point. Everything that follows from the bulb, from the flower to the foliage and stem, radiates or grows from that point.

– National Floral Design Manager, Corporate Office, Hudson, Ohio

Simple *Swags*

A swag can be just the accent your room needs to fill an empty space or add some color. Hang a swag above a doorway, window, or picture to soften the room's decor, or use one as wall decor in place of a picture or mirror. Beautify your front door with a burst of color and change your swags with the passing seasons.

Grapevine Swag

Arches and swags are created on a variety of bases that include foam, straw, wire, and grapevine. Choose the swag form based on the type of materials you are using. For example, it is easy to push stems of silk flowers or clusters of silk or dried florals wired to floral picks into foam. But pushing stems of dried florals into foam most likely will break the stems.

A new and slightly different way to create arches or swags is to cut a vine wreath in half. Each half becomes a separate form to make different designs. The delicate flower stems are worked into the weave of the vine and are held in place with hotmelt adhesive. This makes a lighter, more airy finished design and provides a good base for delicate stems.

1. Using wire cutters or pruning shears, cut the grapevine wreath in half. To help hold the wreath branches together, wrap floral wire around the swag toward each end and in the middle of the arch (see Photo A).

2. Apply hotmelt adhesive to the ends of the dried eucalyptus and other longer dried stems. Insert the stems beginning at the left side of the arch and working out toward the ends of the swag.

3. When the longer stems are in place, begin adding dried flowers until you are pleased with the arrangement. Start with form flowers; add finishing touches with filler flowers (see page 145).

A

Floral – Simple Swags

WEDDING

Personalize your wedding
by designing your own

floral arrangements, corsages, and headpiece
to express your personal style and taste.
Combine unique embellishments and family heirlooms
to make these pieces
better than anything you can purchase.

Basic *Head Pieces*

Whether you prefer a simple floral spray or an elaborate crown of jewels, head pieces are easy to assemble.

Follow these simple instructions, and include embellishments such as pearls, crystals, beads, silk ribbons, and

flowers. Once you have completed the band, add a handmade or purchased veil to complete the process.

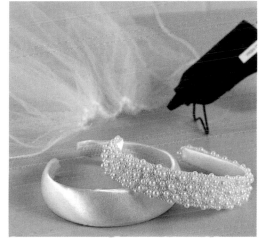

Photo A

Floral Headband

Begin with a pearl headband as seen in Photo A. Make a Perfect Bow (see Bow-Making Basics on pages 148–151), and glue the bow to the top of the headband. Let the glue cool. Apply purchased clay flowers, clusters of small silk flowers, and embellishments of your choice to the band. Fill in all spaces across the headband using additional silk flowers and leaves as desired. (See the finished band, *above left*.)

Rhinestone Headband

Begin with a plain satin headband as seen in Photo A. Purchase rhinestones, pearls, and fancy buttons to create a "tiara" type headband. Place all the buttons in a bowl and mix them up. Pull buttons or pearls from the bowl at random, and glue them to the headband. Finish the "tiara" by clustering a stack of jeweled buttons in the center of the headband (see the finished band, *above right*).

Tulle Veil

You can either purchase or make a veil to add to the headband. To make a veil, position the band on the bride's head and measure from the band down to where the veil will end. Determine the number of layers the bride wants for her veil and cut accordingly. (Example: If the bride wants a 2-layer, 42-inch veil, cut an 84-inch long piece of tulle.) Round off all corners.

Run a gathering stitch across the width at the center point (most tulle is 45 inches wide), then flip the tulle on one side of the stitching over and pull the gathering stitch to gather the doubled layers. For a layered veil of different layer lengths, simply gather closer to one side instead of the middle. Attach the veil to the headband with clear sewing thread.

Note: *To hem the edges, make a rolled hem with a serger.*

✑ Creative Tip

For my daughter's veil, I stitched a narrow ribbon along the edges of the veil. It gave it a lot of body that my daughter just loved. Because tulle is so inexpensive, I recommend getting a yard extra and playing with it to see what look the bride prefers.

– Apparel Fabric Specialist, Independence, Missouri

167 ✑

Corsages *and Boutonnieres*

Worn by members of the wedding party, these small, but very important floral nosegays have become an integral part of the wedding attire. They identify honored members of the party. Each one should be as special as the person who wears it. Follow the basic instructions for the corsages and boutonnieres to make your own versions.

Corsage

When assembling a corsage, keep in mind that there is a top, middle, and bottom portion.

1. Cut the stems for the top portion down to 1 inch and attach 22-gauge wire to each flower stem. Wrap what will be the top flower in your design with floral tape, beginning at the blossom base. Continue wrapping down the stem, adding and wrapping in the blossoms, filler flowers, and any special elements you would like to include. When you complete the top portion, all floral elements will have been wired into one stem (see Photo A).

2. Create a bow from ½-inch ribbon (see Bow-Making Basics, pages 148–151), and secure the center of the bow with 22-gauge wire. Add the bow to the middle portion of the wrapped bundle directly under the flowers (see Photo B). Set it aside.

3. The bottom portion of the corsage contains the larger dominant flowers. Cut the stems of these flowers down to 2- to 3-inch lengths, and wire each element. Add and tape the filler flowers and special elements to the bottom portion as you did for the corsage top.

4. Combine the top and bottom elements as follows. Hold the top section in your hand and bend the elements so that the holes and spaces are filled between the flowers and the bow. Add the bottom portion below the bow, stems running in the same direction, and position the flowers by bending the wires until you are pleased with the design. When you are satisfied with the placement of the flowers and

Photo A

Photo B

special elements, wrap sections together with floral tape to create one unit.

5. Give the corsage a decorative touch by coiling the stem around a pencil or small dowel to create a spiral effect (see Photo C). Add two pearl-headed corsage pins for attaching the corsage to the garment.

Boutonniere

While boutonniere is French for "single flower," many floral and wedding designers today are using up to three blossoms. For this look, use flowers that grow in your garden rather than more formal blossoms.

1. Cut the stem on the dominant flower to measure about 4 inches. Begin wrapping the stem with floral tape. Remove extra branches and leaves from any other flowers or leaves you plan to use. Trim the stems to 3 inches.

2. Assemble the boutonniere in your hand. When you are satisfied with the placement of the flowers, trim the stems with wire cutters to graduated lengths, and wrap with floral tape to create one bundle.

3. Give the boutonniere a decorative touch by coiling the stem around a pencil or small dowel to create a spiral effect (see Photo C). Add a black-headed boutonniere pin for attaching it to a garment.

Photo C

Bridal *Bouquet*

During medieval times, bridal bouquets were created from herbs and garlic that were thought to ward off evil spirits. Although the floral choices have changed with the fashions of the times, the bouquet remains one of the most important bridal accessories. With the array of luscious ribbons and lifelike silk flowers available, the design possibilities are limitless. Complete collections of classic bridal flowers are available, or you can choose non-traditional blossoms for one-of-a-kind bouquets like the one shown, *opposite*.

ᴓ Creative Tip

Make a bridal bouquet more personal by including items the bride holds dear. Incorporate things like a mother's handkerchief or a grandmother's pearls for a special touch. The item might also count for the "something old" for good luck!

– Floral Designer, Knoxville, Tennessee

Hand-tied Bouquet

1. Select a collection of flowers and berries in different sizes, textures, color shades, and shapes. Remove all of the foliage from the stems, and wrap each stem with floral tape. Begin arranging the flowers and berry stems in your hand to create a tight, compact ball of flowers (see Photo A). Wrap the stems together with floral tape just below the flower blossoms.

Cut the stems from seven large grape leaves, and make stems using 22-gauge wire (refer to the the Rose Topiary instructions on page 174). Arrange the leaves around the flowers to form a collar, and join all stems into one main stem cluster with floral tape (see Photo B).

2. Using 2½-inch coordinating ribbon, begin wrapping the handle at the top of the stem cluster by holding the bouquet in your hand so that the flowers are facing away from you (see Photo B). Leave a tail of ribbon about 2 feet long on the left side. With one hand, pinch and hold the ribbon together at the stem top. With your other hand, tightly wrap the ribbon down the stem, covering the pinch with the first wrap. As you wrap, make sure that the ribbon remains flat.

3. When you have reached the bottom of the stem handle, fold the ribbon over the bottom end of the handle so that the back of the ribbon is facing up (see Photo C), and begin wrapping back up the handle. When you are finished there will be ribbon tails on both sides of the bouquet. Tie a large, full bow at this point.

Secure the ribbon in place with 2-inch pearl-headed corsage pins. Trim the tails of the ribbon to the length desired.

Photo A

Photo B

Photo C

Pew Decorations

Depending on the style of your wedding, pew bows can be made with minimal ribbon and flowers or created with elaborate additions of pearlized fruit, decorative cording, strings of pearls, and softly draped swags of tulle flowing from one pew to the next.

Small Pew Bow

1. Select a flower with a large bloom such as a hydrangea. Add three stems of small secondary flowers (see Photo A). Secure the stems of the small flowers to the stem of the larger flower with floral tape. Attach the bouquet of flowers to a plastic pew clip with a dry foam pew clip, floral tape, or sticky clay.

2. Clip the leaves off of a grape cluster and attach them to the back of the flower bouquet using a hot-glue gun (see Photo B). The leaves should form a "collar" around the back of the flowers.

Make a 3-loop bow, referring to Bow-Making Basics on pages 148–151. Attach the bow to the main stem of the arrangement. Wire and tape two small grape clusters together, insert the wire between the loops of the bow, and secure it to the flower stems with floral tape.

3. Add any additional embellishments and secure with floral tape.

Photo A

Photo B

Photo C

Photo D

Large Pew Bow

1. Cut the stems on two large dominant flowers to the desired length. Make a 9-loop bow referring to Bow-Making Basics on pages 148-151. Insert the bow into the middle of a dry foam pew clip (see Photos C and D). Place the two large dominant flowers into the top of the dry foam above the bow.

2. Wire large and small leaves referring to the Rose Topiary directions on page 174.

Place the leaves around the large flowers using the leaves as a "collar." Place the smaller leaves into the center of the arrangement just above the bow. (See the photo, *above.*)

3. Cut pearl berry clusters into several small pieces. Attach them to 3-inch wooden wired picks, and secure with floral tape. Place picks in the pew arrangement. Leave a few berries to attach to the ends of the decorative cording. (See the photo, *above.*) Make a simple bow with decorative cording.

Secure with 22-gauge wire and insert it into the dry foam through the center of the satin bow. Hot glue the individual berries into a cluster at the bottom of the decorative cording. Make additional single loops from the decorative cording as desired and secure with 22-gauge wire and floral tape. Pick into the loops of the satin bow.

Elegant *Centerpieces*

Create elegant topiary decorations for your wedding or reception using your favorite silk flowers and spectacular ribbons. For formal celebrations, add embellishments of sheer tulle, pearl sprays, and hanging crystals. By making your own wedding florals, you can add a bit of your own personality to each and every piece.

Rose Topiary

1. Cut all of the leaves and branches from the stems of seven roses. Wrap each of the bare stems with floral tape. Cut large leaves off a greenery bush, and using 22-gauge wire, bend the wires in half, and poke both ends of wire through the bottom of the leaf just above the stem. Secure the leaf to the stem with floral tape (see Photo A). Continue to tape and wire five additional large leaves. Set aside.

Arrange the roses in your hand.
Note: *Using seven roses, it is easy to place one rose in the center, and surround the center rose with the other six.*

When the arrangement of roses pleases you, secure the grouping by wrapping the bunch of stems with floral tape at the top and bottom. Arrange the large leaves just under the roses in your hand, and secure the stems in place with floral tape (see Photo A). When you are satisfied with the arrangement, wrap the entire stem cluster with floral tape.

2. Beginning directly under the leaves, wrap 2-inch-wide satin ribbon in the same direction of the floral tape. Secure the top and bottom with a dot of hot glue. In the opposite direction and overlapping the first ribbon, wrap a second ribbon around the stem. For a decorative touch, and to hold your work in place, insert 2-inch pearl-headed corsage pins up the stem at 1½-inch intervals (see Photo B).

Photo A

Photo B

3. Fill an urn with dry foam. Cover the foam with Spanish moss and secure with greening pins.

4. Insert the rose stems into the center of the dry foam and secure with hot glue. Make a large 3-loop bow (referring to Bow-Making Basics on pages 148–151), using the same ribbons that you used on the stem, and place it in the front of the urn. Leave the tails of the bow long and cut them later as desired.

Add flowers, berry clusters, and greenery to finish, allowing the foliage to trail out over the container edge. (See the finished design at *left*).

At the top of the topiary, make 2- and 3-loop bows out of the ribbon, and attach them under the roses and leaves. Allow the ribbon tails to softly wrap around the topiary stem cluster.

Note: *For an inexpensive but pretty container, paint a clay pot and clay saucer. On the pot shown, a light green base coat was applied. Once dry, the pot was dry-brushed with gold paste finish (see pages 41–42 for gilding instructions).*

Creative Tip

Make your own birds' nests in any size to add to florals. In a bowl, mix Spanish moss (cut into small bits) with a tacky glue. Use enough glue to hold the mixture together without over-saturating it. Cover an inverted bowl with plastic wrap. Mold the mixture over the bottom of the bowl. Let it dry, and remove.

– Certified Framing Specialist, Temecula, California

Altar or Table *Centerpieces*

Taking front stage with the bride and groom on their special day will be the altar and table arrangements. The floral design may incorporate a unity candle and can be very simple, or as elaborate as you like.

Low Formal Arrangement

This arrangement has the flexibility to fit any size table or altar by varying the lengths of flowers used. Leave the taper candles out of the design or use it on a reception buffet or dining table.

1. Cut a piece of dry foam to fit into a flat, round utility container. Secure the foam to the container using hot glue. Insert a 3-inch candleholder into the top of the dry foam toward the back. Secure the candleholder with ¼-inch waterproof tape (see Photo A). Cover the dry foam with Spanish moss and secure with greening pins (see Photo B).

2. Place a 3×9-inch pillar candle in the candle cup.
Note: Remember to keep all floral materials a safe distance from any candles.

Cut the line flowers to the desired length, and insert them into the dry foam on both sides of the arrangement. You will begin by first outlining the arrangement with the longest line flowers. Establish the overall height of the arrangement by cutting one line flower stem to the desired height. Insert it into the foam on one side of the arrangement, behind the pillar candle (see Photo B). Cut two more stems and insert them in front of the candle so that they will come forward over the edge of the altar. Cut additional stems of line flowers into shorter lengths, and attach 3-inch wood picks. Wrap the picks with floral tape. Place these flowers in the arrangement between the longer line flowers.

3. Cut the stems to the desired length on two stems of dominant flowers (see the off-white flower Photo C). Place the two dominant flowers into the front of the

Photo A

Photo B

arrangement on either side of the pillar candle. Cut large leaves from a greenery bush; tape and wire the stems. (Refer to the Rose Topiary instructions on page 174 for wiring and taping large leaves). Fill in the altar arrangement with small pieces of greenery and large wired leaves.

4. Cut coordinating secondary and filler flowers. Wire the stems using 3-inch wood picks. Wrap the picks with floral tape, and place in the front and in back of one side behind the candle (for correct placement see photo of completed arrangement on page 176). Cut small grape clusters off the main stem of grapes and attach to a wood pick. Finish the arrangement by placing the grape clusters throughout.

Photo C

Wedding — Altar or Table Centerpieces

Small Formal Arrangement

1. Follow the directions for the low formal arrangement on page 177, except that the flowers are cut smaller and the stems are shorter in this version.

2. Insert the line flowers first to establish the height and width of the arrangement (see Photo B, page 177). By beginning with the line flowers, you will be able to establish the shape of the arrangement.

3. Fill in around the line flowers with dominant flowers (see Photo C, page 177). Use individual blooms from a stem of flowers. Wire new "stems" to these blooms. Wrap the new stems with stem tape. Insert flowers at different lengths to achieve depth. Continue working with the shape of the arrangement.

4. Add the greenery and filler flowers.

5. Cut five ribbons to different lengths. Fold lengths in half and secure to a wood pick. Cut the ends of the ribbons on angles for a pleasing look, and pick them into the arrangement.

✤Creative Tip

For a bridal pen to use with your guest book, place a floral

stem or a group of stems toward the top of the pen, and wrap

green floral tape around the pen to the tip.

– Hardlines Supervisor, Visalia, California

FRAME
Gallery

Frames and mats
are more than just utilitarian methods

of displaying your artwork and photos—
they are integral to the finished beauty of the piece.
Learn how to arrange and hang your own home gallery
with tips from the professionals.

Frame *Gallery*

Many things are combined to complete the decor of a room, but interior designers will tell you that the accessories in a room make a big impact. After you've painted the walls and set the furniture in place, it is the arrangement and placement of the wall decor that makes the difference.

Arranging Your Picture Gallery

Whether you are looking for a way to exhibit photo memories or add a finishing touch to your home decor with a focal impact, knowing where to start can be the most intimidating part. It is a simple process to arrange your framed keepsakes if you use the following steps.

Tools and Materials

Antiquing Gel
Use antiquing gel to turn new frames into antique-looking ones in a matter of minutes. The degree of antiquing is controlled by brushing the gel on and wiping it off until it is the desired color. Refer to Antiquing and Distressing on page 214.

Frames
Use a wide variety of shapes and sizes to create a visually interesting wall gallery. Depending on your own taste, keep the frames similar in style or use a variety of shapes, styles, and colors. Ready-made frames are more popular than ever; look for them in the frame department of your Jo-Ann Store, or have custom frames and mats made for your prints and photos.

Mats: Precut and Custom Cut
Bevel cut mats used with prints and photos can make a major difference in the overall appearance of framed pieces. Some framing departments carry a limited selection of sizes and colors of mats, but for an outstanding wall presentation, consider having your artwork framed with custom cut mats.

Frame Gallery Basics
To create a formal effect, center a framed grouping over a piece of furniture such as a sofa or table. For an informal look, consider arranging the frames off center, perhaps next to a wall shelf or other dimensional object.

Large framed photos or prints should be centered in an arrangement, with smaller equal-size prints on either side to create a visual balance. Other possible groupings to consider are "T" shape, triangle shape, "L" shape, or a "cross" arrangement.

Large pieces of framed art look great over a sofa or displayed in multiples on a large wall. They should be approximately eye-level, or five feet from the floor. For optimal visual effect, leave about 12 inches of space from the bottom of a framed piece to the tabletop or sofa. Be sure to hang frames so a seated person will not bump them.

Mirrors can make a visual impact in a room and can be considered works of art. Use them to enlarge a room, reflect light, and repeat interesting features of a room.

Hardware

A variety of hardware items is needed to hang your frame gallery. If you are hanging lightweight pictures, drive a nail in the wall at an angle, or use a small screw or a steel picture hanger. Steel hangers do have weight limitations; read the instructions on the package. For medium to heavyweight pictures and mirrors, drive a strong nail into wall stud. Toggle, molly or hollow wall anchors may be necessary if a wall stud isn't available.

To install a toggle or molly (see Diagram A, page 182), drill a hole large enough to push the shank through the hole. When the shank is pushed through the hole, it will expand and prevent the shank from coming back out of the hole (see Diagram B).

Plastic anchors are installed by first drilling a hole in the wall large enough to accommodate the anchor. Tap the anchor into the hole with a hammer (see Diagram C). When you drive a screw into the anchor, it will expand for a snug fit (see Diagram D).

Use two nails, bolts, or screws in the wall 2 to 3 inches apart if you are hanging a

181 ❧

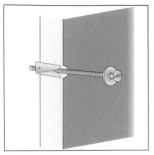

Diagram A

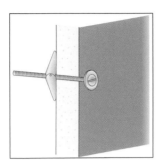

Diagram B

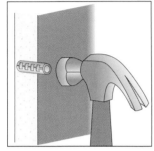

Diagram C

Diagram D

long, thin frame. This will prevent the frame from shifting off level. Be sure to have the proper hardware on your picture frames. Use sawtooth hangers, or attach picture wire to the back of the frame with screw eyes. Read the wire package for weight limitations, especially when hanging mirrors, which tend to be extra heavy.
Note: *To fill nail holes, use spackle or a product designed for that purpose.*

To cut the wire to the proper length, measure across the top of the frame from corner to corner and add an additional four inches to the wire. If the frame is 16×20 inches or larger, add six inches to the wire measurement. The additional lengths will be used to secure the wire by twisting it back around itself after it is threaded through the screw eye. Measure one-third of the distance from the top of the frame for proper placement of the screw eyes.

Getting Started

Note: *For a monochromatic frame decor, spray-paint the frames all one color. Spray painting can also cover damaged areas, making old frames reusable.*

1. Spray-paint the frames with the color of your choice.

2. Using plain newsprint paper from a crafts store, place the frames on the paper, draw an outline of each frame, and cut out the frame shapes. Mark each piece of paper with the frame size. Use painter's tape to hang the paper outlines on your wall, moving them around until you are pleased with the overall arrangement (see photograph *above*). Step away from the wall to view the paper shapes, making sure that the placement, spacing between frames, and distance from the floor (sofa or table) are balanced and in the correct proportion to the wall and room decor.

3. Mark a faint pencil or chalk line along the top center edge of the newsprint paper to indicate placement on the wall, and remove the paper. Measure the distance between the edge of the frame and the hanger. Using that measurement, determine how far below the edge of the paper mark you will need to place the nail or screw, and mark that spot. (For example, if the hanger is ½ inch below the top edge of the frame, you will need to make the hole ½ inch below the mark on the wall.) Insert wall hardware in the appropriate marked locations, and attach wire or sawtooth hangers to the frames using small nails to prevent splitting or cracking the frame. Hang your picture gallery.

FINE ART and
Decorative PAINTING

Learn to see the world
as an artist sees it

and express your creativity through color and design.
Whether you're painting on canvas,
faux finishing a wall, or pulling brushstrokes
on a piece of furniture, the satisfaction
you feel will be your greatest reward.

Fine Art *and* Decorative Painting *Tools*

Knowing and understanding the wide array of painting products is overwhelming for the beginner. Determining your painting needs will help you make the best buying decisions.

Tools and Materials

Brushes

Angular Shader – A
An angular shader is a flat brush with short bristles on one side that gradually lengthen to longer bristles on the other side.

Chisel Blender – B
A chisel blender is similar to a flat brush, but it has shorter bristles that come to a fine chisel edge.

Dagger Striper – C
A dagger striper has long, full bristles cut in a quarter oval (dagger) shape. It is used to make long, sweeping strokes without reloading. Thick to thin strokes are created by the amount of pressure applied to the downward stroke. This makes it excellent for painting ribbons, borders, and similar designs.

Deerfoot Stippler – D
A deerfoot stippler is a short, full-bristled, round brush similar to a stencil brush, except the bristles are cut at an angle. It is used to stipple the textured strokes for shrubbery, fur, etc.

Detailer – E
A detailer is a thin, short-bristled brush that forms a fine point.

Round – F
A round brush has full bristles that come to a fine point. It is used to create a stroke from thick to very thin.

Flat – G
A flat brush has squared-off bristles that form a fine chisel edge.

Fan – H
A fan brush has bristles shaped like a fan. It is often used for special effects, such as flecking or dry-brushing.

Filbert – I
A filbert brush is a flat brush with bristles cut in an oval (fingernail shape).

Liner – J
Liner brushes contain a few long bristles that form a fine point for doing work such as hair, grass, liner work, scrolling, and other fine details.

Mop Brush – K
A mop brush has soft, full bristles usually made of camel hair. Available in several sizes, it is used to soften and blend all types of media.

Rake – L
A rake brush has bristles that are thinned and uneven at the edge. Its "rake-like" shape, when wet, is ideal for creating

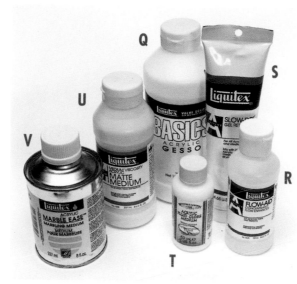

Mediums and Additives for Acrylics

Paint additives are mixed with acrylic paints to change the characteristics of the paints, making them thicker, transparent, or shiny. They also slow down or speed up the drying time, and they create better absorption.

Mediums are the binder (glue) of acrylic paint. They have great flexibility and are chemical, water, and ultraviolet resistant. They are added to acrylic paints to alter paint handling characteristics, appearance, or volume.

interesting line work. It is excellent for dry-brushing grass, fur, and hair, as well as wood graining. Flat and filbert types are available.

Wash/Glaze – M

A wash/glaze brush is a flat brush used to base-coat, varnish, or apply washes.

Brush Basin – N

Available in different sizes and used for cleaning brushes with water, the brush basin has compartments for cleaning and rinsing. One side has special cradles in the bottom, preventing the brushes from laying on the bottom and being damaged, and the other side has ribs for cleaning and removing paint.

Canvas, Stretched – O

Stretched canvas is available in standard
sizes such as 8×10 inches, 9×12 inches, and
rger. Ready-primed and stretched canvas is
ideal surface for oils and acrylics.

Decorating Paste – not shown

Achieve a variety of accents and textures on many surfaces using three-dimensional decorating paste. Create delicate roses, similar to those on decorated cakes, and other bold dimensional designs.

Erasers – P

Use erasers specifically designed for removing pencil marks from drawing surfaces. Kneaded erasers are good for removing and highlighting pastels, pencil, and charcoal sketches.

Gesso – Q

Gesso is used to prepare painting surfaces for acrylic and oil painting. It is non-yellowing, flexible, and non-cracking, and it provides the perfect "tooth" and adhesion to a wide variety of surfaces such as canvas, paper, and wood. Mix with the paint and apply, or use alone.

Flow and Absorption Medium – R

This medium improves the flow, absorption, and blending of any water-soluble paints such as acrylics, inks, or dyes. It minimizes brush marks by reducing the friction of paint application.

Gel Retarder – S

Gel retarder increases the "open" time of acrylic paint, giving the artist up to 50 percent longer working time.

Gel Mediums – T

Available in gloss and matte finishes, gel medium is an ideal extender. It increases the transparency of the color without changing the thickness of the paint, eases the flow, and increases the flexibility. To obtain paint similar in color depth to oil paint, mix with gloss medium. Use the matte when a dull, non-reflecting finish is desired.

Matte Opaque Extender Gel Medium – U

This translucent, white gel has a high density and a high solids content. When mixed with paint, the opaque extender medium provides high opacity relative to other mediums.

Marbling Fluid – V

Mix this fluid into acrylic paint to produce the proper spread and control of colors when creating a marbling technique.

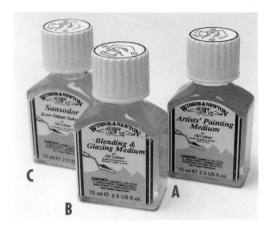

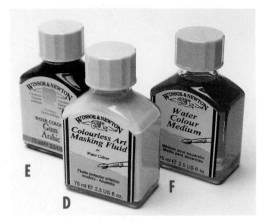

Texture Paste, Extra Thick – not shown
  Use texture paste to build heavy textures on rigid supports, and to create three-dimensional forms. It dries to the hardness of stone and can be sanded or carved when thoroughly dry.

Mediums for Oils

Artists' Painting Medium – A
  This linseed oil/petroleum distillate is used to thin the consistency of oils. It dries to a flexible film with a minimal tendency to yellow, wrinkle, or crack.
Blending & Glazing Medium – B
  This all-in-one blending and glazing medium is used to blend oil colors without making them too transparent or too fluid to cover well. It allows time to slowly build up glazes of highlights and shadows before becoming tacky.
Thinning and Quick-Dry Medium – C
  This durable, non-yellowing medium is for thinning oil and alkyd colors and speeding drying time. This medium is excellent for glazing and producing fine detail.
Refined Linseed Oil – not shown
  This is the traditional (and most popular) medium for oils, since it is the binder used in most oil colors. Linseed oil generally maintains the drying time of the colors.

Mediums for Watercolors

Art Masking Fluid – D
  Use this colorless fluid to protect or mask off a particular area of a painting to make certain areas resistant to watercolor. When the masking fluid is dry, colors cannot penetrate the paper.
Gum Arabic (acacia gum) – E
  Gum arabic increases watercolor brilliancy, gloss, and transparency, and it gives greater depth to each color. It slows down the drying time of the paint and helps to control the spread of wet-on-wet painting.
Watercolor Medium – F
  Similar to gum arabic, watercolor medium also increases the wetting of the paper. Watercolor medium helps to improve the flow of washes across the surface of the paper.

Paints

Acrylics
Tube Acrylics – G through K
  A wide variety of acrylic paints are available for the artist, from basic student grades to professional quality. These thick opaque paints allow for oil-like painting; they retain peaks and brush marks. They can also be thinned with water and used on paper like watercolor paints. Because of their versatility, acrylics can be used for almost any painting technique you desire.

Tube acrylics have a somewhat limited color range; mix paint colors to create a broader color palette.
Liquid Acrylics – L and M
  Usually found in the crafts section of your store, these permanent pigment paints are water soluble when wet, and dry quickly to a water-resistant surface. Available in a wide range of colors (some brands have more than one hundred colors), they are ready to use without mixing or thinning. Liquid acrylics have the consistency of cream, and they dry to a smooth, even surface that shows few brush marks. These paints are ideal for covering a wide variety of porous surfaces, fine line detail, glazing, underpainting, and fabric painting (when used with textile medium).

Oil Paints – N
Oil paints are considered to be opaque and have a thick creamy consistency which requires thinning prior to painting. They are primarily painted on stretched canvas but work well on a variety of surfaces. Oils are slow to dry, giving the artist plenty of time to work. Depending on your artistic preferences, oils can be used to paint anything from realism to abstracts. Oils have a somewhat limited color range, making it necessary to mix oil paint colors to create a broader color palette.

Watercolor Paints – O
There are two types of watercolor paints: translucent (the most common) and gouache (pronounced gwäsh), which is opaque. One of the charms of watercolors is they are unpredictable, so you can never be completely sure of the final results. For this reason, they can be intimidating for beginners; however, for those who persevere, the rewards can be exciting. Although watercolors are most often used in a loose style, they can be controlled for very realistic results.

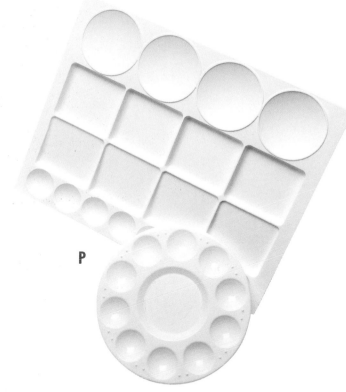

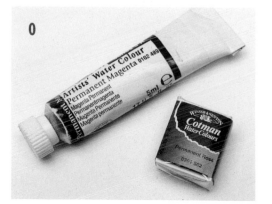

Palette Tools

Plastic Palettes – P
Water and acrylic palettes are usually made of plastic. The palettes are designed with "wells," circular indentations or squares with borders that prevent colors from mixing together. The paint is squeezed into larger areas for mixing colors or mediums.

Palette Cups – Q
Available in different sizes, palette cups attach to palettes and are used to hold a variety of mediums used for mixing with oils and acrylics.

Palette Paper Holder – R
This rectangular plastic container is used for holding palette paper. An air-tight lid helps to temporarily slow the drying of oil and acrylic paints on the palette. It aids in transporting wet paint.

Papers

Bristol, Smooth

This acid-free paper is available in two finishes: medium and high. The high has a smooth finish, which is excellent for mechanical drawing, pencil, pen, and ink. The medium surface has a slight grain and works well with most techniques.

Bristol, Vellum

Translucent vellum paper is excellent for any dry media, including pencil, charcoal, and pastel. This acid-free surface is also ideal for practicing airbrush techniques.

Canvas Paper

Use canvas-textured paper for practicing techniques with oils and acrylics.

Charcoal

This textured, strong, natural white paper provides an ideal foundation for charcoal and pastel. It is also suitable for oil pastel and crayon.

Drawing

This is a student-grade, acid-free paper that is intended for use with any dry media, pen, and ink. It is invaluable to any artist who uses dry media.

Newsprint, Rough

This is an economical, rough surface sheet for sketching or preliminary drawings.

Newsprint, Smooth

This economical, smooth surface sheet is used for practice sketching and preliminary drawings.

Palette Paper

This paper is a disposable paint-mixing palette made of poly-coated paper or parchment paper. Available in 9×12" and 14×18" size pads, the sheets can be torn off and thrown away as they are used.

Sketch

This lightweight sketching paper is suited for classroom experimentation, practicing techniques, or quick studies with any dry media.

Tracing

This is a transparent parchment tracing paper. It accepts pencil, markers, and ink.

Watercolor Paper

Watercolor papers are available in a range of weights expressed in pounds. The weight determines the thickness of the paper. The most commonly used is 140-pound paper.

Watercolor paper is also available in three different textures: Hot-Pressed (HP), Cold-Pressed (CP), and Rough. Hot metal rollers are used in the manufacturing process to "hot-press" the paper for the smoothest, least textured of the finishes. It works well for pen, pencil, and detail. Cold-Pressed paper has been pressed between cold rollers covered with textured felts, and it has more texture than Hot-Pressed. Rough refers to paper that has a great deal of texture because it is left natural.

Additional Tools

Sea Sponges – A

Sponges play an important part in artwork. They can be used with most media such as watercolor, tube acrylics, decorative painting, and faux finishes.

Sketching and Drawing Tools – B

Charcoal sticks, sketching pencils, and graphite art sticks are ideal tools for drawing and sketching. Charcoal and graphite art sticks are good for bold lines and broad background strokes. Sketching pencils create finer details.

Snow — not shown

Use this thick paste to create wintery scenes in your painting, or to apply to a surface for additional texture. Some snow products contain glitter to make it look more realistic.

Solvents – C

Available in the fine arts and crafts sections of your store, a variety of petroleum solvents are available for cleaning oil painting tools and brushes. Solvents also are mixed with oils and other mediums to create washes and techniques.

Tube Wringer – D

This handy tool crimps the end of paint tubes, pushing the paint toward the neck of the tube and making it easier to squeeze the paint out.

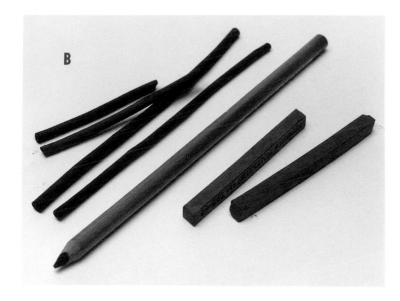

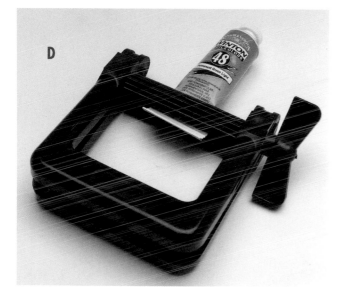

ҙCreative Tip

Odorless paint thinner is great as far as smell,

or lack of, goes; however, it still has "fumes"

and should be used with the same caution and

ventilation as thinner with odor.

– Team Member, Hudson, Ohio

Varnishes – E
Acrylic Varnishes
Available in the fine arts and crafts sections of your store, acrylic varnishes are brushed over dried paints to change or unify the surface sheen (gloss, matte, or semi-gloss). Use it to protect the painting surface from the environment, to protect colors from ultraviolet light, and to protect the finish.

Oil Varnishes
Dammar Varnish
Used on oil paintings, this traditional, high-gloss final varnish dries quickly and remains soluble in turpentine or mineral spirits.
Dammar Retouching Varnish
This is used for temporary protection of recently-executed oil paintings, and for retouching dull patches on oil paintings.

Color *Theory*

Knowledge of color basics will help you achieve stunning

results. Understanding the relationship between colors and

how they impact your creative endeavors will make your

color choices so much easier.

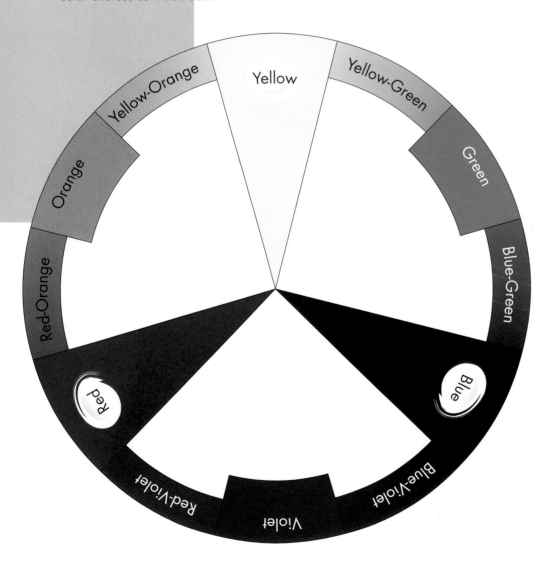

Color Properties

A good place to start is to describe the properties of color—hue, value, and intensity.

Hue
This refers to the name of a color (for example, green, blue, etc.). There are 12 color families. Hue also can refer to the special names given to various paints (for example, Forest Green, Wedgwood Blue, Rose Mist).

Primary Colors
Primary means "first." Red, yellow, and blue, located an equal distance apart on a color wheel, are the three primary colors from which all other colors are mixed. They are pure colors and do not contain white, black, or any other color additive.

Secondary Colors
Mixing two primary colors together creates a secondary color. The three colors are orange (red + yellow), green (blue + yellow), and violet (blue + red).

Tertiary (Intermediate) Colors
Tertiary means "third." Mix a primary color with an adjacent secondary color on the wheel to create a tertiary (intermediate) color. The six tertiary colors are red-orange, yellow-orange, yellow-green, blue-green, blue-violet, and red-violet. "Tertiary" and "intermediate" are synonymous terms.

Value
Value refers to how light or dark a color is, compared on a scale from white to black. All colors have values between these two extremes. For example, on the high end of the scale, blue may be so pale that it almost appears to be white, but on the low end of

a value scale, it is so dark that it appears to be black. The value of a color can be changed by adding white, black, or a lighter or darker color.

Correct value placement is of vital importance in a painting. Besides creating dimension, it helps establish a center of interest and leads the viewer through the painting.

Intensity (Chroma)
This refers to the brightness, dullness, purity, or strength of a color. Words often used to describe intensity are "muted," "grayed," "toned," "vivid," "harsh," etc. The words "intensity" and "chroma" are synonymous.

To change the intensity of a color, add white, black, gray, or an earth tone. Using these colors to change the intensity also will slightly change the color. Complementary colors (colors that are directly across the color wheel from each other), also can be used to neutralize a color without significantly changing it (for example, mixing orange with a small amount of blue).

Use an intense color to draw the eye to a given area of a painting. Use a variety of color intensities to create the illusion of dimension or to create moods.

Color Harmony
Color harmony is another way to describe color schemes, which are simply colors that work well together and act as a "color plan." They fall into two categories: Related and Contrasting.

The most common related color schemes are Analogous, Monochromatic, and Neutral. The contrasting color schemes are Complementary, Double Split Complementary, Split Complementary, and Triadic.

Related Color Schemes

Analogous
There are two interpretations of this color scheme: The first indicates the colors should range from one primary to the next (for example, from red to blue). The second interpretation is that the color scheme is composed of three to five neighboring colors on the wheel, and should have one color in common.

Monochromatic
Derived from the words "mono " (one), and "chroma" (color), this color scheme utilizes variations of one hue. Texture, value changes, and subject matter create the interest in this type of painting.

Neutral
This is similar to the monochromatic scheme, but the colors are neutralized almost beyond identity, and several colors of very low intensity are used.

Contrasting Color Schemes

Complementary
This consists of two colors. They are directly across from each other on the color wheel (for example, red and green, orange and blue, etc.).

Split Complementary
This uses three hues from the color wheel. Select a dominant color, and then use the color on each side of the complement. For example, if red is the dominant color, the other two colors would be yellow-green and blue-green (the colors on each side of the complementary color).

Double Split Complementary
This is similar to the split complementary. The difference is that both sides of the chosen complementary are split. This results in four hues.

Triadic
This uses three colors equally divided on the color wheel (for example, red, yellow, and blue).

Selecting Color Schemes

Once a color scheme is selected, there are additional ways to create color harmony.

Dominance is an important factor. One color must stand out more than the others and be used more abundantly throughout the design.

To achieve color harmony, add a bit of one of the other colors used in the design to all colors used. This helps to pull the design elements together. The exception is when one area is to appear more prominent.

The background color is also important in creating color harmony. It affects how the colors will appear. Remember that colors relate to each other. For example, a lemon painted on a blue-violet background will look vibrant. If painted on an orange background, it will look more subdued.

Warm and Cool Colors

When people refer to color in terms of warm or cool, they may also discuss color in terms of "temperature." Warm colors, which are red, orange, and yellow, tend to move toward the viewer or advance; cool colors, which are green, blue, and violet seem to move away or recede. However, warm and cool colors may vary depending on the color they are located next to. For example, consider three colors of yellow: yellow, yellow-green, and yellow-orange. Relative to each other, yellow-orange is the warmest of the three, and yellow-green is the coolest.

Contrast

Contrast brings a painting to life by using highlights, shading, tints, etc. Creating contrast is a multi-faceted subject. For new painters, a good way to start is with shading and highlighting.

To discuss contrast, it helps to understand what "value" means. Value refers to how light or dark one color is. For example, petals on a flower are not just one shade of color. They are comprised of light, medium, and dark values. These variations are caused by the light source, the angle of the petal, and so forth.

A highlight is the lightest area on a particular object. It is the area where the object receives the most light, such as a ray of sunshine hitting the top or outer edges of an object. Shading is placed on the darkest areas. It's in the shadows or behind another object.

To show the separation between objects that are touching, shading and highlights provide the contrast needed to create dimension.

Flower Diagram

Referring to the Flower Diagram, *upper right*, the white "Xs" indicate highlight placement, and the pink dots represent shading. The three back petals (see A, B, and C) are shaded where they go under the front petal. The front petals are highlighted where they meet the three back petals. To provide contrast on a single petal or object, shade one area and highlight another.

Think in terms of where the light is hitting various objects in a design. Highlight these areas. Shade areas that appear to be farther away from the light. Following these simple steps will enhance your first projects.

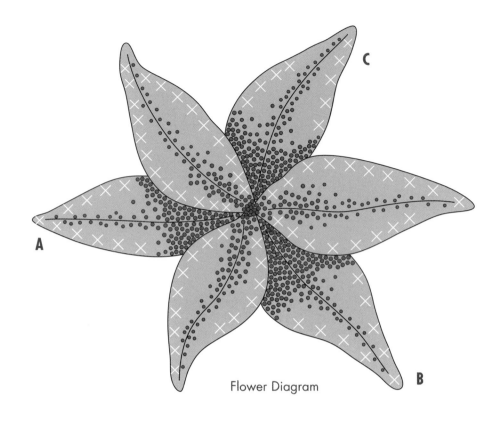

Flower Diagram

First Value Dark

This is the first shading color. It should be slightly darker than the base coat and should cover the largest area. For example, when shading a petal, cover almost two-thirds of it. Use this shading to separate objects.

Second Value Dark

This is slightly darker than the first shading color. It goes inside the first shading area and covers less space.

Third Value Dark

This is the darkest shading color. It is placed inside the second value dark areas and should cover only the smallest areas, such as triangular crevices and other tiny "nooks and crannies."

Highlights and Accents

Build up highlights in the same way. The first one should cover the largest area and be slightly lighter than the base coat. Each subsequent highlight should cover less space (within the boundaries created by the first highlight) and be slightly lighter in value.

Use tints to accent certain objects in the painting; they help tie design elements together and add contrast. They are subtle tints of color. For example, if the design contains a burgundy colored rose with green leaves, tint a small area on a few leaves with burgundy. This helps tie the design together.

For acrylic decorative painters, the most popular method to create layering is with floated color. For detailed information on floating with color, refer to Paint Basics, Floating, on page 201.

Types of Paints

Acrylic Paints

Acrylics are water-base paints that are a mixture of pigment and acrylic polymer resin (the binder). They are packaged in tubes, jars, and bottles, with bottles being the most popular among decorative and crafts painters.

Tube acrylics have a thick paste-like consistency similar to oil paints. Jar acrylics are a thick creamy liquid, and bottled craft acrylics are the thinnest of the three.

Acrylics differ from other paints in several ways. They are water-base, nontoxic, and dry in a few minutes. Cleanup is with soap and water, making them the most popular paint choice for all ages.

Bottled and jar acrylics offer a wide range of colors, often making color mixing unnecessary. Tube acrylics have a limited color palette, and mixing is generally required for a broader range of colors.

Although tube acrylics can be used undiluted, it is generally necessary to thin the paint with a medium or water. A wide variety of mediums and additives are available for tube acrylics (see Tools and Materials on page 185). Look for mediums for crafts paint in the crafts section of your Jo-Ann Store.

Read the label for directions or cautions before painting on glass or dishes that come in contact with food.

Oil Paints

Oil paints are made of finely ground pigments mixed with linseed or safflower oil. They are the consistency of toothpaste and packaged in tubes. Paint coverage varies from transparent to opaque depending on the type of pigments that are used.

Some pigments are considered toxic and are marked as such; mediums and solvents used with oil paints also are generally toxic.

Unlike acrylics, oils can take several days to dry, depending on the colors used (oil paint colors dry at different rates), climatic conditions, the surface used, and the method of the application.

Like tube acrylics, mixing oil colors is necessary to obtain an adequate range of colors. It is possible to mix numerous colors from a few basic colors and an understanding of color theory (see Color Theory on page 190). The color variations achieved by mixing can greatly enhance your painting.

Although most oil paint requires solvents for cleanup, a new type of oil that cleans up with soap and water is now available. The water solubility appeals to painters who have health problems or environmental concerns about using turpentine or other toxic aromatic solvents that are typically required with traditional oils.

Watercolor Paints

Watercolors offer a great deal of painting freedom and flexibility, although it can be frustrating until you learn to control the paint. Whether you want to make quick sketches or detailed paintings, all you need to begin is a piece of watercolor paper, a painting board, a few brushes, and some basic colors. Watercolors can be exciting or

Understanding the basics of working with different kinds of paints, brushes, and surface preparation will make it easier for you to achieve stunning results.

maddening because there is always an element of surprise when the paint moves in unexpected ways.

Watercolors are a mixture of dry pigments and gum arabic. They are available in tubes, blocks of color arranged in a small tin case called a "pan," or dry cakes. Tube colors have a creamy consistency, the blocks are semi-moist, and the cakes are dry.

As with oils, colors are mixed, so it is not necessary to have a large number of paints to create a wide range of colors.

Identifying Brush Parts

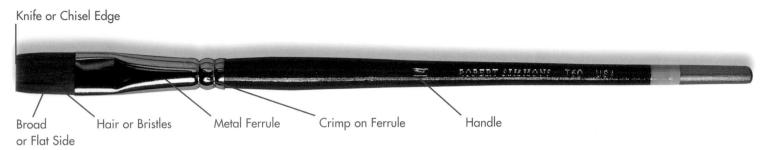

Knife or Chisel Edge

Broad or Flat Side

Hair or Bristles

Metal Ferrule

Crimp on Ferrule

Handle

Watercolor paints are generally considered to be transparent when they are mixed with water, but become more opaque with less water. Cleanup is with soap and water.

Gouache (pronounced gwäsh) is a type of watercolor paint that is opaque. It is a combination of pigment, gum arabic, and white chalk, which dries to a matte finish.

Brush Basics

Whether you choose natural or synthetic brushes, they may seem costly. However, considering their impact on the final quality of your project, good brushes are worth the investment. Most artists have a set of brushes to use with acrylic paints and a different set for use with oil paints.

Brush Types – See Tools and Materials page 184 for photo reference and shapes.

Liners
Liner brushes are used for detail work, curved and straight lines, outlining, scrolls, and strokework.

Natural Hair Brushes
Natural hair brushes are made from a broad range of hair types, such as red sable (a member of the weasel family), kolinsky (an animal found in the cold regions of Russia), ox hair, camel hair, or squirrel hair. Natural

hair brushes may have one, or a combination, of these hair types. They are available in a wide variety of sizes and shapes.

White Bristle Brushes
Made from bleached hog, pig, or boar bristles, white bristle brushes are quite stiff and durable. Use them with heavy mediums such as oils and tube acrylics.

Lucite™ Handle Flats
These brushes are usually made of a natural hair and synthetic combination. The most unusual feature is the clear lucite handle with a wedge shape on the end. This brush is used with all media; the tip of the handle is used to "cut" into or scrape away the paint to create interesting textures.

Mop Brushes
These soft, full-bristled brushes are used to soften the texture of oils and acrylics, blend colors, and apply washes. They can also be used as make-up brushes or for applying gold leafing.

Short-Handle Synthetic Brushes
Made of synthetic fibers, these brushes have short handles, making them ideal for "up-close" painting such as decorative painting, and work well for all media.

Note: *An inexpensive brush wheel can be purchased that will assist you in the selection of the perfect brush for every application.*

Surface Preparation, Painting, and Finishing

Surface preparation, such as cleaning and sanding, is a vital part of painting. A project that is properly prepared will help ensure that the finished piece will last for many years.

A

Candles – A (varnish method)
Look for candle paints and paint additives that are designed to make candle painting easier. The following method of candle preparation is appropriate for acrylic and oil paints.

Handle the candle with a clean, soft cloth. Oils from your hands can cause paint adhesion problems. Gently rub the sides of the candle with a clean, soft cloth to remove excess gloss and scratches. Prior to painting, wipe the candle with rubbing alcohol (avoid the wick) to remove any silicone coating or oils, then wipe the candle with a paper towel.

Apply one coat of brush-on water-base matte varnish. Use even strokes and pull them in the same direction (up and down, not around the candle) to prevent streaking. Let the varnish dry 15 to 30 minutes, depending upon the brand used.

Brightly colored candles may bleed color through the painting. To reduce the risk, apply a second coat of matte varnish.

Trace the pattern on tracing paper with a pencil. Retrace the back of the pattern using a soft, pastel pencil in a color that will show up on the candle. Position the tracing on the candle with the pastel pencil side down. Lightly trace the main pattern lines—a heavy touch will cause an indentation on the candle.

Paint as desired, and let dry completely. Varnish with a product that is compatible with the type of paints used. Cover the sides and top of the candle, but avoid the wick.

The need for varnish depends on the brand of candle medium used (if any) and the desired finish. Some mediums serve a dual purpose as sealer and finish.

Canvas and Floor Cloths

Canvas Accessories
Canvas checkbook covers, waste baskets, and similar accessories are excellent painting surfaces.

Using graphite or transfer paper, trace the pattern onto the canvas using a light touch (see "Transferring Patterns" on page 203). Heavy marks are difficult to remove and may show through the painting. Paint the design with acrylics or oil paints.

When painting is complete, apply several coats of varnish, making sure it is compatible with the type of paints used. Varnish makes the surface more durable and easier to clean. Use a spray varnish for pen and ink designs to prevent the possibility of smearing when a brush-on varnish is used.

Floorcloths
To minimize preparation time for floorcloths, purchase double-primed artist canvas available by the yard. Choose a heavy weight canvas for greater durability.

Cut the canvas to the desired size including a 1-inch hem. On the front edge of the canvas, make pencil marks, using a ruler as a guide, to indicate where the hem will be turned.

Base-coat the front of the canvas with acrylic, using a large sponge brush or sponge roller. Let it dry completely.

Take a piece of tracing paper the size of the floorcloth, fold it in half, then in quarters to determine the center, and mark it with a pencil. Trace the pattern onto the tracing paper, using the center mark to position the design. If a border is part of the design, draw a pencil line on the tracing to indicate the proper placement. Transfer the design to the floorcloth using graphite or transfer paper. Paint the design as desired and allow to dry completely.

The floorcloth should be hemmed to prevent the edges from curling. When the paint is dry, lay the floorcloth with the right side facing up. With a crafts knife, lightly score along the pencil line but do not cut through the canvas (this will make the hem easier to turn under). Using a brayer or rolling pin, turn the hem and crease the fold. To miter the corners follow the instructions in the Table Coverings section on page 257. Flatten the fold, and affix

½-inch double-faced carpet tape on the edge of the floorcloth. The tape has a brown paper backing. For ease of application, apply the tape around the entire floorcloth, then peel off the paper, and fold the hem over the tape. If the tape lifts, apply glue to secure it, making sure to press out any air bubbles.

Apply five to seven coats of varnish to both sides of the floorcloth. Sand in between coats with very fine sandpaper or a piece of unprinted brown paper sack.

B

Concrete – B
Acrylics or oils are appropriate for concrete surfaces. Specialty paints for outdoor use are also available for stepping stones and similar objects that will be exposed to the weather.

Brush the stone with a stiff brush to remove dirt. Wipe off with a lint-free cloth and apply two coats of sealer with a large, flat brush. Let it dry between coats.

Transfer the pattern (see Transferring Patterns on page 203). Paint as desired using older brushes or fabric brushes because rough surfaces will ruin good brushes. Allow the painted surface to dry. Read the paint label to determine if varnishing is necessary.

C

Glass – C
See Glass Painting, page 208.

Fiberboard – not shown

Fiberboard (commonly call Masonite™) is available at hardware stores in two varieties—tempered and untempered. Tempered fiberboard comes with an oil coating; untempered does not. Because oil is not compatible with some paints, the untempered variety is a better choice for a painting surface. Fiberboard, when cut to fit, is suitable for framing.

Sand any rough edges, then wipe with a tack cloth (a special cloth used to remove sawdust or sanding grit from a painting surface). The surface must be clean and dry. Tape the cut edges to prevent fiber particles from getting in the paint. Prime the fiberboard with gesso, then base-coat using acrylic paint. Transfer the pattern and paint as desired. Let the painted design dry, then varnish as desired.

D

Metal – D

New paints are now available for painting on metal. These paints have been specially formulated to adhere to slick, nonporous metal surfaces. Also, look for metal primers that help make acrylic craft paints adhere to metal.

Before painting, remove rust from the metal project. For light rust, use sandpaper to remove it, or use a rust remover for heavier rust. When the rust has been removed, wash the metal with a mixture of half water and half white vinegar. Dry completely.

Apply a metal primer to prevent further rusting. Then apply several thin layers of paint, instead of one thick base coat. Let each coat dry thoroughly.

Transfer the pattern with graphite paper, then paint. Allow the finished painting to dry completely. Varnish as desired.

E

Papier-Mâché – E

Papier-Mâché is inexpensive to purchase and requires minimal preparation. Although sealing or sanding is not required, sealing with a decoupage finish or all-purpose sealer will reduce the number of paint applications. When the sealer is dry, apply one to three coats of acrylic paint.

Transfer the pattern using an appropriate color of transfer paper (see Transferring Patterns, page 203). Paint the surface as desired.

Let the paint dry, remove any remaining transfer lines, then varnish.

Terra-Cotta – F

Terra-cotta is a popular painting surface, is inexpensive, and requires little preparation before painting.

F

Look for paints that have been formulated for patio or outdoor use and are recommend for porous surfaces. Read the paint label for proper sealing or varnishing suggestions. In general, sealing with a matte spray, gesso, or brush-on water-base sealer is recommended. Flowerpots should be

sealed inside and out, including the drainage hole.

Clean the terra-cotta with soap and water. Let it dry completely before sealing or painting. Paint with acrylic craft paints or a specially formulated outdoor type of paint. Avoid getting fingerprints on the area to be painted by handling the surface with a clean cloth.

After sealing, transfer the pattern onto the surface (see "Transferring Patterns," page 203) and paint as desired. Varnish as desired or use a finish recommend as compatible with the type of paint you are using.

Tile – G

G

See "Glass Painting," page 208.

Tin – H

Painting on tin has been popular for many years and there seems to be no end to the wide variety of available shapes and sizes.

To prepare old, rusty tin for painting, remove the rust with a rust remover. For lightly rusted pieces, scrub with a wire brush. To prepare new shiny tin, sand it lightly with fine-grade, soapy steel wool and hot water. This

H

gives "tooth" (a slight texture) to the surface for better paint adhesion.

Wash old or new tin in unscented dishwashing liquid. Rinse in a solution of half white vinegar and half water. Wash again in dishwashing liquid, rinse well in plain water, and allow to dry.

Prime the tin with either a spray or brush-on metal primer. Apply several thin coats rather than one heavy one. New metal primers (also used for tin) are also available that help make acrylic crafts paints stick to tin and other metal objects. Be sure to read product labels for specific instructions. The background can be left the natural tin color, or it can be painted with acrylic paint or one of the new metal paints specially formulated to adhere to slick, nonporous surfaces.

After the tin has been washed and primed, transfer the pattern using an appropriate transfer paper color or chalk (see Transferring Patterns, page 203), paint and varnish as desired.

Watercolor – Stretching Paper

Watercolor paper responds to water in different ways depending on the weight, quality, and sizing in the paper. Most paper will stretch when wet and shrink when it dries. As the paper dries, it will buckle and fold if it is not properly stretched. A dried, unstretched painting will have puddles of color caused by ridges in the paper (called cockling).

You will need the following items to get started: A wood board or similar surface (if the wood is new, waterproof it by varnishing several times to seal the surface), watercolor paper cut to the desired size, gummed paper tape, a water tub, and a sponge (see Photo A).

Getting Started

1. Submerse the paper in water, holding it down with your hand until it no longer floats. Let the paper soak for 20 to 30 minutes (see Photo B). Heavy paper may need to soak slightly longer. While the paper is soaking, wet the sponge with water, and cut four strips of gummed paper tape to measure about 2 inches longer than the length and width of the paper.

Photo A

Photo B

Photo C

Note: *The tape should reach about 1 inch beyond the edge of the paper. For example, if the watercolor paper is 9×12 inches, you will need two strips of tape cut to 11 inches and two strips cut to 14 inches. Never use masking tape for this purpose because it will not stick to a wet board or paper.*

2. Remove the paper from the water and lay it on the board. Smooth the paper with your hands to remove air bubbles. Dampen the gummed tape with the sponge. Lay the tape along the edges of the watercolor paper, overlapping the tape at the corners of the paper (see Photo C). About half of the width of the paper tape should be on the watercolor paper and half on the board.

3. When the paper is dry, begin painting without removing the tape. Rewet the paper with a sponge or spritz with water before painting, if desired. When the painting is finished and dry, cut the tape with a crafts knife and remove it from the board.

Wood – I

Sand or strip old wood that is flaking, cracking, or chipping. Use a commercial wood stripper if necessary.

For old wood that doesn't require stripping, thoroughly clean with a soap recommend for wood surfaces. Rinse well, and let it dry.

The following instructions apply to old and new wood: Prepare the wood for base-coating by sanding the surface with 100- and then 150-grit sandpaper. Fill nail holes, if necessary. Remove the sanding dust with a tack cloth. Apply sealer to all surfaces, let the sealer dry, resand with 150-grit sandpaper, and wipe clean.

Determine if the wood will be painted with acrylic paint, stained, or left a natural color.

When the paint is dry, transfer the pattern (see "Transferring Patterns," page 203), if desired, and paint the design or embellish with a faux finish. When the painting is complete and dry, varnish as desired.

Brushstroke *Basics*

Traditional decorative painting originated in Europe several hundred years ago where it was used to embellish furnishings and home interiors. This technique doesn't require an art degree, previous experience, or color theory. All you need is a desire to be creative combined with a willingness to practice the strokes and learn the basics.

Brush Strokes

Refer to page 194 to identify parts of a brush.

Broad Stroke
(Flat Brush)
This is a basic stroke from which many other strokes are formed.

Fully load a flat brush by picking up paint on one side of the brush and stroking back and forth on the palette, then turn the brush over and repeat the process for the other side. Angle the handle slightly toward you. Start at the top of the stroke with all the bristles touching the surface. Pull down and maintain an even pressure throughout the stroke. Slow down toward the end and lift the brush straight up. If the edges of the stroke have ridges of paint, the brush has too much paint in it.

Chisel Stroke (Flat Brush)
This is a basic stroke that is also known as a knife or line stroke. When combined with the broad stroke, it forms the narrow portion of the comma, "C" stroke, and "S" stroke.

Fully load a flat brush. Stroke it back and forth on the palette to get a good chisel edge. Start at the top of the stroke with the flat part of the brush in a six o'clock position (vertical), and pull down. Keep the brush in an upright position; maintain even pressure throughout the stroke. The width of the stroke should not vary. It should remain a fine line without any bulges.

C-Stroke (Flat Brush)
This is also referred to as a "Crescent" or "U" stroke.

Hold the brush in an upright position. Set the brush down on the chisel edge (tip of bristles) using light pressure and pull a horizontal chisel stroke (see Chisel Stroke). Increase the pressure as you pull down and flatten the brush onto the "broad" part of the brush (see Broad Stroke) to form the curved, wide part of the "C." Gradually decrease pressure, slowing down to allow time for the bristles to return to a chisel, then slide the brush in the direction you began.

Circle Stroke
(Flat Brush)
Hold the brush in an upright position on the chisel edge. Press the bristles onto the surface and roll the brush handle between your fingers as the bristles make a circle on the surface. Maintain even pressure while painting around the circle.

Comma Stroke
(Flat/Round Brush)
This is sometimes called a "Polliwog," "Squiggle," "Tadpole," or "Daisy" stroke (when painted without a curve). The instructions apply to both brush types. Start with the top of the comma. Using a

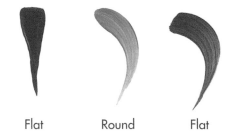

Flat   Round   Flat

fully loaded brush, press down on the bristles causing them to spread slightly. Gradually release pressure as the stroke is pulled toward you, then slow down to allow the bristles to return to the chisel edge for flats or the pointed tip for rounds. Gently slide and lift the brush for the thin part of the comma. Key words to keep in mind while painting this stroke are: "Press, pause, pull, and lift."

Crescent, Sliding
(Flat Brush)
Paint this the same as a "C" stroke. The only difference is the thin beginning and endings are closer together than they are with the "C."

Begin on the chisel edge (refer to "Chisel Stroke," *opposite*) and gradually apply pressure to flat the bristles across the top curve. On the way back down, decrease the pressure, slow down, and end on the chisel edge.

Dot Hearts (Liner Brush)
A Using the tip end of a brush handle, dip into paint and place a dot on the project surface. Reload the tip and place another dot next to the first.

B Using a liner brush, quickly pull the paint in the dots down to form a "V."

C Fill in the "V" with paint to form a heart.

Dot Swirl Roses
(Any Brush)
A Using the tip end of a brush handle, dip into paint and place one dot color on the project surface.

Reload the tip and place another dot color next to the first.

B With the tip end of a brush handle, stir the paint in a circular motion to mix the two colors and make a rose flower.

Leaf Stroke (Round Brush)
A Using a small round brush, pull a series of loose comma strokes. As you reach the end of the stroke, lift and "flip" the tip. Make a series of double leaves, getting smaller as you reach the tip.

B With a liner brush, pull a long thin comma stroke up the center.

"S" Stroke (Flat/ Liner/Round Brush)
Start on the chisel edge (see "Chisel Stroke," opposite) for flat brushes, or the pointed tip for rounds. Hold the brush in an upright position. The handle must not change position throughout the entire stroke. Make gentle curves. Start at the top of the stroke on the chisel edge and pull down with a chisel stroke. Gradually increase pressure to create the thick part of the "S." Begin to release the pressure and slow down at the end of the stroke, ending on the chisel edge.

Border or Ribbon Stroke (Flat Brush)
A continuous "S" stroke is effective for creating borders or ribbons. Hold the brush upright with the handle facing in the same

direction throughout the stroke. Start at the top of the "S" with the brush on the chisel edge, pull a short thin line toward you at a 45-degree angle, then press the bristles down for a broad stroke in the middle of the "S." Release the pressure so that the brush comes back up to the chisel edge, pull a short thin line with the 45-degree angle, then press down to make another broad stroke. Repeat the sequence until you run out of paint, reload and continue. For ribbon, vary the length of the "S" strokes to create a realistic appearance.

Teardrop Stroke
(Liner/Round Brush)
This is also referred to as a "Reverse Tear" or "Norwegian Teardrop."

Load the brush with plenty of paint. Twirl the bristles by rolling the brush handle between your fingers so that a point is formed. Hold the brush in an upright position and start on the thin end of the stroke using light pressure. Pull a thin stroke toward you, gradually adding pressure to form the round head. Stop and lift the brush straight up.

Z Stroke (Flat Brush)
Start on the chisel edge (see "Chisel Stroke," opposite) and pull a chisel stroke. Stop abruptly without lifting the bristles off the surface. Change direction and pull a broad stroke. Finish with another chisel stroke. The brush handle should face the same direction throughout the entire stroke.

Special Brush Techniques

Crosshatching

This refers to crisscrossed lines that are usually painted with a liner or round brush (see *below*) as on the center of the plate on page 205. Crosshatching is used to fill in spaces,

Photo A

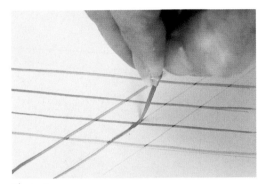
Photo B

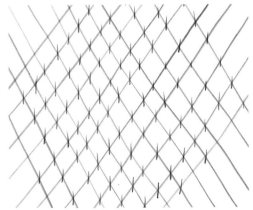
Photo C

to form borders, and give relief to busy floral designs.

For best results, freehand the crosshatching instead of transferring a pattern. This helps avoid transfer lines showing through the thinned paint. Also, transfer lines tend to inhibit the artist so the crosshatching doesn't look free and easy.

1. Thin fresh paint with water or extender until it flows like ink. Paint that has started to dry on a palette will not be fluid enough to achieve good crosshatching.

Fully load a script liner brush with the fresh, thinned paint (see Photo A). The fully loaded brush should have a reservoir of paint in the middle of the bristles. Pull the brush away from the puddle of paint on the palette, and turn the handle making the bristles come to a fine point. Wipe off any excess water from the ferrule. Practice the lines on a scrap of paper first.

2. Hold the brush perpendicular to the surface. Paint the lines using gentle pressure (see Photo B). Stay relaxed; tension makes it more difficult to paint even lines. Pull the brush toward you and turn the project as needed.

3. To achieve uniform results, paint all the lines going in one direction first, then paint the lines going in the other direction to complete the design (see Photo C).

Photo D

Curlicues

This is a form of liner work used to embellish a design. For best results, add the curlicues after the painting is complete so they can be placed in the right places to enhance the design.

1. For acrylics, thin fresh paint with water until it is an ink-like consistency. Fully load a liner brush with this mixture and turn the handle making the bristles come to a fine point. Pull away from the blending area to allow the bristles to form a fine point as shown in Photo A.

2. Hold the brush perpendicular to the surface, relax, and use gentle pressure to paint free, flowing strokes (see Photo D). It is important to paint on the tip of the bristles only. Slow down when painting curves to keep the bristles from bending, which will distort the form.

Photo E

Double Loading

Although any brush can be double-loaded, the flat and angle brushes are most commonly used.

A double-loaded brush carries two different colors at the same time, each on opposite sides of the brush.

1. To double load the brush, put two different colors of paint on a palette in separate puddles (see Photo E). For example, use pink and lavender paint. Dip one side of the bristles in pink and the other side in lavender.

2. Turn the brush so the wide, flat edge of the bristles touches the palette. Stroke it back and forth until the colors blend into each other in the center. If there isn't enough paint in the bristles, load more on the appropriate sides.

3. Blend back and forth on the palette. Soon the pink and lavender will blend together and create another color in the middle of the bristles.

Photo F

Loading a Brush
Load the bristles with paint or medium, then stroke them back and forth on the palette to work it into the bristles (see Photo F). Blend until there is no excess paint or medium on the bristles.

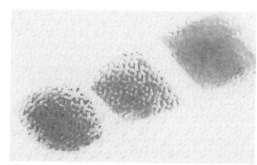
Photo G

Dry Brushing
This is one of the techniques used to apply highlights, shading, graining, or to create a flowing, yet irregular look (see Photo G). It can be used for making hair, beards, fur, wispy smoke, and other textural painting. Try using a rake, fabric, stencil, deerfoot, or mop brush for this technique (see brush descriptions on page 184). Dry brushing can be very hard on brushes, so it's best to use an old one.

1. Dip the bristles in the paint and work the paint into the bristles. Pounce them on a clean area of the palette to distribute the paint across the bristles. Then scrub the brush back and forth on a dry paper towel to remove the majority of the paint. You will need to repeat this until the paint on the brush is almost dry (see Photo G).

2. Apply paint to the surface with a circular or sweeping motion, depending on the object. For example, use a sweeping motion to shade or highlight a dress, or a circular motion on a balloon. Start with little pressure, increasing as necessary.

Photo H

Flecking (Spattering)
Flecking has several different names: flyspecking, spattering, or splattering. Use this technique to put tiny specks of paint on a surface.

Flecking is most commonly done on a dry surface. To create a soft, ethereal effect, slightly dampen the surface before flecking.

Make sure any previously applied paint is dry. Spread newspapers around the work area and wear an apron. Flecking can be messy.

Four things influence the appearance of flecking: (1) paint consistency, (2) working distance from the object (4 to 12 inches), (3) pressure applied to the brush, and (4) how quickly the flecking tool is moved over the surface.

Apply flecking with a fan brush or a toothbrush. There are also specialty tools created for flecking.

1. Mix paint with water until it is an ink-like consistency. Dip a clean fan brush in the diluted paint mixture. Practice over a paper towel or a palette first.

2. Gently pull a crafts stick or a palette knife across the top of the bristles, pulling toward you. Adjust the distance from the surface and the pressure on the fan brush until the specks are the desired size, and then spatter the surface (see Photo H).

Photo I

Photo J

Floating
Floating is one of the most important techniques used in decorative painting. It is sometimes referred to as "sideloading."

Use a flat brush or angle brush to float color. An ideal float must have a gradual fading of color across the bristles, ranging from the paint color on one side to clear water on the other. There should not be any sharp lines of paint. "Gradual fading" are the key words. Floating mediums are now available. If desired, use them in place of water for blending floats. Their purpose is to make it possible to make a longer floated stroke before the paint dries.

1. Put out a fresh puddle of paint; use clean water and a clean, flat or angle brush. Dampen the brush with water.

Lightly blot each side of the bristles on a paper towel to remove excess water. Dip one corner of the bristles into the paint (see Photo I).

2. On a clean area of the palette, stroke the bristles back and forth to blend, using some

201 ✖

pressure (see Photo J). The blending strip should be 1 to 1½ inches long. Stroke back and forth as many times as necessary to get a gradual fading from paint color to clear water, usually 5 to 10 strokes.

Have a clean paper towel handy before floating on the actual surface. If the float isn't good enough, wipe it off and start over. Use light pressure to apply the float. For straight floats, apply in one flowing motion. For shading around leaves and other irregular shapes, try applying short strokes for greater control.

Every new painter will probably make some common mistakes when floating paint. It is important to know how to fix them:

- If there is too much water in the brush, the float will look watery. Remove the float, clean the brush, and remove more water from the brush by blotting on the paper towel.

- If the float doesn't blend well and looks rough, it doesn't have enough water in the bristles. Add more water to the bristles on the side without paint, reblend on the palette, and reapply to the surface.

- If the float creates a harsh line, it wasn't loaded properly. Remember to blend floats 5 to 10 times on a palette before applying. Wipe off the problem float, clean the brush, and start over.

- If the float is too dark and has already dried, try floating on top of it with the base-coat color.

Liner Work

This is used for outlining, painting curlicues, crosshatching, and more. The paint consistency is extremely important; it should vary depending on the type of liner work. For curlicues and crosshatching, use an ink-like consistency. For more opaque lines (i.e. for detail work) use a cream-like consistency.

Use a script liner and fresh paint. Dip the bristles in water and mix the water on the brush with the paint (see Photo A on page 200). The paint should have an ink-like consistency. Pull the bristles away from the puddle and roll the handle between your fingers while the bristles are in the paint to create a fine point (refer to Photo A on page 200 for loading the brush with paint).

Hold the liner brush with the handle perpendicular to the surface. Paint on the tips of the bristles and think "loose." Slow down while painting curves. This helps keep the bristles from bending, which creates an unattractive line.

Stippling

The stippling technique is created by pouncing (tapping) a brush up and down on a surface to apply the paint. There are a number of applications for this technique, such as fur, trees, and snow.

1. Dip the brush or sponge into undiluted paint. Pounce it up and down on a palette to remove any excess paint.

2. Use a light pouncing pressure as you apply paint to the surface. See "Stippling" on page 223 for more details.

Creating a Wash

The technique known as a "wash" can be described as thinning paint with water to create a transparent paint that is then brushed over a painted surface. A wash is used to enhance certain areas of the painting. For example, a river painted blue will not have depth, but add several layers of transparent colors over the blue and it will begin to look real.

Put a small puddle of paint on a palette. Gradually mix in a little water. There is no exact ratio because paints vary in viscosity (thickness). A good starting place, however, is 2 parts water and 1 part paint. Adjust the mixture by adding more water until it looks like tinted water.

1. Use a large, flat brush. To lessen the chance of streaking, use as wide a brush as possible for the area. Fully load the brush with the thinned paint.

2. Lightly touch the loaded brush on a dry paper towel to wick out some of the moisture. This helps to prevent puddling.

3. Paint in one direction, pulling strokes toward you (see Photo K). If streaking occurs, brush in the opposite direction. There is no limit to the number of washes that can be used.

Photo K

Special Techniques

Embellishing with Glitter

Glitter can be used on most surfaces, except fabric. Dry, iridescent glitter adds sparkle to projects and it is especially effective on holiday projects. Glitter is available in different grades and colors. Apply it after all painting is complete and dry.

Apply at least three coats of brush-on water-base varnish to the project before adding glitter. Allow each coat to dry thoroughly before applying the next one.

Brush varnish on the areas that will have glitter. While the varnish is still wet, sprinkle glitter on the area. As the varnish dries the glitter becomes "glued" to the surface. It is not necessary to varnish over the glitter.

Wait to shake off the excess glitter until the varnish has completely dried.

Note: *Glitter should not be used on dishes or glassware that will come in contact with food.*

Transferring Patterns

Patterns for decorative painters are available in books, magazines, packets, and on the Internet. Directions are usually included to guide the artist through the entire project.

Transfer Paper Method
These steps apply to any type of transfer paper.

To trace a pattern, put a sheet of tracing paper or vellum on top of the pattern. Use a pencil or pen and trace the entire pattern.

Position the tracing as desired. Secure one side of the tracing with a piece of tape or hold it down with one hand (see Photo L). Slide the transfer paper under the tracing with the shiny side down. Use a dark color (such as graphite) for light backgrounds and a light color for dark backgrounds. Use a stylus or an empty ink pen to transfer the design.

Regardless of the method used, transfer only the lines required for initial color placement; don't trace any detail lines. After tracing a few lines, carefully pull a corner of the tracing paper back to see that the pattern is transferring properly (see Photo M). The traced lines should be just dark enough to be seen. Dark, heavy lines will show through the paint and are difficult to remove.

Chalk Method
Turn the tracing face down. Use a color of chalk that will show on the background. Rub chalk over the back of the pattern and then shake off any residue. Another option

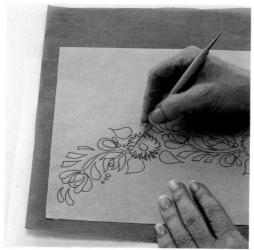

Photo L

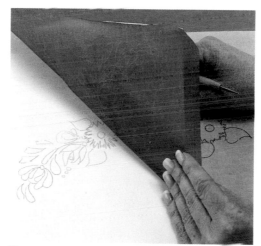

Photo M

is to carefully retrace all the lines on the back of the pattern with chalk.

Position the tracing paper on the surface, chalked side down. Secure with masking tape. Trace the main pattern lines with a stylus. Press gently to avoid damaging the surface.

Transfer Paper Method
These steps apply to any type of transfer paper.

Template Method
Transferring a pattern to stepping stones and other coarse surfaces is difficult. When traditional transfer methods don't work, try

transferring the pattern to a piece of lightweight cardboard. Cut out only the main design elements (for example a flower or leaf). Place cutouts on the surface and trace around them using a washable fabric marker. Once the base-coat is applied, it is easier to transfer the detailed lines using a more traditional method. If any transfer lines remain after the painting is complete, remove them with water.

The above methods also work well on fabric; however, first position the fabric on a firm surface.

Bridal Veiling Method
This is effective for wearable art such as sweatshirts. Lay the pattern on a firm surface and place a piece of waxed paper or food wrap on top to protect it. Place a piece of bridal veiling material on top of this. Trace the pattern with a black felt tip marker onto the bridal veiling. Pin the veiling to the fabric and, using a fabric transfer pencil, retrace all the pattern lines onto the fabric. Place cardboard or other firm plastic-covered surface under the fabric before painting or the paint may bleed through. Paint as desired. If the painting does not cover all the transfer lines, wipe them off with a clean, damp cloth.

Transfer Pencil (Iron-On)
These are effective for transferring a pattern onto light-colored fabric. Retrace the back of the tracing with an iron-on pencil (it will be the reverse of the finished image). Secure the pattern to the fabric with pins or tape. Set the iron to a setting that is appropriate for the type of fabric. Iron one small area of the pattern at a time for about 30 seconds. Before continuing, carefully pull the pattern back to see that the transfer was successful. Avoid sliding the iron over the surface because this can cause the tracing to shift.

Getting Started

Combine the brushstrokes you have just learned to make the plate on page 205. Make the flowers, leaves, and crosshatching by following these examples:

Note: *Be sure to use glass paint on ceramic and glass surfaces. Read labels for cautions to make sure the paint is nontoxic and can be used on food surfaces. Also, follow the manufacturer's instructions regarding glazing or baking certain brands of glass paint.*

Folk Art Rose – Rim of Plate
1. Using a #6 flat brush, make a closed crescent stroke with pink paint.

For the stem: With a #4 round brush, pull an extra long comma stroke in medium green.

2. On either side of the closed crescent stroke, use a #6 round brush, and pull pink comma strokes on either side. Brush mix some pink and white paint and pull smaller comma strokes on top of the closed crescent.

For the stem: Add a thinner yellow comma stroke using a #4 round brush.

3. Brush mix pink and white and add additional flourishes with various sizes of comma strokes on top of the existing flower strokes. Place two comma strokes above the rose flower.

For the leaves: Using a #4 flat brush, pull comma stokes with medium green and allow to dry. With yellow, pull light comma strokes over the green leaves.

Cornflower – Rim of Plate
1. Using a #2 round brush, pull teardrop strokes with dark blue to form a circular flower.

Folk Art Rose

Cornflower

Folk Art Tulip

Pansy Bud

For the leaves: Using a #4 flat brush, double load the brush, half in medium green and half in yellow. Make a loose "S" stoke, then a comma stroke beside the "S" stroke with the flat brush.

2. Using the same brush size and stroke as in Step 1, add more petals to the flower with medium blue paint.

3. Using the same brush size and stroke as in Step 1, use white paint to pull more strokes on top of the medium blue strokes.

Flower center: Using the tip end of a brush handle, dip into the dark blue, make three large dots, and connect them with the tip of the handle. Add three small white comma strokes in the center.

Folk Art Tulip – Rim of Plate

1. Using a #4 flat brush, double-load with medium yellow and a small amount of medium green. Make a loose "S" stroke, then make a double-loaded comma stroke (flat brush) beside the "S" stroke using the same colors.

2. Using a #4 flat brush and medium green, make "S" strokes on either side of the yellow petals. Place a green and yellow dot at the base of the flower with the tip of the brush handle. Make three green and yellow dots that decrease in size. Place one red dot between the yellow petals with the tip of the brush handle.

Pansy Bud – Rim of Plate

1. Using a #4 flat brush, make a closed crescent stroke with purple paint.

2. Brush mix lavender and purple paint, and make two smaller closed crescents on top of the first one. With the tip of the brush handle, make three green and yellow dots that decrease in size below the pansy bud.

Crosshatching – Center of Plate

1. Using a liner brush, thin the paint to an ink-like consistency. Carefully pull long straight lines across the center of the plate. Paint all the lines in the same direction, then turn the plate and paint the lines in the opposite direction.

2. Allow the paint to dry, then add the small lines shown in yellow at the cross-hatching intersections.

Creative Tip

When blending two colors of paint, use two brushes, one for each color, so you don't have to wash your brush each time, and to make the blended edge nearly invisible.

– Team Member, Hudson, Ohio

Fabric *Painting*

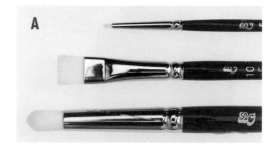

A

C

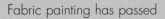

Fabric painting has passed through many transitions over the years. Today people seem to prefer simple designs that are often used in conjunction with stamping, and tie-dying is enjoying a resurgence with young people.

Tools and Materials

Fabric Brushes – A
All varieties have short, stiff synthetic bristles that are sturdy enough to withstand stenciling on fabric and other surfaces. Shown *above* from top to bottom are detail, flat and round brushes.

Foam Stamps – B
With dozens of designs to choose from, foam stamps are a quick and easy way to apply designs to fabric. Some act as an outline, while others also fill in the design.

B

Paints – C
There are a number of fabric paints and textile dyes specifically designed for painting on fabrics. Some paints are used for outlining, while others are

E

D

used for filling in patterns or embellishing with glitter. Acrylic paints also can be used for this purpose, but they should be mixed with a textile medium.

Textile Medium – D

Use textile medium to mix with acrylic paints. This product will make the paint more flexible, softer, and help the paint bond to the fabric.

Tie-Dye Paints – E

Kits contain everything you need for tie-dying except the garment. Follow the manufacturer's instructions.

Fabric Basics

The ideal fabric for wearable art is a blend of 50-percent cotton and 50-percent polyester; 100-percent cottons tend to shrink, and acrylics may develop fuzzy nubs. For best results, paint with fabric paints or dyes designed for that purpose.

There are a variety of ways to apply the paint. Apply it with a brush onto dry fabric, or use a wet-on-wet technique to blend the colors. Consider using fabric marker pens to write or draw on the fabric. Also try outlining with dimensional paints, spraying with fabric glitter products, or stamping with a stamp or sponge.

Wash the fabric to preshrink it and remove any sizing. Avoid using detergents with a built-in fabric softener or bleach. Don't use fabric softener sheets, as they may cause paint adhesion problems. Dry according to the instructions for the fabric used. Iron if needed.

Painting mistakes are difficult to remove. It may be possible to remove paint if it hasn't dried. Use rubbing alcohol on the spot immediately and dab it with a paper towel.

The garment may be worn when the paint is dry, but wait at least five days before laundering it. Turn the painted garment inside out for washing. Use a mild detergent that doesn't contain bleach, whiteners, lemon scents, or other additives. Wash in the gentle cycle and cold water. Avoid using fabric softener and softener sheets. For best results, treat painted fabric as a fine washable. Hang the garment up to dry on padded hangers with the right side out, or lay flat if decorated with dimensional paints and/or jewels.

Getting Started

1. Place the fabric on plastic-treated cardboard. This provides a firm surface on which to paint; it also prevents paint from soaking through to other layers of fabric. Secure the fabric with tape. To protect against accidental spills, use a piece of plastic to mask any areas that aren't to be painted.

2. If you are using a pattern, use transfer paper, an iron-on pencil, or chalk the back of the pattern. For specifics on each method, see Transferring Patterns on page 203.

3. Paint the pattern as desired. If you are using stamps (as shown on the opposite page), you may want to paint a solid area slightly larger than the foam shape to highlight it, allow it to dry, then paint the stamp and apply to the painted area. Embellish with dimensional paints.

4. Remove any cardboard (if used) as soon as the painting is complete, as the painting will stick to the board when dry. Hang the painted fabric up to dry unless it is decorated with dimensional paints and/or jewels. In these cases, dry flat.

Heat set if required. Refer to the manufacturer's instructions for heat setting. Do not iron dimensional paints.

Using Textile Medium

Regular acrylics work well for fabric painting when it isn't important to maintain the "soft hand of fabric," (e.g. painting on canvas shoes, or totes that are stiff to begin with). Use textile medium to change the consistency of the paints, enabling them to better penetrate the fabric and bond around the fibers. It also reduces the tendency for the paint to bleed outside the pattern areas.

Brush textile medium on the design area, then brush on the paint. Another method is to mix the paint and medium together on a palette, then apply it to the fabric.

Follow the manufacturer's instructions for the correct ratio of paint to textile medium.

Glass *Painting*

Handpainting is an excellent way to personalize glassware. Using basic techniques, you can create designs of your own, or you can take inspiration from patterns on antique china.

Tools and Materials

Brushes
Use good quality synthetic artist's brushes for glass painting, available in many sizes and shapes. See Tools and Materials on page 184 for a description of brushes.

Paint
Both acrylic and oil paints work well for glass painting, or try one of the specialty paints made to adhere to slick surfaces. Read the instructions on glass and tile paints; some of them require the use of special cleaning and glazing products that will need to be purchased with the paint.

Glass Markers
Glass markers are also available if you prefer using a marker.

Glass Painting Basics

Wash the glass with soap and water to remove all oils. Rinse with a mixture of half white vinegar and half water, or use rubbing alcohol. Dry well. To keep the surface oil-free, avoid touching the areas to be painted.

Painting on glass is a challenge because of the slick surface. To add tooth to the surface, lightly spray the object with a coat of clear acrylic spray to create a "frosted" appearance, brush on matte varnish to the design area, apply a glass and tile medium, or etch the glass.

Transfer the pattern. For clear glass (for example, a wine glass), tape the pattern inside the glass and use it as a guide. If the glass is opaque, use chalk, nonwaxy graphite paper, or freehand the pattern with

a nonwaxy pencil. Don't use a marking pen because the ink will mix with the paint and change the color. Waxy graphite will repel the paint.

Paint with a medium thick coat of paint instead of using heavy applications. Avoid overworking the paint. If the paint grabs, leave that area and paint another area, or the paint will lift. If more than one coat is required, allow the first coat to dry completely. Drying time will vary depending on the paint used, climatic conditions, etc. Varnish when the paint is completely dry. For brush-on varnish, use a light touch on the first coat to avoid lifting the paint.

Getting Started

Note: *Paint should only be applied to the areas that don't come in contact with food. Read all paint instructions; some require that the finished piece be baked.*

Avoid overstroking painted areas to prevent wiping off or smearing. Refer to Brushstroke Basics on page 198.

1. Clean and wash the glass as described in Glass Painting Basics. Use the paint and colors of your choice.

2. Refer to the rose and leaf strokework shown at *right*. Dip the tip of the handle into a puddle of paint, and make a dot on the glass for the center of the rose (see A). With a #4 round brush, make two comma strokes on either side of the dot (see B). Vary the petal color by occasionally picking up a small amount of white paint along with the petal color to lighten some of the petals on the right side (see C).

3. To make leaf strokes, refer to Brushstroke Basics on page 198. With a #4 round brush, make comma strokes with medium green to form the leaves (see D). Keep the strokes loose, and randomly place them around the roses. Vary the leaf color by occasionally picking up a small amount of white paint along with the leaf color to lighten some of the leaves.

4. Make tiny dots using the tip of the brush handle, and scatter them around the flowers and leaves. Use more than one color for added interest (see E).

5. Using a #6 flat brush, paint stripes on the foot of each glass.

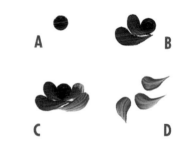

Faux *Finishes*

For years, artist's oil paints, waxes, powders, pastes, and other solvent-base products have been used to produce a wide variety of faux finishes with beautiful results. However, they can be difficult to use without the benefit of training and the understanding of color mixing. Today there are numerous water-base acrylic products available that are easier to work with, are low in odor, clean up with water, and produce similar results.

The word "faux" literally means to create a painted surface that looks so real that it appears to "fool the eye." While it is desirable to paint finishes that come close to the look of real elements such as wood patterns, stone, marble, and verdigris, to name a few, faux finishing gives you a great deal of artistic license. Therefore, you're free to use your imagination to develop your own special versions.

Tools for All Faux Finishes

Acrylic Paint – A
Acrylic paint is a latex water-base crafts or fine art paint that is low in odor and cleans up with water. It is readily available in bottles, jars, and tubes, but the liquid type requires no mixing.

Antiquing Medium – B
Antiquing medium is used to darken an object or surface to make it look old or aged (see Antiquing and Distressing on page 214).

Brushes – C to E
Choose from the following brushes for a variety of faux techniques:
French Brush – C
This brush has a handle and short, stiff white bristles that are used for combing through glazes to create stripes and textured designs.
Liner Brush – not shown
The liner brush is used to make long, thin lines, outlines, and vein lines for faux finishes such as marble (see Tools and Materials, page 184.

Synthetic Brushes – not shown
A variety of shapes and sizes of synthetic brushes are used in creating faux finishes (see Tools and Materials, page 184).
Stippler Brush – D
Stippler brushes are available in a variety of sizes and shapes; some have long handles, while others are square blocks of wood with bristles. The brush is used to create subtle results by pouncing or tapping it into wet paint and glazes to softly blend or transition from one color to another.
Sponge Brush – E
Available in several sizes, disposable sponge brushes are inexpensive and work well for many applications.

Cloths – not shown
Use clean, lint-free cloths when you are creating faux finishes. Besides the obvious use for cleaning and wiping tools and surfaces, cloths may be used for rag rolling and applying or removing paint from a wall to create a textured effect.

Combing Tool – F

Available in a number of shapes and sizes, combing tools are usually made of rubber and have "teeth" cut into the edges that create designs as the tool is pulled through glazing medium.

Crackle Medium – G

Crackle mediums are used to create an aged, crackled appearance on a surface. There are two basic types of crackle: One produces large, coarse cracks, and the other kind makes fine eggshell cracks. The size and amount of cracking will vary according to the method and thickness of the application.

Crafts Knife – H

Also commonly called an X-ACTO knife, this tool comes in handy for cutting away tape, trimming, and scraping.

Drop Cloth –

not shown

Drop cloths are large, plastic sheets available in home improvement stores and are used to cover floors, furniture, and other surfaces to protect them from paint splatters.

Denatured or Rubbing Alcohol –

not shown

Alcohol is used to soak acrylic paint from brushes and remove unwanted dried paint. Acrylic paints are water soluble if the paint is still damp, but require the use of alcohol for stubborn dry areas.

Feather – not shown

Use a feather to simulate vein lines in marble finishes.

Glazing Medium – I

Glazing medium is a clear, transparent gel mixed with acrylic paints to extend the drying time and thicken the paint. It is also available in colored gel medium.

Graining Tool – J

The wood graining tool (also called a rocker tool) has a curved surface with rubber or plastic grooves on the surface. This tool is available in varying widths and sizes of grain. When the rocker is pulled through the glaze medium, it forms a simulated wood grain finish.

Latex Gloves – not shown

Use latex gloves to protect your hands, if desired.

Paint Pan and Roller – not shown

Use paint pans and rollers if you are working on large projects such as walls. The roller carries more paint and medium, and it makes application faster than with a brush.

Painter's Tape – not shown

Painter's tape is a low-tack tape used by house painters to mask around windows, moldings, and ceilings. Use painter's tape (usually a blue color), to protect areas on walls and projects you don't want painted.

Plastic Wrap or Bags – not shown

Plastic wrap and bags create interesting textures and patterns when they are wrinkled and pressed into glazing medium on a surface.

Plumb Line – not shown

A plumb line is a line or string with a weight at one end that is temporarily attached to the ceiling or a wall to determine a vertical line. The string may be chalked so that you can snap the line against the wall to mark a line. A plumb line is commonly considered to be a wallpaper hanging tool.

Sea Sponge – K

Sea sponges are available in numerous dimensions. The sponges are usually light brown, and they have holes of various sizes and small finger-like protrusions that make good faux finish textures (see Sponging, page 222).

Spray Bottle – not shown

A spray bottle is filled with water to mist or spritz surfaces while working on faux finishes.

Varnish

Varnish seals and protects faux finishes from wear, tear, and environmental elements (see Tools and Materials, page 189).

Marbling *Basics*

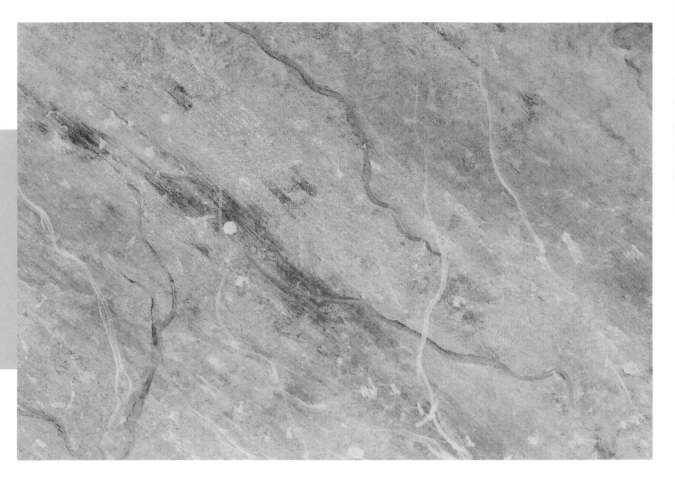

Faux marble gained popularity during the Renaissance period, when the technique was used to replicate the look of stone by people who could not afford the real thing.

Creative Tip

When faux finishing a room, take time to work paint into the corners. It creates a more finished look, with no obvious bare spots.

– Team Member, Hudson, Ohio

Marbling Basics

Marbling, also incorrectly known as marbleizing, can be achieved through the use of several different tools. Practice with these implements until you find the combination that works best for you. When you are learning this technique, spend some time studying different types of real marble until you have perfected your skills.

Faux marble is best achieved by applying several layers of transparent paint. Thin applications of color and veins, painted one on top of the other and allowing the previous layer to show through, will produce the most realistic results.

Use masking tape or painter's tape to protect adjacent areas such as moldings or other walls that aren't being marbled. Remove the tape as soon as possible. Use a crafts knife to gently run a cut line along the edge of the tape.

Work from the top down if you are working on large projects such as a wall, fireplace mantel, or column.

Dispose of leftover glaze mixes at the end of the day and prepare new mixes as needed.

Once you have mastered the basic steps, adjust the marble colors to suit your decor. Choose the paint colors that work best with your decorating scheme by selecting light, medium, and dark values of color. When choosing a base-coat color, pick an off-white or similar paint color for lighter marble. For dark marble, choose colors such as black, deep green, deep blue-gray, or gray.

Use a piece of real marble as a reference to create a more realistic faux finish.

For best results, try to complete a project in one session. The continuity of the color and design work may be difficult to replicate at another time. Never mix oil and acrylic paints on the same surface, because they are not compatible and can cause cracking or peeling of the paint.

Photo A

Photo B

Photo C

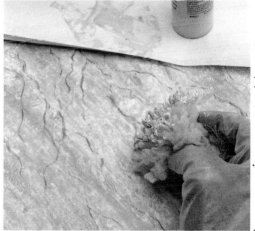

Photo D

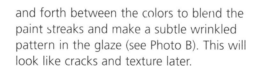

Getting Started

1. For the pink marble shown, base-coat the surface with an off-white paint. Create three glaze mixtures (dark dusty pink, medium dusty pink, and tan). If you are marbling on a wall, work in small sections of 2×2 feet, working wet into wet paint. Complete each section before moving on to the next. With the appropriate size brush, pick up a small amount of each of the glaze mixes and make random streaks at an angle (see Photo A). Keep the paint wet by misting with a spray bottle of water.

2. While the paint is still wet, use a section of "scrunched" plastic wrap to dab back

and forth between the colors to blend the paint streaks and make a subtle wrinkled pattern in the glaze (see Photo B). This will look like cracks and texture later.

3. Using a liner brush (or feather) and tan paint thinned with a small amount of water and glazing medium, make vein lines. Keep the lines thin and "shaky," fading in and out (see Photo C). Keep the surface damp with the spray bottle of water.

4. Mix the off-white base-coat paint with the medium pink to make a light pink, then

mix with a small amount of glaze medium. Sponge it on the surface to soften the streaked lines and veins (see Photo D).

5. Repeat the process of adding veins using the off-white paint. Lightly sponge to soften the vein lines.

6. Let the finish dry completely. Seal the surface with several coats of high gloss water-base varnish, allowing ample drying time between coats. For an aged look, apply antiquing medium, let it dry, and apply a final coat of varnish.

Antiquing *and Distressing*

Antiquing and distressing are two distinct techniques used to simulate the effects of aging. Use one of these two methods to create an aged look with very different finishes on your projects.

Antiquing Basics

Antiquing is accomplished by brushing on and wiping off transparent color (usually dark brown) to produce depth and an aged effect. Antiquing helps emphasize fine detailing of carving, ornamentation, molding, trim, and textures.

Always test the antiquing color in a hidden area before you begin the application.

Accentuate crevices, corners, and edges by leaving additional antiquing in these areas.

Getting Started

1. Quickly apply the antiquing medium with a cloth or brush (see Photo A).

A soft stencil brush works well to apply antiquing in areas with carving and texture.

2. Remove most of the antiquing with a clean cloth until you are pleased with the depth of color (see Photo B). If desired, re-apply antiquing to create greater depth.

3. Let the antiquing dry thoroughly and varnish, if desired. Test brush-on varnish in a hidden area to make sure the varnish won't lift the antiquing, or use a spray varnish.

Distressing Basics

Distressing creates a worn, country look that is the new, trendy finish called shabby chic. It is created by removing parts of the first layer of paint to reveal a darker undercoat (see the flower pot, *upper left*).

Work with contrasting paint colors so the base coat will show up better. The base coat is usually the darker of the two colors.

A variety of methods and tools can be used to achieve a distressed finish, such as sanding, scratching, piercing, or denting the surface. Try using a nail, key, chain, ice pick, hammer, tin can lid, or other metal objects to make the project look old and worn.

Rub paraffin or white candle wax on areas where you want the most distressing. It will make paint removal easier.

If desired, protect the project with a matte varnish.

Photo A

Photo B

Getting Started

1. You will need to choose light and dark colors of paint. Base-coat the project with one or more coats of the darker color and allow it to dry thoroughly. If desired, rub wax on the areas that would normally receive the most wear, such as corners and edges.

2. Apply one or more coats of the lighter paint color. Let the paint dry thoroughly.

3. Using the tools of your choice, distress the paint to reveal the darker undercoat. It will be easier to remove the paint in the areas where the wax was applied. Sand areas that are rough to the touch due to the distressing.

Combing *Techniques*

Combing Basics

Practice with the combing tool on illustration board or cardboard before beginning your project.

Drying time for the glaze medium will vary according to the temperature and humidity in the room. The more humidity, the longer the drying time.

Combing options are endless—let your imagination and creativity be your guide. Some suggested designs are basketweave, moiré, swirl, and crosshatching (criss-crossing lines).

Since the glaze stays wet for several minutes before it begins to "skin over," you can correct an error by brushing over the glaze and recombing.

Combing is particularly effective on walls, tables, doors, floors, and other flat surfaces. Be sure the combing design is the correct scale for the surface or room size. For best results, complete a project in one session. The continuity of the color and design work may be difficult to replicate at another time.

Getting Started

1. Base-coat the surface with the color of your choice (see Photo A). This is the color that will show through the combed marks.

Let the base coat thoroughly dry. If you are working on a wall, mask adjacent walls, ceilings, and baseboards to protect them from over-painting.

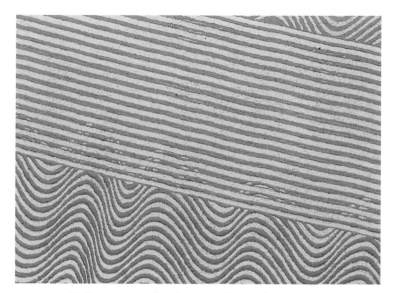

2. For easy application, mix the glazing medium with the paint color of your choice in a paint pan. Follow the manufacturer's instructions for specific mixing ratios and drying times. Apply the colored glazing medium with a roller or an appropriate size brush. If you are working on a large project such as a wall, and the pattern can be worked in squares, complete a section at a time before moving to another section. However, if you are doing straight combing down a wall, it is best to work in narrow, vertical strips.

3. Set the teeth of the comb on the edge of the prepared surface, and drag the comb through the fresh wet glaze without lifting or stopping. Raising the comb will cause an interruption in the combing pattern. Rinse or wipe off the comb after dragging to prevent a buildup of medium and to ensure sharp lines with each pass of the tool (see Photo B).

4. Let the glaze dry thoroughly, then apply several coats of varnish.

Create projects or wall designs by using special tools in various sizes to rake through a coat of wet glaze, revealing the base coat underneath. This technique offers more flexibility and freedom of creativity than many faux finishes.

Photo A

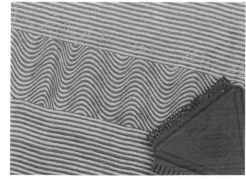

Photo B

Decorating — Combing Techniques

Wood *Graining*

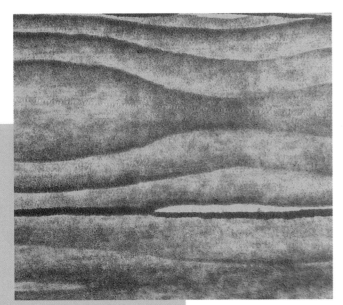

Wood graining was originally

applied to surfaces to produce the

appearance of rare, expensive

woods. Use traditional wood tones

to create believable finishes or

fantasy colors to produce faux moiré

fabric designs.

Wood Graining Basics

If you are working on a large project such as a wall, ask a friend to help you so that one of you can work from the top and the other from the bottom.

Some rockers are made so that they can be removed from the handle and reversed to create a variation in the grain pattern.

Practice and test the pressure needed to create the ideal wood grain before starting the project. Consider using a combing tool in combination with the graining tool to give a more realistic look to the grain. Alternate pulling one or more strips with the graining tool and the comb. Use a soft brush to soften and blend hard lines.

Getting Started

1. Base-coat the project with the color of your choice. Let the base coat dry thoroughly.

2. For easy application, mix the glazing medium with the paint color of your choice in a paint pan. Follow the manufacturer's instructions for specific mixing ratios and drying times. Apply a thin coat of the colored glazing medium with a brush or roller that is the appropriate size for the job (see Photo A). If you are working on a large project such as a wall or door, work in long, narrow sections the length of the surface.

3. While the glaze is wet, pull the wood graining tool through the glaze (see

Photo A

Photo B

Photo B). As you pull, slowly rock the tool back and forth down the entire length of the surface without lifting or stopping. (Raising the graining tool from the surface will cause an interruption in the combing pattern.) Wipe off the graining tool frequently to prevent a buildup of glaze and to ensure sharp graining lines.

4. Let the glaze dry thoroughly, then apply several coats of varnish.

Verdigris *Basics*

As copper and bronze oxidize, a soft turquoise-green color forms on the surface of metal. While verdigris technically only forms on the surface of metal objects, the finish has become so desirable for home decor that it is being replicated on numerous surfaces. These surfaces include wood, metal, clay, plaster, and garden accessories.

Verdigris Basics

Real verdigris is created by rainwater running over the surface of metal, making it look streaked. For this reason, create runny streaks on your project to simulate real verdigris.

Getting Started

1. Use a drop cloth or table cover to protect the floor or table top, since this technique can be messy. Base-coat the surface with a metallic color, such as copper or bronze. Let the paint dry.

2. Mix dark brown paint with water to a runny consistency, and quickly apply the paint with random vertical streaks using a sponge brush (see Photo A). The surface should be in an upright position so that the paint will run.

3. Before the dark brown paint dries, mist it with water and allow the color to run (see Photo B). Use the sponge brush or another appropriate size brush to create additional streaks and runs. Be careful not to get the color too dark.

4. While the surface is still wet, mix a small amount of turquoise paint with water and a small amount of brown paint. Dab the thinned turquoise paint to the top of the wall or project surface with a brush that is the appropriate size for the project. Let the paint run to create additional streaks. Use old cloths or paper towels to soak up excess water at the bottom of the wall. Adjust the colors, adding more turquoise, or if the project begins to get too bright, a small amount of thinned brown paint.

5. Finish with a matte varnish. Refer to the photo, *above left*, for a completed verdigris wall.

Photo A

Photo B

Crackle *Basics*

Under normal circumstances, crackling or crazing occurs when paint and varnish expand and contract as a result of temperature changes. To speed up the process, a variety of crackle mediums have been developed to instantly add years of aging to new finishes.

Crackle Basics

Some crackle mediums produce fine, delicate crackled finishes, and others have a variety of larger, coarse cracks. With some products, a crackle medium is applied over a base coat of paint and allowed to "set." When a coat of paint is applied, the top layer will crack (see the photo at *left*). Other crackle mediums work by cracking the base coat.

Two-part crackle medium (see the photo, *top opposite*) is brushed on top of the base coat. Apply the first step crackle medium and let it "set." Then apply the second step crackle medium over the first. A chemical reaction will occur, causing the top layer of medium to crack. Finish by brushing antiquing medium over the dried surface to emphasize the cracks.

The application method of crackle mediums varies between brands and types. Different degrees of cracking can be obtained by varying the amount of crackle medium and acrylic paint you apply on the surface. The direction the crackle is applied will be the direction of the cracks. Apply the medium horizontally, then brush vertically for even, "eggshell" cracks. To create a more consistent pattern, apply the crackle medium with a sea sponge. The general rule is: The thinner the layer of crackle medium, the finer the cracks; the thicker the crackle medium, the larger the cracks.

It is extremely important that you read all of the instructions on the container before beginning a crackle project. Crackle mediums have different methods of application and drying times that vary from brand to brand. Use the same manufacturer's brand of paint and crackle medium to be assured of compatibility.

Do not brush over previously painted areas or you will smear the paint.

Getting Started

Coarse Crackle – see photo *left*
1. Base-coat the surface with the color of your choice. Remember that the base-coat color will show through the cracks, so be sure to choose two colors that will create a pleasing combination. Let the base coat dry thoroughly.

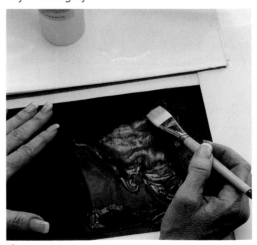

Photo A

2. Follow the manufacturer's instructions for applying the crackle medium (see Photo A, *opposite*). Remember that the direction of the brushstrokes will be the direction of the cracks.

3. Allow the medium to dry for the suggested period of time, according to the instructions. Working quickly, apply a coat of paint over the crackle medium. The cracks will begin to appear within minutes (see photo, *top opposite*). Let the paint dry thoroughly, sand lightly with 150-grit sandpaper, and wipe off the sanding dust. Apply several coats of spray varnish.

Eggshell Crackle – see photo *right*

Eggshell crackle is generally a two-step process, making it necessary to purchase two bottles of crackle or a kit (usually step 1 and step 2) to make this technique work.

You will need to apply an antiquing medium or a gold metallic paint mixed with a glazing medium to make the fine cracks more visible.

1. Base-coat the surface, and apply any designs such as decorative painting or decoupage papers to the surface.

2. Apply step 1 crackle following the manufacturer's instructions (see Photo B). Let it dry.

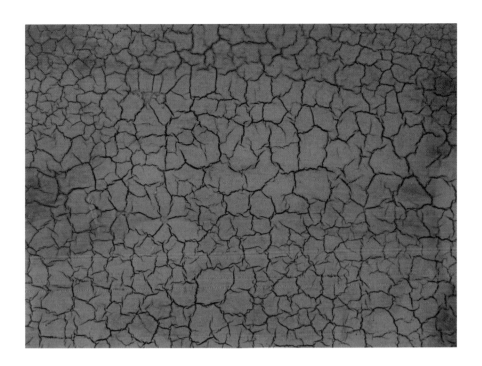

3. Apply step 2 crackle following the manufacturer's instructions (it will look the same as Photo B, since both mediums are clear).

4. As the crackle dries, cracks will begin to form. Let it dry according to the

manufacturer's instructions, and apply an antiquing medium or a gold-colored finish to enhance the cracks (see Photo C). Refer to Antiquing and Distressing, page 214.

Photo B

Photo C

Dragging *(Strié)*

Photo A

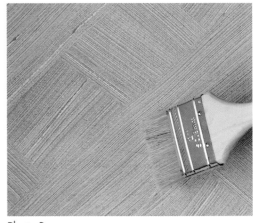

Photo B

Also known as strié (pronounced stree-ay), the word means to create a soft, irregular stripe with obvious graining by dragging a brush with stiff bristles through a colored glaze.

Dragging Basics

Dragging requires a fairly steady hand, some speed, and possibly the help of another person if you are creating strié on walls. For straight line stripes running down a wall, attach a plumb line from the ceiling and slightly in front of the wall. Drag the brush down the wall alongside the plumb line. Since it is necessary to drag the brush in one continuous stripe down a wall, one person should stand on a ladder and the other person on the floor.

Begin the stripe at the ceiling. Continue down the wall with the person on the ladder, handing the brush to the person on the floor without lifting or interrupting the brush pattern. This will take some practice and team coordination. Use painter's tape on the wall to guide you with designs such as crosshatching, where the grain runs at a 45-degree angle to the ceiling. Work one section following the line of the tape, then remove the tape and move to the next section.

Getting Started

1. Base-coat the project surface with the color of your choice. Remember that the base-coat color will show through the glaze and affect the overall look of the finish. Be sure to choose a base-coat and glaze color that will create a pleasing combination. Let the base coat dry thoroughly.

2. For easy application, mix the glazing medium with the paint color of your choice in a paint pan. Follow the manufacturer's instructions for specific mixing ratios and drying times. Use painter's tape around the ceiling and baseboards or other areas that need to be protected. Apply the colored glaze medium with a brush or paint roller of the appropriate size (see Photo A). If you are working on a large project such as a wall, and the pattern can be worked in squares or long rectangles, complete a section at a time before moving to another section.

3. Use a French brush or dragging brush to create the desired pattern (see Photo B). If you are working on a furniture piece, let the paint dry for the recommended time, then apply several coats of varnish. Walls do not need varnishing (see the finished example, *above left*).

Rag *Rolling*

Create interesting textures with this simple technique. All you'll need to get started is fabric for rolling, glazing medium, and paint.

Rag Rolling

The term ragging encompasses several different techniques. Two of the methods are similar to sponging, although the end results are very different. Both methods use a rag rolled into a ball. With one method, ragging on, you apply glaze to the surface with a dabbing or rolling motion. With the other method, ragging off, you remove the glaze using the same type of motion.

The third method is rag rolling, which requires the rag to be folded into a "sausage" shape, twisted as though you were wringing it out, and rolled across the wall or surface. The pattern created tends to be more linear and controlled than the first two techniques.

Rag Rolling Basics

The fiber content of the rags will determine the degree of texture you create. Fabrics such as cheesecloth, burlap, t-shirt material, or old sheeting material work well. Try to avoid fabrics that contain synthetic fibers, since they will not absorb the glaze. Fabrics with cotton fiber content work the best. Avoid fabrics that fray or lint.

Getting Started

1. Base-coat the surface with the color of your choice. Remember that the base-coat color will show through the glaze and affect

Photo A

the overall look of the finish. Be sure to choose a base-coat and glaze color that will create a pleasing combination. More than one glaze color can be used, if desired. Let the base coat dry thoroughly.

2. For easy application, mix the glazing medium with the paint color of your choice in a paint pan. Follow the manufacturer's instructions for specific mixing ratios and drying times. Use painter's tape around the ceiling and baseboards or other areas that need to be protected.

3. Cut several rectangular pieces of fabric about 2×3 feet. Thoroughly wet a rag with the glazing mixture. Fold the rag into a "sausage" shape, and twist it to wring out the excess glaze. Be sure the glaze has been distributed throughout the rag.

4. Hold the rag at both ends and begin rolling it across the surface, making sure the rag remains twisted (see Photo A). Be sure to maintain an even pressure while rolling. When the texture becomes less defined, it is time to reload the rag with glaze. Follow the procedure as described. When the glaze begins to dry on the rag, dispose of it and use a new piece of cloth.

5. Completely rag roll the surface using the first color. If you plan to use a second color, let the first glaze dry, then follow steps 2 through 4 for applying additional colors (see the finished example, *above left*).

Sponging

Sponging on is the easiest faux finish technique to do. To sponge on a faux finish, use a natural sea sponge, pick up one or more colors of glaze, and dab it on the wall to create interesting texture and color. This method will make a slightly stronger design than stippling.

Sponging Basics

Test the color combinations you have chosen before starting your project. Similar colors look better together. Apply the darkest color first and work up to the lightest.

Use a natural sea sponge, paying careful attention to the holes and protrusions in the sponge, since this will determine the surface design.

Be careful not to rotate the sponge while it is still in contact with the surface. It will smear the design.

To get into tight areas or corners, tear off a small section of the sponge.

Periodically step back from the surface to look for areas that need additional sponging. Strive for a consistent pattern.

Getting Started

1. Base-coat the surface with the color of your choice. Remember that the base-coat color will show through the glaze and affect the overall look of the finish. Be sure to choose a base-coat and glaze color that will create a pleasing combination. More than one glaze color can be used, if desired. Let the base coat dry thoroughly.

2. For easy application, mix the glazing medium with the paint color of your choice in a paint pan. Follow the manufacturer's instructions for specific mixing ratios and drying times. Use painter's tape around the ceiling and baseboards, or other areas that need to be protected.

3. Dampen the sponge with water, then squeeze it dry. Dip the sponge into the glaze mixture , squeeze out the excess, and blot it on a piece of paper. Working in areas of about 3×3 feet, sponge using a pouncing motion. To create a random design, lift the sponge away from the surface, rotate, then touch the surface (see Photo A). Continue until the entire surface has been sponged. Varnish if desired (see the finished sponged example, *above left*).

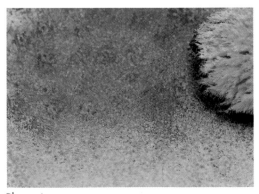

Photo A

Stippling *Techniques*

Create a subtle suede-like texture on walls using a glazing medium and a stippling brush. This is one of the most subtle faux finish techniques, often used on furniture in combination with more dominant designs. Because of the understated nature of this finish, it is ideal for people who prefer less dramatic statements in their home decor.

Stippling Basics

Stippling brushes are available in a variety of sizes and shapes. Buy the largest one you can afford, since small brushes mean double the work. Use a stencil brush to get into tight corners.

Stippling is a great way to produce shaded color without definite texture or design.

Keep the glaze thin unless you want texture. More texture can be created by adding fine sand.

Getting Started

1. Base-coat the surface with the color of your choice. Remember that the base-coat color will show through the glaze and affect the overall look of the finish. Be sure to choose a base-coat and glaze color that will create a pleasing combination. More than one glaze color can be used, if desired. Let the base coat dry thoroughly.

2. Mix the glazing medium with the color of your choice, following the manufacturer's instructions. Use painter's tape around the ceiling and baseboards, or other areas that need to be protected.

3. Using a pouncing or tapping motion, apply the colored glaze medium with the stippling brush (see Photo A). You should be leaving a fine bristle design in the wet glaze. Be sure to pounce the bristles flat on the surface so that full contact is made with the brush. Let the paint dry (see the finished sponged example, *above left*).

Photo A

Stenciling

Dress up your home and furniture with simple or elaborate multi-layer stencil designs. Even a beginner can accomplish pleasing results by following these easy techniques.

Tools and Materials

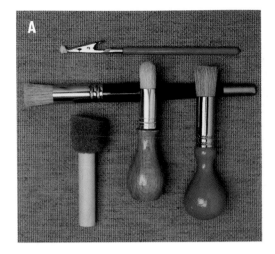

Brushes – A

A variety of stencil brushes and sponges are available to fit everyone's needs. Some have long slender handles, while others have rounded handles to prevent tiring of the hand. The common feature of most stencil brushes is the flat part of the bristles or sponge that comes in contact with the surface. An unusual stenciling tool is a long slender handle with a clip on the end to hold a tiny piece of sponge that helps to access hard-to-reach areas.

Brush Cleaner – B

Use a brush cleaner to remove the paint from your brushes and keep them in good condition.

Stencil Paint – C

Use water-base acrylic paint for stenciling or one of the specially formulated stencil paints. Gel stencil paint is thick, does not run, has adequate open or working time, and cleans up with water. Stencil cremes have a lipstick-like consistency that can be cleaned up with soap and water.

Stencil Adhesive and Painter's Tape – D

Use stencil adhesive or painter's tape to secure your stencil to a surface to prevent it from slipping. Adhesives are available in a liquid applicator or a spray can.

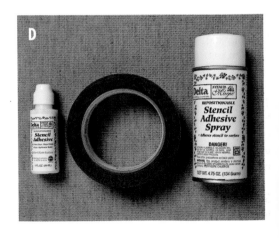

Stencil Basics

Consider creating your own stencil by drawing inspiration from wallpaper, fabric designs, prints in books, or clip art. Purchase stencil acetate at your local Jo-Ann Store. The best stencil material is glossy on one side and frosted on the other. Less paint will stick on the glossy side, and the frosted side will provide better adhesion.

To cut your own stencil, tape the edges of stencil film to a piece of glass and place your pattern under the glass. Use an X-ACTO knife, crafts knife, or electric stencil-cutting tool for cutting the design.

It is best to use a different stencil sponge or brush for each color; washing applicators between paint colors leaves moisture in the brush or sponge and tends to thin the paint.

Successful stenciling depends on the care you use in loading the brush with paint. It is important to fill the brush and apply the paint properly. If you are using liquid acrylic paint, pick up paint on the brush, work it into the bristles using a rotating motion, and then tap most of the paint off on a paper towel. It is better to apply less paint and have to add more, than to apply too much. Overloading the brush causes paint to seep under the stencil, which will ruin the image. Gel and stencil creme paints are less likely to seep under the stencil, but a buildup will accumulate around the edge of the design if the brush is overloaded.

The method of application is different for liquid paints and stencil cremes. A tapping or pouncing "up-and-down" motion is used with liquid paints; a rotating or circular motion should be used with stencil cremes.

Some stencils have openings so close together that it may be difficult to prevent

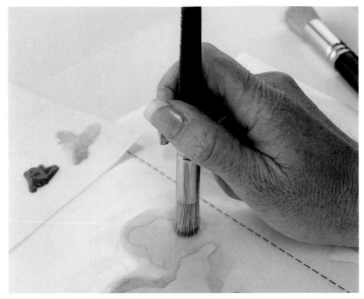

Photo A

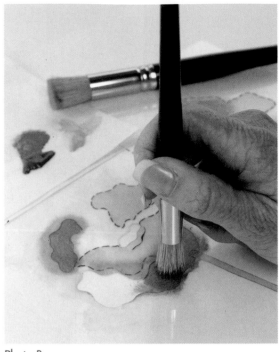

Photo B

Photo C

the paint from creeping into adjacent areas. Prevent this from happening by placing a small piece of tape (called masking) over the surrounding area.

Hold the stencil brush or sponge in an upright or 90 degree position when stenciling.

Getting Started

Multi-Layer Stenciling

Today, multi-layer stencils are available in many trendy and sophisticated designs. While stencils with several layers can be a challenge, the stunning results are well worth the effort (refer to the photo on page 225).

1. Base-coat the surface with the color of your choice. Study the stencil layers to determine the order in which they will be painted. Most multi-layer stencils have letters or numbers indicating the order; some also have dotted lines that help with placement by outlining the design from the previous layer. Many stencils have tiny holes in the corners; place a pencil mark at the location of the hole and line up the next layer with the mark.

2. Apply a stencil adhesive or tape. The first layer uses a light color which acts as a highlight on the flowers (see Photo A). Paint the first layer, following all directions on the stencil and paint packaging.

3. Remove the first stencil layer, then allow the paint to dry for a few minutes before applying the next stencil layer. Place the second layer over the design. Notice that the black dotted lines are placed over the previously stenciled areas as a guide for the proper placement (see Photo B). Apply the desired colors.

4. Remove the second stencil layer, allow the paint to dry, and line up the third stencil layer (see Photo C). Apply the desired colors and carefully remove the last layer. Allow the paint to dry completely, then varnish to protect the colors.
Note: *It is not necessary to varnish designs stenciled on walls unless they will be cleaned often, such as in a kitchen.*

Photo D

Photo E

Single-Layer Rose – Light background

1. Base-coat the surface with the color of your choice. Affix the stencil to the surface using a stencil adhesive or tape.

2. Apply the colors of your choice, using the appropriate method of application for the type of paint you are using (see Stencil Basics, page 225). The colors should be in a mid-value color range (see Color Theory, page 190), since darker colors for shading will be applied later (see Photo D). Let the paint dry.

3. Keeping the stencil in place, add darker colors to create the shading (see Photo E). To create highlights (the lightest value on your stenciling), use a lighter color than the mid-value color. Carefully stencil this lighter color on top of the color already in place.

4. Remove the stencil and allow the paint to dry. If you are using stencil creme, let it dry for at least 24–48 hours before varnishing. If the paint has been heavily applied to a glossy surface, let the paint dry for up to 10 days.

227 ✿

Photo A

Photo B

Single-Layer Rose – Black background
If you are working on a black or dark background, the stencil colors will be much clearer and brighter if the stencil design is first painted white.

1. Base-coat the surface with the dark color of your choice. Affix the stencil to the surface using a stencil adhesive or tape.

2. Stencil the entire design area with white paint and allow it to dry (see Photo A). *Note: If you are using stencil creme, it is not necessary to let the paint dry.*

3. Blend the colors of your choice into the white stencil creme (see Photo B). Follow the steps for the Single-Layer Rose (light background) beginning with Step 2,

page 227. If you are using acrylic paint, stipple on top of the dried paint with your chosen colors.

Photo C

Photo D

Photo E

Dimensional Stenciling

Use dimensional stenciling to add texture, relief, and dimension to a wall.

1. Base-coat the surface with the color of your choice. Choose a single-layer stencil with fairly large openings (it is best not to use stencils with multiple layers or a small, intricate design). Affix the stencil to the surface using a stencil adhesive or tape. Using a light modeling or texture paste, apply the paste with a palette or spackling knife. The surface of the paste should be as smooth as possible (see Photo C).

2. Slowly and carefully lift the stencil so that the texture paste is not disturbed, and allow it to dry (see Photo D).

3. Paint the dimensional stencil with the colors of your choice (see Photo E).

HOME DECOR
SEWING

Custom window treatments, made-to-fit slipcovers,

linens for your bed and table, and

clever accessories for the home can be yours

by learning the following techniques.

Decorate your home in style

when you use these simple sewing

instructions, beautiful fabrics,

and handsome trims

to embellish every room

in your living space.

Tools *and Materials*

Although some tools are specific to home decor sewing projects, many of them are used in fashion sewing and quilting. Refer to pages 232 and 272 for additional descriptions of sewing tools and materials.

Heading Tape – not shown

Ready-made heading tape is made with cords running through heavy, stiff material that is sewn to curtain headers and valances. The cording is pulled from both ends of the tape to make gathers and pleats. Choose from pencil pleating or triple pleating for the style you prefer.

Hook-and-Loop Tape – C

Commonly known as Velcro®, this tape has two strips—one with tiny hooks, the other with looped pile. The strips mesh to hold in place when pressed together. It works well for attaching items to a wall, cornice, furniture, or header boards.

Marking Pens and Pencils – D

Test marking tools on fabric scraps before using them on fabric. Use specially designed temporary (air, water soluble, or erasable) pencils and pens to mark seam allowances, measurements, and much more.

Mats – E

Thick self-healing cutting mats are used with rotary cutters to protect surfaces and to keep fabric from shifting during cutting.

Measuring Tools – not shown

Use a metal measuring tape to measure large areas. A soft dressmaker's tape works well for smaller areas or for round and curved objects.

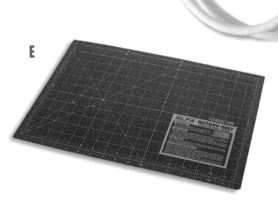

Batting – A

Batting is used to add bulk and padding to cornices, headboards, and quilted items.

Cording – not shown

Cording is available in several sizes and can be purchased by the yard. It is generally used to make piping.

Fray Stop – B

Use fray preventative products to stop fabrics from fraying on a cut edge. It also is ideal for buttonholes.

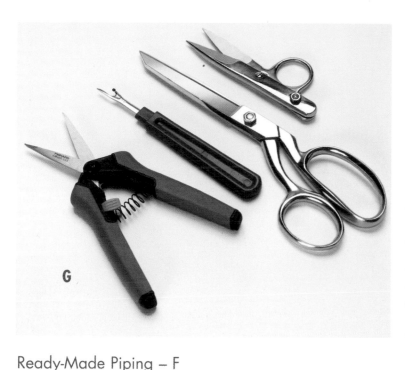

Staple Gun – J
The staple gun is used to attach fabric and batting to wooden items such as furniture frames, headboards, and cornices.

Zippers – not shown
Zippers create an ideal opening and closure in a seam and allow for insertion and removal of pillow forms or comforters.

Glues have become a quick and popular way to permanently fasten fabrics together without sewing. In most cases, however, fabric glues cannot be used on lightweight or sheer fabrics because they will either show or stain. Glues can be messy looking, so be sure they will be hidden from view in the finished project.

Getting Started

Snaps
Individual snaps work as closures, to fasten trim to the body of a project, or to hold two or more fabric segments together. Place the ball (raised) part of the snap against the right side of the item and the socket (indented) side to the wrong side of the project. Sew the snap to the fabric through each hole, knotting and cutting the thread between holes. Sew the ball end in place first, then align the pieces (see Diagram A). Slip a pin through the hole in the end of the snap to mark the placement of the socket end of the snap.

Ready-Made Piping – F
The cording is covered with bias-cut piping. Available in numerous colors and sizes, piping is used to accent seams and embellish many home decor items, such as pillows, duvets, bedspreads, and upholstered furniture.

Scissors and Clippers – G
Choose from a variety of specialty scissors, such as spring-action clippers, seam rippers, shears, and thread snippers. Each cuts threads and fabrics with a minimum of effort. Keep blades sharp by using them only on fabrics and threads.

Snap Fasteners – H
Available in numerous sizes, snaps are suitable for closing cushions, covers, and pillows.

Snap Tape – I
Snap tape has snaps along the length of two strips of tape to sew on each side of the fabric. It is ideal for use as a closure on pillows and cushions. Snap tape can be purchased in small packaged quantities or by the yard.

Fastener Basics

Use fasteners for home decor coverings to easily remove pillows and comforters and to launder the covers. Some are better suited for certain weights of fabric than others. For example, heavyweight fabrics, such as canvas, call for grommets, large snaps, or extra-strong hook-and-loop tape. Small snaps, snap tape, or hook-and-loop dots work better on lightweight materials.

Snaps are available in a wide variety of sizes. Consider use, because they pull apart with moderate strain. Once relegated to awnings and other utilitarian objects, grommets are now a home-decorating trim used to lace fabrics together or in place of buttonholes at the top of draperies and shower curtains.

Home Decor – Tools and Materials

Diagram A

To use snap tape, position it so that the ball of the snap is first attached to the fabric. Align the socket section. Sew along both lines of the tape, using a zipper foot if necessary (see Diagram B).

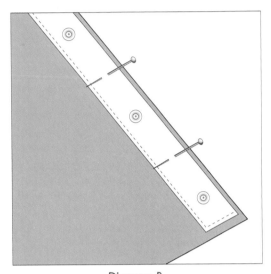

Diagram B

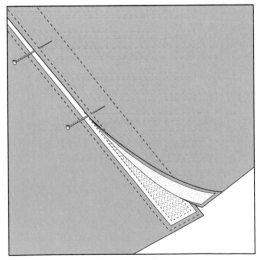

Diagram C

Grommets

Grommets are two separate pieces—a male piece with a shank and a flat female piece (see the photo *above*).

The fabric is cut or snipped slightly, inserted between the grommet pieces, and the grommets are permanently joined. The basic methods of joining grommets are with grommet pliers or a grommet tool and hammer.

Hook and Loop Tape

Hook-and-loop tape (commonly known as Velcro®) seals openings tightly, holds skirts and valances to headers, or adheres trims that can be removed to launder a project. It is available in different weights and widths, in sew-in and self-adhesive styles, and in spots, squares, and by the yard. Always read the label carefully and follow the manufacturer's directions for usage. Sewing through self-adhesive hook-and-loop tape can gum up a sewing machine needle and bobbin case. If only one side of the project will be laundered, place the soft loop side of the hook-and-loop tape on that section to help prevent snags (see Diagram C).

Glues

Hotmelt adhesive (also known as hot glue) is often recommended for home-decorating projects, although it may not be the best choice. Hot glue often dries with a slight ridge, can soften and melt when exposed to high heat or direct sunlight, and cracks and peels when it becomes cold. Look for fabric and specialty glues instead. Read the labels and choose the glue that matches your needs most closely. Check for washability, dry cleaning instructions, color when dry, flexibility, permanence, and material compatibility.

Bias Basics

Determine the width of the bias strips, allowing for seam allowances, then determine the length needed. To join bias strips, include the additional fabric needed for seam allowances.

Getting Started

Cutting Bias Strips

1. Fold the fabric diagonally to match two straight raw edges. The diagonal fold line will be the true bias, which is a 45-degree

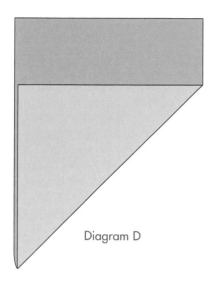

Diagram D

Diagram E

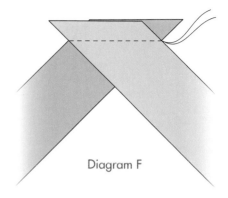

Diagram F

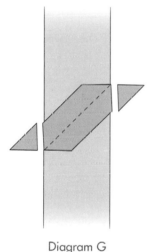

Diagram G

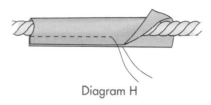

Diagram H

angle to both the lengthwise and crosswise grains (see Diagram D). Press the fold. There are rulers available to make marking and cutting bias strips easier and quicker.

2. Using a fabric marker and a long ruler, mark bias strips parallel to the bias fold line (see Diagram E). Cut the bias strips using a ruler, mat, and rotary cutter or scissors.

3. To join several strips for the length needed, place the strips right sides together at right angles and stitch (see Diagram F).

4. When the two strips are joined, press the seam open. Two small triangles of fabric will

extend beyond the fabric edges; trim them off (see Diagram G). Trim the seam allowance, if needed.

Piping Basics

Follow the instructions *above* to cut bias strips to make piping. Purchased cording is available in several sizes. Cut bias strips wide enough to cover the cording and to have enough fabric for a ⅜-inch seam allowance.

Getting Started

1. Fold the bias strip in half lengthwise with the right side of the fabric out. Slide the cording between the layers of fabric and against the fold. Pin the fabric edges together, encasing the cording. Using a zipper foot or piping foot attachment, sew the fabric layers together. The stitching should tightly encase the cording (see Diagram H). Do not trim the seam

allowance because it will be used to attach the piping to your project.

2. Cut self-made or purchased piping 2 to 3 inches longer than the dimension of the project. Place the piping on the right side of the decorator fabric aligning the seamline of the piping and the seamline of the project. The raw cut edge of the piping should align with the raw edge of the decorator fabric, and the rounded side of the piping should face toward the center of the project. Pin and baste the piping in place using a basting stitch and a zipper foot or piping foot. (Special sewing machine feet allow for closer stitching to the cording.)

3. Pin the backing or lining fabric to the decorator fabric, right sides facing and raw edges aligned. The piping will be inserted between the fabrics. Using a zipper foot or piping foot, sew along the seamline through all fabric layers. When sewing piping around all sides of a project that requires turning, such as a pillow, leave an opening.

4. Turn the project to the right side. If the project requires stuffing, insert the pillow form, cushion, or other filler through the opening and work it into the corners. Slip-stitch the opening closed.

Comforters *and Duvets*

Half the fun of owning a soft, fluffy down comforter or duvet is being able to switch the shell and change the look of the whole room. Because of the simple construction, a project can be made in a single day.

Comforter and Spread Basics

For most comforters or bedspreads, standard-size fabric is not wide enough to accommodate the width of a bed. You'll need to add side panels to increase the width. Do not piece the cover down the center; add a panel to each side instead.

To make the side panels, cut a second panel of fabric the same length as the first. Divide this panel in half, cutting the halves to the necessary width plus the seam allowances. The process of joining side panels is similar to making a tablecloth (see page 258, Diagram A), for an example. Be sure to match the patterns as necessary. For example, if the comforter needs to be 86 inches wide and the fabric is 54 inches wide (53 inches of usable fabric; 1 inch will be seam allowances), an additional 33 inches will be needed. Divide 33 into two panels of 16½ inches each and add 1 inch for seam allowances. The side panels will each measure 17½ inches before stitching. Cut the backing fabric in the same manner for the center and side panels.

To determine the yardage needed for a comforter, measure the width and length of the bed, and overlap the sides of the bed by 10 to 12 inches. If you make a bedspread, measure it in the same way, with the overlap on the sides of the bed measured to the floor.

If the top and lining fabrics are the same, double the yardage for the comforter plus ¼ yard; add 2 inches for each side. If the top and lining fabrics are different, add the additional measurements to the top and separate lining fabric as indicated. The additional allowances are for seams and the hems.

To determine the amount of cording needed, measure the perimeter of the comforter or spread. Add 2 inches for securing the ends. To make matching piping, refer to Bias Binding and Piping on page 235.

Getting Started

Making a Comforter or Spread

1. Refer to Diagram A on page 238 to make a comforter or spread. Cut a center panel the necessary length, adding the seam allowances. Cut the side panels plus seam allowance and hems.

2. Right sides together, match the long raw edges of the center and side panels. Pin and stitch, using a ⅝-inch seam allowance. Open the seams and press. Repeat for the lining.

3. Pin the cording to the right side of the comforter or bedspread as seen in Diagram A on page 238. Machine baste in place using a zipper foot to stitch close to the cording. Tuck the ends of the cording into the seam to prevent fraying.

4. Pin the front and back together with right sides facing and the raw edges matching. Stitch around three sides using a zipper foot. Trim the seams and turn right side out.

5. Insert a down comforter or synthetic filling, tucking it into the corners and smoothing out lumps or wrinkles. For a bedspread, baste quilt batting to the wrong side of the back piece before sewing the front to the back. If desired, spot-tack the batting in place with fabric glue before basting the edges. Trim the batting from the seam allowances before turning.

6. Turn in the seam allowance at the top, and close the opening by hand-stitching or machine topstitching with the zipper foot.

Make a Duvet

Duvets are made similar to large pillowcases, with a down comforter or filling tucked inside. Unlike closed comforters and bedspreads, duvets are not permanently sewn closed, so the filling can be removed and the cover laundered.

Getting Started

1. To make a duvet with a flap (see Diagram B), determine the yardage needed by measuring the length of the cover, doubling the measurement, and adding 16 inches for the flap and seam allowances. Measure the width, which should include a 10- to 12-inch drop on the sides, plus seam allowances of ⅝ inch for each side. Cut top and bottom panels for the duvet, with the lower panel having the additional 16 inches for the flap.

For most duvets, standard-size fabric is not wide enough to accommodate the width of

a bed. You will need to add side panels. Do not piece the duvet down the center; add a panel to each side instead. The process of joining side panels is similar to making a tablecloth (see page 258, Diagram A), for an example.

2. To hem the duvet opening on the side with buttons, turn under ¼-inch hem and press. Then turn up 1 inch, press, pin, and stitch.

3. To hem the duvet flap, turn under ½ inch, press; then turn under 1½ inches, press, pin, and stitch.

4. Right sides facing, pin and stitch the duvet cover together on three sides. The flap should extend about 14 inches beyond the duvet opening (see Diagram B). Turn right side out and press.

5. Create small hems on both sides of the flap by turning under ¼ inch, pressing, then turning ¼ inch and stitching. Fold the flap up over the top of the duvet and press. Pin the flap in place.

6. Determine and mark the button and buttonhole placements. Make the buttonholes (see page 346–347) and attach the buttons.

Option: To finish the duvet with ties (see Diagram C), cut a 3-inch wide facing, long enough to go around the top of the duvet, plus the seam allowance. Hem one side of the facing and join the ends of the facing. Follow the instructions for making pillow ties on page 243. Pin the ties to the right side of the duvet fabric, evenly spacing them across the duvet and aligning the raw edges with the duvet. Pin and sew the facing to the duvet, ties inserted between the duvet and the facing.

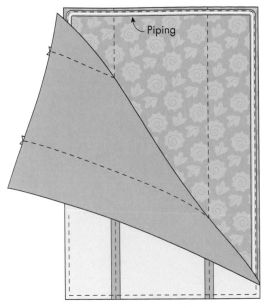

Diagram A

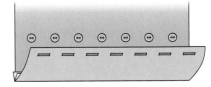

Diagram B

Diagram C

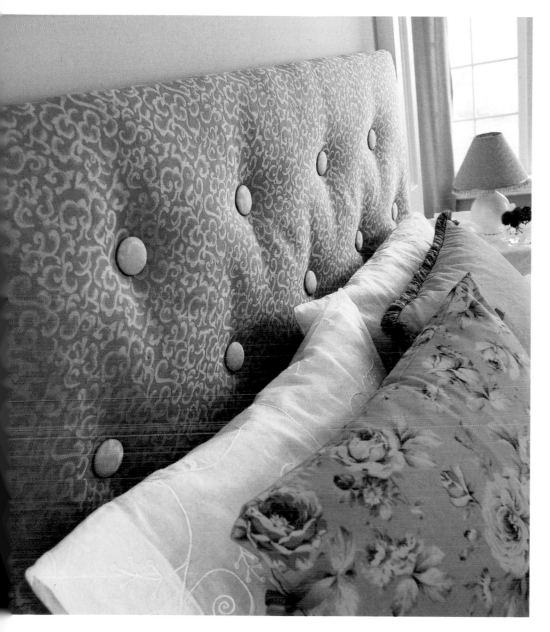

Covered
Headboard

An upholstered headboard
tufted with hand-covered
buttons is the perfect focal
point for any bedroom.
Choose a matching or
coordinating decorator fabric
along with contrasting buttons
to tie the entire bedding
ensemble together.

⊱Creative Tip

*Different thicknesses of batting can
be used when padding a headboard.
Before positioning the batting,
spray the surface of the headboard with
repositionable spray adhesive.
The adhesive secures the batting in place
while wrapping and stapling the batting edges
to the back.*

– Team Member, Hudson, Ohio

Headboard Basics

To determine the size of the headboard,
measure the width of your bed frame.
Calculate how tall you want the headboard
to be by measuring from the top of the
mattress to this point. Cut ½-inch plywood
to the size of the headboard measurement.

Note: *The headboard measurement
for the full-size bed shown, above, is
56×32 inches to accommodate a
54-inch-wide mattress.*

Determine the length of the legs by
measuring from the floor to the top of
the mattress and adding 25 inches.

(This measurement is for a 32-inch-tall headboard. For a taller headboard, add height so that the legs are within 5 inches of the top of the headboard.) Using this measurement, cut two legs from 1×4-inch lumber.

Drill four evenly spaced holes in the upper part of the legs (see Diagram A for screw placement) and attach the legs to the headboard with wood screws. Also determine the placement and drill the holes where the headboard attaches to the bed frame.

Determine button placement holes, then mark the placement on the back of the headboard. Drill small pilot holes through the headboard at these locations.

Getting Started

Make the wooden headboard as described above. To figure the size of the headboard fabric, use the dimensions of the headboard and add 8 inches of fabric to each side for plenty of fabric to wrap and staple to the back.

1. Cut three layers of lofty polyester batting to fit the headboard, adding 4 inches for wrapping around each side. Wrap the batting over the headboard and to the back, cutting around the legs as needed. Staple the batting to the back of the headboard with a staple gun that uses ½ inch staples (see Diagram A).

2. Stand the headboard upright, with the back toward you. Lay the fabric over the batting to cover the front (right side out) and wrap over the top of the headboard. Turn under the top raw edge ½ inch and staple it in place with the staple gun. Continue stapling the fabric to the headboard all the way across the top.

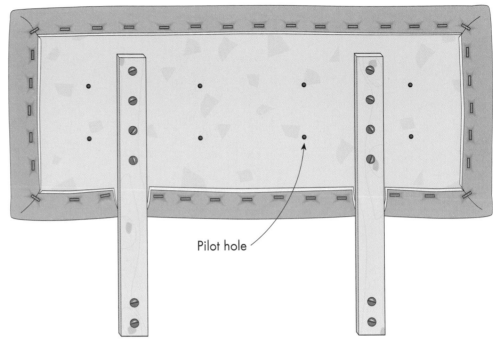

Pilot hole

Diagram A

3. Lay the headboard front down. Pull the fabric taut around the remaining three sides, wrapping the fabric to the back. Turn under a ½-inch raw edge and staple. The amount of fabric pulled to the back is determined by the thickness of batting on the front. Adjust as needed. Clip around the legs as needed, and continue stapling across the back in both directions.

Periodically look at the front of the headboard to make sure that the fabric is evenly pulled and stretched to avoid distorting the pattern. The fabric should be tight, but allow give so that the fabric will tuft when the buttons are attached.

4. Cover 12 buttons with a coordinating fabric; refer to Covering Buttons on page 346.

5. Thread 22-gauge wire in an upholstery needle. Push the needle through the button hole from the back and out through the fabric in front. Slide the button shank onto the wire at the front, then back through the hole. Before pulling the button tight, place a dot of fray-check liquid on the fabric where the wires enter and exit the fabric. Pull the wire tightly to the back, twisting the wire firmly to hold it in place. Clip off excess wire.

6. Place the headboard against the bed frame. Using bolts, attach the legs of the headboard to pre-existing holes in the bed frame.

Bed *Skirt*

A bed skirt made to match bedding provides a completely finished look to the bedroom. Add a contrasting border, as shown here, or stitch a ruffle using one fabric.

Dust Skirt Basics

If you prefer a tailored look, substitute pleats for gathers; or use flat panels of fabric with inverted pleats at each corner to add fullness around the curve. Both pleated and flat panels hang better without a contrasting border or lining. A 1¼-inch hem works best for these skirts in a fabric with medium body and crispness.

Getting Started

1. Measure the top of the springs. Cut a piece of heavy lining fabric this size, adding ½-inch seam allowances to all sides. This will form the fabric top that fits between the mattress and box springs.

2. For the skirt, measure line A and line B as shown, *right*. For a bed that is placed against the wall, such as a day bed, or one that has a headboard to the floor, determine the total fabric measurement by adding two of measurement A, 1 of measurement B, plus 12 inches. This will allow the skirt to wrap around the corners of the bed at the headboard.

For a bed that can be viewed from all sides, add two of measurement A and two of measurement B.

When you have determined the A and B measurements, multiply by 2½ to figure the length of the skirt strip. (Use this figure if you plan to add a trim to the bottom of the skirt.) For the depth (measurement C in the diagram, *right*), measure from the top edge of the box springs to the floor; for a skirt

without a border, add 1¼ inches for the hem. To hem the skirt without a border, turn under ¼ inch, press, then turn under another 1 inch and stitch.

If the skirt has a border as shown *above*, use two measurements—one for the depth of the skirt and one for the depth of the border. Add ⅝ inch for a seam allowance for the skirt (top and bottom edges), ⅝ inch for the border seam allowance and 1¼ inches for the border hem. Cut the border strips, piecing them for the length of the skirt. To hem the border, turn under ¼ inch, press, then turn under another 1 inch, and stitch.

3. For a skirt with a border, sew the border to the skirt. Finish the seam as desired to prevent fraying (see Seams and Finishes on page 348). Finish the ends of the skirt with a simple hem.

4. To gather the skirt, run two sets of gathering threads along the top edge, ½ inch

from the raw edge. Gently pull the threads to gather until the skirt fits the liner fabric cut in Step 1.

5. To evenly balance the gathers, fold the skirt in half, then in half again. Adjust the gathers in each quarter section of the skirt. Unfold and pin the skirt to the liner. The skirt should wrap around the front corners at the head of the bed about 6 inches on each side (see the diagram *below*).

6. With right sides together, stitch the skirt to the liner with a ⅝-inch seam.

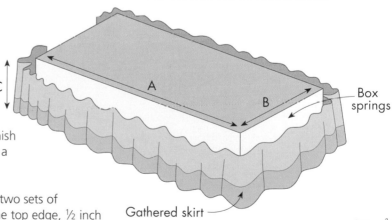

C

A

B

Box springs

Gathered skirt

241

Elegant
Pillows

Whether tossed on the bed, strategically lined up on the sofa, or used to soften a chair, pillows are the perfect accessories for adding interesting shapes and personality to a room.

Pillow Basics

When choosing pillow fabrics, consider the way in which the pillow will be used. This will help to determine the type of fabric, the style (relaxed or formal), whether the material is washable, and if the pillow should have a removable cover to be laundered.

Choose the right style of pillow for your room decor. Formal or traditional furniture calls for tailored pillows, while pillows with ruffles create a soft, feminine effect. Use pillows to tie color schemes together, color-coordinate pillows to walls and

furnishings, or to enhance neutral color sofas and chairs. A variety of pillow shapes with coordinating fabric will add interest to a sofa or bed.

Choose filling by the desired decorative effect and how the pillow will be used. Fiberfill, made of polyester or acrylic, is a popular filling and is fully washable when stuffed in a fabric liner. Pillows should have an inner lining that holds the filler so that the cover can be removed to launder.

Tightly pack fiberfill to prevent lumps. Kapok is made from vegetable fiber and works well for cushions and pillows, but it cannot be laundered. The combination of feather and down stuffing is less expensive than pure down. Feathers require a casing made of tightly woven fabric, such as ticking, and must be sewn with French seams to prevent feathers from poking through.

Getting Started

Tucked-and-Tied Pillow

1. Measure the dimensions of the pillow panels and add ⅝ inch all around for seam allowances. Cut out the panels.

Cut two facings. One should be 7½ inches long and the same width as the pillow plus a ⅝-inch seam allowance. The second facing is 3 inches long and the width of the pillow plus the seam allowance.

If ribbon ties will be used, cut 1⅓ yards of ribbon into four pieces (for two bows).

2. To make fabric ties, cut four strips 6×12 inches each. Fold each fabric strip in half lengthwise, right sides facing, and raw edges aligned. Sew along one short side and the long raw edge, using a ¼-inch seam allowance. Trim the seams, turn right side out, and press.

3. Lay the front and back pillow panels right sides up. Pin two ties on the right side of each panel, evenly spacing the ties across the pillow opening and matching the raw edges. The ties should face toward the center of the pillow. Pin and baste the ties in place along the raw edges (see Diagram A).

4. Hem each facing by turning under the edge ¼ inch, press, turn under another ¼ inch, and topstitch (see page 326).

Pin the narrow facing to the tie edge of one panel, right sides together, matching the raw edges.

Insert the ties between the facings and the panels (see Diagrams B and C). Stitch the facings to the panels using a ½-inch seam allowance. Trim the seam, press, and turn the facings to the back of each panel.

5. To sew the cover together, open out the wider facing (this becomes the flap) and pin the panels right sides together. The narrow facing remains turned back with the ends stitched into the seam. Stitch the three sides using a ½-inch seam allowance (see Diagram D). Trim the corners.

6. Turn the pillow cover right side out and press. Turn under the edges of the flap ¼ inch to form a hem, then turn another ¼ inch, press, and stitch (see Diagram E).

7. Insert the pillow form into the cover. Tuck in the lower flap to cover the pillow form (see Photo E). Tie the ribbons or ties, allowing some of the flap to show on the end (see the photo *opposite*).

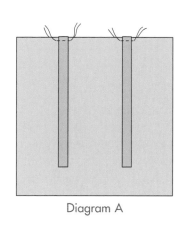

Diagram A

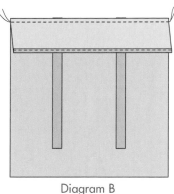

Diagram B

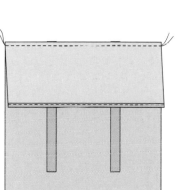

Diagram C

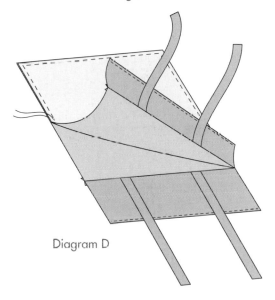

Diagram D

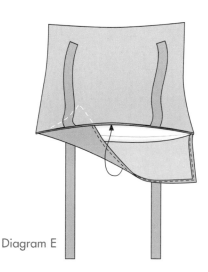

Diagram E

Diagram A

Getting Started

Pillows with Gussets

Although pillows without gussets or side panels are easy to make, the finished tailored style of gusseted pillows makes them well worth the extra work.

1. Determine the size pillow you want, add a ⅝-inch seam allowance all around, then cut out two round or square pieces of fabric for the pillow front and back. Since it is difficult to get a perfectly round shape, you may first want to make a template from heavy paper or cardboard. Lay the template on the fabric, mark around the circle with tailor's chalk, and cut it out.

To figure the length of the gusset or strip, measure the distance around the pillow and add ⅝ inch for each seam allowance. The gusset shown above is cut 5 inches deep, including the ⅝-inch seam allowances. Determine the length of piping needed by multiplying the length of the gusset by 2. To make matching piping from the fabric, see page 235.

Determine the size of covered button for the pillow. The button used in the photo *above* is 1½ inches in diameter.

2. Place the gusset right side up. Cut the length of piping in half and pin it to the front of the strip, matching the raw edges of the fabric, with the piping turned toward

the center. Refer to the piping placement in Diagram A to stitch the piping in place.

3. Pin the short ends of the gusset together, right sides facing. Stitch the seam with a ⅝-inch seam allowance to make a circle (see Diagram B). Trim the seam and press open. Fold the gusset into quarters and mark each quarter with contrasting thread or tailor's chalk.

4. Fold the top and bottom pillow circles into quarters and mark each quarter with contrasting thread or tailor's chalk (see Diagram C).

5. Baste ½ inch from the raw edge of the top and bottom pillow circles. Start and stop the stitching at each quarter mark (see Diagram C). Pin the gusset to the top of the pillow (right sides facing), matching quarter marks and pinning. Pull the threads to ease each of the quarters to fit the gusset (see Diagram D). Evenly distribute the gathers in each quarter and pin the gusset to the pillow. Stitch the top to the gusset using a ⅝-inch seam allowance.

6. Repeat to sew the bottom, leaving a 14-inch opening. Turn the pillow cover right side out, press, and insert the pillow form. Hand-sew the opening closed.

7. Following the manufacturer's instructions or the directions on page 346, assemble two covered buttons. Use a double length of heavy thread plus 8 inches. Run the thread through one button shank, leaving plenty of thread. Go down through the pillow form, through the button shank on the opposite side, and back through the pillow form. Pull the thread taut, knot the two ends at the base of the button, and tie off.

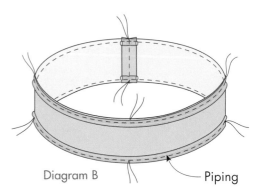

Diagram B   Piping

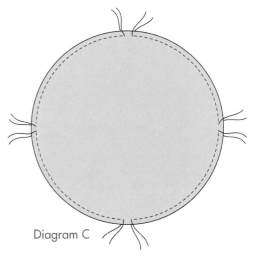

Diagram C

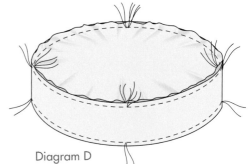

Diagram D

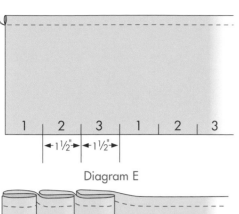

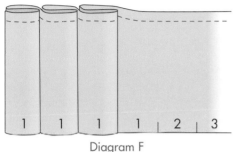

1 | 2 | 3 | 1 | 2 | 3
←1½"→←1½"→

Diagram E

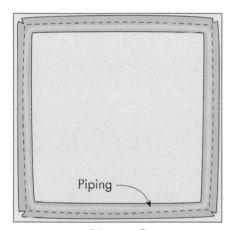

1 | 1 | 1 | 1 | 2 | 3

Diagram F

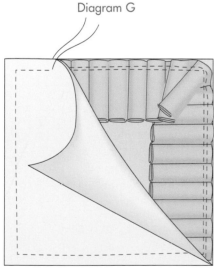

Piping

Diagram G

Diagram H

Getting Started

Knife-Pleated Pillow

A knife-pleated edging is a welcome alternative on formal or casual pillows.

1. Cut two squares or rectangles the desired size, and add ⅝ inch on all four sides for seam allowances. Figure the length of the cording or piping by measuring one side of the pillow and multiplying by 4. To make piping, see page 235.

The width of the pleated edging is your choice; however, a knife-pleat edging wider than 3 inches tends to droop. Because the edging is folded in half, double the fabric to the desired finished width. Add ½ inch to the width for the seam allowance. To determine the length of fabric for the edging, measure around the pillow and multiply by 3, plus 1½ inches for each seam. Piece the strip as needed, then fold it in half lengthwise.

2. Referring to Diagram E, use tailor's chalk to mark the fabric along the opposite edge from the hem, starting 1¼ inches from the end. Repeat across the length of the edging. Mark each section at 1½-inch intervals with consecutive 1, 2, and 3 (see Diagram E).

3. Hand-press the pleats by folding along each mark so that all the 1s are on top, as shown in Diagram F. Pin the pleats in place and machine baste.

4. Pin the cording or piping to the right side of the fabric and baste it in place (see Diagram G).

5. Pin the pleated edging on the cording or piping on the right side of the fabric. Carefully ease the pleats around the corners of the pillow, as shown in the photo, *above*. Baste in place (see Diagram H).

6. With right sides together, place the fabric backing on the front square or rectangle, with the cording or piping inserted between the two squares of material. Stitch three sides using a ⅝-inch seam allowance. Turn the pillow to the right side and insert a pillow form or fiberfill. Hand-stitch the opening closed.

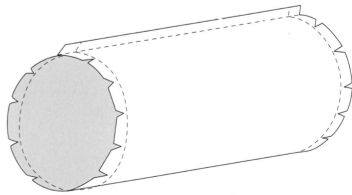

Getting Started

Double-Ruffled Bolster

1. Purchase a bolster form. Determine the amount of fabric needed by measuring the length and circumference of the bolster form (see Diagram A), and add a ⅝-inch seam allowance all around. Cut a rectangular piece of fabric from these measurements. Measure the diameter of the end of the bolster (see Diagram A), and add a 1¼-inch seam allowance. It is best to draw the circle on a piece of paper, then use the template to cut two pieces of fabric for the end pieces.

2. Sew a staystitch (see page 325) along both ends of the rectangular fabric ⅝ inch from the edge of the fabric. Make shallow snips across the ends, but do not cut through the staystitching (see Diagram B). Fold the rectangular fabric in half, right sides facing, and stitch a seam along the length of the tube.

Diagram A

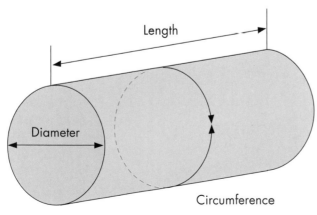

Diagram B

 — Length, Diameter, Circumference labels

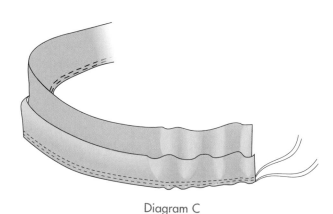

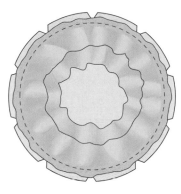

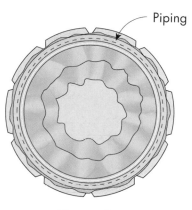

Piping

Diagram C

Diagram D

Diagram E

3. Determine the amount of piping, needed. To make the bias strips and piping, see page 235.

To calculate the length of fabric needed for each ruffle, multiply the circumference of the bolster by 2 (two ruffles for each end). Cut two 7-inch strips and two 4-inch strips to make double ruffles.

4. To make the ruffles, sew each strip together with a ⅝-inch seam to form four circles. Press the seams open. Fold each ruffle in half lengthwise, right sides out, and press (see Diagram C).

Slip one narrow fabric circle over one wide fabric circle, raw edges aligned. Pin and stitch a double row of running stitches along the raw edges (see Diagram C). Leave an ample length of thread to pull the threads and create gathers. Repeat for the remaining circles.

5. Pull the double threads, gathering until the double ruffle is the correct diameter.

6. To attach the piping and ruffle, pin the ruffle on the circular fabric as shown in Diagram D, adjusting and bunching the gathers as needed; machine baste. Stitch the ends of the piping together to measure the correct diameter; pin it on the ruffle and machine baste (see Diagram E).

7. To attach one end of the bolster, place the right sides together, as shown in Diagram F. Align the raw edges, pin, and stitch. Trim the seams. Turn right side out and press. Insert the bolster form. Pin and hand-stitch the other end of the bolster to close.

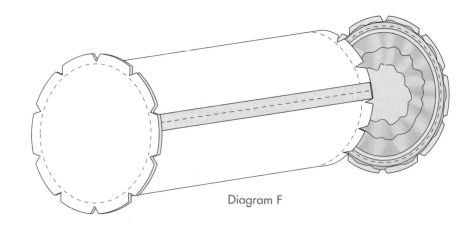

Diagram F

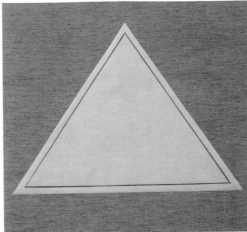

Photo A

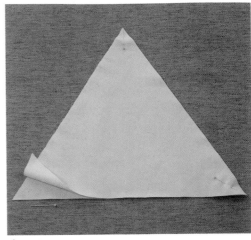

Photo B

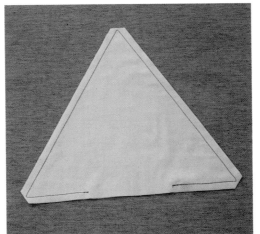

Photo C

Photo D

Getting Started

Specialty Shapes

1. Pillow forms in traditional shapes—squares, rectangles, or circles—are available ready-made to insert in finished covers. Unusual shapes mean the form must be handmade. Cut the desired shape from paper, adding seam allowances to each side (see Photo A). Cut two of these shapes from muslin. Save the pattern to use for making the decorative fabric cover. Pin the shapes together, right sides facing (see Photo B).

2. Sew around all the sides, leaving a small opening for turning and stuffing. Clip the corners and any curves (see Photo C).

3. Tightly pack polyester fiberfill stuffing into each corner, using your fingers or a corner tool. Add stuffing to the remainder of the pillow, packing it as tightly as possible (see Photo D). If the stuffing is lumpy, pull it apart to remove any masses before placing it in the pillow.

4. Slip-stitch or narrowly topstitch the opening closed. Fluff the pillow to evenly distribute the stuffing. The finished form should be smooth and even with no lumps or dimples (see Photo E).

5. Repeat steps 1 and 2 to sew the decorative cover. Insert the pillow form into the pillow cover, and slip-stitch the opening closed.

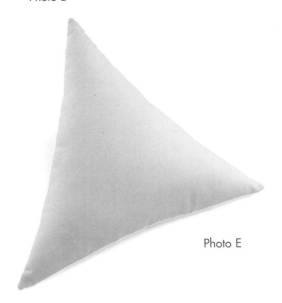

Photo E

Getting Started

Bed Pillowcase

1. Measure the length and width of the bed pillow. Add 9¼ inches to the length of the pillowcase for the hems and seam allowances, and add 1¼ inches to the width of the fabric for a seam allowance.

2. Cut a rectangular piece of fabric to the dimensions of the pillow plus 3 inches for fullness and 8 inches for the hem (see Diagram A).

3. Fold the fabric in half lengthwise, wrong sides together (see Diagram B). Pin and make a French seam by first sewing a ¼-inch seam; then turn the pillowcase wrong side out and stitch a ⅜-inch seam (refer to Seams and Finishes on page 348 to make a French seam). The second seam will enclose the raw edge and prevent fraying. Press the seams to one side.

4. With the pillowcase wrong side out, measure 4 inches from the opening, fold, and press (see Diagram C). Measure an additional 4 inches; turn, press, and pin. Stitch along the edge of the hem (see Diagram D).

5. Turn the pillowcase right side out and press. Insert a bed pillow.

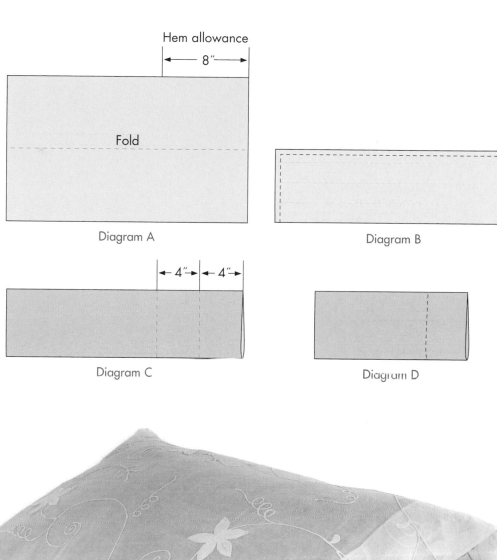

Hem allowance
8"
Fold
Diagram A

Diagram B

4" 4"
Diagram C

Diagram D

Home Decor – Elegant Pillows

Window
Treatments

Shades, curtains, draperies, and valances do more than offer privacy. When both the style and fabric are right, they'll give the room a unified, coordinated look, and complete the room decor.

Window Basics

Choosing the proper style of window dressing and fabric for your room is one of the most important decisions you will need to make. Besides color and pattern, window treatments also provide privacy, filter light, completely block light, or frame a window for an incredible view.

Keep in mind that fabric hanging in a window may look quite different than it does on a bolt of material. Strong patterns can become garish, texture more prominent, and the fabric color may change in strong light, or with the addition of a liner. Hold the fabric up to a similar light exposure as the intended window to determine whether

it will meet your needs. Place a piece of fabric behind it if there will be a lining.

Choosing the proper fabric for your curtain is also important. Check to see whether the material is washable and if it will possibly shrink. Loose weave fabrics may stretch and should be lined.

Fiber content is very important. Always find out what type of fabric you are buying and use thread with the same fiber content. Some of the most common types of fabrics are:

Polyester fabrics are often blended with natural fibers such as cotton, are very strong, fade resistant, and work well for both opaque and sheer window treatments.

Acrylic fabrics are lightweight, strong, and crease-resistant. Some are washable, while others need dry cleaning.

Cotton is a natural fiber that is strong, washable, and wears well. Some fabrics have a shiny finish that helps to resist soil.

Acetate is a synthetic fiber that is silky looking and drapes well, but is not strong unless it is combined with fibers such as cotton.

Decorator fabrics are available in fairly standard widths. If you are making a window treatment for a fairly large opening, the fabric will probably not be the necessary width. You may need to join several widths of fabric to get the size you need.

Join the panels using a flat-fell or French seam (refer to page 348). When you sew the panels together, trim off the selvages because they are more tightly woven than the rest of the fabric and can cause the seams to pucker.

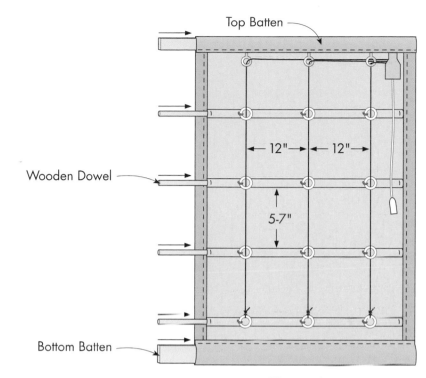

Diagram A

Roman Shade Basics

Determine the size of the finished shade by measuring the length and width of the window. If the shade is to fit inside of the window, subtract ⅜ inch from the width so it will slide smoothly.

You will need decorator fabric for the front of the shade and lining for the back. You also will need two pieces of wood (called the batten) for the top and bottom of the shade. The bottom batten should be about 2 inches wide and 1½ inches shorter than the width of the shade. The top batten should be about 1 inch wide and 1½ inches shorter than the width of the shade. You also will need ½-inch wooden dowels, screw eyes, plastic rings, cord, and a cord pull.

To determine the decorator fabric yardage, measure the length and width of the window. Add 3⅛ inches to the width for the side hems, and add 8 inches to the length. If the window is wider than the fabric, join lengths of fabric, being careful to match the patterns, if necessary.

The lining fabric should be 1½ inches less than the width of the decorator fabric and 9½ inches longer than the finished size of the shade. Add 2½ inches for each dowel casing.

Getting Started

1. Begin working on the shade lining first. Fold under both sides of the lining fabric 1½ inches to make a hem and press, but do not stitch.

To determine where to mark the stitch lines for the casings, subtract 2 inches from the top of the lining, then divide the remaining fabric until you get a number that is between 5 and 7 inches (see Diagram A). On the right side of the lining, measure down from the top of the lining 2 inches and begin marking each section in a straight line with tailor's chalk or a fabric marker with disappearing ink. Fold the fabric along the lines and press.

Pin each fold and stitch 1¼ inches from the fold to create a casing for each dowel.

2. At the bottom of the liner, fold up ½ inch to the wrong side and press. Then measure 3½ inches from the fold for the bottom hem; turn and press.

3. Lay the decorator fabric for the shade facedown on a flat surface. Center the lining fabric on top of the decorator fabric with the dowel casings facing up. The lining fabric will be tucked under the hem at the top, sides, and bottom.

4. At the bottom of the shade, tuck and pin the lining fabric under the 3½-inch hem. Check to make sure that the wood batten will fit inside the hem. Stitch at the edge of the hem across the blind, sewing through the lining and decorator fabric. Tuck and pin the lining under the edges of the decorator fabric all the way around. Stitch a line up the sides of the shade to secure the shade and lining together.

5. Move up to the first dowel casing. Pin the lining and decorator fabric together at this point, making sure that both fabrics are smooth and flat. Following the stitching line of the dowel casing, stitch over this line as you sew through both pieces of fabric. Double stitch at the beginning and end of each row. Make sure that the stitch line is straight (it will show on the front), but do not stitch into the dowel casing. Repeat this process until you finish all the stitching.

6. To finish the upper part of the shade for the top batten, lay the shade on a flat surface and measure from the bottom of the shade for the finished length. Mark the finished length at the top of the shade. To make the top batten hem, follow Step 4 instructions, adjusting the hem if needed; press and stitch. Check to make sure that the wooden batten will fit in the top hem before stitching.

7. Cut the top and bottom battens 1 inch shorter than the finished width of the shade. Drill two vertical pilot holes in the top batten about 3 to 4 inches from each end. The pilot holes will be used to attach the batten to L-brackets for mounting to the wall. Slide the battens in the top and bottom hems and hand-stitch the ends closed.

Cut the dowels to the same length as the top and bottom battens, insert, and hand-stitch the casings closed.

8. Lay the shade on a flat surface with the liner side up. On the casings, measure and mark the ring placement using tailor's chalk or a fabric marker. The distance between the rings should be at 12-inch intervals beginning in the center of the shade (see Diagram A, page 251) with the distance between the end rings at the edges smaller. Stitch the rings to the lining.

Attach the screw eyes through the fabric into the lower edge of the top wooden batten and directly in line with the rings.

9. Determine whether to hang the cords to the right or left side, and place a screw eye or metal pulley on the lower edge of the top batten. Tie a cord to each of the bottom rings, thread it through the upper rings in the row and through the screw eye at the top (refer to Diagram A), then over to the screw eye or pulley at the side. Repeat for all the cords. Trim the cords, gather them, and make one large knot about 15 inches from the end, or attach an endcap. Attach a cleat to the wall or window frame to secure the cords when the shade is pulled up.

10. Attach small L-brackets to the wall and attach the shade to the L-brackets where the pilot holes were drilled. The batten can also be attached to the inside of the window frame.

11. Pad and cover a header board with matching fabric and install it in front of the shade, if desired, referring to the finished Roman shade shown on page 250.

Optional: Pre-pleated fabric is available for making Roman shades (see *below*). Available in several widths, it offers insulation to make rooms warmer and creates a soft look. Similar fabrics are available for non-insulated window treatments and black-out shades that darken a room. Simply add a decorator fabric to the front along with the necessary hardware.

Pocket Curtain Basics

A pocket curtain works best when it can stay permanently open, closed, or swagged with tiebacks. Some curtains and valances have a ruffle above the pocket (casing) as shown *opposite,* and others are plain. If you make a curtain without a ruffle, eliminate the additional measurements and instructions.

Note: *Sheer curtains are made using the standard pocket curtain instructions as described below and opposite.*

Getting Started

Pocket Curtain without Ruffle

1. Determine the length of the valance or curtain and add 2 to 4 inches for the hem. To figure the size of the casing, follow this formula: Measure the diameter of the rod, add ¾ inch, and divide by 2. For example, if the rod is 6 inches diameter:
6 inches + ¾ inch ÷ 2 = 3⅜-inch casing.

The casing should slide easily on the rod. The side hems will be double-turned to give body to the curtains. Figure 2½ inches for each side seam, with a finished width of 1¼ inches. Based on the size of the curtain and fabric, a smaller curtain or light fabric will have a smaller-size hem. For instructions on mitered corners, see page 259.

Determine the fabric dimensions needed for the valance by measuring the rod width and multiplying by 2½. To figure the fullness for rod pocket curtains, multiply the width of the rod by 1½ or 2.

2. To hem the sides of the curtain, turn under 1¼ inches, press, turn another 1¼ inches, and press. Pin in place and stitch.

3. To make the rod casing, turn the raw edge under ½ inch, then turn under the necessary width to accommodate the rod (see Diagram A *opposite*). Press in place, pin,

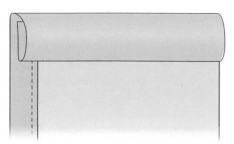

Diagram A – No Ruffle

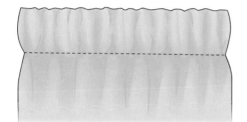

Diagram B – No Ruffle

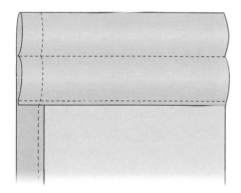

Diagram C – Ruffle

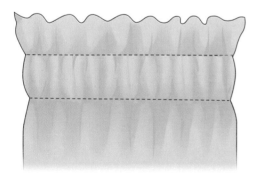

Diagram D – Ruffle

and stitch. Turn up the bottom hem and finish as desired. To make a mitered hem, see Table Coverings on page 259. See Diagram B for a completed curtain without a ruffle.

Pocket Curtain with Ruffle

1. To hem the sides of the curtain, turn under 1¼ inches, press, then turn another 1¼ inches and press. Pin in place and stitch.

2. To make a rod casing with a ruffle, turn under the top raw edge ½ inch. In general, the top ruffle is 2 inches deep. Determine the size of the rod pocket needed plus the width of the ruffle. Fold this width to the wrong side of the curtain; pin and stitch along the half fold. Measure half the distance between the stitching and the top edge of the curtain, and stitch across the curtain to form the rod casing (see Diagram C).

3. Turn up the hem at the bottom of the curtain and finish as desired. To make a mitered hem, see Table Coverings on page 259.

4. Insert the rod through the casing, gathering the fabric (see Diagram D).

Tabbed Curtain Basics

Tabbed curtains are great looking and add interesting detail to window treatments. Make sure the tabs slide easily if the curtain is to be pulled back. The measurements given here will make 4-inch-long tabs. For larger diameter rods, measure the diameter of the rod and allow 1 inch between the rod and valance. Adjust the measurements accordingly.

Getting Started

1. Measure the curtain rod to determine the width of the curtain; double that figure for fullness, and add 2 inches for narrow side hems. Measure the desired length and add 2½ inches for the hem and ½ inch for the top seam. Remember, the tabs will drop the valance approximately 2 to 2½ inches. Cut a facing the width of the valance and 6 inches wide.

2. Determine the number of tabs by measuring in 3 inches from each side. Divide the remaining space into even increments, about 6 inches apart. Mark each point with a pin (see Diagram A).

3. For the tabs, cut a 2½-wide strip. Make one long tube that can be cut into numerous tabs. With the wrong side out, fold the strip in half lengthwise and stitch along the raw edges using a ¼-inch seam allowance (see Diagram B). Turn the strip right side out and press it so the seam falls at the center back of the strip. Cut the strip into 6½-inch lengths. Fold the pieces in half, matching the raw edges and center back seams. Pin the tabs to the top edge so the center of one tab falls at each mark and the raw edges align.

4. Sew a hem across one edge of the facing as follows: Turn under ¼ inch, press, then turn under ½ inch, pin, and stitch. Align the right sides of the facing and the upper raw edges. Pin and stitch the facing to the top of the curtain to encase the tabs (see Diagram C). Open out the facing, press, and make a 1-inch hem on the sides of the curtain and facing. Turn the facing to the wrong side along the upper seam line and press. Topstitch or hand-stitch the end of the facing to the hemmed edge of the curtain.

5. Determine the length of the curtains. Turn up ¼ inch, then 1¾ inches for the lower hem of the curtain or valance. Pin and stitch the hem in place.

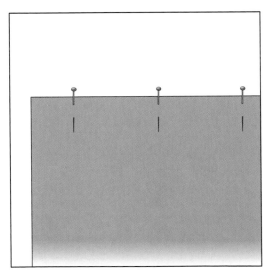

Diagram A

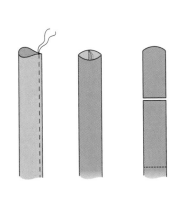

Diagram B

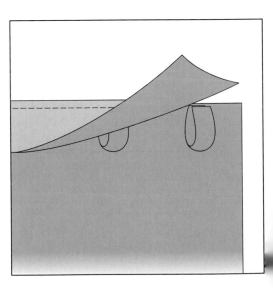

Diagram C

Pleated Drapery Basics

A drape with top pleats gives a traditional look to a window. Heading tape makes it easy to form pleats of even sizes and spacing. Tape brands differ slightly in assembly, but all of them work on the same principle. Read the manufacturer's instructions before beginning.

Getting Started

1. To determine the amount of tape needed, measure the curtain rod for the width required, depending on the manufacturer's instructions.

2. Figure the required width of fabric needed. Cut the curtain fabric 5 inches wider than the pleating tape length for side

hems. Add 4 to 8 inches for the bottom hem and add 2 inches at the top. (If a standard double-turned hem is 4 inches wide, then the hem allowance would be 8 inches.)

3. Double-hem the sides of the curtain by first turning under 1¼ inches, pressing, turning another 1¼ inches, and stitching. The appropriate width of the side hems will depend on the type of fabric used and the overall size of the curtain.

4. At the top of the curtain, turn under 2 inches toward the wrong side of the fabric. Line up fabric pattern details (see roses on panel at *left*), if needed, and press. Pin the heading tape to the wrong side of the curtain, fold the ends of the heading tape under, and pin the cords out of the way. Stitch across the top and bottom of the tape, going in the same direction each time so that the tape lays flat (see Diagram A).

5. To measure for the hem, lay the curtain on a large flat surface. Measure from the top of the curtain to the bottom, and mark the desired length with tailor's chalk. Adjust the length to accommodate the curtain rings. To make the hem, fold up the bottom fabric edge in a double-turned hem, press, and stitch in place. To make a mitered hem, see Table Coverings on page 259.

6. Tie off one end of the drawstrings. Grasp the free end of the drawstrings and pull the strings to pleat the tape. Tie off the drawstrings (see Diagram B).

7. To hang the curtain, attach clip-style rings to the top of the pinch pleats (see the photo at *top left*).

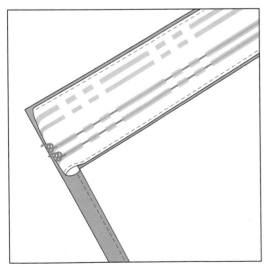

Diagram A

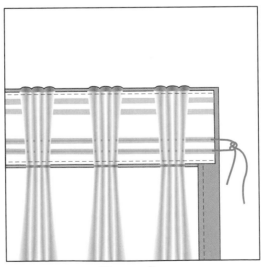

Diagram B

Table *Coverings*

Ready-made tablecloths and skirts in the perfect color, pattern, style, and size are often impossible to find. Two basic methods allow you to make coordinated coverings that are great for your decor or special celebrations.

The projects shown here have simple finished edges, and you can change the look with trims for a traditional or contemporary look.

Creative Tip

On washable fabrics,
use a glue stick instead of pins to hold trims,
lace, etc., in place.
After sewing, the first washing
will remove the glue.
—Team Member, Washington, Pennsylvania

Table Covering Basics

Table coverings used for dining normally have a drop that extends to the top of the chair seat. For decorative tables, the drop usually extends to the floor.

Whether you make a round, square, or rectangular table cover, the fabric will probably not be wide enough to reach the desired length or width. Add equal-size panels to each side to make the fabric wide enough, matching the patterns, if necessary (see Diagram A). Do not piece the fabric down the center. Seams on the sides of the tablecloth will be much less noticeable and the cloth will lie flat when the seams are sewn off center. Stitch the side panels to the center panel using a ½-inch seam allowance, and press the seams open.

Getting Started

Round Table Cover

1. Measure the diameter of the table (see measurement AB, Diagram B). Measure the desired drop (see measurement CD, Diagram B), double this measurement, and add the diameter. Add an additional 1 inch for a narrow hem or 2 inches for a wide hem.

2. If the fabric is not wide enough, follow the instructions in Table Covering Basics to join the fabric panels. Fold the fabric into quarters to make a square (see Diagram C). The square should be equal to the cutting diameter measurement established in Step 1, plus 2 inches.

3. Pin a piece of string to the folded corner. Tie the other end of the string to a fabric marker or tailor's chalk, and adjust the length so it is half the diameter of the table cover. To make a compass to create a perfect circle see Diagram D. Starting at one edge, swing the marker along the fabric, keeping the string taut and the marker at a 90-degree angle.

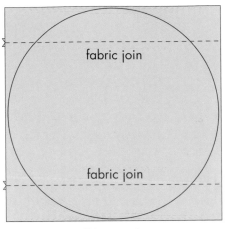

fabric join

fabric join

Diagram A

Diagram B

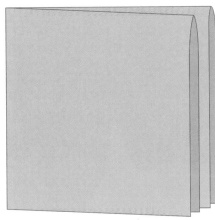

Diagram C

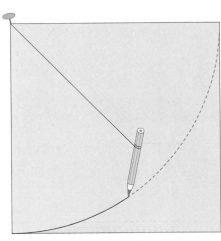

Diagram D

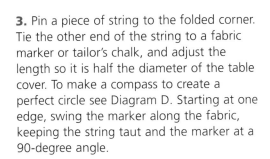

Diagram E

4. Cut along the line, through all four layers of the fabric (see Diagram E.) Hem the lower edge of the table cover using the measurement you calculated in Step 1.

Getting Started

Square or Rectangular Table Cover

1. Following Diagram F, measure the length AB and width CD of the table. Determine the length of the drop EF and add 1¼ inches for a hem. Double the drop measurement and add it to both the length and width measurements of the table.

2. To hem the table cover and make mitered corners, press under ¼ inch on all sides (see

Diagram G), turn up 1 inch for the hem, and press; do not stitch. Open out the pressed hem and turn each corner diagonally (see Diagram H). Trim the corner as shown, leaving enough fabric for the hem.

3. Fold the hem back in place. The corners will a 45-degree angle (see Diagram I). Pin the mitered corner and hem in place.

4. Slip-stitch (see page 326) each mitered corner in place (see Diagram J). Stitch along the folded hem edge, pivoting at each corner.

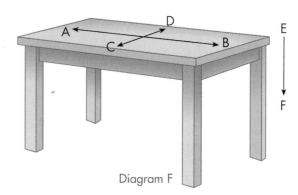

Diagram F

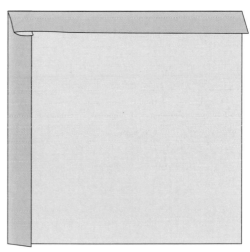

Diagram G

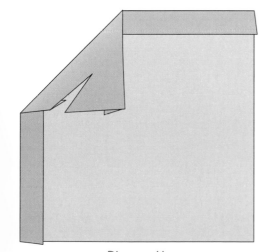

Diagram H

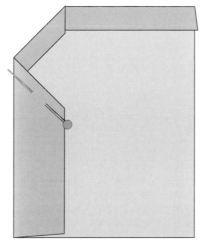

Diagram I

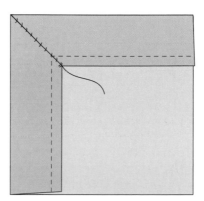

Diagram J

Easy *Slipcovers*

Fitted slipcovers are an ideal way to freshen the appearance of comfortable chairs and ottomans. Fabric colors and textures update home furnishings while providing a designer look at minimal expense. Coordinate fabrics with room decor, change slipcovers with the seasons, or add an elegant touch to the dining room.

Chair before slipcover

Slipcover Basics

Coordinate fabrics with the room decor to cover existing furniture. For slipcovers that will receive frequent use, choose fabrics that are easily laundered. Polyester-blend fabrics wear well without wrinkling and are easy to sew. Prewash fabrics before cutting and sewing, if appropriate, to test for color bleed and shrinkage. Check the manufacturer's care label. Avoid open-weave or loosely woven fabrics because the threads will catch on clothing or furniture and will not wear well.

The following instructions are for a chair and ottoman. Commercial patterns are available at fabric stores. If you choose stripes or large-pattern fabrics, calculate extra yardage to center the pattern and to match designs along the seams and trim areas. Trimming the slipcovers gives the furniture a professional, finished appearance.

Carefully measure the furniture piece to determine the amount of fabric to purchase, including seam allowances, hems, and extra fabric to match patterns. When working with expensive fabric, make a muslin cover first to use as a pattern for the finished cover. You'll avoid making costly mistakes and having to purchase additional fabric.

After measuring and making paper tracings or patterns, cut the fabric and pin it along the seam allowances, wrong side out, before sewing the seams. Seam pinning allows you to adjust the fabric to get an accurate, smooth fit for the slipcovers.

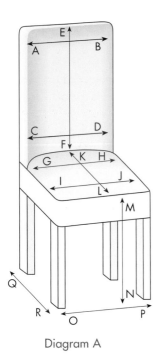

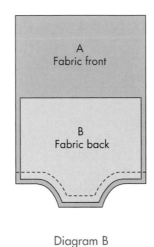

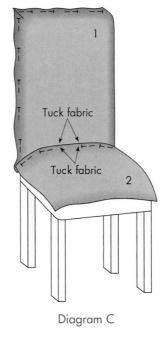

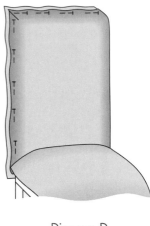

Diagram A   Diagram B   Diagram C   Diagram D

Getting Started

Cushioned Chair Slipcover

Note: *Add ½-inch seam allowances to each fabric panel measurement for the slipcovers.*

1. Referring to Diagram A, measure A to B and C to D for the chair back width, including the fabric that will wrap around the sides of the back. Add 1 inch to the measurements to allow for ½-inch seam allowances on each side.

Measure E to F for the chair back length and cushion depth. Add 5½ inches to the length for the apron (see Diagram B), plus a ½-inch seam allowance. (See the shape of the apron in Diagram B for tucking between the chair back and seat.)

2. Referring to Diagram A, measure the seat from G to H, I to J, and K to L, adding a ½ inch for seam allowances. Add 5½ inches for the apron tuck-in plus a ½-inch seam allowance, as shown in Diagram B.

3. For the skirt panel depth, measure from M to N. Add 4 inches to the measurement to include a ½-inch seam allowance and 3½ inches for the hem. Referring to Diagram A, for the skirt panel length, measure O to P and Q to R. Double the measurement for the chair circumference, then add 33 inches. The resulting measurement includes seam allowances and four inverted box pleats (8 inches each) for the corners (see the diagrams, *opposite*, to make box pleats).

From the measurements, cut out muslin or paper patterns to check for fit. Position the patterns on the chair and make any adjustments. Use the muslin or paper patterns to cut out the fabric.

4. To determine the amount of yardage needed for piping or cording trim, measure the seat edge all the way around the chair and add 1 inch seam allowances. Use purchased piping, or cover cording to coordinate with the slipcover fabrics, or make your own (see Bias Binding and Piping on page 235).

5. Referring to Diagram C, place the chair back front panel (C-1) on the chair right side out and temporarily pin it in place, wrapping the front panel around the sides to the back edges of the chair back.

Place the seat panel, right side out, on the chair and pin it in place.

To join the seat cover (C-2) and front of the chair back (C-1) at the apron, tuck the apron between the seat and chair back, then pin the seat panel to the back panel along the back edges as shown in Diagram C. Remove the panels. Right sides together, sew the seat panel to the back panel along the seam allowance, as shown (see Diagram B showing the stitch lines of the apron). Clip corners and curves, and trim the seam allowance. Place the joined panels on the chair to check the fit.

6. To join the front and back panels of the chair back (see Diagram D), place the joined back and seat panels (C-1 and C-2) on the chair, wrong side out. Pin the panel for the back side of the chair back, wrong side out, to the seam line of the front panel. Make small tucks in the fabric along the chair corners, if needed. Mark the seam lines with tailor's chalk; remove the panels from the chair.

Baste the front and back together. Turn the chair back panels right side out, slip it on the chair to check for a smooth fit, and make necessary adjustments. Remove the panels, sew the seams, and press.

7. To attach the piping to the seat cover, turn the chair back, front, and seat cover right sides out, and slip it on the chair. Begin pinning the piping to the fabric at the back of the chair. Leave 1 inch of extra piping on both ends to be tucked into the seam allowance later. Matching the raw edges of the piping with the seat cover, pin the piping and clip the piping at the corners of the chair for a better fit (see Diagram E). Pin and machine baste the piping all the way around the seat cover. Place the slip cover back on the chair with the wrong side out.

8. To make the skirt, with right sides together, sew the skirt panel seam allowances together to make a tube. Press the seam open. With the seam line as a guide, use pins to divide and mark the skirt into quarters. With the skirt wrong side out, center the skirt seam at the back of the chair and pin it in place. Pin the center of the skirt at the front, the third, and fourth quarter marks along the seat panel sides.

Make box pleats in the skirt at each seat corner, folding under 2 inches of fabric at each side to make a 4-inch pleat (see

Diagram F). When the skirt is turned to the right side, the pleats will be inverted. Pin the pleats to the seat panel and pin the pleated edges to the skirt, as shown in Diagram G. Pin remaining raw edges to the seat cover.

Remove the slipcover panels and baste the skirt to the seat and chair back panel, tucking in the seat piping at the back seam. Turn the panels right side out and place the slipcover on the chair to check for a smooth fit. Make adjustments if needed. Sew the skirt to the panels; press.

9. Place the slipcover on the chair and mark the skirt hem with pins. Remove the slipcover; turn and press the hem. Turn under ½ inch along the raw edge and press. Stitch the skirt hem in place and press. Sew fringe along the hemmed edge of each outer skirt panel, turning under the raw edges of the fringe. Sew tassels at each inverted box pleat, if desired.

10. Turn the slipcover right side out and place it on the chair.

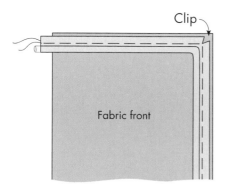

Diagram E

Diagram F

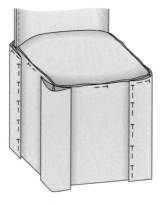

Diagram G

Getting Started

Ottoman Slipcover

1. Referring to Diagram A, measure the top panel of the ottoman slipcover from A to B and C to D. Add 1 inch to each measurement for seam allowances. Measure the circumference of the ottoman for the piping, adding 2 inches for the seam allowance. Also determine the yardage needed for the fringe, adding ½ inch for turning under at each end.

2. Measure the width and depth of each ottoman skirt panel, from E to F and G to H. Add 5 inches to each width for side hems and 3½ inches to the depth for the hems on the skirt panels. There should be ½ inch left over for the top seam allowance.

3. The finished corner inset panels are 10 inches wide. Add 2 inches for the hem allowance to the width; add 3 inches to the depth for each panel. There should be ½ inch left over for the top seam allowance.

4. To hem the panels and inset, turn under ½ inch and press; turn under 2½ inches and pin. Stitch the hems in place.
Note: Inset panels should be slightly shorter than the ottoman skirt.

To finish the side hems on the skirt panels and inset panels, turn under ½ inch along each side and press. Turn under the skirt panel side hems 2 inches each, press and pin. Turn the inset panels side hems another ½ inch and pin. Stitch the hems in place.

5. Place the top panel right side up on the ottoman. Position and pin the fringe along the seam allowance (see Diagram B), aligning raw edges. Baste the fringe to the panel. Repeat for the piping (see Bias

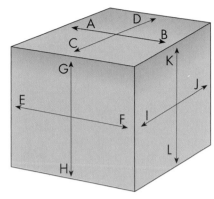

Diagram A

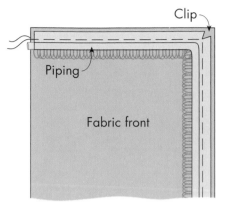

Diagram B

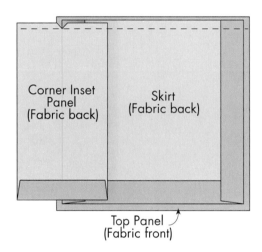

Diagram C

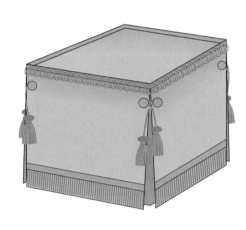

Diagram D

Binding and Piping on page 235 to make piping). Clip the piping at the corners to fit.

6. Place the top panel right side up on the ottoman, as shown in Diagram C. Position and pin each skirt panel along the seam allowances to the top panel, right sides facing. Center the inset panels at each corner, cutting notches at the corners. Baste the skirts to the top panel (see Diagram C) with the piping sandwiched in between. Check the slipcover for fit and make any

adjustments. Sew the seams, clipping the seam allowances at the corners. Press the seams.

7. Sew rope tassels and covered buttons (see Covered Buttons on page 346) to the ottoman corners (see Diagram D), if desired. Sew fringe along the hem edge of the skirt.

Chair *Cover*

Dress up your chairs with seat cushions that make even the plainest chair an important design element in the room. These pads are so simple, you can change them with the seasons or make special versions just for the holidays.

ᴈCreative Tip

When you attempt a big project, such as curtains, quilts, etc., wind a couple of bobbins ahead. It saves having to stop in the middle of a seam to do this task.
—Team Member, Salisbury, Massachusetts

Chair Cover

Make a quick chair cover to match a tablecloth, valance, or place mats. Depending on the type of fabric you choose, you can get a traditional or casual look.

Chair Cover Basics

Measure the seat following the arrows in Diagram A. Make a paper pattern for the seat. The skirt is one continuous length of fabric. Measure the distance around the seat, add a seam allowance plus 8 inches for each of the corner box pleats. The skirt is 7 inches deep.

Getting Started

1. Measure around the chair seat and make enough piping to go around the chair and to sew the ends into the seam allowance (see Diagram B). Refer to Bias Binding and Piping instructions on page 235.

2. Cut out the seat fabric following the pattern, then cut the fabric for the skirt.

3. Hem the skirt by turning under ¼ inch, press, then turn under another ¼ inch and stitch. Press the hem.

4. Pin and baste the piping to the seat cover, clipping the piping seam allowance at the corners of the seat cover to ease the fit (see Diagram C).

5. Stitch the two short ends of the skirt together, wrong sides facing. Pin the skirt to the seat, making 4-inch-wide box pleats (2-inch turn-backs on both sides of the pleat) at the chair corners (see page 263 to make box pleats). Clip the skirt seam allowance at the seat cover corners to ease the fit; stitch.

6. To make the chair ties, cut a 2×72-inch strip of fabric. Fold the the raw edges toward the center ½ inch, then fold in half again. The strip should be ½ inch wide. Sew along the folded edges. Cut the strip in half and tie knots in the ends. Hand-stitch the ties to the back corners of the seat cover.

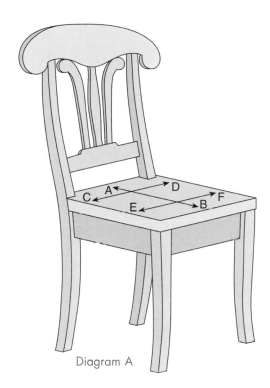

Diagram A

Diagram B

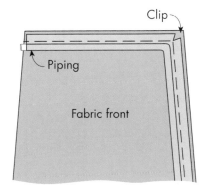

Clip

Piping

Fabric front

Diagram C

Covered *Lampshade*

Custom-made lampshades need not break your decorating budget. Whether you use self-adhesive shades or cover a ready-made lampshade, it is much easier than you might think.

❧ Creative Tip

*Stick pins in a bar of soap
before working with or stitching
heavyweight fabrics.
The soap helps the pins to
slide easily through heavy layers.*
—Team Member, Hudson, Ohio

Lampshade Basics

Choose fabrics and trims that match your room, scaling them to the appropriate size for the lamp and shade. If you use a self-adhesive lamp kit, follow the manufacturer's instructions. Or purchase a shade that is made of plastic material or heavy paper.

Getting Started

Simple Covered Lampshade

1. To determine the amount of fabric, tape a large piece of paper to a flat surface. Lay the lampshade in one corner of the paper, noting a starting point, such as the seam. Using a pencil, roll the shade across the paper and mark the arc of the shade until you reach the beginning point (see Diagram A). Add a ½-inch seam allowance and a ½-inch margin to the top and bottom. Cut out the paper pattern. Check the pattern against the lampshade to ensure the correct size and fit.

2. Using repositionable spray adhesive or stencil adhesive, spray the lampshade; set aside to tack-up. (Spray in a protected area so that the spray does not drift onto other household items.) This type of glue will remain tacky, so there is no need to hurry. Read the manufacturer's instructions on the spray can.

3. Lay the pattern on the fabric or decorative paper, and pin or tape it in place. Cut out the shape following the pattern.

4. With a ruler, mark a ½-inch fold line at one end of the fabric or paper to create a seam allowance. Using fabric glue, make a very small line of glue along the length of the seam to hold it together. Fold the seam over and hand press. (Test the glue

on a scrap of fabric to make sure that it doesn't stain.)

5. Referring to Diagram B, apply the fabric or paper to the lampshade, starting with the seam and continuing around the shade, wrapping and smoothing out ripples or air bubbles with your fingers. Use clothespins on the top and bottom rims to secure the material to the shade (Diagram C).

6. Clip the top and bottom margins to make the fabric or paper easy to wrap to the back of the shade. Turn under the material along the top and bottom margins and glue it along the inside edge.

7. Use a small, continuous bead of fabric glue or hot glue to apply additional trims to the top or bottom edges of the shade.

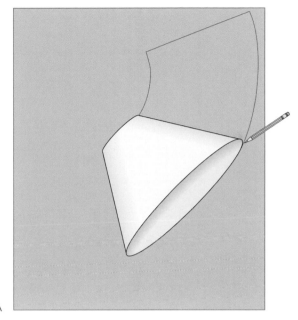

Diagram A

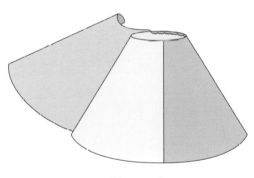

Diagram B

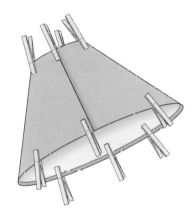

Diagram C

QUILTING

Be part of an American tradition,

and discover the joy of quilting.

Make and give colorful quilts

in a variety of styles—traditional,

whimsical, and folk-art—

and discover why

this technique has survived

for centuries.

Tools *and* Materials

The right tools make the job enjoyable, and there is a tool for nearly every imaginable quilting need. Learning to use the tools correctly ensures success and adds beauty and value to the finished project. The expanded interest in quilting over the past two decades has been enhanced by the development of a wide variety of tools that makes quilting quicker and easier with professional results.

Experiment to find the tools that work best for the projects you create.

Accessories – A

Beeswax (in the plastic holder) coats hand quilting thread to reduce tangles. Needle threaders aid in pulling threads through tiny needle eyes. Thimbles and small disks that adhere to skin protect fingers from needle jabs, prevent calluses, and relieve the pressure required to push threaded needles through fabric and batting layers.

Adhesives – B

Basting spray, glue sticks, and fusing agents in sheets and strips temporarily or permanently keep quilt pieces in place. Specialty adhesives can eliminate the need for pins and stitching.

Machine Attachments – C

An even-feed walking foot attachment "walks" across the fabric while it is sewn, simultaneously feeding the top and bottom fabric layers under the presser foot.

A quilting foot is a ¼-inch-wide presser foot that enables quilters to sew accurate, narrow seam allowances.

A quilting bar helps to stitch even rows without quilting marks on the fabric. **Note:** *See your sewing machine dealer to purchase attachments.*

Marking Pens and Pencils – D

Test marking tools on fabric scraps before using them on a quilt top. Use specially-designed temporary (air or water soluble, or

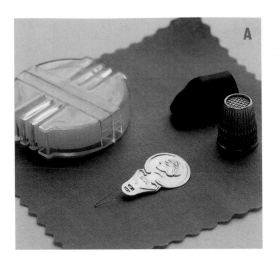

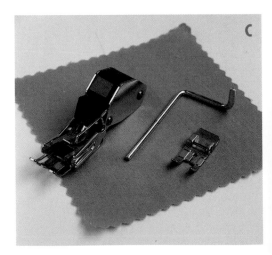

erasable) pencils and pens to transfer quilt designs to fabric. Use permanent pens to make quilt labels.

Mats – E

Thick, self-healing cutting mats are used with rotary cutters to protect surfaces and to keep fabric from shifting while it is cut.

Measuring Tools – F

Several sizes and shapes of durable transparent acrylic rulers are marked with measurements and angles to use with rotary cutters, pencils, or chalk. Flexible measuring tape, 100 to 120 inches long, is a necessary and handy tool for quilters.

Needles – G

Sharp needles are a must for machine piecing, hand piecing, and quilting. Needle sizes vary, with larger numbers indicating smaller needle sizes. Quilting needles are labeled as such or as "betweens," and common sizes are 8, 9, and 10. Size 8 is suggested for beginners. Curved needles are used to tie quilts, the shape making it easy to pierce the fabric and batting layers and return to the top in a continuous motion.

Other Marking Tools – H

Use chalk, pounce (for use with stencils), and specialty tapes to temporarily mark quilt tops and to mark the width and spacing of quilting lines.

Pins – I

Sharp, narrow pins hold fabric pieces in position for piecing and appliqué. Glass-head pins hold up to heat; plastic-head pins do not. Long flower-top pins are easy to grip and easy to see. Rustproof safety pins hold the quilt top, batting, and backing together prior to quilting.

Quilting Hoop and Frame – J

Choose square, rectangular, or circular frames to hold assembled quilts for quilting. Lightweight frames are portable; large traditional quilt frames can accommodate many quilters at a time.

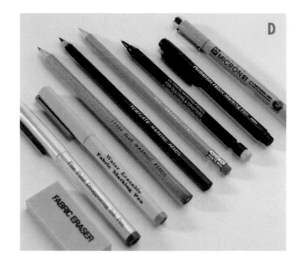

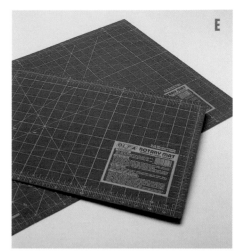

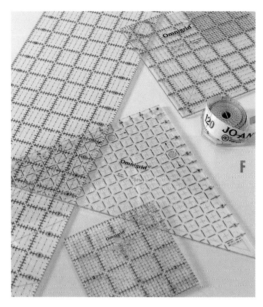

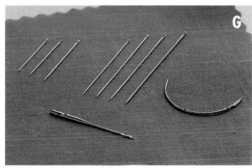

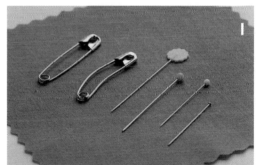

Rotary cutters – K

Rotary cutters take the place of scissors and have sharp, round blades to cut through multiple fabric layers. Rotary cutters are used with self-healing cutting mats and thick acrylic rulers that provide cutting guides. Rotary cutters are available in a variety of handle configurations and blade sizes, as well as specialty blades.

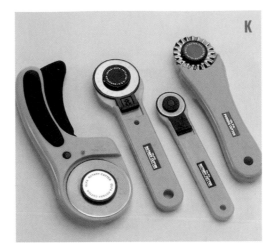

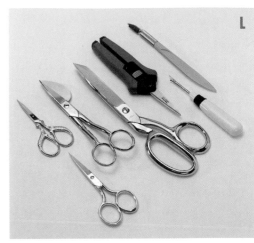

Scissors and Clippers – L

Choose from a variety of specialty scissors, such as duck-billed appliqué scissors, shears, and clippers. Each snips threads and fabrics with a minimum of effort. Keep blades sharp by using them only on fabrics and threads. Keep secondary scissors for cutting paper and templates.

Specialty Threads – M to R

Choose thread to match the fabric content (using cotton thread with cotton fabric, for example). Consider using a neutral thread to blend into the fabric when working with multicolor fabric.
Clockwise—threads for quilting, appliqué, and embellishment:
M. Monofilament in transparent and invisible smoke
N. Cotton-covered polyester
O. 100 percent cotton quilting
P. Cotton Embroidery
Q. Metallic, specialty
R. 100 percent cotton mercerized

Stencils and Templates – S

Stencil patterns of rigid plastic and other materials are used to transfer designs to fabric with pencils, pounce, or chalk. Templates made from sturdy materials can be traced around many times without the edges wearing away. Acrylic templates are commercially available, as is material to make your own. Machine-piecing templates include seam allowances; hand-piecing templates do not.

Pressing Tools –
not shown
Steam irons are used to press patchwork after each state of stitching—a critical sequence to the finished project. A good quality iron and a clean bottom plate make pressing, not ironing, easy.

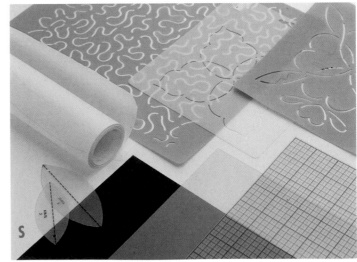

Choose Your Fabrics

Just as Grandmother carefully chose fabrics for her quilts, you'll want to choose the best fabrics available to make your quilt. Most quilters agree that 100 percent cotton fabrics provide the quality and durability needed to make long-lasting quilts. Widely available, cotton fabrics press crisply, sew with minimal seam distortion, and are easy to quilt.

Quilt patterns generally specify quantities of 44/45-inch-wide cotton fabrics allow for fabric shrinkage and cutting differences. Read the ends of the fabric bolts. The 40/42-inch-wide fabrics are becoming common in fabric stores, and you'll want to know the difference to calculate for extra fabric. Convenient and widely available "fat quarters" (18×22-inch pieces) provide quilters with fabric assortments without having to purchase full yardage.

To ensure that you have enough fabric for a quilting project, add ¼ yard or more to each fabric requirement. Matching fabrics if you run short may be difficult.

Color and Pattern Mixing

Choosing fabric colors for a project is half the fun of creating a quilt. To get started, select a focus fabric or print, then select fabrics in the colors of the print to enhance the scheme. Consult the "Color Theory" chapter on page 190 to establish a color palette and to work with dark, medium, and light fabrics. Using color and patterns in unexpected ways adds dimension and character to quilts.

Prepare Your Fabrics

Talk to a dozen quilters and you'll get a dozen opinions on whether or not to wash and dry fabrics before cutting. Because prewashing fabric is optional, you'll have to decide this step for yourself.

Prewashing fabrics provides assurance to many quilters. Although quality fabrics resist color running and shrinkage, some of each may occur. If the colors are going to run, they will do so in the prewash cycle. Some experienced quilters add a large square of white cotton to the prewash; when the wash cycle finishes, the white square offers clues to the dye stability.

Working on crisp, unwashed fabric appeals to many machine piecers. If you use fabrics with the same fiber content throughout the quilt, shrinkage that occurs in the first washing should be uniform.

Test a scrap of each new fabric for shrinkage and bleeding. When prewashing fabric, unfold it to a single layer. Wash it in warm water with quilter's soap added to the wash bath and allow the fabric to shrink or bleed. Rinse the fabric until the water runs clear. Don't use fabric that has not stopped bleeding. Hang fabric to dry or tumble it in the dryer until slightly damp. Press the fabric before cutting it. If desired, restore crispness to the fabric with spray fabric sizing before pressing it.

Fabric selection is critical to the overall quality of the quilt. Although choosing a color scheme may be the most challenging part of the process, looking through bolts and bolts of fabric to select just the right ones can be a delightful experience. Quality fabrics and batting ensure that your quilt will wear well to be enjoyed for years—just like the antique quilts that have been passed along from generation to generation.

Select a First Project

Because of the multitude of patterns available from magazines, books, and fabric stores, choosing your first project may be confusing. Be confident in the advice you receive from experienced quilters and your fabric store team members. Knowledgeable employees will guide you to success.

Sign up for a quilting class. In a small group, you'll learn quilting techniques quickly and easily. Demonstration-oriented, hands-on classes practically guarantee success. Experienced instructors choose the projects, and you choose the materials or buy a supply kit. With the instructor's help, you'll learn quilting step-by-step.

Tips for selecting a first project:

- Choose a project, such as a wall hanging, baby quilt, or table runner, that will be completed in a few hours.
- Buy a kit that includes pattern, directions, and the fabric you'll need to complete the project, such as a quilt-block-of-the-month program.
- Choose a simple project. Pieced projects that are made up of squares and rectangles are among the easiest. If you choose appliqué, select simple motifs and fusible-adhesive material for your first project.
- Read through this quilting chapter to build your quilting confidence. Study the photographs and step-by-step instructions for machine and hand-piecing techniques.
- Attend a quilt show, join a quilt guild, and ask local quilters for advice. Most quilters are eager to share their passion for fabric, sewing, and quilting with newcomers.
- Fall in love with what you choose. If you really like the picture or model of what you've selected and you're wild about the fabrics you've chosen, you'll be eager to finish the project.

Select Batting

The batting is a layer of filler sandwiched between the quilt top and the backing. Select from these basic types of batting (see Photo A):

Photo A

Cotton batting, a good choice for beginners (see Photo A, top triangle), is easy to stitch and adheres well to cotton fabrics, resulting in less basting or pinning. Most cotton batts are washable. Cotton batting requires more rows of quilting than polyester batting to keep the batting from shifting and bunching during washing and drying. Follow the batting package recommendations for distance between rows of quilting. Cotton batting also is a good choice for garments because it has give that shapes and conforms to the body. Because cotton batting should not be quilted using long, widely spaced stitches, cotton flannel, which provides less loft and a flatter finished quilt top, is sometimes substituted. Cotton flannel often is used in quilts when an antique appearance is the desired result.

Polyester batting, a good choice for puffy quilts (see Photo A, left triangle), is lightweight and generally returns to its original loft when compressed and released. Polyester batting may "beard" (work out between the fabric weave) more than natural fibers. Polyester fleece is dense and works well for pillows, place mats, and table runners. Most cotton/polyester and polyester batts are washable.

Wool batting, which retains loft and absorbs moisture, is a practical choice for cool, damp climates (see Photo A, right triangle). This natural fiber is more expensive than other battings and requires special handling and care. Use lukewarm water and gentle wool detergent to wash quilts made with wool batts, and allow them to air dry to prevent shrinkage. Follow specific care instructions on the batting package.

Fusible batting eliminates the need for pins and basting. The special low-loft polyester batting (see Photo A, bottom triangle), layered between the backing and the quilt top, is pressed with a warm iron from the center to the edges. The repositionable fusing material imbedded on both sides of the batting washes out after quilting.

Consider Fabric Grain

Quilt pattern instructions usually list a cutting order to make the best use of the fabric. When cutting order isn't provided, cut large pieces first and conserve the fabric. Follow these basics for cutting:

- One or more sides of the pattern piece should follow the grain line of the fabric. If the pattern has an arrow to indicate grain line, place the arrow along the lengthwise or crosswise grain of the fabric (see illustration on page 277).

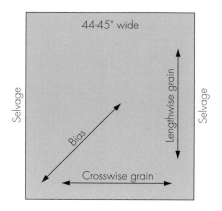

Fabric Grain Diagram

- Lengthwise grain is the most stable and has the least amount of stretch. Cut fabric pieces that will be along the outer edge of blocks and quilts on the lengthwise grain.
- Crosswise grain has more give. Cut lengths of fabric to make binding on the crosswise grain for flexibility.
- Bias grain has the most give and stretch. Cut on the bias when flexibility is desired to make appliqué stems that will meander or binding that will curve, for example.
- Do not use fabric selvages (the woven edges) in quilts. Selvages shrink and become distorted when washed.

Choosing Fabrics

Most quilters choose 100 percent cotton fabric because it feels good to the touch, is absorbent, and will withstand daily use and many washings. Although polyester and cotton combinations are strong, colorfast, and wrinkle resistant, there are some inherent problems with blends. It is often difficult to get polyester to press flat, and there is a problem with pilling (groups of short and broken fibers that come to the fabric surface and form tiny balls or nubs on the fabric).

Threads and Needles

Thread and needle choice ultimately affect the sewing project. Understand when to use the numerous types and sizes of threads and needles available, and choose the appropriate size for the fabric you work with.

Needles

Choosing the appropriate sewing machine needle size and type for the thread and fabric you use is important to the finished piece, and can make the difference between a trouble-free or a frustrating project. Using needles with eyes that are too small for the thread to easily pass through may cause the thread to fray and break. When the needle eye is too large, unattractive and weak seams result. Change the needle frequently and read needle package information and sewing machine instructions to ensure you use the correct size needle for the fabric.

Hand sewing needles are classified by size and type. Determine appropriate needle type and size according to the fabrics you work with. Dressmaking needles range from size 1 through 10 and from 14 through 22. The best hand sewing needles range from size 7 through 10.

Cotton Thread

The naturally strong fibers of cotton thread make it the first choice for general hand and machine sewing. It keeps consistent tension and resists shrinkage; however, it is not recommended for knits because it has little stretch. Use mercerized cotton thread that has been treated for added luster and strength and is receptive to dye with little or no color bleeding. When you work with 100 percent cotton fabrics (especially for quilting), use the same thread content as the fabric. Use cotton threads with delicate fabrics such as gauze, organdy, and voile; lightweight to medium fabrics such as muslin, chambray, cotton blends,

broadcloth, percale, and corduroy; and heavyweight fabrics such as duck, fleece, gabardine, denim, canvas, drapery fabric, and sailcloth.

Purchase quality threads with long fibers. Avoid threads with short, fuzzy fibers, which tend to present sewing problems. Avoid threads that have been glazed or waxed. Glazes and waxes wear off, creating sewing machine tension problems.

Polyester Thread

Polyester thread is made with either long or short strands of multifilament fibers that stretch and recover. Purchase the best quality polyester thread available. Use polyester threads on knits; extra-fine, lightweight, regular, and heavyweight synthetic fabrics and fabric blends; and for topstitching, basting, and hand-stitched buttonholes. Polyester thread is not recommended for cotton fabrics because the minuscule sharp edges of the polyester filaments tend to cut soft fibers.

Nylon Thread

Available in transparent and smoke, nylon thread is usually used in projects that require strength and stretch, such as canvas or crafts projects. Fine nylon thread is used to stitch dress, skirt, and pants hems because the thread is invisible and will stretch without breaking.

Cotton/Polyester Thread

This thread combination has a minimum core fiber of two-ply twisted polyester wrapped with mercerized cotton. It has some stretch, is more resistant to heat than pure polyester thread, and is less damaging to cotton fabrics. Use versatile cotton/polyester thread with many fabrics.

Metallic and Embellishing Thread

Threads of this type are used for decorative purposes, adding sparkle and shine to quilts, wall hangings, crafts

Thread Size and Fabric Use Chart

P= Polyester, C=Cotton Sewing Threads

Size of Thread	C30/2	P30/3	C40/3	C50/3	C60/2	P70/3	P100/3
Blended Fabric		●			●	●	●
Chiffon	●						
Cotton Fabric			●	●	●		
Denim			●	●			
General Purpose	●						
Home Decor Fabric		●				●	
Jersey						●	●
Knit						●	●
Leather		●					●
Linen			●	●	●		
Silk	●				●		●
Synthetic	●			●	●	●	
Tricot						●	●
Wool		●	●	●	●		

projects, and fashion garments. Specialty threads, however, tend to be fragile and delicate and will not hold up well on projects that receive wear and tear. Use specifically designed machine needles when sewing with metallic threads.

Thread Size
Thread size is referred to with number combinations, such as 80/2. The first number designates thread thickness or weight and diameter. The higher the number, the finer the thread. The second digit represents the number of plies twisted together to make the strand of thread and indicates thread strength.

Machine Piecing Threads
Match thread fiber with fabric content, using 100 percent cotton thread or cotton-covered polyester thread to piece 100 percent cotton fabric. Use matching or contrasting thread for stitching that is intended to show from the right side of the finished project.

Thread Color

Quilters generally aren't concerned with matching thread color when machine piecing. Instead they rely on light, medium, or dark neutral threads, depending on the color values of the fabrics. You may choose to use thread to match the fabric. With fabrics that have contrasting values, use one thread color on the top and another in the bobbin.

Cutting *Fabrics*

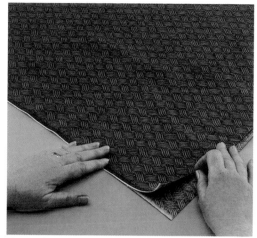

Photo A

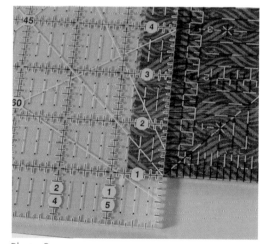

Photo B

Photo C

Cutting Basics

Rotary cutters have revolutionized quilting, making precision cutting faster and easier for even novice quilters. Using specialty rulers and cutters, quilters can cut myriad patchwork shapes in record time.

Sharp, round, rotary cutter blades will cut through as many as six fabric layers. Use rotary cutters carefully—the blade is very sharp. Purchase a cutter with a safety guard and make it a practice to cover the blade every time you finish cutting. Use the rotary cutter only with a self-healing mat and a heavy acrylic ruler. Treat your cutter with care—avoid cutting over pins and dropping the cutter, both of which damage the blade and cause frequent replacement.

Note: *ALWAYS use the safety cover for the blade when the cutter is not in use. NEVER leave a rotary cutter where a child can reach it.*

Stand while cutting and cut away from you. Hold the cutter at a 45-degree angle to the cutting surface and apply even pressure on the rotary cutter. The surface of the self-healing mat and the weight and the acrylic ruler help to prevent the fabric from shifting while you cut. If you are unable to cut through multiple fabric layers easily, check the following:

• Is the blade dull? If yes, sharpen or replace it.
• Is there a nick in the blade? If yes, replace it.
• Did you put enough pressure on the rotary cutter? Practice on fabric scraps to learn the amount of pressure that works for you.

Many quilters will tell you that much of the pleasure of putting together a quilt begins with cutting the fabric. This tactile process gets them in touch with the fabric before the construction begins. Experiment with the tools of the trade, learning the methods of using templates as well as rotary equipment, to discover the joy of the hands-on approach with fabric.

Photo D

Rotary Cutting

1. Press the fabric. Lay the fabric facedown on the cutting mat, selvage edges parallel to the mat. Fold the fabric wrong sides together to match the selvages (see Photo A, page 279). Fold the fabric in half again and align the fold with the selvages. Lightly crease the folds by hand.

2. To ensure straight cuts, align a large acrylic ruler along the bottom fold of the fabric. Align the 1-inch mark on a second ruler with the fold of the fabric, leaving a small amount of fabric under the ruler edge for trimming (see Photo B, page 279). Remove the first ruler. Use the second ruler as a guide (see Photo C, page 279) and the rotary cutter to trim away the fabric edge.

To Cut Strips

Align the desired width mark on the ruler with the edge of the fabric. Hold the ruler firmly in place with one hand, one finger resting on the mat for stability.
Note: Some quilters arch their hand; some hold the ruler with their hand almost flat. Hold the ruler so it is comfortable for you and in a manner that prevents slipping and ensures that the blade does not come in contact with your fingers.

Photo E

Hold the rotary cutter in the opposite hand with the blade next to the ruler edge of the ruler. Roll the blade across the fabric for a clean cut (see Photo D).

To Cut Squares

Turn the cutting mat clockwise 90 degrees. Align the same width mark used to cut the strip (see Photo E) along the fabric edge, ensuring that the top and bottom edges of the strip are accurately aligned. For example, align the 2½-inch mark along the left edge of the 2½-inch strip. Roll the cutting blade along the edge of the ruler to cut accurate 2½-inch squares.

To Cut Rectangles

Align the desired measurement on the ruler with the lower edge of the strip to cut rectangles. For example, align the 4½-inch mark along the lower edge of the 2½-inch strip and roll the cutter blade along the edge of the ruler to cut 2½x4½-inch rectangles (see Photo F).
Note: Check your pattern to determine whether measurements include seam allowances. If not, add ¼ inch to each outside edge of the strips, squares, or rectangles before cutting.

Photo F

Photo G

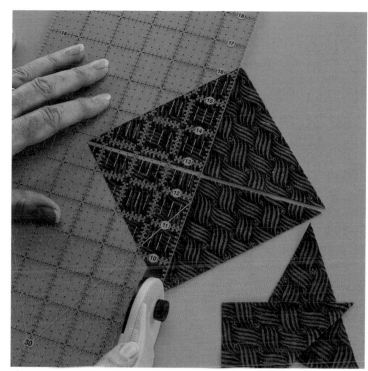

Photo H

To Cut Half-Square Triangles
(two triangles from one square)
Align the edge of the ruler diagonally with opposing corners (see Photo G) and cut along the ruler edge for two half-square triangles. When two half-square triangles the same size are joined along the center seam, they make one square.

To make a 4-inch finished half-square triangle block:
- Cut a 4⅞-inch-wide fabric strip.
- Cut a 4⅞-inch square from the strip.
- Cut the square in half diagonally as shown in Photo G.
- Join two 4⅞-inch half-square triangles to make one 4½-inch triangle-square, which finishes to 4 inches square when joined to additional 4½-inch blocks.

Note: *To figure cutting measurements that include seam allowances, add ⅞ inch to the finished size of the half-square triangle block before cutting the square.*

To Cut Quarter-Square Triangles
(four triangles from one square)
Align the ruler diagonally with opposing corners and rotary cut in half. Keep the triangles together, reposition the ruler along the opposite corners, and cut again (see Photo H). Sew four quarter-square triangles together to make one square.

To make a 4-inch finished quarter-square triangle block:
- Cut a 5¼-inch-wide fabric strip.
- Cut a 5¼-inch square from the strip.
- Cut the square in diagonal quarters (in an X) as shown in Photo H.
- Sew together four 5¼-inch quarter-square triangles to make one 4½-inch quarter-square triangle block, which finishes to 4 inches square when joined to additional 4½-inch blocks.

Note: *To figure cutting measurements that include seam allowances, add 1¼ inches to the finished size of the quarter-square triangle block before cutting the square.*

To Cut Fabric Wider Than the Ruler Length
Align the ruler along the fabric to cut as you would for strips. Cut along the length of the ruler, nearly to the end. Leave the rotary cutter in place on the fabric and slide the ruler ahead several inches, aligning the ruler edge with the cut fabric edge. Continue cutting and sliding the ruler along the fabric edge to cut the length of fabric needed.

Traditional Template Making and Cutting

Using ready-made templates of heavy plastic, acrylic, or metal to cut curved and irregular pieces ensures accuracy. Make your own permanent templates from sturdy template plastic to trace a pattern many times without wearing away the edges.

1. Lay template plastic over the quilt pattern and trace the pattern onto the plastic using a permanent marker and a straightedge. For hand piecing, trace the exact size of the finished piece without seam allowances (see Photo A); dark lines indicate the sewing line. For machine piecing, include the seam allowances in the template size (see Photo B); dashes indicate the sewing line, the solid line is the cutting line. Make pinholes in template corners to mark corner points. With a permanent marker, indicate the piece number, grain line, and block name on the template. Check for accuracy. Templates must be accurate or the error, no matter how small, will compound many times as you assemble a quilt top.

2. *For hand piecing or appliqué,* position the template on the wrong side of the fabric and trace the template, leaving at least ½ inch between each pattern. Draw narrow, accurate sewing lines with a pencil, chalk, or quilt marker (see Photo C). Mark cutting lines or estimate seam allowances around each piece by eye as you cut with sharp scissors, adding ¼-inch seam allowances for hand piecing; add ³⁄₁₆-inch seam allowances for hand appliqué.

For machine piecing, position the template on the wrong side of the fabric and trace (see Photo D), leaving little space between templates. Use sharp scissors or a rotary cutter and ruler to cut precisely on the cutting lines.

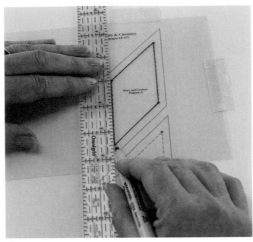
Photo A

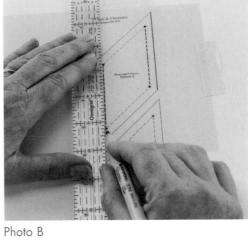
Photo B

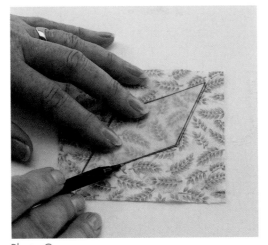
Photo C

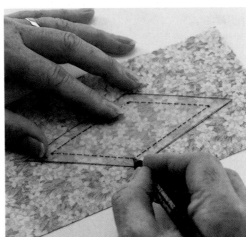
Photo D

Creative Tip

When rotary cutting large quantities of strips, place self-adhesive notes on the back of a clear acrylic ruler to mark the desired increments.

– Store Team Member, Taunton, Massachusetts

Hand Piecing

1. Mark the seam lines on the wrong sides of both fabric pieces to be joined. Accurately drawn seam lines are critical to matching and sewing fabric pieces to result in a predetermined unit or block size. Place the fabric pieces right sides together, matching the seam lines as closely as possible. Hold the fabric edges between your thumb and index finger and pin the edges, if desired. Thread a needle and knot one end of the thread or backstitch at the starting point of the seam. In one continuous motion, insert the needle at the beginning of the seam line on the top fabric, push the needle through the bottom

Photo A

Photo B

fabric on the seam line, and bring the needle to the top along the seam line. Repeat the motion to take one, two, or more stitches (see Photo A). Pull the thread evenly along the seam line without pulling it too tightly. Backstitch at the end of the seam line and cut the thread.

2. To join two units or rows of patchwork, hold the fabric between your thumb and index finger, matching the seam lines as closely as possible. Begin and end the seam line as for the two fabric pieces (see Photo B). Butt seam allowances, using your fingers to press opposing seams in alternate directions to reduce bulk. Take fewer continuous stitches over the bulk to ensure that all fabric layers are caught together. Press the seams flat.

Machine Piecing

You'll get quick results with a sewing machine. Although it's not necessary to mark seam allowances, it is necessary to be consistent. Slight differences are compounded as units and blocks are assembled. Use a ¼-inch foot if your sewing machine has one, and follow the guidelines *below* to ensure seam accuracy.

Seam Allowance Accuracy

1. Use a ¼-inch quilter's seam allowance to join two 2½-inch-wide fabric rectangles along the long edges (see Photo C, page 284), right sides together.

2. Press open the pieces and measure the width of the unit—it should measure exactly 4½ inches from raw edge to raw edge (see Photo D, page 284).

Patchwork refers to the process of joining fabric patches to form a textile surface. Patchwork also refers to the finished product that has been pieced, assembled with backing and batting, and quilted. Often associated with utilitarian quilts, patchwork frequently consists of fabric scraps, reflecting the desire of past generations to make the best use of their resources.

If the strip does not measure accurately, make adjustments to the sewing machine seam gauge. Join additional 2½-inch-wide fabric pieces until the unit measures exactly 4½ inches across.

When the seam allowance is accurate, insert the needle into the seam line and place a small strip of masking tape on the sewing machine needle plate, using the fabric edge as a guide. Sew with the fabric edge butted against the inside edge of the tape for an accurate ¼-inch seam allowance.

Photo C

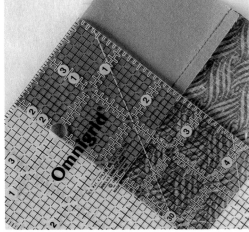

Photo D

Machine Chain Piecing

Save time and thread by continuously joining fabric pieces on a sewing machine. This method is especially useful to join many same-size fabric pieces. For example, squares that make up a unit or block can be joined in twos or threes. Units are combined in larger units to complete the block.

1. Match two fabric pieces right sides together along the seam edges. Feed the pieces under the machine needle and sew an accurate ¼ inch. Without lifting the

presser foot or clipping the thread, insert another unit and sew along the ¼-inch seam line. Continue feeding and sewing fabric pieces to complete a length of chained units (see Photo E). Clip the threads between the patches. Press the seams.

2. Blocks and rows of blocks also can be chained by machine. Feed the rows of patches or blocks under the machine needle, continuing as for the smaller units. Press or finger press seam allowances to lie in alternate directions to reduce seam bulk.

Pressing Matters

Pressing is key to accuracy in quilting. Press rather than iron seams after each step of sewing. Use a light pressure with the iron, picking it up and moving to from one position to another. Sliding the iron across the fabrics distorts the seams. Allow fabrics to cool to prevent distortion. Follow the pressing sequence to join units, blocks, rows, and strips.

1. Lay the sewn unit on the ironing table. Set the stitches by pressing the seam flat.

2. Open the unit facedown and press the seam allowance to one side (or press it open if directed to do so). Some quilt pattern instructions suggest which way to press seam allowances. When in doubt as to which direction, press the seam allowances toward the darker fabric.

3. Press the seam from the right side of the unit or block. Pressing from the right side of the fabric prevents creases that may result from pressing only from the wrong side of the fabric. Allow the fabric to cool.

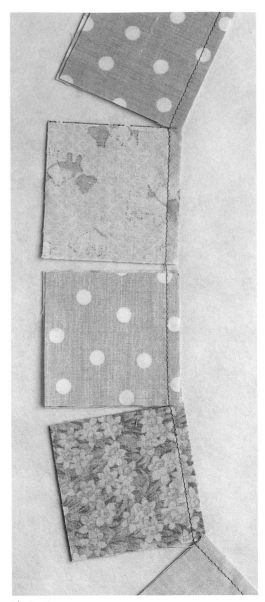

Photo E

4. Reduce seam bulk by alternating the direction of seams along a strip of blocks when joining units or blocks.

Note: *Press appliqué and dimensional patchwork facedown on a clean, white terry towel to avoid flattening the design.*

Piecing *Basic Quilt Blocks and Units*

Timesaving Techniques

Strip Piecing

1. Right sides together, cut two contrasting fabrics into strips. Sew the strips together lengthwise (see Photo A, wrong side of green fabric). Rotary-cut the joined strips into segments (see Photo A, wrong side of yellow fabric) to make squares or rectangles.

2. Press the seams and then join the segments by alternating color placement (see Photo B) or use them in combination with other units to make a block. After joining segments into a unit, press the seams to one side (see Photo C, four-patch unit example).

Note: *Make strip sets using more than two fabric strips to make nine-patch blocks (see pages 286–287).*

Easy-to-sew blocks, such as four-patch, nine-patch, half-square triangle, and Flying Geese, continue to be fun to assemble long after you've acquired the skill to put them together effortlessly. These time-honored blocks adapt to many settings and fabric combinations. Assemble a quilt top using a repeat of the same block or sew several block designs to combine in a sampler quilt.

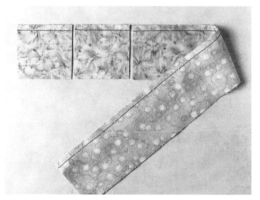

Photo A

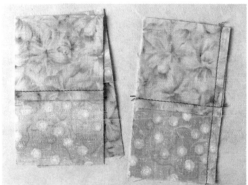

Photo B

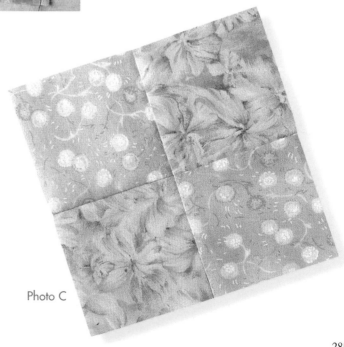

Photo C

Figuring Four-Patch Blocks

1. Two strips sewn together and cut into segments make the units for a four-patch block. For quick piecing, cut two 42-inch strips to the width of one finished segment size plus ½ inch for seam allowances.

Use the chart *below* to guide you in making ten sizes of four-patch blocks. To make a finished 4-inch square four-patch block, cut fabric as follows:
- From dark fabric cut one 2½x42-inch strip
- From light fabric cut one 2½x42-inch strip

2. Place the strips right sides together, matching raw edges, and sew the length of the strips. Press the seam allowance toward the dark fabric (see Photo A, page 285).

3. Cut the strip set into 2½-inch wide segments. From a 42-inch strip set, you can cut 16 segments (see the chart *below*).

4. Reverse one of the segments to match light to dark fabric (see Photo B, page 285). Match the raw edges of the segments and interlock the seams, one seam up and one seam down. Join the segments to make one four-patch block. Press the seam to one side. Repeat to make eight 4½-inch four-patch blocks. When joined together, the blocks will finish to 4 inches square.

Note: To cut squares with scissors rather than a rotary cutter, use the Segment Size column in the chart below to cut four squares to make one four-patch block.

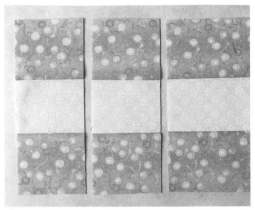

Photo D

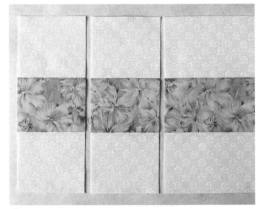

Photo E

Finished Size of Four-Patch Block	Strip Width Cut Two Strips	Segment Size
2"	1½x42"	28—1½" wide
3"	2x42"	21—2" wide
3½"	2¼x42"	18—2¼" wide
4"	2½x42"	16—2½" wide
4½"	2¾x42"	15—2¾" wide
5"	3x42"	14—3" wide
5½"	3¼x42"	12—3¼" wide
6"	3½x42"	12—3½" wide
8"	4½x42"	9—4½" wide
10"	5½x42"	7—5½" wide

Figuring Nine-Patch Blocks

1. Three strips sewn together and cut into segments make the units for a nine-patch block. For quick piecing, cut six 42-inch strips to the width of one finished segment size plus ½ inch for seam allowances.

Use the chart *opposite* to guide you in making four sizes of four-patch blocks. To make a finished 6-inch square four-patch block, cut fabric as follows:

- From dark fabric cut two 2½x42-inch strips
- From light fabric cut three 2½x42-inch strips
- From medium fabric cut one 2½x42-inch strip

Photo F

Photo G

2. Right sides together and matching raw edges, join one light to one dark strip along one long edge. Join a second dark strip to the opposite side of the light strip. Press the seams toward the dark fabric.

3. Right sides together and matching raw edges, join one light strip to one medium strip along the long edge. Join a second light strip to the opposite side of the medium strip. Press the seams toward the darker fabric.

4. Cut the strip sets into 2½ inch segments (see Photos D and E, *opposite*), the same width as the original strips. Lay out the segments (see Photo F).

5. Join one dark-light-dark segment to a light-medium-light segment. Join a second dark-light-dark segment to make a nine-patch block that measures 6½ inches square, including seam allowances (see Photo G). Press the seams in one direction. The finished size of the block, when joined to other nine-patch or 6½-inch blocks, will be 6 inches square.

Note: *It takes twice as many dark-light-dark segments as light-medium-light segments to make this nine-patch block. Cut and sew an additional dark-light-dark strip set to use all of the segments for nine-patch blocks, alternate the block by having the* light-medium-light segments to the outside of the block, or use leftover segments in another quilting project.

Finished Size of Nine-Patch Block	Strip Width Cut Six Strips	Segment Size
3"	1½×42"	28—1½" wide
6"	2½×42"	16—2½" wide
9"	3½×42"	12—3½" wide
12"	4½×42"	9—4½" wide

Half-Square Triangle Units

Half-square triangle units are basic pieced units that can be used alone or as part of larger or elaborately pieced quilt blocks. To quickly piece half-square triangles, begin with two squares of contrasting fabric cut to the same size. Two squares of fabric placed together, sewn, and cut apart will result in two half-square triangle units.

Method A

1. Right sides together and matching raw edges, place two squares of contrasting fabric together. Lay the squares, lighter fabric on the top, on a piece of 220-grit sandpaper to prevent the fabric from shifting while it is marked. Place a ruler diagonally on the fabric and use a pencil to draw a line from corner to corner across the lighter square (see Photo A). Alternately, you can place the fabric squares on a cutting mat and hold it firmly in place with the ruler while you draw the diagonal line.

2. Stitch ¼ inch on both sides of the line (see Photo B). Cut along the line with a rotary cutter to make two half-square triangle units (see Photo C). Press the seams toward the dark fabric.

Method B

1. Right sides together, stack one light and one dark fabric square. Place the rotary ruler diagonally across the squares and use a rotary cutter to cut the squares in half (see Photo D, *opposite*).

2. Sew together one light and one dark triangle (see Photo E, *opposite*). Press the seam toward the dark fabric to complete one half-square triangle (see Photo F, *opposite*). Repeat to make a second half-square triangle with the remaining light and dark triangles.

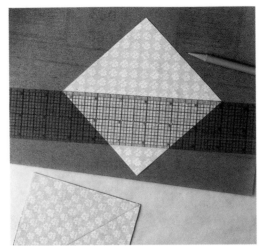

Photo A

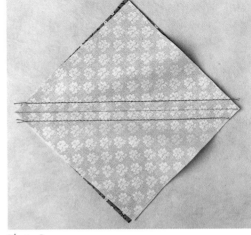

Photo B

Photo C

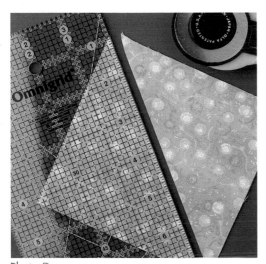
Photo D

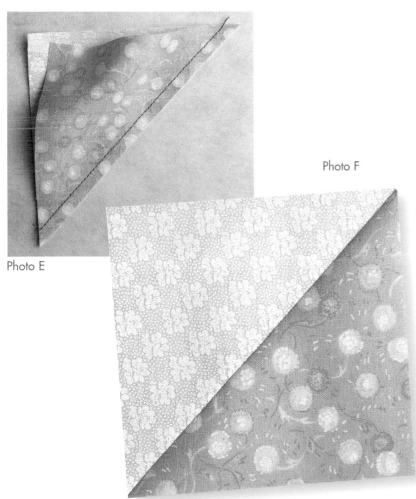
Photo E

Photo F

Finished Size	Cut Size	Number of Squares Cut From 42" Strip
1"	1⅞"	21
2"	2⅞"	14
3"	3⅞"	10
3½"	4⅜"	9
4"	4⅞"	8
4¼"	5⅛"	8
4½"	5⅜"	7
4¾"	5⅝"	7
5"	5⅞"	7
5¼"	6⅛"	6
5½"	6⅜"	6
5¾"	6⅝"	6
6"	6⅞"	6

Figuring Half-Square Triangles

1. Use the chart, *above,* to guide you in making several sizes of half-square triangle blocks. For example, to make two finished 4-inch half-square triangles, add ⅞ inch to the finished size, and cut two 4⅞-inch squares from contrasting fabric.

2. Place the squares right sides together and use Method A or Method B, *opposite,* to make two half-square triangle units. Press the seam toward the darker fabric.

Note: *To make quarter-square triangle units, add 1¼ inches to the finished size before cutting squares. (For example, cut 5¼-inch squares for a 4-inch finished quarter-square triangle unit.)*

Flying Geese Units

Flying Geese is a basic quilt block unit that can be combined with squares to make star blocks, pieced to make rows or borders, or creatively joined with other blocks.

To make one Flying Geese unit you will need two light squares and one dark rectangle that is twice the length of the finished size of one light square, plus seam allowances. For example, to make a finished 2×4-inch Flying Geese unit, use two light 2½-inch squares and one dark 2½X4½-inch rectangle (see Photo A, *opposite*).

1. For accurate sewing lines, place the light fabric squares on 220-grit sandpaper and use a quilter's pencil to mark a diagonal sewing line along the wrong side of the squares (see Photo B, *opposite*).

2. With right sides together, align the edges of one marked light square along one end of the dark rectangle (see Photo C, *opposite*) and stitch on the drawn line. Trim the seam allowance to ¼ inch.

3. Open the unit and press the seam toward the dark fabric to complete half a Flying Geese unit (see Photo D, *opposite*). Sew a second marked light square to the opposite end of the rectangle. Trim and press the seam (see Photo E, *opposite*) to complete one Flying Geese unit (see Photo F, *opposite*).

⚜Creative Tip

When I cut templates for quilt projects, I store them in

heavy zipper-type freezer bags and label the bags with

the project name. I can easily see what's in each bag.

– Store Team Member, Springfield, Missouri

Photo A

Photo B

Photo C

Photo D

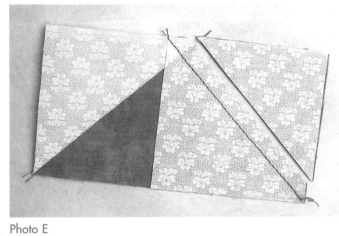

Photo E

Photo F

Photo G

To Make a Star Block

1. To make a Star Block using Flying Geese, use four Flying Geese units, one 4½-inch light square for the center, and four 2½-inch dark squares for the corners.

2. Referring to the photo, *left,* to assemble the Star Block, sew dark squares to each short side of two Flying Geese Units. Press the seams toward the dark squares.

3. Sew a Flying Geese unit to opposite sides of the large light square, noting the position of the Flying Geese units. Press the seams toward the large square.

4. Sew the rows of units together to complete one Star Block (see Photo G). Press the seams to one side.

Note: To make a table runner as shown on page 290, assemble three Star Blocks side by side. See pages 310-311 to layer and bind the table runner.

Figuring Flying Geese Blocks

1. Use the chart at, *right,* to guide you in making five sizes of Flying Geese blocks. For example, to make a 4×8-inch Flying Geese block, from contrasting fabric cut one rectangle 4½×8½ inches and cut two 4½-inch squares.

2. Following the instructions on page 290, join the squares to the rectangle to make one Flying Geese unit. Trim the seams and press them toward the dark fabric. Press the unit from the right side.

Note: To figure additional sizes for Flying Geese units, cut the squares to equal the width of the rectangle.

Finished Size	Cut Rectangle Size	Cut Square Size	Pieces from Strip 42"
2×4"	2½×4½"	2½"	16—2½" wide
3×6"	3½×6½"	3½"	12—3½" wide
4×8"	4½×8½"	4½"	9—4½" wide
5×10"	5½×10½"	5½"	7—5½" wide
6×12"	6½×12½"	6½"	6—6½" wide

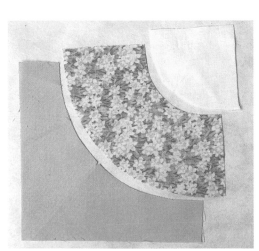

Photo A

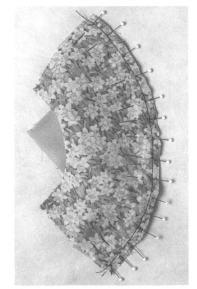

Photo B

Photo C

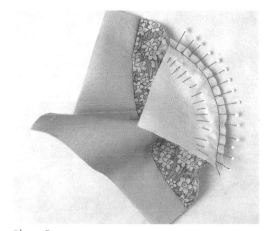

Photo D

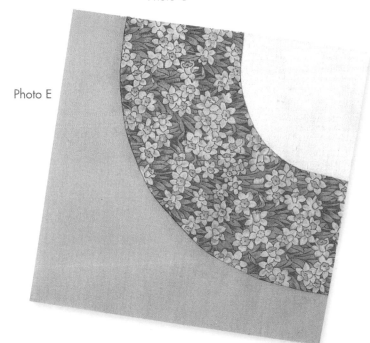

Photo E

Piecing Curved Seams

The key to easy alignment on curved pieces is to clip a small center matching notch in both curved edges (see Photo A).

1. Clip into the seam allowance of the inner curve, without cutting into or beyond the seam lines. Do not clip outer curved edges.

2. Align pieces right sides together, matching center notches. Pin at notches, seam ends, and liberally along the seam line (see Photo B), easing fabric as needed. Sew the pieces together with a ¼-inch seam allowance.

3. Clip the curve, if necessary, to lie flat. Press the seam allowance toward the inner curved piece (see Photo C). Join subsequent curved pieces in the same manner (see Photo D) to complete a curved block (see Photo E).

Setting In Seams

To sew angled pieces, such as the units that make up a LeMoyne Star, carefully align marked matching points. Start and stop sewing precisely at the matching points, ¼ inch from the edge, and backstitch to secure the seams.

1. Using the template or rotary cutter method, cut eight diamonds, four half-square triangles, and four squares.

2. Join two diamonds right sides together along one edge and sew between the matching points (see Photo A) to make one two-diamond unit.

3. Right sides together, align and sew the inner side of the two-diamond unit to one short edge of a triangle (see Photo B), matching and sewing to the ¼-inch marks. Remove the unit from the sewing machine, or turn it if you are piecing by hand. Match the second short edge of the triangle to the opposite inner edge of the two-diamond unit. Stitch between the matching points (see Photo C). Press the seams toward the diamond unit (see Photo D, *opposite*) to complete one diamond-triangle unit. Repeat to make four diamond-triangle units.

4. Match two diamond-triangle units along the diamond points (opposite the triangle), and sew them together. Press the seams. Sew one side of a square along the diamond edge adjacent to a triangle, (see photos E and F, *opposite*). Remove the unit from the sewing machine. Rotate the square to match and sew it to the adjoining diamond edge. Press the four-diamond and square unit (see Photo G, *opposite*). Set the unit aside. Repeat to make a second four-diamond and square unit. Press the seams.

5. To join the two units, refer to Photo H, *opposite,* and match and finger-press the seams in opposite directions to reduce bulk. Pin the units together. Carefully sew over the star center for crisp center points. Press the seams.

6. Join the final two squares, matching, turning, and setting in the seams to lie flat (see Photo H, *opposite*). Carefully press the block, right side up, to avoid distorting the seams and raw edges.

Photo A

Photo B

Photo C

Photo D

Photo E

Photo F

Photo G

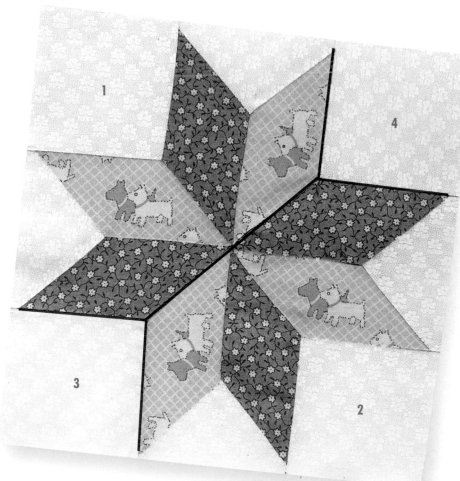

Photo H

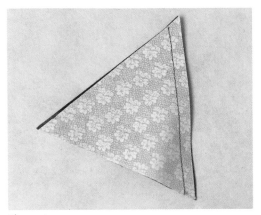

Photo A

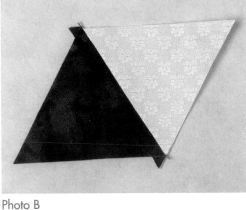

Photo B

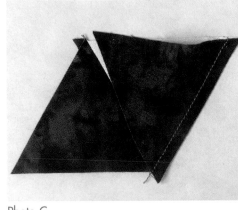

Photo C

Photo D

Photo E

Equilateral Triangle Units

Triangle motifs are popular for making patchwork blocks, using two or more colors for contrast. Join four equilateral triangles to create a larger equilateral triangle.

1. Cut three dark and one light equilateral triangles. Join one light and one dark equilateral triangle (see Photo A). Press the seam allowance toward the dark fabric (see Photo B).

2. Join a second dark triangle to the opposite side of the light triangle (see Photo C). Press the seam allowance toward the second dark triangle (see Photo D).

3. Join a third dark triangle to the remaining side of the light triangle (see Photo E). Press the seam allowance toward the third dark triangle to complete an equilateral triangle block (see Photo F).

Note: *When working with equilateral triangles, avoid stretching the bias edges. Lift and lower the iron on the seams without sliding it across the fabric.*

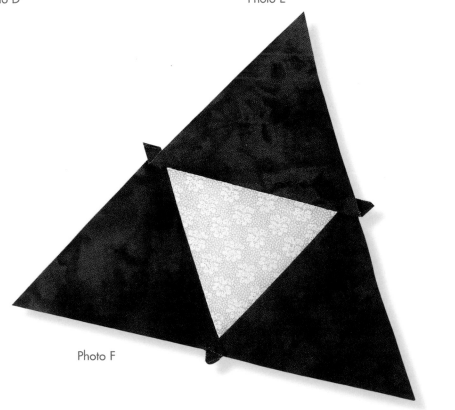

Photo F

Appliqué *Artistry*

Appliqué lends itself to graceful, curving shapes and layers of pattern and color. Whether you use tiny invisible stitches or folk art blanket stitches, you'll be able to achieve diverse expressions of art with appliqué. Because the stitching can be done by hand, you can tote the work along with you as you travel—filling your time creatively.

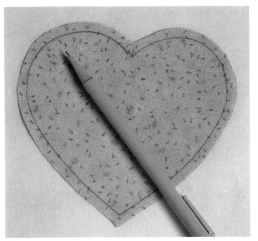

Photo A

Photo B

Photo C

Appliqué

Create a fabric picture by applying textile shapes to a foundation block. Traditionally, fabric edges are turned under and sewn to a foundation fabric, using slip stitches (see Photo B) or embroidery stitches (see pages 90-94). Appliqué shortcuts provide an easy way for busy quilters to accomplish similar results in a fraction of the time.

Traditional Hand Appliqué
Use long milliner's needles or straw needles for hand appliqué. The extra needle length aids in tucking under fabric before taking the slip stitches.

1. Trace a template onto the reverse side of the appliqué fabric. Cut out the fabric shape, adding ³⁄₁₆-inch seam allowance (see Photo A).

2. Place the fabric shape right side up on the foundation fabric and pin it in place. With the needle tip, turn under the seam allowance along the edges of the shape as you hand-sew it to the foundation fabric. Use tiny slip stitches and pull the thread taut every few stitches to raise the appliqué

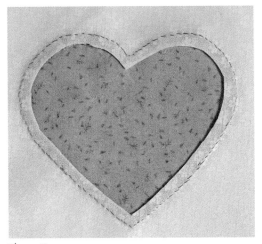

Photo D

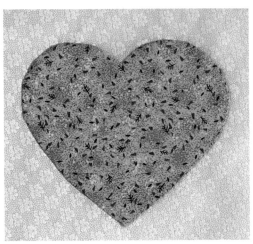

Photo E

above the level of the foundation fabric (see Photo B). Clip curves on complex shapes so seam allowances lie flat when turned under.
Note: *You may baste and press seam allowances before stitching.*

3. Turn the fabric to the reverse side of the appliqué to reveal the stitches around the shape (see Photo C).

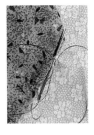

4. On the reverse side, trim away the foundation fabric to within ¼ inch of the sewing line (see Photo D). On the right side of the appliqué, the shape should be smooth (see Photo E).
Note: *To press, place the appliqué facedown on a white terry towel. Press lightly to avoid flattening the dimension of the appliqué.*

Photo A

Photo B

Photo C

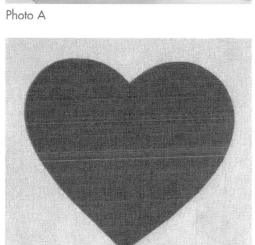

Photo D

Photo E

Fusible Appliqué

Either fuse the entire appliqué shape to the foundation fabric or fuse just the outer edges of the shape. The heart in the foreground of Photo B shows how to cut the fusing-adhesive material to fuse the entire shape. The heart in the background of Photo B shows fusing adhesive material cut to fuse only the outer edges of the

shape to eliminate stiffness in the finished applique project.

1. Lay fusing-adhesive material paper side up over the appliqué pattern. Trace the pattern with a pencil (see Photo A).

2. *Fusing the entire shape* (see Photo B, foreground): Cut the shape roughly ¼ inch

outside the line. Following manufacturer's instructions, press the fusing adhesive onto the back of the appliqué fabric and allow it to cool.

Fusing the shape edges (see Photo B, background heart): Cut the shape roughly ¼ inch outside and inside of the traced line. Following the manufacturer's instructions, press the fusing-adhesive material onto the back of the appliqué fabric and allow it to cool.

3. Cut out the shape on the drawn line. Peel off the paper from the fabric (see Photo C).

4. Place the shape on the foundation fabric and press to fuse it in place (see Photo D). Allow the fabric to cool.

5. If desired, make blanket stitches by machine or hand around the edges of the shape (see Photo E).

Photo A

Photo B

Photo C

Double Appliqué

To ease the challenge of turning curved edges, face appliqué pieces with sheer, nonfusible, nonwoven interfacing.

1. Trace the pattern onto the wrong side of the appliqué fabric. Right sides together, stack the appliqué fabric on a similar size square of interfacing (see Photo A).

2. Sew pieces together along the pattern line (see Photo B). Trim the interfacing slightly smaller than the fabric.

3. Clip the inner curves, and make a small clipped opening in the center of the interfacing. Turn the shape to the right side through the clipped opening (see Photo C, facing side of appliqué shape). Press the piece from the fabric side.

4. Pin and stitch the shape to the foundation fabric. If desired, use a blanket stitch to appliqué the edges of the shape (see Photo D) to the foundation fabric.

Photo D

Photo A

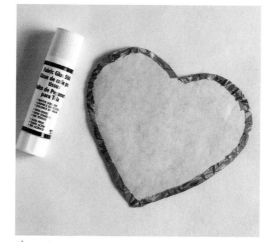

Photo B

Photo C

Freezer Paper Appliqué

Whenever accuracy is critical, use the freezer paper appliqué method. Use a warm iron and freezer paper to temporarily adhere the waxed side of the paper to fabric.

1. Cut a freezer paper pattern and press it to the wrong side of the appliqué fabric (see Photo A). Cut out the fabric shape, allowing a scant ¼-inch seam allowance.

2. Apply dabs of temporary-hold adhesive to the freezer paper edge. Finger fold the seam allowance over the edge of the freezer paper and press into place (see Photo B), clipping the seam allowance curves as necessary.

3. Pin and blind-hem the appliqué shape on the foundation fabric by machine (see Photo C).

4. Turn over the appliqué and trim away the foundation fabric to within ¼ inch of the sewing line. Gently pull the freezer paper away from the stitching (see Photo D).

Photo D

Bias Stems and Vines

Because appliqué stems and vines generally curve gracefully, cut strips on the bias for flexibility. Use one of these two methods to makes stems and vines.

Quick Method No. 1:

1. Cut the bias strip three times the desired finished width. Fold and press the strip in thirds (see Photo A).

2. Right sides facing, sew the bias strip to the background fabric along the right hand fold. Use the fold line as a stitching guide, matching the fold with the desired background curve. Clip curves in seam allowance as necessary. (See Photo B).

3. Turn bias strip over the stitching line and secure with hand or machine stitches along the opposite folded edge. (see Photo C).

Quick Method No. 2:

1. Cut the bias strip twice the desired finished width plus ½ inch. (For example, cut the bias strip 1½ inches wide for a ½-inch wide finished strip.) Fold the bias strip in half lengthwise, right sides out, and press (see Photo D).

2. Using a ¼-inch seam, sew folded bias to background, aligning raw edges with desired background curve. Clip curves in seam allowance as needed (see Photo E).

3. Turn bias strip over the stitching line and secure with hand or machine stitches along the folded edge (see Photo F).

Photo A

Photo B

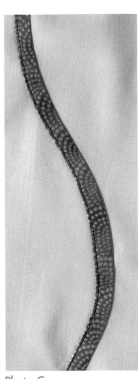

Photo C

Photo D

Photo E

Photo F

Setting *Quilt Tops*

After the blocks are pieced, assemble them into a quilt top. There are so many layout designs in which to set pieced blocks that the same blocks arranged in a variety of ways create entirely different quilt tops. Starting with these familiar block layout designs, arrange and rearrange finished blocks to achieve the look you want for your quilt top.

1. Blocks in a straight set (see Photo A): Blocks are joined horizontally or vertically to form rows. The rows are sewn together to complete the quilt top.

2. Blocks combined with sashing strips and corner squares (see Photo B): Strips and squares add dimension as well as size to the quilt top, often providing contrast or detail to the pieced blocks and a surface for additional quilting designs. Blocks also can be combined with sashing strips without corner squares.

3. Blocks set on point (see photo C): Pieced blocks take on a different look when joined on the diagonal with setting triangles. Notice how the movement changes from the blocks that are set straight in rows or with sashing strips.

Laying out the blocks before joining them creates a visual for reviewing the total design of the quilt top. Whether you set blocks in tidy rows, encase them in sashing strips and setting squares, or set them on point with setting triangles, you'll have fun discovering the design possibilities.

Photo A

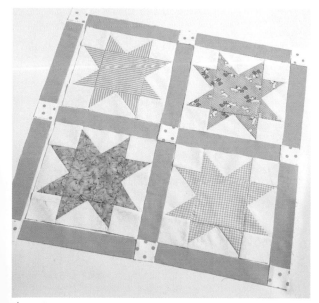

Photo B

Photo C

Making *Borders*

Borders are the frames for your pieced or appliquéd quilt tops. Get as fancy or as plain as the quilt fabrics and design dictate, using a variety of techniques to contribute size, color, or pattern to quilt tops. Follow these step-by-step directions to learn how to frame the pieced quilt top with borders to complement, set off, and finish the quilt while adding to its function and beauty.

Plain Border with Butted Corners

The fastest and easiest border to cut and sew, this method uses two strips cut the length of the pieced quilt top. The two remaining strips are cut to fit the quilt top width including the first two borders.

Before sewing on borders, square up the quilt top. Measure the width and length of the quilt top in several places. Lengths and widths should match for opposing quilt edges. Use an acrylic ruler or square to check that the quilt top corners are 90-degree angles. Trim the corners with a rotary cutter or scissors for neat corners.

1. Measure the quilt top from top to bottom edges along the center of the quilt. Determine the border width and add ½-inch seam allowances. For 3-inch finished borders on a quilt that measures 24 inches from top to bottom, for example, cut two 3½×24-inch border strips. Right sides together, sew a border strip along one side of the quilt top (see Photo A). Sew the remaining strip to the opposite side. Press the border strips open, pressing the seam allowances toward the border strips.

2. Measure the quilt from side to side along the center of the quilt top, including the borders. For example, to make 3-inch wide finished borders on a quilt that measures 18½ inches across (including the borders), cut two 3½×18½-inch border strips. Right sides together, join the strips to the top and bottom edges of the quilt (see Photo B). Press the borders open, pressing the seam allowances toward the border strips (see Photo C).

Pieced Border with Pieced Corner Squares

Pieced borders add dimension, design, and movement to quilts.

1. Measure the quilt vertically and horizontally along the center. You will

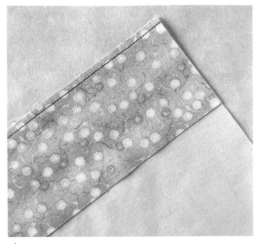
Photo A

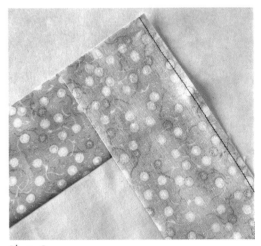
Photo B

Photo C

Photo A

Photo B

Photo C

cut and piece four dark strips and two light strips to equal each length. For example, for a finished 6-inch pieced border on a quilt top that measures 48 inches long by 36 inches wide, cut four dark and two light 2½×48 inch strips. Cut four dark and two light 2½×36 inch strips. Join the strips with the light strip between the two dark strips to make four strip sets. Press the seams toward the dark strips.

2. From 2½-inch dark and light strips, cut and piece four nine-patch units to use as border squares. The pieced nine-patch blocks should measure the width of the pieced border strips.

3. Right sides together, sew a long pieced border to each long side of the quilt top (see Photo A). Press the border open, pressing the seam allowance toward the border.

4. Right sides together, join a pieced corner square to each end of the two remaining pieced borders (see Photo B). Press the seam allowances toward the pieced border.

5. Right sides together, sew the pieced borders to the top and bottom of the quilt top, matching seams at the corners. Press the borders open, pressing seam allowances toward the borders (see Photo C).

Note: *To figure cutting measurements that include seam allowances for pieced strips, divide the finished border width by three and add ½ inch to each strip. For example, a 6-inch wide finished border is made up of three 2½-inch strips.*

Quilting – Making Borders

305 ✿

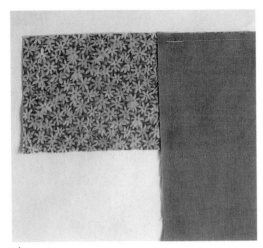

Photo A

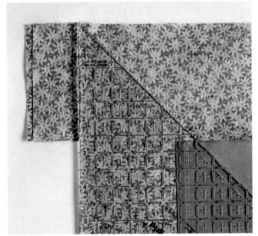

Photo B

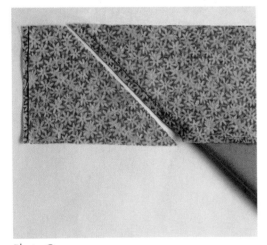

Photo C

Photo D

Mitered Border

Mitered corners are stitched after the border strips have been sewn to the quilt top, leaving the ends free. To make multiple borders with mitered corners, piece together strip sets and treat them as a single border strip.

Measure the length and width of the quilt along the center. To the length and width measurements, add two times the width of the finished border strip plus seam allowances. For example, for a 3-inch finished border on a 24-inch square quilt, cut four 3½×31-inch border strips.

1. Center each border strip along the quilt top edges, excess border fabric extending beyond the quilt edges. Sew the borders to the quilt top. Begin and end sewing ¼ inch from the quilt corner edges and backstitch to secure stitching (see Photo A). Press the seams toward the border fabric.

2. With the quilt facedown, press the overlapping border strips. Turn the quilt to the right side and align the edge of a triangle or the 45-degree mark on a ruler with the raw edge of the top border strip, long edge of the triangle intersecting the corner seam (see Photo B). With a pencil, draw along the edge of the triangle from the corner border seams to the raw edge. Place the bottom border strip on top and repeat the marking process.

3. Place adjacent border strips right sides together and match and pin the seam lines. Beginning with a backstitch at the inside corner, stitch exactly on the line to the outer border edge. Check the right side of the mitered border to ensure that it lies flat. Trim the excess fabric to a ¼-inch seam allowance (see Photo C). Press the seam open. Mark and miter the remaining corners. Press the border from the right side (see Photo D).

Quilting Components

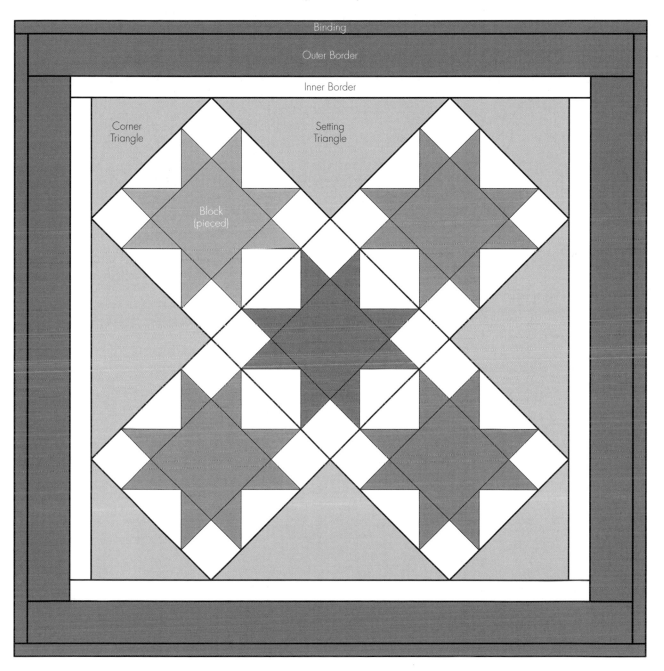

This illustration of a finished quilt shows the fabric units pieced to make the blocks, the blocks joined with setting and corner triangles to assemble the quilt top, and the inner and outer borders that frame the quilt. A narrow binding strip finishes the edges of the quilt.

Finishing: *Marking, Quilting, & Binding*

Photo A

Finishing the quilt top is the culmination of the efforts you have poured into selecting the pattern and fabrics, cutting and piecing or appliquéing the blocks, and adding the borders. This step becomes your gift to you—even if you plan to give your quilt away—because of the sense of accomplishment you achieve for completing a work of art.

Marking the Quilt Design

Quilt designs are generally marked on the quilt top after it has been pieced and before it is assembled with the batting and backing. To prevent the fabric from shifting while you mark it, secure the quilt top to a surface with masking tape. Using one of the methods described below, start marking from the center of the quilt and work outward, repositioning the fabric and design to completely mark the quilt top.

1. Trace the quilting design from a template onto the quilt top (see Photo A) with a fine-point nonpermanent marker.

2. Use chalk or pounce to transfer the quilting design to the quilt top (see Photo B). Although chalk may wear away easily, it also can be reapplied as needed.

Photo B

3. Adhere quilter's tape before or after the quilt layers are sandwiched together to mark straight quilting lines (see Photo C). Reposition the tape as needed to complete the quilting. Do not leave tape on fabric for extended periods of time because tape residue is difficult to remove.

Choose the Batting

Choose batting according to fiber content, loft, warmth, ease of needling, softness, and washability, as well as to complement your quilt and to hold up to its intended use. Pattern instructions generally specify the quantity of batting needed; however, plan to use quilt batting that extends at least 3 inches beyond each edge of the quilt top. For more information, refer to "Select Batting" on page 276.

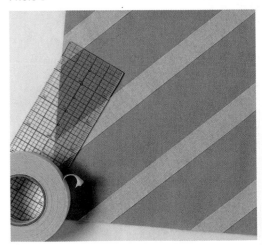

Photo C

Assemble the Layers

Cut and piece the backing at least 6 inches wider and longer than the quilt top. When it is necessary to piece backing fabric, press the seams open. Layer and assemble the quilt on a large flat surface.

1. Place the backing facedown on a smooth, flat surface (see Photo A).

2. Tape, clip, or otherwise secure the backing to the surface. Smooth the batting over the backing (see Photo B).

3. Place the quilt top right side up on top of the batting (see Photo C).

4. Beginning at the center of the quilt top, pin or baste the layers together every 4 to 6 inches, smoothing the fabric as you work toward the edges (see Photo D). Eliminate this step when using fusible batting.

Quilting

Hand Quilting

Quilters often strive for small, evenly spaced stitches. Running or stab-quilting stitches should be 6 to 12 per inch and equally spaced to look the same on the back of the quilt as they do on the front. Secure beginning and ending stitches with small knots pulled to the inside of the quilt.

To make running stitches, work from the top of the quilt and load the needle with as many stitches as possible before pulling out the needle with your upper hand (see Photos E and F). Optional: Beginners may choose to start with one or two stitches on the needle.
Note: *Consistent stitching is more important than the number of stitches per inch.*

Photo A

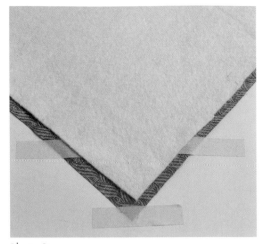
Photo B

Photo C

Photo D

Photo E

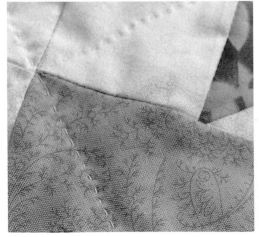
Photo F

To make stab stitches, work from both the top and bottom layers of the quilt. Push the needle through the quilt with one hand and pull it out the back with the other. Pull the thread completely through the quilt each time, push it back up, and pull through.

Machine Quilting

Once considered to be inferior to hand quilting, machine quilting has become appreciated for its artful appearance and technique. Use a quilting foot or even-feed walking foot for machine quilting. Adjust the stitch length for 6 to 12 stitches per inch and loosen the upper tension when you use invisible thread. Begin from the center of the quilt top and quilt outward in all directions. Use tiny backstitches to begin and end stitching or knot the thread, and embed long thread ends in the batting, similar to the hand quilting method.

Tying a Quilt

Tying or tufting the layers results in a puffy comforter look and is a quick alternative to quilting. Loftiness can be increased further by using thick or multiple batting layers. Tying is especially appropriate for quilts that will receive lots of wear and tear. Read the batting label suggestions to ensure that it is appropriate for tying.

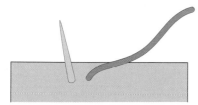

Quilt Tying Diagram 1

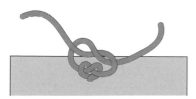

Quilt Tying Diagram 2

Use pearl cotton, sport-weight yarn, or narrow ribbon to tie quilts through all the layers. Tie a square knot or a bow on the top or the back of the quilt (see Diagrams 1 and 2 *below* for tying a quilt).

Binding the Quilt

To provide a durable finished edge to the quilt, easy-to-apply double-layer French-fold binding is recommended. Cut enough 2½-inch fabric strips on the cross grain to equal a length a little greater than the circumference of the quilt top.

1. Seams joined on the bias add strength to the binding, reduce bulk as the binding is folded, and are less conspicuous than straight seams. To piece the strips for the required length, overlap facing fabric edges and draw a diagonal line across the top strip (see Photo A). Sew binding strips together

along the line. Repeat for the length of strips required. Trim excess fabric to ¼-inch seam allowances (see Photo B), and press open the seam allowances (see Photo C). With wrong sides together, fold and press the binding strip in half lengthwise.

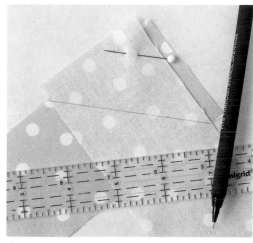

Photo A

Photo B

Photo C

Creative Tip

To give your quilt an antique look, use beige instead of white thread to quilt. I like Coats and Clark color #18.

– Store Team Member, Prescott, Arizona

Photo D

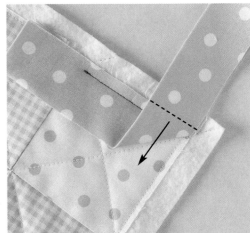

Photo E

Photo F

Photo G

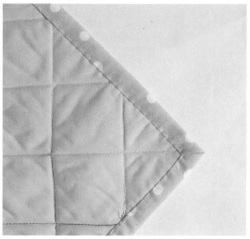

Photo H

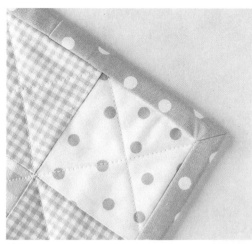

Photo I

2. Turn the short raw edge of the binding strip to the inside (see Photo D, *opposite*). Match the raw edges of the binding strip and the quilt top, beginning the binding along the center of one side. Begin sewing 2 inches beyond the turned under end of the binding, sewing the binding to the quilt top through all layers.

3. Stop sewing ¼ inch from the corner of the quilt top. Backstitch and clip the threads. Remove the quilt top from under the sewing-machine presser foot. Fold the binding strip up, creating a diagonal fold (see Photo E, *opposite*). Hold the fold in place with a finger; fold down the binding to create a fold at the top edge and to align with the adjacent quilt edge. Sew through the top fold, stitching through all layers (see Photo F, *opposite*). Continue around the quilt, sewing binding to all the quilt edges.

4. When the binding meets at the starting point, insert the end of overlapping binding into the folded binding (see Photo G) and continue stitching. Clip the threads and remove the quilt from the sewing machine.

5. Trim excess batting and backing even with the quilt top. Fold the binding over the seam to the back of the quilt. Hand-stitch

the binding to the backing fabric to cover the machine stitching (see Photo H).

6. To make mitered corners in the binding on the quilt back, hand-stitch the binding up to a corner. Fold a miter in the binding and take a stitch or two in the fold to secure it (see Photo H). Continue stitching to complete the binding (see Photo I).

Bias-cut Quilt Binding

Stripes and plaids make playful bindings when cut on fabric bias. Cut and piece 2½-inch-wide bias strips (see page 311) to make continuous binding for a quilt top. Sew the binding to the quilt top and miter the corners as you would for binding strips cut on the cross grain of fabric.

Quilt Label

Complete your quilt with a label that includes information about who made the quilt, where and when the quilt was made, and for what occasion. Press freezer paper to one side of a muslin square to stabilize the fabric for writing. Inscribe and embellish the muslin using permanent fabric markers. Remove the freezer paper, turn under the muslin edges, and secure the label to the back of the quilt with slip stitches.

Basics of Quilt Care

Eventually quilts require cleaning—even decorative wall hangings attract dust. Follow these suggestions to keep quilts in good condition to enjoy for years.

Wash cotton and cotton-blend quilts in warm water with a small amount of quilt soap or mild detergent either by hand or in the gentle cycle of a washing machine. Lay quilts flat between two sheets to dry. Do not hang quilts to dry; the weight causes stress on the stitches and unevenly redistributes the batting.

Fragile and old quilts can be gently vacuumed by placing a fine net or stocking over the vacuum attachment to reduce suction. For valuable quilts, seek the advice of a textile professional to determine whether to vacuum, launder, or leave as is.

Keep quilts away from sunlight, heat, and humidity. For storage, fold quilts flat, wrap them in acid-free paper, and place them in a cotton bag or pillowcase. Periodically air and refold the quilts differently to reduce stress on the fabric.

FASHION
SEWING

Jazz up your wardrobe

with garments made from stylish

fabrics and patterns.

Whether you want to know how

to sew a zipper,

attach a collar, or set in a sleeve,

you'll learn to achieve

professional results

with these step-by-step instructions.

Tools *and* Materials

Using the right sewing tools makes fashion sewing more enjoyable and ensures professional-looking results every time. Invest in quality tools designed for the type of sewing that you do; they'll serve you well for many years.

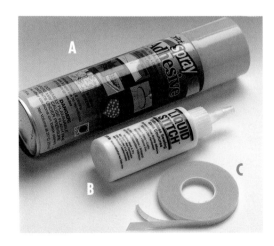

Tools and Materials

Adhesives and Tapes – A to C

Spray adhesive (A) and tape (C) are handy for temporary placement of fabrics or papers, and they eliminate the need for pinning or basting. Use permanent bonding glue (B) for hems, crafts, trims, appliqués, and home-decorating projects.

Cutting Tools – D to H

Lightweight spring-action clippers (D) with soft-grip handles cut threads and get into small spaces cleanly with minimum stress on the hand and wrist.

Seam rippers (E) have a sharp point to reach into the seam to remove basting threads or to unsew seams.

Quality sewing shears and scissors (F) are forged of high-grade steel and honed to fine-cutting edges that can be sharpened when they dull. Blades are joined with an adjustable screw. Scissors are made for both left- and right-hand use, usually are constructed with a bent handle, and have finger and thumb grips for cutting control.

Pinking and scalloping shears (not shown) cut shaped edges and are used to finish seams to prevent fabric from raveling, as well as for decorative uses.

Thread clippers (G) have a small spring that keeps them in the open position that makes snipping threads quick and easy.

Use rotary cutters (H) instead of scissors to cut through multiple layers of fabric. Choose rotary cutters along with special self-healing mats to protect the work surface and to prevent the fabric from shifting while cutting.

Electric scissors (not shown), corded or cordless, are used to cut large quantities of fabric without the stress of opening and closing the scissors many times.

Note: As with all sharp tools, keep shears, scissors, and rotary cutters stored away from small children.

Elastic – I to L

Elastic is available in a variety of widths and weights to suit many purposes. Extra wide waistband elastic (I) is designed to prevent rolling and twisting. Woven and knit elastics (J and K) are available in widths of ¼ inch to 3 inches. Sew elastic directly into a garment or use a casing. (Braided elastic becomes smaller as it stretches and should be used only in casings.) Elastic thread (L) is used to shirr fabric (small gathers made in multiple rows most often made at the waist, yoke, or bodice).

Marking Tools – M to P

A tracing wheel (M) and dressmaker's tracing paper (N) are used to transfer the pattern and sewing markings to fabric. Single- and double-sided tracing papers are available in white and colors. Use caution with the tracing wheel as it may damage specialty and fragile fabrics. Test the tracing wheel and tracing paper on scrap fabric before using it on garment pieces.

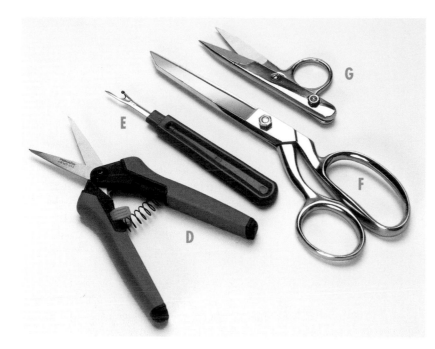

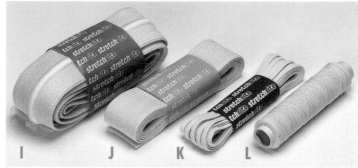

Tailor's chalk (O), available in white and colors, is used to mark temporary construction and fitting markings. Chalk brushes off or washes out of most fabrics.

Water-soluble and air-soluble fabric marking pens and pencils (P) are used to transfer sewing marks and alteration marks to garment fabric. Test marking pens on scrap fabric to ensure that the marks will wash out of the fabric.

Measuring Tools – Q to T

Flexible, stretch-resistant measuring tapes (Q) are used to take body measurements and for soft-furnishings dimensions. Choose one that is reversible with markings on both sides, preferably with both inch and centimeter marks. Cloth measuring tapes will not melt under a hot iron.

Seam gauges (R) made of plastic or metal with a sliding marker are handy tools for measuring seam allowances, buttonhole and button dimensions, and pleat spacing.

Use metal, heat-resistant hem gauges (S) to simultaneously mark and turn hem allowances on straight and curved hems.

Transparent acrylic rulers (T) with increments of ¼ or ⅛ inch aid in altering patterns, squaring straight edges, and determining grain line.

Use clear acrylic French curves (not shown) to aid in altering curved pattern edges and to make rounded corners on garments.

Hardwood, metal, or acrylic yardsticks (not shown) are used to mark hems and buttonholes, to measure yard goods, and to check fabric grain line.

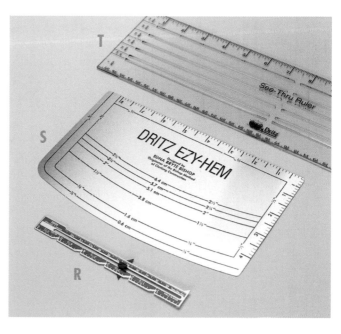

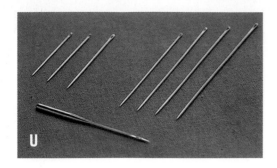

Needles – U

Match hand-sewing needles to the intended use. Use sharps for hand sewing, "betweens" for fine hand stitching and quilting, and milliner's needles for basting and gathering stitches. Needles are numbered according to size. The larger the number, the shorter and finer the needle.

Choose machine-sewing needles in the size and point to correspond with fabric weight and finish. For medium-weight fabrics and for general sewing, use sizes 9 to 18. The lower the number the finer the needle. Use sharp-point needles for woven fabrics to penetrate the fabric crisply. Use ballpoint needles for knits and stretchy fabrics to spread the weave and avoid snagging the fabric.

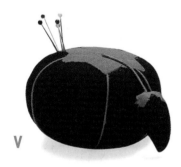

Pins and Pincushion – V

Sharp, rustproof pins and needles are essential home-sewing tools. Pins suitable for fashion sewing are available in brass, nickel-plate, and stainless steel. Use glass-head or T-pins when leaving pins in place while pressing because they hold up to the heat; plastic head pins do not. All are easier to see on the fabric than pins with small heads. Choose silk pins for light- to

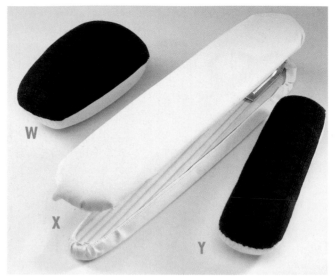

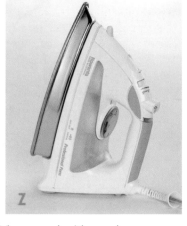

medium-weight fabric, pleating pins for delicate fabric, quilting pins for heavy fabric, and ballpoint pins for knits.

Pincushions are used as a convenient place to store your pins and needles. Often pincushions have a small emery bag attached for sharpening and removing the rust from pins and needles. Pincushions come in a variety of shapes and sizes including those worn on the wrist.

Pressing Tools – W to Z

Pressing at each stage of construction is vitally important to the professional appearance of the garment. Develop the habit of pressing each seam, dart, and tuck as you sew, unless otherwise instructed.

Tailor's hams (W) and pressing mitts (not shown) are used to press curved seams. Both tools usually are purchased covered with wool on one side and cotton on the reverse. Use the side that is most compatible with the fabric for pressing. To press small or hard-to-reach areas, place the pocket of the mitt on your hand or over a sleeve board. Place the fabric to be pressed over the mitt and press.

Sleeve boards (X) are used to press small or narrow areas, such as sleeves, necklines, and pants hems.

Seam rolls (Y), covered with wool on one side and cotton on the other, are firm cylinders that are used to press seams open. Place the seam allowance face up on the roll and press to prevent a seam allowance imprint on the finished side of the fabric. When pressing seams, match the most compatible fabric to the fashion fabric.

Use a steam/spray iron (Z) to press your sewing, such as darts and seams. Purchase an iron that offers steam and spray options at all temperature settings so it can be used with synthetic, cotton, and linen fabrics.

Pressing cloths (not shown), available in wool, cotton, cheesecloth, and transparent fabrics to correspond with fashion fabrics, are used to make flat seams without causing a shine on the finished fabric. Transparent pressing cloths allow the fabric to show through and are useful for working with fusibles. Leftover fabric pieces from fashion fabric also can be used as pressing cloths. Moisten pressing cloths or use steam heat to press professional-looking seams.

Sewing Machine - not shown

Sewing machines are an important tool and a good investment for home sewing. Although many brands of machines work basically the same, machines vary widely in the functions they are capable of performing. Sewing machines are available in models from very simple with only straight stitching capabilities (forward and backwards) to the most complex computer-generated pattern functions. Costs of sewing machines vary according to the functions and accessories.

For proper sewing machine operation, read the owner's manual to learn about appropriate needle sizes to use, proper threading techniques, correct stitch lengths, and regular maintenance recommendations. Consider investing the time to take classes that familiarize you with your new machine.

Thread – AA to HH
Select quality sewing threads that are strong, durable, and resilient. With so many threads available, take the time to select the appropriate thread for the fabric from the chart *right*.

Select compatible needle and thread sizes, with the needle eye large enough to accommodate the thread and small enough to fill the needle puncture with thread. Select thread one shade darker than the fabric; thread appears slightly lighter when embedded in the fabric. For prints and plaids, select the thread color closest to the dominant fabric color. The pattern you select will often make a recommendation for specialty threads such as metallic and variegated. The threads shown are only a sampling of those that are available and include:

AA Sulky 40 (rayon)
BB 100% Polyester
CC 100% Polyester
DD Nylon (Twice the tensile strength of cotton for same size thread)
EE Variegated Metallic Yarn
FF All-purpose, 37% cotton/63% polyester
GG Color Twist Rayon for machine stitching, topstitching, and embroidery.
HH Silver Metallic with color

Creative Tip

When you are hand sewing, run thread through beeswax to help prevent knotting.

–Team Member,

Milwaukee, Wisconsin

Thread Chart

Thread	Suggested Fabric and Uses
Polyester	Acrylic, action knits (two- and four-way stretch), cotton, double knit, interlock knit, jersey, leather, linen, polyester, rayon, terry cloth, spandex, synthetic suede, vinyl, wool
Cotton-wrapped Polyester	Acrylic, action knits (two- and four-way stretch), cotton, double knit, interlock knit, jersey, leather, lycra , linen, polyester, rayon, terry cloth, spandex, synthetic suede, vinyl, wool
Mercerized Cotton	All fabrics (except stretch knits, spandex)
Nylon	Nylon, triacetate, heavy fabrics (e.g. canvas)
Rayon	Rayon, nylon, chiffon, organdy, tulle, voile, batiste, crepe, jersey, and all fabrics suggested for polyester thread
Silk	Silk, chiffon, organdy, tulle, voile, batiste, crepe, jersey, and all fabrics suggested for polyester thread

Fashion Sewing – Tools and Materials

Specialty Items – II and JJ

Use fray preventive products (II) to stop fabric seams from raveling. Iron-on fusible bonding tape (JJ) can be used as a shortcut to hemming by hand or in making belts. Fusible bonding also is available in various weights to be used as interfacing.

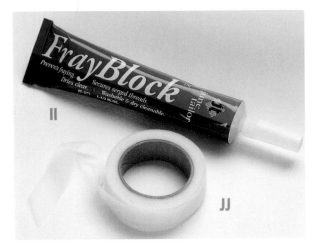

Zippers and Fasteners – KK to RR

Zippers (KK), manufactured with metal, nylon, or polyester coils, are available in colors, lengths, sizes, and weights for specific purposes, such as trouser zippers, invisible seam zippers, separating jacket zippers, and decorative zippers. Patterns often list the type of zipper suggested to finish garment projects.

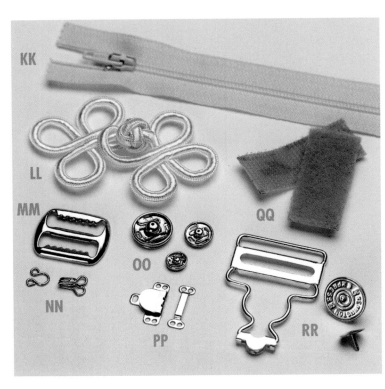

Fasteners are for decorative and practical purposes. Decorative fasteners (LL) made of satin cording are commonly referred to as frogs. Buckles (MM) are available in sizes, shapes, and materials (such as metal, wood, plastic, and leather) to be used for belts, decorative ties, lacing, and vests.

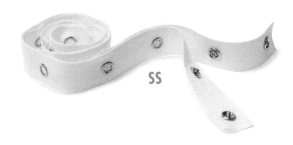

Hook-and-eye fasteners (NN) are available in sizes 00 to 5 to use for hidden closures. Snaps (OO) are used for closures in children's and adult's clothing. Snaps range in size from tiny, size 4/0, for delicate clothing, to heavy-duty coat snaps at size 4. Heavy duty hooks and eyes (PP) are designed as waistband fasteners on skirts and pants. Hook-and-loop tape (QQ) consists of two strips, one with tiny hooks, the other with a looped pile. The strips mesh to hold in place when pressed together and pull apart to unfasten. Metal buttons and buckles (RR) are commonly used on the straps of overalls.

Snap Tape – SS

Cotton snap tape is ideal for babies and children's clothes, particularly sewn into inner leg seams to facilitate diaper change. Spaced snaps are attached to twill tape, ready to sew into garments that require easy opening and closing.

Sewing Basics

Selecting Patterns

Choose patterns for garment styles that you know flatter your figure, either from previous experience or by trying on ready-made garments. Because commercial pattern companies follow fashion trends, you can be assured that pattern books include patterns that replicate fashionable ready-made styles.

Refer to the size chart on the pattern back for finished garment measurements to ensure fit with minimal alterations. Although there are variables, commercial patterns generally follow size standards. The size chart also indicates how much fabric you will need from each fabric width and for lining, interfacing, and trims.

Patterns often provide skill level guides. Look for "easy," "quick," or "time-saving techniques" for simpler projects. As a general guide, the fewer pattern pieces, the simpler the garment construction. If you are a beginning sewer, choose from the recommended fabrics listed on the pattern envelope. Analyze the line drawing and the project description to determine whether design details are within your range of sewing. If the pattern looks too difficult or too time consuming, put it aside to select from easier projects. Attempt difficult projects after you master basic sewing skills and techniques.

Select the notions for the project at the time you purchase the pattern and fabric. Patterns list the notions, such as thread, zipper, buttons, and trims that are required to complete the garment project. The pattern will also contain full-size tissue patterns, general instructions, a cutting layout, and step-by-step project directions.

Selecting Fabric

Choose fabric for your fashion project, considering the many fabrics available, as well as where and how you will wear the garment. Choose fabrics in fibers, textures, colors, and designs that appeal to you. The hours that you spend cutting, assembling, and pressing the fabrics to complete the project should be as enjoyable as wearing the finished garment.

Quality fabric is a joy to sew and a pleasure to wear. Cost doesn't necessarily indicate quality. Many reasonably priced fabrics offer great value.

Examine fabric quality to judge woven fabrics by thread count, or threads per inch. The higher the thread count, the higher the quality. Hold the fabric to the light to determine whether you can see through it and whether the threads are evenly woven. Tightly woven fabrics fray less than loose weaves and are generally easier to sew.

Printed fabrics should be printed on the straight grain to allow for uniform pattern repeat. Fabric dyes should penetrate the facing of the fabric through to the wrong side. Even the back of the fabric should look appealing. Plaid, stripe, and patterned fabric, whether woven or dyed, must be matched when sewing garment seams, and extra yardage will be required. Determine how seams might look when choosing large fabric designs or motifs to make into garments.

As you shop for fabrics, determine how they feel in your hand. Do they wrinkle or crush easily? Are they soft, heavy, flimsy, stiff, rough, or smooth-textured? Select fabrics that fit well into your existing wardrobe and that are appropriate for the pattern, season, and occasion. Determine whether you have the necessary skills and tools to sew the fabric. Also determine whether the cost of the fabric and the required notions fit your budget. How much are you willing to invest in the maintenance of the finished garment? Will it be reliably low maintenance (wash and wear), require little to no ironing, or be expensive to dry clean?

Woven Fabric The tightly woven edges of the fabric running along the fabric length are called selvages. It is not recommended that selvage edges be used in garment construction because the weave differs from the grain of the fabric and it may shrink or pucker. One exception is to use a selvage in making a waistband.

The lengthwise grain, or threads, of the fabric run parallel to the selvages. The lengthwise threads are the strongest threads in the fabric. Generally pattern instructions indicate, with a long arrow printed on the pattern pieces, when to place patterns on the lengthwise grain of the fabric. Match the arrow along a long thread as closely as possible, pinning it in place.

The crosswise grain runs from selvage to selvage, perpendicular to the lengthwise grain. Crosswise threads have more resilience or give than lengthwise threads.

Bias refers to any diagonal line between the lengthwise and crosswise threads. True bias is an exact 45-degree angle to lengthwise and crosswise threads. Bias cuts provide the maximum stretch and are used to make bindings and trims that can be stretched or eased to fit curves.

Knit Fabric Knit fabrics are made up of interlocking loops of yarn, or ribs, that run parallel to the length of the knit fabric. Select a rib to establish the lengthwise grain of knit fabric. Cut tubular knits into a single layer along a selected rib.

The crosswise courses of a knit fabric run perpendicular to the ribs and have more stretch and give than the ribs.

Fiber Content Fiber content, which determines fabric care and wear, is printed on the fabric bolt along with recommendations for fabric care. Some wools are washable; some cottons and linens are not. Determine what you are buying. While at the fabric store, write the information on a slip of paper. At home, attach the information to a fabric swatch for care reference.

Fabrics are made from natural fibers, synthetic fibers, or a combination of the two. Natural fibers include cotton, linen, silk, wool, ramie, fur, and leather. Synthetic fibers include rayon, acetate, triacetate, nylon, polyester, acrylic, modacrylic, olefin, and spandex. From these basics types, fabrics are woven, knitted, or felted.

Some fabrics require preshrinking before they are cut and sewn. Wash and dry fabrics that will be made into washable garments, using the methods that assure that the garment you make may be washed with no damage. Fabrics that will be dry-cleaned are best steam-shrunk by professional dry cleaners.

To test fabrics that you think may shrink, cut and measure an exact 4-inch square. Cover the fabric with a press cloth and steam with a hot iron for ten seconds without allowing the iron to touch the fabric. Allow the fabric to air dry and cool. Measure the swatch to determine whether it is still 4 inches square. Shrinkage, no matter how little, indicates that the fabric would benefit from pre-shrinking or professional steaming before being cut and sewn into a finished garment.

Layout & Cutting

After pre-shrinking, press the fabric and make any necessary alterations to the pattern. Use a large, flat, level surface to lay out the fabric. Then establish the fabric grain line before laying out the pattern and cutting the fabric.

Laying out the Pattern
Refer to the pattern layout directions to position the patterns on the fabric, selecting the view, fabric width, and pattern size for the selected sewing project.

To prepare the fabric for pattern placement and cutting, most fabrics are folded right sides together, wrong sides out, and selvage edges aligned. If it is difficult to determine a right and wrong side to the fabric, select one side, marking it with chalk that will brush off later, to use throughout the garment construction.

Place the pattern pieces according to the layout directions, laying pattern pieces on folds, along lengthwise grain, and reversing or cutting multiple pattern pieces as indicated. Shaded pattern pieces usually indicate to place the printed side down or to reverse the pattern piece before cutting. Pattern pieces that are half shaded are typically cut along folded fabric.

On woven fabrics, align straight-grain pattern pieces on the fabric, aligning the grain line arrow with the selvage edge. On knit fabrics, align straight-grain pieces, using the arrow and a selected rib. Using a flexible measuring tape, align both ends of the arrow equally from the selvage. Adjust as needed and pin the arrow in place before pinning the remainder of the pattern.

Pin each pattern piece to the fabric inside the cutting line and perpendicular to the pattern edges, approximately every 3 inches. Pin diagonally into corners, and pin more closely along curves or on slippery fabric.

Plaids, stripes, and large motif fabrics require adjustments to ensure that patterns and seams match when the pieces are sewn. Lay out pattern pieces on single layers of fabric, matching fabric designs for seams and noting design placement for finished garment pieces. Avoid placing large or busy designs along significant body curves.

Napped or directional fabrics, such as corduroy, velveteen, taffeta, satin, faux fur, and prints with one-way design, require special handling. Use a touch test to determine the nap of the fabric. Run your fingers across the length of the fabric in one direction; run your fingers in the opposite direction. Fabric that feels smooth runs with the nap, fabric that feels slightly bumpy or rough is against the nap.

If the nap isn't obvious, determine the directional nap by holding the fabric to look at the lengthwise grain in one direction. Reverse the fabric 180 degrees to look at it in this direction. If there is a noticeable difference, lay out and cut pattern pieces following the pattern instructions for "fabrics with nap." Cut all pattern pieces in the same direction. Garments that have the nap running down usually look lighter and wear longer. Garments made with the fabric against the nap look darker and have richer shading.

Cut one-way fabric designs with the design or motif in the appropriate direction and placement for balance and symmetry. Cut pattern pieces from shiny or polished fabrics all in the same direction, whether they are positioned up or down.

Cutting

With the fabric spread on a large, flat, level surface and the patterns pinned securely in place, cut with sharp scissors along the cutting line.

Cut the pattern notches outward. Do not cut notches into the seam because it will weaken the finished seam. Use short snips, making double or triple notches for a single unit, in the seam to mark center front, center back, fold lines, stitching lines for sewing details, sleeve centers, etc.

To cut multiple fabric layers, bias strips, slippery fabric, vinyl, faux suede, or leather, use a rotary cutter and cutting mat. Save fabric scraps to test fabric markers, stitch length, and tension.

Measuring and Fitting

Fitting problems cause more frustration for home sewers than any other issue. Entire books are devoted to the subject and the basics remain the same. Measure the body, compare the measurements with the pattern, and make adjustments to the pattern before cutting out the fabric.

Measure the Body

Have a friend help you; it's nearly impossible to take your own measurements accurately. Wear the type of undergarments you plan to wear with the garment you are making. Using a nonstretch flexible tape measure, take the following measurements:

Bust (see Diagram A) – Measure across the fullest part of the bust line. If there is more than 2 inches difference between the bust and the high bust, use the high bust measurement to select the pattern size.

Waistline (see Diagram A) – Measure at the natural location. When in doubt, tie a string or narrow piece of elastic around the middle. Raise your arms and allow the tie to settle at the natural waistline; measure over the tie.

Hips (see Diagram A) – Measure around the fullest part, which may be 7 to 10 inches below the natural waistline, depending upon height and body type.

Front Neck to Waist (see Diagram B) – Measure from the indentation at the center neck to the waist.

High Bust (see Diagram B) – Measure from about 3 inches below the neck from armhole to armhole.

Front Shoulder to Waist (see Diagram B) – Measure from the high point of the shoulder next to the neck to the waist.

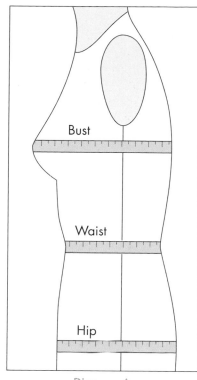

Diagram A

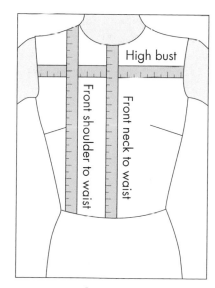

Diagram B

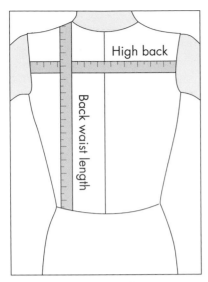

Diagram C

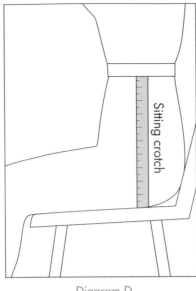

Diagram D

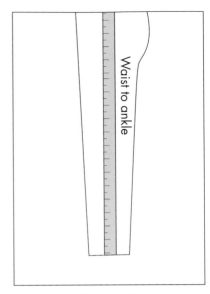

Diagram E

Back waist length (see Diagram C) –
Measure at the midpoint of the highest
point of the shoulder next to the neck
and down to the natural waistline.

High back (see Diagram C) – Measure
about 5 inches below the neck from
armhole to armhole.

Sitting crotch (see Diagram D) – Measure in
a sitting position from the natural waist to
the chair.

Waist to ankle (see Diagram E) – Measure
at the natural waist to the ankle.

You may also wish to measure sleeve
length, inside leg, shoulder width, and
overall height.

Keep a record of your measurements and
update them semi-annually, more often if
you experience weight fluctuations.

Compare Pattern Measurements
Few people have measurements that
coincide with pattern size charts. For a
custom fit, adjust the pattern to fit

your measurements. Compare your
measurements with individual pattern
pieces and make allowances for ease (the
difference between your measurements
and the fit of your clothes) before
making changes.

Simple Pattern Adjustments
Make simple pattern adjustments using
tissue paper, paper scissors, measuring tape,
pattern tape, and a pencil.

To shorten patterns, cut the pattern along
the lengthen/shorten lines and overlap the
pieces the appropriate amount, keeping the
grain line straight. Tape pieces together.
Realign and blend cutting and stitching lines
before cutting out the pattern pieces.

To lengthen patterns, cut the pattern on
the lengthen/shorten lines. Place tissue
between the pieces to add the appropriate
measurement, keeping the grain line
straight. Tape the pattern to the tissue
paper insert. Realign the pattern arrows,
cutting lines and stitching lines before
cutting out the pattern pieces.

Interfacing

Interfacing gives garments shape and
stability. Choose from sew-in and fusible
interfacings in a range of weights to suit
most fabrics. Fusible interfacing, a favorite
choice of many home sewers because it is
easy to use, contributes more firmness than
sew-in types. Although fusible interfacing is
limited to specific fabrics, sew-in interfacing
can be used with any fabric. Consult with
fabric salespeople to determine appropriate
interfacing for the fabric, pattern, and style
of garment you intend to make. See the
diagrams *opposite,* showing the most
common interfaced areas of a garment.

To ensure the results you want with fusible
interfacing, non-woven fusibles, dry-clean
only, and sew-in interfacing, follow the
manufacturer's directions to preshrink.
Always preshrink the interfacing and the
garment fabric to prevent them from
shrinking at different rates.

Areas Commonly Interfaced

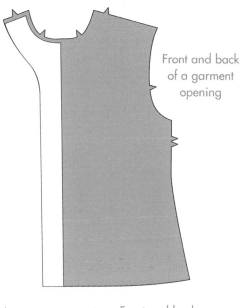

Front and back of a garment opening

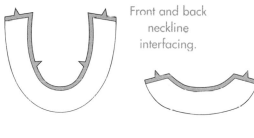

Front and back neckline interfacing.

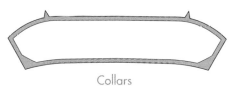

Collars

Cuffs or waistbands

Pocket flaps

Pressing Matters

Follow the motto: "Press as you sew, press as you go" and don't stitch over a seam until it has been pressed. Good pressing is evident in the finished garment. Set up an ironing surface close to the sewing machine, and keep press cloths and other accessories nearby to develop the habit of pressing each step of the way.

The difference between pressing and ironing is significant. Pressing involves picking up the iron, moving it to an area, and laying it on the fabric while applying pressure with the iron. It involves little, if any, sliding motion of the iron across the fabric. The iron should contact the fabric in the same direction as the fabric grain. Ironing involves sliding or gliding the iron across the fabric, which can cause distortion in unfinished seams and across grains. Although ironing is useful for many finished items, use pressing during garment construction.

Press after completing each sewing step, before stitching intersecting seams, and on the wrong side of the fabric to prevent shine. Use dry, steam, and steam/spray options depending on the fiber content of the fabric. After pressing, allow the fabric to cool to prevent fabric distortion.

Before pressing seams, remove pins and basting threads. Press seams flat on the wrong side of the fabric along the stitching line to set the stitches. Press seams open (if directed to do so) or press them to one side, using a seam roll to prevent the seam from imprinting the right side of the fabric. Use a seam roll and press cloth to press the seam from the finished side of the fabric. Allow the fabric to cool.

To finger press, run your thumb along the seam line, supported by a hard surface, and apply light pressure.

Basic Machine Stitches

Topstitching is most commonly used as a decorative finish and often calls for a specialty thread. Stitch ¼ inch from the edge of a pocket, along finished seams, cuffs, collars, or as desired.

Stitch-in-the-Ditch is used to hold two seams together and prevents the need for hand sewing. It is most often used on waistbands, facings, cuffs, and collars.

Staystitching is used to prevent bias and curved edges from stretching out of shape. Stitch ½ inch from the raw edge. Be sure to stitch between the raw edge and the seam allowance.

Understitching keeps facings from turning to the outside at the seam. Open the facing and press the notched and trimmed seam allowance toward the facing. Stitch the facing and the seam allowance together just inside the seam.

Hand Sewing

For hand-sewing, use a sharp needle appropriate to the fabric weight, finish, and thread content. For permanent hand stitching such as hems, use 18 to 24 inches of matching thread. Begin and end stitching with tiny, unobtrusive slip stitches rather than knotting the thread.

Basting and temporary stitching is usually done with white or light colored thread so it will contrast with the fabric. Avoid dark thread colors because the dye may leave marks on the fabric. Knot or backstitch to secure the stitches. Polyester thread is a good choice for hand sewing because it blends without leaving marks in the fabric when it is pressed.

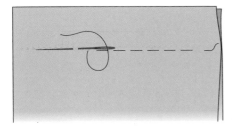

Diagram A

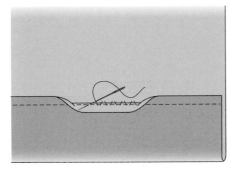

Diagram B

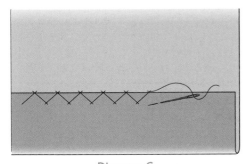

Diagram C

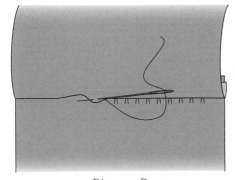

Diagram D

Hand basting (see Diagram A) is used to temporarily join fabrics together when pin basting isn't accurate or secure enough. Weave the needle and thread in and out, making uniform ¼-inch stitches.

Blind stitches (see Diagram B) are used to permanently hem knits and bulky fabrics. Prevent ridges from forming and showing at the hemline of the finished side of the garment by folding back a clean finished hem edge. Secure the thread at the hem edge and stitch from right to left, taking tiny, evenly spaced, V-shape stitches alternately between the garment and the hem edge.

Catch-stitching (see Diagram C) is a permanent method of hemming knits and holding facing edges in place. Secure the thread at the hem edge. Stitch from left to right, taking tiny, loose backstitches alternately in the garment and hem edge, forming Xs the length of the hem.

Slip stitches (see Diagram D) are used to permanently stitch an invisible hem. Secure the thread in a fabric fold and stitch from right to left. With the needle, pick up a single garment thread below the folded hem edge. Insert the needle directly above the stitch, bring it out ¼ inch away, pick up another single thread, and continue stitching, alternating between the garment and folded hem edge. Secure the thread end in a fabric fold.

Sewing for Children

Making children's clothes is fun. Small, untailored garments are quick to sew, the fabrics are bright and lively, and construction techniques usually are streamlined.

When making children's clothes, select patterns and fabrics to please the children as well as the parent. Make clothes that the children will enjoy wearing. Older children may help select fabrics and patterns for their clothes, learning about style, fabric, and garment construction in the process. Your child even may be interested in learning to sew some of the simpler designs that you have chosen together. This is an excellent opportunity to introduce your kids to the fun of sewing.

Choose children's wear fabrics that are washable and durable. Select patterns that replicate ready-to-wear styles and have minimal details. Make clothes that are easy to put on and take off, using elastic waistlines, snaps, and hook-and-loop tape closures. Avoid using buttons and zippers on the backs of clothing. For fabrics, stretchy knits are stylish, comfortable, and long wearing.

Incorporate room-to-grow designs into children's clothing, adding tucks at the hem or bodice or sewing double cuffs. Reinforce knees in pants to provide longer wear. Double-stitch seams to make them strong. Kids love pockets and adding one or two makes the clothing more fun for them.

Sew safety reflector tape to outdoor clothing such as jackets and coats. Most tapes are washable; some may have to be replaced after repeated washings. The safety provided is worth the effort in stitching on the colorful tapes. For security reasons, avoid adding children's name labels to clothing.

Collars

Collar style is a dominant garment detail.

No matter what type of collar you choose,

learning basic construction techniques will

ensure a professional finished appearance

for the clothing you make.

Getting Started

Notched Collar
Basic notched collars, also referred to as rolled collars, are constructed to softly and neatly finish dress bodices, blouses, shirts, and jackets.

1. Cut out the collar pieces and interfacing. Fuse with an iron or sew the interfacing to the wrong side of the under collar, matching notches and center seam marks. With the right sides of the collar together, matching notches and center marks, stitch the outer edges of the collar. Press the seam to set it. Trim the seam allowances, clip the points, and clip into the seam allowance along the curves (see Diagram A).

Turn the collar to the right side, easing out the corners. Press the collar from the right side, gently rolling the seam to the under collar to prevent it from showing on the finished garment. Topstitch around the outer edges of the collar.

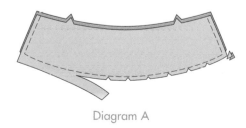

Diagram A

Collar Basics

Two basic collars, notched and neckband, are similarly constructed. For beginning sewers, notched collars provide ease of assembly and good looks. Neckband collars, frequently used in shirts and jackets, are constructed of a collar and band, or stand, and provide a more structured look than notched collars.

To prevent stretching the garment neckline while pinning and sewing the collar, always stay-stitch (see page 325) inside the seam allowance. For collar shape and definition, apply interfacing to the underside of the collar and neckband pieces, selecting the appropriate weight of fusible or sew-in interfacing for your fabric (see Interfacing, page 324).

To make precise collar points, stitch diagonally across corners rather than making sharp turns. Use one diagonal stitch for fine or lightweight fabrics, and up to three stitches for heavyweight fabrics. Before turning the stitched collar right side out, press, trim the seam allowances, and clip curves to help the finished collar lay flat. Turn the collar right side out, easing out the points with your fingers or a small, dull tool (such as the handle of a crochet hook). Press the collar, working the seam to the underside before sewing it to the neckline, taking care to avoid stretching seams, curves, and points.

Notched Collar

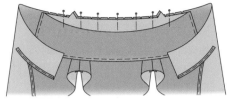

Diagram B

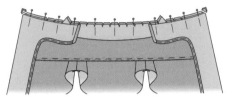

Diagram C

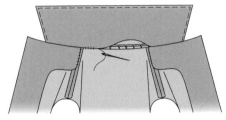

Diagram D

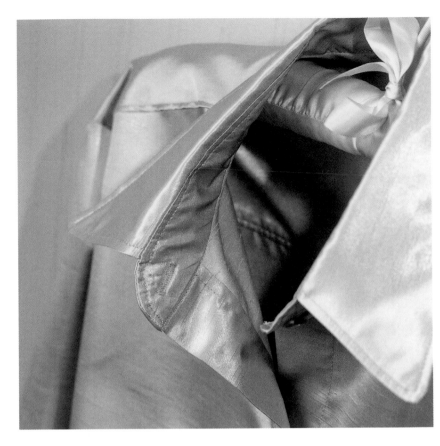

2. Stay-stitch (see page 325) the neck edge of the collar close to the seam line. Transfer the center back, front, or shoulder seam marks to the collar pieces with pins or tailor's chalk, clipping up to the stay stitching.

3. With the right side of the garment facing you, pin only the underside of the collar to the right side of the garment neckline (do not pin the top side of the collar), matching notches, shoulder seams, and center marks (see Diagram B). Keep the front facing free as you pin the collar and keep the upper collar free between the notches.

4. With the underside of the collar pinned, fold the facing toward you over the garment and collar, right sides together, along the fold line of the facing, keeping the upper collar free (see Diagram C).

Match notches and pin the facing to the collar and the neckline.

With the right side of the garment facing you and the upper collar facing up, stitch along the seam line, catching the neckline, the under collar, and facing, keeping the upper collar free between the notches. Press the seam flat. Press the neckline seam to the inside of the collar. Trim the seam allowances. Turn the facing to the inside of the garment as shown in Diagram D.

5. Turn under the unnotched upper collar neckline seam allowance and press (see Diagram D). Machine-edgestitch (see page 326) or hand-stitch the collar seam to the stitching line of the under collar. Tack the facing at the shoulders. Press the collar and facing.

Collar with Neckband

A neckband collar *opposite*, can be made using two separate pattern pieces (the collar and a neckband sewn together), as shown, or from a collar with a neckband extension. The construction and finished look are similar using either method.

1. Cut out the collar and neckband pieces. Cut out the interfacing. Fuse the interfacing pieces to the under collar and to the collar band. Set aside the collar band pieces.

2. With right sides together, match, pin, baste, and sew the under collar to the upper collar, leaving the neck edge open (see Diagram A). Trim across the points, clip the curves, and trim the seam allowances. Press the seams toward the under collar.

3. Turn the collar right side out, gently pulling out the points and working the seam toward the under collar. Use a pressing cloth to press the collar. Following the pattern instructions for stitch placement, topstitch (see page 326) the collar all the way around (see Diagram B).

4. Before sewing the neckband and collar together, turn under and press the seam allowance on the unnotched edge of the neckband as shown in Diagram C. With right sides facing, pin the raw collar edges to the notched edges of the two neckband pieces, (neckband made in Step 1). The neckband extends beyond both sides of the collar. Baste, then stitch the collar and neckband together along the seam line, leaving the turned edge free. Remove basting stitches. Trim the seam allowances and clip curves (see Diagram C).

5. Turn the neckband down and press (see Diagram D).

6. With the wrong side of the garment facing you, pin the notched side of the neckband to the garment neckline (see Diagram E). Stitch the seam, clip, and trim the seam allowance. Press the seam allowance up toward the collar.

7. Referring to Diagram F, lay the garment flat with the collar extended and the right side of the garment facing you. The neckband will extend down on the right side of the garment to cover the inside neckband. Topstitch the turned edge of the neckband to the inside neckband and stitch where the collar attaches to the neckband.

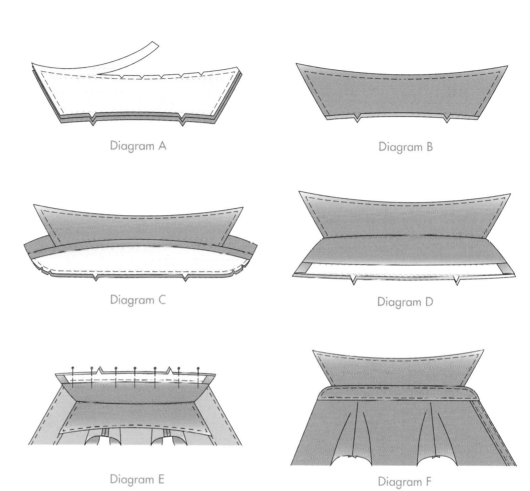

Diagram A

Diagram B

Diagram C

Diagram D

Diagram E

Diagram F

Creative Tip

Cut the under collar 1/8 inch smaller than the upper collar all the way around. This will cause the upper collar to roll slightly to the underside, hiding the under collar seam.

– Team Member, Hudson, Ohio

Sleeves *and* Cuffs

Beautifully set-in sleeves are the mark of a
well-constructed garment. Follow the step-by-step
directions to learn how to mark, sew, and finish
sleeves for blouses, shirts, jackets, and more.

Sleeve Basics

Set-in sleeves come in many styles. The
steps for constructing them are similar for a
gathered cap sleeve or a smooth tailored
sleeve. Depending on the style, the sleeve
fabric is gathered or eased along the seam
edge to fit into a sleeve opening.

Getting Started

The example shown is a typical one-piece
sleeve with an underarm seam.

1. Transfer pattern markings to the sleeve
fabric and remove the tissue pattern from
the fabric.

2. Set the sewing machine stitch length at
10 stitches per inch to sew two lines of
basting stitches along the sleeve cap. From
the right side of the fabric, from notch to
notch, stitch just inside the ⅝-inch seam
allowance (see Diagram A). Stitch a second
line ⅜ inch from the seam edge.

3. With right sides together, join the
underarm seams (see Diagram B).

4. Press the seam allowances flat, then
press the seam open. Finish the seam
allowances (see Diagram C); also see Seam
Finishes, pages 348–349.

5. Turn the sleeve to the right side and the
garment to the wrong side. Insert the sleeve
into the sleeve opening, right sides together,
matching and pinning the notches, seam

Diagram A

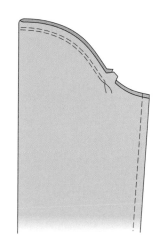

Diagram B

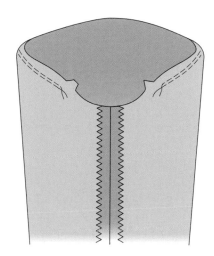

Diagram C

lines, and pattern markings (see Diagram D). Pull up the bobbin threads of the basting to ease the fit of the sleeve cap to the sleeve opening. Wrap the thread ends of the basting stitches around a pin at each of the notches. Distribute the fullness and pin the sleeve to the opening at close intervals. *Note: The top 1 inch of the sleeve cap along the shoulder seam should be relatively flat and free of puckers. Turn the sleeve to the right side to check the seam and adjust fullness as needed.*

6. Sew the sleeve and the sleeve opening together along the seam line (see Diagram E). Reinforce the underarm seam between the notches with an additional row of stitching as shown in Diagram E. Trim the seam allowance to ¼ inch between the notches at the underarm. Do not trim the sleeve cap seam. Finish the seam allowances with zigzag stitches if desired. Press the sleeve cap from the right side.

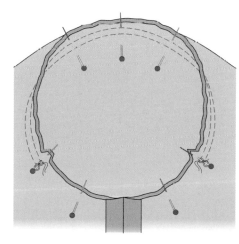

Diagram D

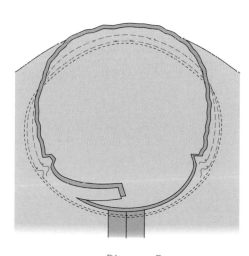

Diagram E

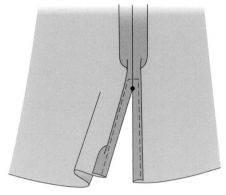

Diagram A

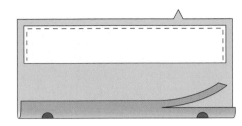

Diagram B

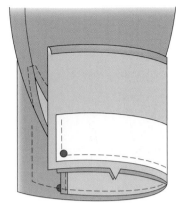

Diagram C

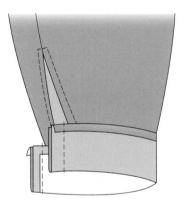

Diagram D

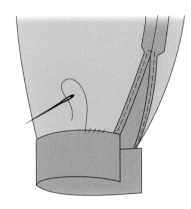

Diagram E

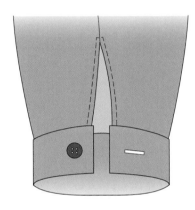

Diagram F

Cuff Basics

Most cuffs are made in a similar manner and size. If you have extra small or large wrists, adjust the pattern to fit your size. Once you are familiar with the installation of cuffs, you can make them any width you choose. Also add additional buttons and buttonholes that are right for the width.

Getting Started

1. Follow the directions for making sleeves on page 331, leaving a 3-inch cuff opening in the seam.

2. At the cuff opening, turn the seam allowance under on both sides to make a rolled hem. Stitch up one side of the small hem, across the seam, and down the other side (see Diagram A).

3. To make the cuff, cut interfacing as shown in Diagram B, and stitch ¼ inch from the raw edges of the interfacing on the two ends and outer edge of the cuff. On the unnotched side of the cuff, turn up a ⅜-inch seam allowance and press.

4. With the right sides together, match the notches and dots on the cuff and sleeve (see Diagram C). Pin the sleeve and cuff together and stitch a ⅝-inch seam from dot to dot.

Trim the seam and press the seam allowance toward the cuff.

5. Fold the cuff in half, with right sides together. Stitch across the ends of the cuff (see Diagram D). Trim the seams.

6. Turn the cuff right side out and press (see Diagram E). With the sleeve wrong side out, finish the cuff with a slip stitch (see page 236) to close the seam. Add topstitching (see page 236) to the cuff if desired.

7. Mark the buttonhole location and stitch with the sewing machine (see Buttons and Buttonholes on page 346). Sew a button on each cuff (see Diagram F).

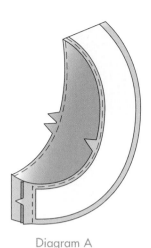

Diagram A

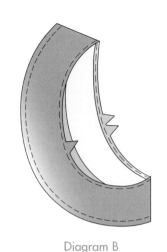

Diagram B

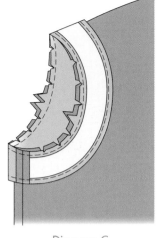

Diagram C

Facings

Hardworking, concealed facings provide a smooth, finished appearance to garment openings. Learn to create facings that lay flat, and they'll neatly finish your finest clothing while adding comfort and style.

Facing Basics

Facing fabric, used to finish the raw edges of garment openings, is typically cut from the garment fabric using a pattern. Always cut shaped or curved facings, matching pattern grain lines of the fabric. Facing pieces should be sewn together before joining them to the garment unless instructed otherwise.

The example shown is for a basic pieced armhole facing that has an interfacing applied; however, a neck facing is finished in the same manner.

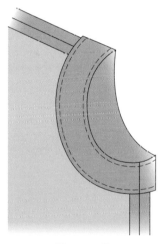

Diagram D

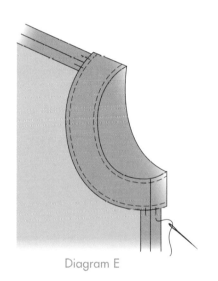

Diagram E

Getting Started

1. Cut the interfacing using the pattern piece marked for facing. Trim away the seam allowances. Center the interfacing on the wrong side of the facing and fuse with an iron, or baste to the facing. To prevent the inner curve of the facing from stretching, stay-stitch (see page 325) ½ inch from the inner curve, inside the seam line (see Diagram A). With right sides together, match, pin, and sew the facing pieces together. Press the seam allowances open.

2. Finish the outer edges of the facing (see Seam Finishes on page 348). The example shown has a ¼-inch turned and stitched hem as shown in Diagram B.

3. With right sides together, match notches, markings, and seam lines; pin and sew the facing to the opening of the garment (see Diagram C). Trim the seam allowances and press open. Clip and notch the curves, then understitch (see page 325) the seam allowance to the facing.

4. Turn the facing to the inside and press (see Diagram D). Understitching can be seen in Diagram D along the edge of the facing seam after the facing has been turned.

5. Align the seam lines and secure the facing to the seam allowance with a few small hand stitches (see Diagram E).

Patch *Pockets*

Pockets can be fun, functional, and decorative. They can be large and obvious or tiny and concealed, positioned to get attention or to blend into the garment inconspicuously. Patch pockets made in a variety of shapes and fabrics complement or contrast garment design.

Pocket Basics

Patch pockets are the most common and handiest type of pocket. They are often used on shirts and blouses, jeans and slacks, and skirts and accessories. As the name implies, the pockets are made from a separate piece of fabric that is stitched to the outside of a garment. Patch pockets are square, rectangular, curved, straight, pointed, or circular. The corners can be rounded or square, and they can have flaps, a button closure, or a neat hem.

Before positioning pockets, try on the garment to determine the best placement. Blindstitch patch pockets to garments by hand- or machine-topstitch.

The example shows the construction of an unlined patch pocket with squared corners. For professional looking results, press the pocket with each step of construction.

Getting Started

1. Cut out the pocket as instructed in your pattern. Turn ¼ inch of the upper raw edge toward the wrong side and press (see Diagram A). Sew a basting stitch (also called an easestitch) around the lower portion of the pocket. Do not clip the threads.

2. Fold the self-facing to the right side and stitch the ends down across the ¼-inch hem (see Diagram B).

ॐCreative Tip

To reinforce the upper corner of a pocket that will get a lot of wear and tear

such as on kids clothing, stitch small triangles at the upper corners.

– Team Member, Independence, Missouri

3. Trim the corners and the self-facing seam allowance (see Diagram C).

4. Turn the facing right side out and press. Clip and notch the seam allowance at the corners. Pull the ease stitching thread to round the curves and press the seam allowance toward the wrong side of the pocket (see Diagram D).

5. Topstitch (see page 326) across the top of the pocket, making sure to catch the facing on the back (see Diagram E). Position and pin the pocket to the outside of the garment as desired. Topstitch around the pocket ¼ inch from the folded edge. Pull threads to the back to tie off rather than backstitching (see Diagram E). Hand-stitch the pocket in place for a plain front.

Diagram A

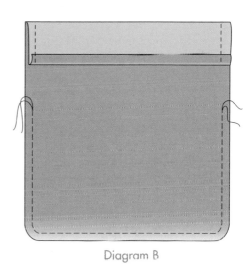

Diagram B

Diagram C

Diagram D

Diagram E

Fashion Sewing – Pockets

335 ✂

Yokes

The yoke of a garment is the section that runs across the back from shoulder to shoulder. Most often used on shirts and dresses, it defines this area of the garment and provides an ideal place to show off patterned fabric, embroidery, or other embellishments.

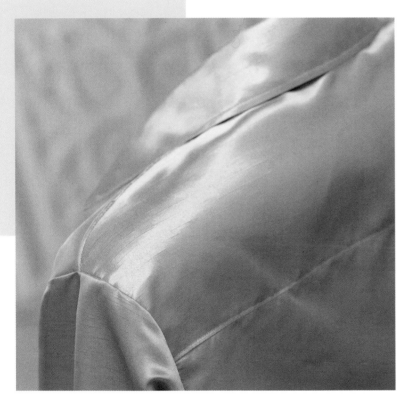

Yoke-Making Basics

The simplest and most common method of constructing a yoke is to topstitch it to the garment. When using this method, it is important to keep stitches even and prevent gathers in your fabric to create a tailored finish. Cut two yoke pieces from your fabric: One will show on the outside of the garment, and the other will be used as the facing.

Getting Started

Topstitched Yoke

1. Pin the top and bottom yokes to the back of the upper edge of the back matching the notches. The top yoke will have the right side facing the right side of the garment back, and the bottom yoke (inside) will have the right side facing the wrong side of the garment. Stitch all three layers together (see Diagram A).

2. Referring to Diagram B, press the top and bottom yokes facing upward, and topstitch (see page 326) the back yoke seam. Press under the shoulder seam allowance on the top yoke. Pin the front sections of the garment with the wrong sides together, and stitch the shoulder seams.

3. Match the folded edge of the top yoke at the shoulder seam and topstitch it to the garment (see Diagram C). Refer to page 327 for making collars and page 330 for sleeves, or finish according to your pattern instructions.

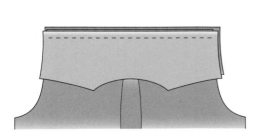

Diagram A

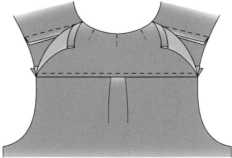

Diagram B

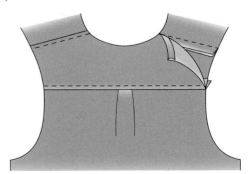

Diagram C

Waistbands

A well-made waistband should be smooth, close-fitting, and stable. Learn to make a faced waistband that will give a tailored look to your skirts and pants.

Waistband Basics

The waistband of a garment undergoes a considerable amount of wear, so it needs to be strong and sturdy. You can custom-make your own waistband by cutting it long enough for comfort, ease, and an overlap allowance.

To calculate length, add ½ inch for ease, 1¼ inches for seam allowances, and 1 inch for overlap to your waist measurement for a total of 2¾ inches. (For example, if your waist measurement is 26 inches, you'll need to cut your waistband 28¾ inches long.) For width, cut the waistband two times the desired finished width plus 1¼ inches for seam allowances. (For example, if you want to make a 1¼-inch-wide band, cut your waistband 3¾ inches wide.)

Getting Started

1. Cut the waistband on the lengthwise fabric grain. Cut purchased fusible waistband interfacing 1¼ inches shorter than the waistband.

2. Fuse interfacing to the wrong side of the waistband following the directions that accompany the product. Allow ⅝-inch seam allowances along the edge of the waistband that will be sewn to the skirt and at both ends of the waistband.

3. With right sides together, pin and sew the waistband to the skirt edge (see Diagram A). Trim the seam allowances (see Diagram B).

4. With the right sides together, fold the waistband in half. Sew a seam at each end of the waistband (see Diagram C).

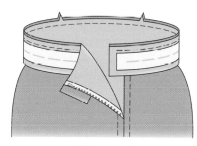

Diagram A

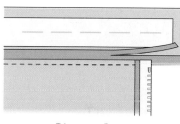

Diagram B

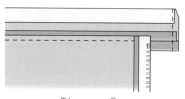

Diagram C

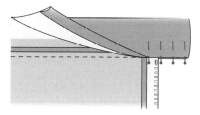

Diagram D

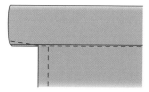

Diagram E

5. Clip the corners of the waistband end and trim the seam allowances.

6. Turn the waistband right side out and press. The open side of the waistband will be on the inside of the skirt (see Diagram D). Tuck the seam allowance of the

waistband up into the waistband and baste it in place.

7. With the right side up, stitch-in-the-ditch (see Diagram E) of the waistline or topstitch the waistband (see page 325) to hold the free edge of the waistband in place. If desired, the waistband can be slip-stitched (see page 326) to the inside waistline of the garment, eliminating the machine stitching.

8. Attach a hook-and-eye closure for skirts and slacks.

Casings *and Bias Binding*

Casings, constructed as a part of the garment or sewn into clothing, provide a snug fit to the body, yet remain comfortable to wear. Sew elastic casings into waistbands in skirts, slacks, and one-piece garments, or make casings for sleeve and leg openings.

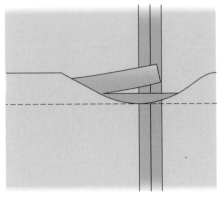

Diagram A – Self-Casing

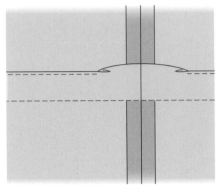

Diagram B – Self-Casing

Casing Basics

Casings provide soft gathers and a smooth fit. Sewing elastic into children's clothing is especially beneficial to wearing comfort and the ease of dressing and undressing.

Make casings wide enough to fit the size of the elastic. A general rule is to make the finished casing ⅛–¼ inch wider than the elastic width, depending on the weight of the fabric.

Select elastic according to the width and weight of the garment fabric. Knitted and woven elastics are soft and supple. They can easily be stitched in place while the garment is flat. Braided elastic is stiff, suitable for swimwear, and tolerates repeated dips in chlorine-treated water. Other stiff elastics are made especially for waistbands. They have horizontal nonroll ribs that prevent them from curling and becoming uncomfortable.

To measure elastic, add approximately 1 inch to the body measurement. The amount of stretch in the elastic determines the needed length.

Pin a safety pin into one end of the elastic to thread it through the casing, or use a threading tool made for this purpose. Secure the opposite end of the elastic to the garment with a safety pin to prevent it from being pulled through the casing. Thread the elastic through the casing, evenly distributing the gathers. Overlap both elastic ends and secure with a safety pin. Try on the garment and adjust if necessary. Stitch the elastic ends together with zigzag or backstitches (see page 326).

Getting Started

Self-Casing
This type of casing is commonly used in garment waistlines that have a bodice sewn to a skirt. The seam allowance at the waist is much wider than normal.

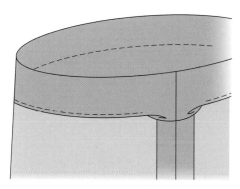

Diagram C – Turned Casing

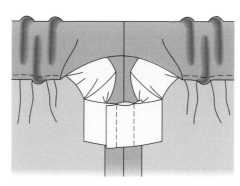

Diagram D – Turned Casing

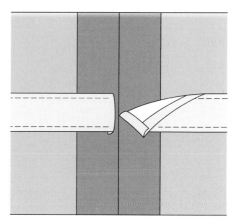

Diagram E – Applied Casing

1. Sew the side seams and the skirt to the bodice. Press the seam allowance at the waist toward the bodice. Trim the inner seam allowance to approximately ¼ inch. Do not trim the outside seam allowance; this will become the casing (see Diagram A).

2. Turn under ¼ inch of the casing and press. Pin and stitch the casing to the bodice of the garment as shown, leaving an opening at a side seam to insert the elastic (see Diagram B).

3. Thread the elastic through the casing. Adjust to fit, sew the elastic ends together, and stitch the casing closed.

Turned Casing

This type of casing is typically used to make quick and simple waistbands for skirts and slacks. A turned casing also eliminates the need for a zipper.

1. Turn under ¼ inch at the waist and press. Determine how much fabric will be turned under and mark the fold line with tailor's chalk, or a fabric marker. Fold to the inside and pin.

2. Stitch close to the folded edge, leaving an opening along a side seam to insert the elastic (see Diagram C). If desired, topstitch the top edge of the garment approximately ⅛ inch from the fold line to prevent the elastic from twisting within the casing.

3. Thread the elastic through the casing. Adjust to fit, secure the elastic, and stitch the casing closed (see Diagram D).

Applied Casing

Applied casings are often used to make a gathered waistband in a one-piece garment, and to create a snug fit at the wrist and ankle. Use purchased bias tape, bias strips cut from the same fabric as the garment, or bias strips cut from lining fabric.

1. Cut a bias strip to the needed length plus 1 inch. Turn under ¼ inch along both raw edges of the bias strips and press (refer to page 234 for making bias strips).

2. Mark the position of the casing on the inside of the garment. Pin the casing in place with the casing ends meeting at a side seam. Edgestitch (sew close to the edge of the fold) the casing to the garment, leaving an opening to insert elastic (see Diagram E). Be sure that the edgestitching is straight and even. Avoid backstitching that will show on the right side of the garment; instead, pull threads to the inside to tie off.

3. Insert elastic through the casing, distributing gathers. Adjust to fit, stitch the elastic ends together, and close the casing with small whipstitches.

Creative Tip

To keep elastic waistbands from rolling, stitch through the casing and elastic at the side seams.

—Team Member, Hudson, Ohio

Zippers

Functional zipper closures can provide added design detail or conceal a zipper in a seam. Although zippers may look difficult to install, following basic instructions simplifies the task.

Zipper Basics

Zippers are available in a range of lengths, weights, styles, and fabrications to install in garments and home decor projects. Use separating zippers for jackets and coats, zippers with metal teeth and pulls for heavyweight articles, and lightweight or hidden zippers in fashion clothing.

If the zipper tape is not 100-percent polyester, preshrink the zipper as you would fabric. Press the zipper tape with a hot iron, avoiding the nylon coils.

Set the machine stitch length at 6–8 stitches per inch and baste the garment seam from the bottom of the opening to the top. The zipper opening should equal the zipper coil length plus 1 inch. Press the seam open.

Use a sewing machine zipper foot to baste and stitch the zipper in place. In lieu of machine basting, hold zippers in place until they are stitched by applying double-sided fabric basting tape or fabric glue, allowing the glue to dry a few minutes before stitching.
Note: After stitching through fabric glue, wipe the machine needle with a piece of cotton lightly soaked with alcohol before continuing to sew.

Use masking or transparent tape on the right side of the fabric as a stitching guide, stitching along the tape edge but not into the tape. Or use a ruler and water- or air-soluble markers to draw a stitching guide on the fabric. Be sure to test the markers on a scrap piece of fabric to ensure that markings will dissolve from your fabric.

Stitch the zipper from the bottom stop, along the zipper tape guide line, to the tape extension. Stitch in the same direction along both sides of the zipper tape to eliminate puckers in the finished installation.

To avoid stitching around the pull tab, which is bulky and sometimes difficult to maneuver around, purchase a zipper longer than required. Position the zipper with the bottom stop in place and the zipper

extension beyond the top garment edge. Sew in the zipper, slide down the pull tab, and cut off the leftover extension. Leave the zipper open until the facing or waistband is applied. Stitch across the top of the zipper to create a stop.

Getting Started

Lapped Zipper Installation
Use lapped zipper installations on dresses, skirts, and slacks to conceal the zipper within a side seam.

1. Baste the garment seam closed and press the seam allowance open.

2. Place the open zipper facedown on the seam allowance with the coils along the seam line. The garment will be folded back away from the seam allowance (see Diagram A). Stitch through the seam allowance only, not through the garment. Baste, pin, or use fabric glue to keep the left hand side of the zipper in place. Using a zipper foot, stitch from the bottom stop to the top stop along the zipper tape guide line.

3. Close the zipper and turn the zipper face up with the garment still folded to the back and the zipper teeth along the fold (see Diagram B). Attach the zipper foot and move the needle to the opposite side of zipper foot. Starting at the bottom of the zipper, stitch along the folded fabric edge from the zipper bottom stop to the tape extension, sewing through the seam allowance and zipper tape.

Diagram A

Diagram B

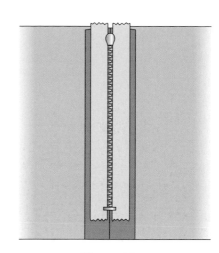

Diagram C

Diagram D

4. Pin or tape the zipper to the opposite seam allowance so it is laying flat on the seam. Turn the garment to the right side (see Diagram C). Adjust the needle with the zipper foot. Using ½-inch masking tape as a guide, stitch along the edge of the tape. Beginning at the seam line, stitch across the bottom of the zipper beginning at the seam, pivot at the edge of the tape, and stitch to the top of the raw edge.

5. Remove the tape and machine basting. Using a pressing cloth, lightly press the zipper area of the garment.

Centered Zipper Installation

Use centered zipper installations for center back and center front garment closures. Select a zipper tape color to closely match the garment fabric.

1. Baste the seam closed and place the zipper flat, facedown on the seam allowance. Pin or glue the zipper in place (see Diagram D).

2. With the garment right side up, center ½-inch-wide masking or transparent tape the length of the zipper over the seam line.

Note: Do not use tape on napped or delicate fabric. Rather, use a basting line or sewing machine guides.

3. Using a zipper foot and the edge of the tape as a guide, starting at the bottom of the zipper, stitch on the right side of fabric across the bottom edge of the tape without backstitching (see Diagram E). Pivot at the corner of the tape and stitch to the top. Move the zipper foot to the opposite side of the needle. Stitch the opposite side of the zipper as described *above*. Pull the threads at the bottom of the zipper to the wrong side and tie off.

4. Turn the garment to the right side. Remove the tape and open the seam by removing the machine basting. Press.

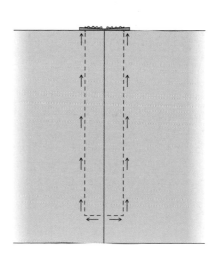

Diagram E

❧ Creative Tip

To keep the bottom of the zipper lying flat inside your garment, stitch across

the bottom edge of the tab through the seam allowance only. This will keep

the zipper from catching and getting bunched up.

—Team Member, Overland Park, Kansas

Pleats, Gathers, *and Hems*

Finishing touches such as hems, soft gathers, and crisp pleats make all the difference in the appearance of a garment. Choose the right technique for your fabric and garment style and give your project a professional look.

Hem Basics

Unless a hem is decorative, it should be invisible. To minimize stitches when hemming by hand, make certain you catch only one or two threads of the garment fabric as you work. You can catch more fabric in the hem allowance to add stability.

Finish the garment hem by hand or by machine. Decide on the technique to use based upon the fabric and design details of the garment. Whatever finish method you choose, the steps for preparing the hem are the same.

Getting Started

1. Before you mark the hem, hang the garment on a hanger for at least 24 hours. This simple step allows the grain line to relax and is critical for knit garments and those with bias- and circular-cut hems.

2. When the hanging period is over, try on the garment with the accessories (including shoes) you'll wear with it. Measure and mark the hemline with pins or tailor's chalk. The hem allowance should be 1½ to 2 inches on an A-line or flared garment, and no more than 3 inches on a straight garment.

3. Trim away the excess hem allowance. Finish the raw edge according to the fabric type.

4. Trim seam allowances that intersect with the hem to ¼ inch to eliminate bulk at the seams.

5. Turn up the hem along the marked hemline, matching seam lines first. Pin the hemline in place and remove the marking pins. Try on the garment again, adjust as needed, and stitch the hem.

Types of Hems

Turned-and-Stitched Hem
Turn up the desired hem allowance. Turn the raw edge under ¼ inch and stitch through the folded hem allowance near the edge. Referring to Diagram A, hem by hand using a slip stitch or blind stitch (see page 326). Diagram B shows a turned-up hem with a side hem.

Zigzag Finish for Knits and Fabrics — not shown
Turn up the desired hem allowance. Using a medium stitch width and length, zigzag close to the raw edge of the hem allowance, then trim fabric close to the stitching. Hem by hand or using a machine blind stitch.

Topstitched Hem
Turn up a 1½-inch hem allowance; finish the edge as desired. From the right side, pin the hem allowance in place. On the right side, topstitch 1 inch from the folded hem edge. Add a second row of topstitching ¼ inch above the first row (see Diagram C).

Hand-Rolled Hem
This type of hem is often used with woven or knit fabrics. Turn the raw edge ¼ inch, roll the hem another ¼ inch and slip-stitch or machine blindstitch (see Diagram D).

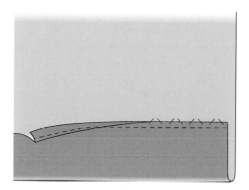

Diagram A – Turned-and-Stitched Hem

Pinked-and-Fused Hem

Turn up a 1½-inch hem allowance; finish the edge with pinking shears. Add a fusible web strip between the garment and the hem. Fuse the layers together following the manufacturer's instructions (see Diagram E).

Gathering Basics

Gathers add fullness and softness to a garment (see page 344 for illustrations). They're used at the waistline, neckline, sleeve cap, cuff, and yoke. Soft fabric makes gathers that drape and fold; crisp fabrics create gathers that stand away from the body. Experiment with a scrap of your fabric to determine the density of gathers. A long gathering stitch (6–8 stitches per inch) is easy to draw up by hand and makes larger tucks in the fabric than a shorter gathering stitch (8–10 stitches per inch). But, the shorter stitch makes softer gathers that are easier to control and distribute.

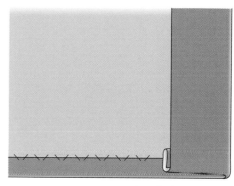

Diagram D – Hand-Rolled Hem

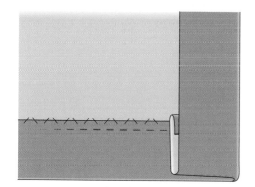

Diagram B – Turned-and-Stitched with Side Hem

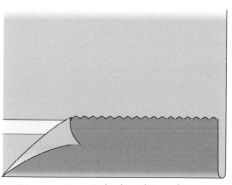

Diagram E – Pinked-and-Fused Hem

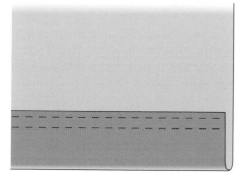

Diagram C – Topstitched Hem

❧Creative Tip

For fabrics that don't press as neatly, such as knits or fleece, first baste stitch at the desired hem line, then fold the hem at this stitching line. Finish as desired. This ensures a crisp fold and an even hem.

– Team Member, Hudson, Ohio

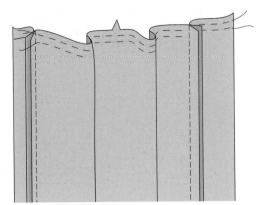

Diagram A

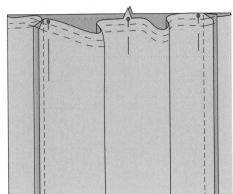

Diagram B

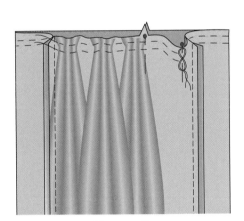

Diagram C

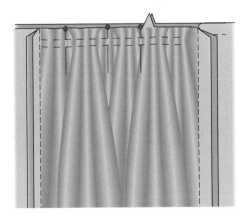

Diagram D

Getting Started

How to Sew Gathers

1. Sew a line of gathering stitches on the right side of the fabric, in the seam allowance just inside the ⅝-inch seam allowance, beginning and ending at seam lines (see Diagram A). Use a contrasting-color thread in the bobbin to tell the two threads apart. Sew a second row of stitches in the seam allowance ¼ inch from the first row. The longer the length of the gathering stitches, the greater the risk of breaking the gathering threads. To avoid this, use heavy-duty thread in the bobbin, and divide the total length to be gathered into several equal sections and stitch each individually.

2. With right sides facing, pin the stitched edge to the garment, matching notches. If necessary, make your own pinning guides by folding straight and stitched edges into quarters. Mark fold lines with pins, then pin edges together, matching marking pins (see Diagram B).

3. Gently pull on both bobbin threads from one end. Slide the fabric along the threads to gather. Secure the threads around a pin (see Diagram C).

4. Pin gathers in place, distributing the fullness evenly (see Diagram D).

5. With the gathered side up, stitch the garment together at the ⅝-inch seam allowance just inside the gathering lines. Adjust the gathers between the pins as you stitch. Remove pins as you sew.

6. Trim the seam allowances; press on the wrong side. Open the garment out and press the seam. Press the seam toward the gathers for a full look, toward the garment for a smooth look.

Pleat Basics

Pleats control fabric fullness. They can be pressed or unpressed, stitched or unstitched, soft or crisp, on the inside or outside of your garment. Pleats require accuracy in cutting, marking, and sewing. Transfer all pleat markings from your pattern to your fabric with tailor tacks, an air- or water-soluble marking pen, or pins.

Getting Started

How to Sew Pleats

1. Mark all pleat lines with tailor's tacks. Make a snip mark for the top of pleat lines within the seam allowance and you'll never lose your guide (see Diagram D).

2. Fold the fabric together and pin or hand-baste pleats along the folded edges (see Diagram E). Sew together each pleat from top to bottom markings (see Diagram F). Backstitch to secure threads at the end of each pleat.

3. Press the pleats. Pleats shown here are pressed on the right side. Pin or baste tucks to hold the pleats in place before proceeding with construction.

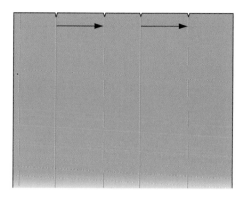

Diagram D

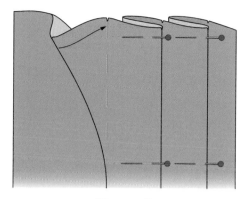

Diagram E

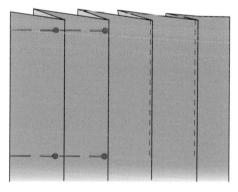

Diagram F

✽Creative Tip

Place brown paper strips (from a grocery bag) in the

fold of each pleat when pressing to prevent an imprint

of the pleat on the right side of the garment.

– Team Member, Hillsboro, Oregon

Buttons *and Buttonholes*

Although making buttonholes may be intimidating, it is really very easy. Once you understand the basics, let your sewing machine do the rest.

Buttonhole Basics

Most of today's sewing machines have buttonhole attachments or can be programmed to make a buttonhole stitch. Be sure to read the directions for your sewing machine before you begin.

Buttonholes should be made on a double thickness of material to give them strength.

Be sure to position buttons and buttonholes where gaps are most likely to occur.

Getting Started

1. Mark the position and width of each buttonhole with a chalk pencil or disappearing pen (see Diagram A). If you are making several buttonholes in a row, make two vertical lines the width of the buttonholes, then mark the horizontal lines where each button will be placed.

2. Follow your sewing machine instructions for making a buttonhole. Stitch around the lines you have marked (see Diagram B).

3. Place straight pins at both ends of the buttonhole before cutting it open (see Diagram C). The pins will prevent you from accidentally cutting through the buttonhole's ends. If you used a chalk pencil, remove the marks.

4. With very sharp scissors, carefully cut the fabric down the center between the buttonhole stitches (see Diagram D). Do not cut beyond the straight pins.

5. Remove the straight pins. If desired, apply a liquid fray-preventing product to the cut edges of the buttonhole to prevent loose threads and unraveling (see Diagram E).

Covered Button Basics

Covered buttons add a professional touch to your garments. They are made from a lightweight material and come in two sections in a variety of sizes.

Select covered buttons carefully to make sure they are both the proper weight and size.

1. Cut a circular piece of fabric approximately half again as large as the button (see Diagram F). Most manufacturers will provide you with a template to follow. Make a running stitch around the edge of the circle. Lay the button with the shank portion in the middle of the fabric circle and pull the threads to gather.

2. Fold the fabric over the edge of the top half of the button (see Diagram G), and cut the thread. Pick up the lower half of the button and gently push it into the upper half, making sure that all the fabric is tucked inside.

3. Attach the button at a right angle to the fabric. Stitch through the material and the shank several times to secure. Finish by tying off on the wrong side of the material.

Reinforcing Buttons

To stabilize buttons that will receive frequent use, or to strengthen those sewn on heavy fabrics, sew a smaller button to the back of the garment, allowing space for a shank. Place a pin or a toothpick on top of the outer button and sew over it (see Diagram H). Remove the toothpick; raise the button to the top of the stitches and make a thread shank under the button by winding thread around the excess stitching. Backstitch to finish.

Diagram A

Diagram B

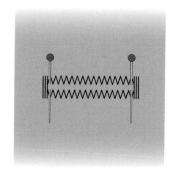

Diagram C

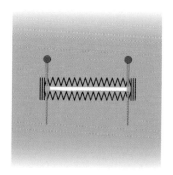

Diagram D

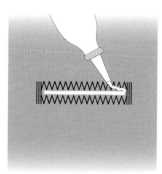

Diagram E

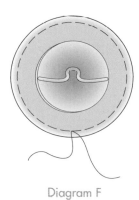

Diagram F

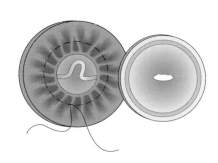

Diagram G

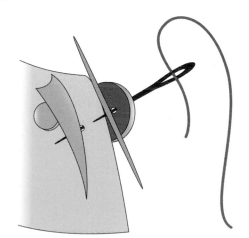

Diagram H

Seams *and* Finishes

The way a seam is sewn and finished is important to the making of a garment. From the pressing of each seam to finishing the edges, it is part of achieving professional results.

⋙Creative Tip

When sewing on buttons, insert the loop end of a doubled thread through the eye of the needle, then knot the end of the thread (see Loop Knot page 61). This procedure adds strength and speed to the process.

—Team Member, Hudson, Ohio

Seams Basics

The seam is the basic building block of fashion, quilting, and home decor sewing. Choose seam finishes according to the type of fabric you are using, the type of wear a garment will receive, and whether the seams will show. If a garment will be lined, it usually does not require seam finishing.

Make seams with care and accuracy. Most seams are ⅝ inch wide; however, patterns differ, so check for special seam allowances. Start and finish seams with a few backstitches for stability and reinforcement. Press plain seams open to enhance the finished look of the garment.

Getting Started

Plain Seam

A plain seam is most often used in garment and accessory assembly. The stitching is generally ⅝ inch from the edge along the entire seam and is made with 10- to 12-stitches per inch. The edges of a plain seam may be finished with a number of techniques. Plain seams are most often used with garments made of fabrics that have little or no fraying.

1. Pin or baste layers of fabric to prevent slippage.

2. Stitch seams with right sides together, removing pins before sewing over them.

3. Press plain seams open unless directed otherwise.

Flat-Fell Seam

This type of seam is commonly used with men's garments, denim fabrics such as jeans, children's play clothes, and reversible garments. Flat-fell seams wear well because the edges are enclosed to prevent fraying.

1. Stitch the seam with the right sides together and press the seam allowances to one side. Trim the lower seam allowance to ⅛ inch along the entire length of seam (see Diagram A).

2. Turn the edge of the upper seam allowance under ¼ inch and press (see Diagram B).

3. Pin the pressed seam allowance to the garment and stitch along the edge. Sew carefully to ensure stitch lines are straight as they will show on the right side of the garment (see Diagram B).

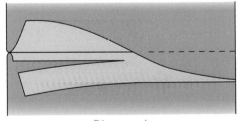

Diagram A

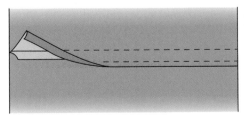

Diagram B

Diagram C

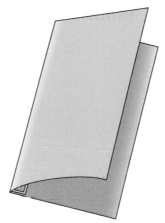

Diagram D

Diagram E

French Seam

The French seam is most often used with sheer fabrics, and is commonly found on children's clothing, unlined jackets, blouses, and lingerie. You can prevent fabrics from fraying by using this technique to enclose the seam edges within the last seam. French seams work best on straight seams, as it is difficult to sew them on a curve.

1. With wrong sides together, stitch a ⅜-inch seam (see Diagram C). Trim the seam allowance to ⅛ inch.

2. Fold the right sides together with the stitching line exactly on the fold and press (see Diagram D).

3. Stitch ½ inch from the fold (see Diagram E). Press the seam allowance to one side. This makes a ⅝-inch seam.

4. Open and press the seam flat to one side.

Turned-and-Stitched Seam
(Clean Finish)

The turned-and-stitched method should only be used with lightweight fabrics or garments such as a blouse or unlined jacket.

1. Make a plain seam and press open. Turn under the edges of each seam allowance ⅛–¼ inch and press. Straight-stitch along the edge of each fold (see Diagram F).

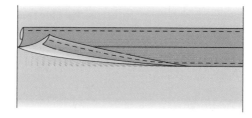

Diagram F

Optional Seam Finishes

Overlock stitch finish: Use an overlock stitch to quickly finish the edge of a seam allowance. This requires the use of an overlock machine (serger), which trims the edge of the fabric and encases it in stitching with one step. Overlock machines may use three, four, or five threads in this single operation. Press the finished seams to one side.

Pinked finish: Use pinking shears for a quick and easy finish. If fabric ravels easily, stitch ¼ inch from each seam allowance edge. Using the pinking shears, trim close to stitching line. Pinking alone will not keep fabric from raveling.

Zigzag finish: Stitch close to or over the seam edge with the stitch width set on medium and at about 15 stitches per inch. Use a machine overcast stitch interchangeably with the zigzag stitch. This stitch can be used for most fabrics, including heavyweight.

Index

Index

Acknowledgments

For the support, assistance in designing projects, and product contributions from the following companies and designers, we extend our sincere thanks and gratitude to:

Binney & Smith, Inc.
Carpenter, Laurie Nelson
Coats & Clark, Inc.
Colart Americas, Inc.
Collins, Laura Holthorf
Darice Craft and Floral Products
DecoArt
DMC Corporation
Duncan Enterprises
Gibb, Helen
Greg Markum, Inc.
Hiney, Mary Jo
Houts, Lenny
Kaisand, Jessie
Kato, Donna
Lion Brand Yarn Co.
Loew-Cornell, Inc.
Luedtke, Julie
Mead, Jill
Natural Science Industries, Ltd.
Parkhurst, Alan
Plaid Enterprises, Inc.
Princeton Art and Brush Co.
Royse, Roberta
Scafidi, Mary
Schmitt, Elaine
Sorensen, Dorris
State, Suzanne
Strathmore Papers
Tracy, Gloria
Walker, Deb

The Fabric of Success

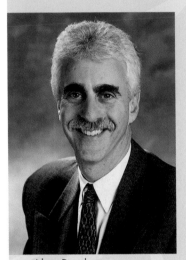

Alan Rosskamm

Pictured from left to right:
Armond Arnson (Kahn &
Kleinman), Martin Rosskamm,
Betty Rosskamm, Hilda Reich,
Alma Zimmerman, Joe
Thomas (McDonald & Co.),
and Justin Zimmerman. This
picture was taken at the
groundbreaking for the office
and distribution center in
Beachwood, Ohio, in 1969.

The Story of JO-ANN. Stores, Inc.

When Alan Rosskamm was 10 years old, he spent his spare time in his grandmother Hilda's store, straightening thread racks and folding fabric remnants. Today he is president and CEO of the nation's leading fabric and crafts retailer. He is the third generation involved in Jo-Ann Stores, Inc., continuing the legacy of vision, quality, and service.

From one 1,400-square-foot store in 1943 to almost 1,000 United States locations today—employing more than 20,000 people—Jo-Ann Stores, Inc., has not only witnessed a creative explosion in sewing and crafts, it has helped inspire it.

> *"We will help you succeed by giving you the confidence to explore your creativity."*
>
> – Alan Rosskamm

Martin & Betty Rosskamm

Alan's grandparents, Hilda and Berthold Reich, along with their friends, Sigmund and Mathilda Rohrbach, founded the business in 1943. Both immigrant couples from Nazi Germany, they came to Cleveland, Ohio, to start a new life. Mr. Reich had been importing cheese in a small east-side storefront when the Rohrbachs approached him to sell fabrics. (The Rohrbachs' son, Max, was a fabric salesman whose company offered to supply them with remnants to start.)

They soon pushed the cheese to the back and opened the doors of the first Jo-Ann store, then named the Cleveland Fabric Shop. "With our European background, we were anxious to please our customers," recalls Alma Zimmerman, the Rohrbachs' now 88-year-old daughter. Alma recalls buying 4-yard cuts from Macy's department store in New York and then reselling them in Cleveland. "We didn't make a profit, but we were able to offer something new to our customers," she says.

Alma & Justin Zimmerman

Over the next five years and after the death of Alma's father, Alma and Hilda Reich became the mainstays of the business. They cultivated the customer base, doubled their space, and added a drapery workroom in the basement. In 1948, with the opening of a second Cleveland store, the Reichs' daughter, Betty, and her new husband, Martin Rosskamm, began delivering fabric bolts every Saturday. "There was no such thing as telling the customer, 'We can't get it for you'," Betty says. Now at age 73, Betty still works at the Jo-Ann corporate office, overseeing the special-order department.

continued

"*If you're going to spend your time doing something, you want the most up-to-date materials. Jo-Ann Stores, Inc., travels the world to find the best and latest products for you.*"

– Dave Bolen

Further expansion in the 1950s and 1960s led to a new name, Jo-Ann Fabrics, which the families came up with by combining the names of their daughters, Joan Zimmerman and Jacqueline Ann Rosskamm. By 1969, the business had grown to 169 stores in 28 states and had become a publicly held corporation, trading on the American Stock Exchange under the name of Fabri-Centers of America, Inc. In 1976, it joined the New York Stock Exchange. In 1999, the corporate name was changed to Jo-Ann Stores, Inc.

Through the 1970s and 1980s, Jo-Ann Stores joined the shopping mall bandwagon by opening its own 4,000-square-foot stores in regional malls. As women began to enter the workplace, sewing and crafts became less of an economic necessity and more of an outlet for relaxation and self-expression. By the late 1980s and early 1990s, Jo-Ann Stores had left the malls for larger stores and strip shopping centers; some had added crafts and floral products to the mix.

The year 1995 marked another turning point when Jo-Ann opened a 46,000-square-foot test store, adjacent to its Cleveland headquarters, stocked with every imaginable creative item to "serve and inspire creativity." "We've learned so much about what our customers want," Alan says. The store

became the pilot for Jo-Ann etc., standing for "experience the creativity." Venturing beyond the ordinary retail experience, this interactive-store concept opens the door to "edutainment," (a combination of education and creative entertainment). According to Alan, Jo-Ann etc. is the only store format that specializes in both sewing and crafts, offering a vast range of products, inventive classes, unique ideas, and a knowledgeable staff dedicated to nurturing each customer's passion for creativity.

"This is a store that can inspire you to enjoy your creativity, a place where you will find the materials, tools, and advice you need to achieve beautiful results," Betty says, confident of Jo-Ann's exciting new direction. In the spirit of its service-minded founders, Jo-Ann Stores, Inc., continues to anticipate sewing and crafting trends and to weave a history that's still in the writing.

"Jo-Ann team members are hobbyists who enjoy sharing their ideas, experiences, and expertise. You can rely on them for guidance, advice, and creative support!"

– Betty Rosskamm

Contributing

A

Addy, Kate
Ahlswede, Jen
Akers, Lucy
Akey, Barb
Allcom, Donna
Altzman, Bettye
Ambrosio, Dianna
Anderson, Pat
Anderson, Peggy
Anderson, Taryn
Arnold, Miriam
Atkinson, Yvonne
Augustyniak, Sandy

B

Bacon, Phillip
Bailey, Angela
Barker, Carol
Barton, Linda
Bates, Laurie
Benfield, Jay
Benton-Logan, Robin
Beranak, Mari
Bergdorf, Jan
Best, Carol S.
Biscocho, Edlyn
Biscocho, Emily

❧ Creative Tip

Make a bridal bouquet more personal by adding items the bride holds dear. It is easy to incorporate items such as a mother's handkerchief or a grandmother's pearls to add a special and personal touch. This could also count as the "something old" for good luck!

— Team Member, Knoxville, TN

Black, June
Bohannon, Patty
Boone, Karen
Borrowman, Helen
Boser, Marilyn
Bossert, Sharon
Brasel, Cathy
Brewer, Ann
Bridgeman, Joyce
Brown, Evelyn
Brown, Jonnell N.
Brown, Muriel
Buchter, Pat
Burton, Amber
Busby, Cindy
Bush, Terri
Bushlack, Judy
Butler, Ruth
Buza, Ann
Byas, Kay
Byrd, Sarah

C

Cahalan, Cathy
Calderone, Debbie
Calvert, Shirley
Campagna, Linda
Campbell, Sandy
Carlos, Rosa
Carney, Debbie
Carr, Marcia
Carrillo, Laurie
Carter, Rich
Caruso, Connie
Casciato, Cindy
Casey, Kelly
Cawley, Ellen
Cemoch, Ann Marie
Chapin, Carol
Chesterman, Elaine
Christerson, Billie
Christy, Lynnell M.
Clark, Charlotte
Claudette, Patricia
Coates, Diane
Connor, Helen
Conocchia, Marci
Cook, Janice
Coughran, Debbie
Cowham, Rebecca
Cox, Dan

Cox, Deborah
Craver, Terrie
Crismer, Carol
Crissey, Judy
Crotts, Georgi
Cuerin, Katie Lyn

D

Dabrowski, Evelin
Dalbec, Cindy
Davis, Robyn
Davis, Suzanne
Davis, Therese
DelGatto, Sandra
Derby, Carolyn
DeVries, Patricia
Dickhausen, Susie
Diebel, Wendy
Doherty, Anne
Dombrowski, Jo
Doolin, Sharon
Duca, Denise
Dybash, Sarah
Dye, Tammie
Dyer, Joanne

E

Eaton, Veronica
Eaves, Cindy
Elliott, Susan
Erickson, Joyce
Esber, Jennifer
Evans, Judy
Everett, Wendy
Everhart, Nancy

F

Fabbro, Joan M.
Farley, Gloria J.
Fedie-Madison, Alexandra
Ferguson, Barb
Ferguson, Catherine
Finch, Laurie
Finochhi, Nicki
Flores, Elizabeth
Floyd, Jennifer
Foster, Sassy
Foster, Sherrlyn
Fox, Wilma
Frejd, Nancy

G

Gaffney, Angie
Gant, Pat
Garcia, Gerda M.
Gaskins, Dianna
Gilly, Pat
Gilmore, Diane
Gorski, Jacque
Green, Debra L.
Green, Patricia C.
Greenwald, Stacey
Gregory, Mary
Grisez, Betty
Guenter, Betty

H

Haburchak, Corless
Hadlock, Amanda
Haese, Anna Marie
Hammel, Marcy
Hanzalik Richter, Cynthia R.
Harbach, Patt
Harbauch, Patt
Hargrave, Amanda
Harper, Rene
Harrigan, Robin
Harris, Dave
Harsha, Kristina
Hartley, Mary
Hartsock, Cynthia
Hawley, Glenora
Hayden, Robyn
Heath, LeeMary
Heil, Heather
Heil-Grover, Stephanie
Hein, Ann
Helvig, Becky
Hennessey, Linda
Henry, Brian
Herbert, Sherry
Hermann, Becky
Hernandez, Carmen
Hetcher, Rose
Hills, Della
Hines, Norma
Hodges, Karen
Hogle, Janet
Holbert, Dee
Holm, Alison
Hoover, Christine
Horak, Michelle

Horton, Pauly
Hribar, Sarah
Huber, Karen
Hudgins, Janna
Hudon, Tracy
Hunt, Donna
Hunt, Svea H.
Hurson, Viola G.

J

Jackson, Angie
Jackson, Natalie
Jenkins, Priscilla
Jeral, Monica
Johnson, Sybil M.
Johnston, Karen
Jones, Anna B.
Jordan, Belinda

K

Kallas, Caryn P.
Karl, Judy
Kellgreen, Sara
Kelly, Anne
Kelly, Mary E.
Kelly, Mary J.
Kelly, Melody
Kelsey, Janelle
Kemener, Lynda
Kendall, Laura
Kindhart, Pam
Kister, Edna
Klick, Terri
Knight, Deb
Knoyer, Marjorie
Koch, Eva
Kralicek, Michael
Krapp, Helena
Kriesel, Sharon
Kuson, Laura

L

Lagasse, Helen
Laszlo, Martha
Lawrence, Maria
Ledversis, Toni
Lee, Laura
Lehre, Monica
Lesch, Gayle A.
LeStourgeon, Janice
Levenson, Linda

*We wish to thank all of our Jo-Ann Team Members
for the hundreds of tips they willingly gave to make
this book a great success.*

Lindgren, Jean
Lisko, Kelly
Liston, Nancy
Lizzano, Kristen
Logan, Robin
Logan, Susan
Lopez, Olga
Lowe, Betty
Lowery, Lisa
Lown, Cheryl
Luther, Violet
Lynch, Christine

M
Maguire, Sharon
Mai, Becky
Mallory, Sue
Malone, Bobbie
Mann, Donna
Marlinski, M.J.
Maron, Kimberly
Marquardt, Rachel
Marquis, Claire
Martin, Jan
Martinez, Virginia D.
Matejka, Holly
Matthews, Charlotte
McAdams, Christie
McCaslin, Ramona
McCommons, Rhonda
McCosh, Pam
McCreary, Judy Kay
McDaniels, Marcia
McFarland, Sue
McGarry, Pat
McKinney, Pat
McLellan, Gerry
Meier, Lynn
Meinke, Dianna
Menczynski, Carol
Mertz, Linda
Meyers, Trish
Michael, Lori
Michaelis, Barb
Miesle, Nancy
Miller, Bonnie
Miller, Fern
Miller, Janet
Minta, Patti
Mitchell, Karen
Mittrucker, Janett

Mongson, Leslie
Moore, Lynn
Moret, Lisa
Morris, Crystal
Morris, Fran
Mortorana, Patricia
Mosca, Patricia J.
Mota, Delores J.
Mullins, Kathy
Musciano, Cheryl
Myers, Ann

N
Nakashima, Julie
Nayes, Inge
Nestlebush, Alma
Niemeyer, Lynne
Noel, Raye
Nolan, Joanne W.
Noss, LuAnn
Nuttall, Thelma
Nyholm, Patricia

O
O'Doul, Vonna
Olivas, Sandra
Oliver, Carol
Oliver, Sandra
Olson, Teri
Ontiveros, Estella
Overholt, Amanda
Oxley, Barbara

P
Paoletti, Christine
Parkhurst, Alan
Pascarella, Cindy
Patynko, Juanita M.
Paulsin, Nancy
Pepinsmith, L.
Perkins, Mary
Peters, Jackie
Peterson, DeAnne
Phillips, Evelyn
Piezer, Jean
Poleshuk, Jolene
Pope, Bonnie
Prokop, Lisa A.
Pyle, Jean

Q
Quiroz, Mary

R
Rafferty, Kathy Lee
Rahn, Cathy
Ramsey, Debra
Ranson, Ernestine
Ray, Nancy
Ready, Linda
Recano, Cazilia
Renea, Cynthia
Renner, Kathy
Resendez, Sarah L.
Reveria, Maria
Reynolds, Korlyn
Rice, Lisa
Richardson, Loretta
Richter, Shirley
Riggin, Mike
Robertson, Kaye
Robinson, Debbie
Robinson, Phillip
Robinson, Ruth
Rosenwinkel, Lori
Ross, Lori
Rowan, Judi
Ruhl, Frances
Rulland, Carol
Ruolo, Ellen
Ruple, Rosalie
Ryan, Bernadette

S
Santucci, Grace
Sarver, Danny
Savery, Marsha
Scafidi, Mary Hyre
Schnabel, Kim
Schneider, Michelle
Schoenleber, Barbara
Semmens, Carol
Serdar, Evelyn
Shafer, Barbara
Shephard, Peggy
Silvernail, Jennie
Skinner, Margaret
Skinner, Marie Lucy
Skoczen, Kathie
Skrivanek, Carissa
Slater, Peggy

Smith, Diane
Smith, Gwen
Smith, Nancy
Smith, Pat
Smith, Sallie
Smolski, Becky
Snyder, Linda
Solomond, Darlene
Sorenson, Lisa
Spears, Valerie
Sprinkle, Andi
Spry, Leslie
Stam, LuAnna
Stelpflug, Linda "Mickey"
Stephenson, Joyce
Sternecker, Diana
Steward, Caron
Stewart, Jaynee
Stone, Kathy
Store, Betty
Suiter, Arla
Sulin, Ann
Sullivan, Carolyn
Suray, Sandy
Surfus, Diana

T
Tangonan, Melody T.
Tavernier, Jane
Teale, Joyce
Teasley, Linda
Teneyuque, Nick
Teska, Jean
Thomas, Amy
Thor, Joyce
Toftner, Jeanne
Tokarz, Wendy
Toon, Rosemary
Towne, Colleen
Trousdale, Teresa

U
Ullam, Marilyn

V
Valanzola, Stephanie
Van Brunt, Nancye
VanDelinder, Barbara
Vann, Kathryn
Vaudry, Micheline
Vera, Janice

Viitala, Tawnya
Vipperman, Sheila K.
Volpe, Terry
Vonkennell, Kathy
Vreeland, Nancy

W
Walker, Deb
Wancha, Jill
Warzel, Lana
Weaver, Susan
West, Aliyah
Wible, Debra
Wight, Carolyn
Wilch, Jeannette
Williams, Debbie
Williams, Vallerie
Williamson, Karin
Wilshusen, Susan
Wilson, Jackie
Wilson, Tina
Witt, Jean

Y
Yater, Susan
Yosch, Betsy
Young, Pat
Yow, Yvonne

Z
Zaretzke, Jane
Zelna, Melissa

JO-ANN®

After reading this book, it is our sincere hope that
you will be challenged to try new techniques, learn by doing,
create from the heart, be more determined when you fail,
and rejoice in your creativity—

Your journey has just begun..........

Crafting · Decorating · Quilting · Sewing